Co-Motion

CO-MOTION

Re-Thinking Power, Subjects, and Feminist and Queer Alliances

Paola Bacchetta

Duke University Press
Durham and London

2 0 2 6

© 2026 DUKE UNIVERSITY PRESS
Project Editor: Ihsan Taylor
Designed by A. Mattson Gallagher
Typeset in Arno Pro
by Westchester Publishing Services

Library of Congress Cataloging-in-Publication Data
Names: Bacchetta, P. (Paola), author.
Title: Co-motion : re-thinking power, subjects, and feminist and
queer alliances / Paola Bacchetta.
Description: Durham : Duke University Press, 2026. | Includes
bibliographical references and index.
Identifiers: LCCN 2025021629 (print)
LCCN 2025021630 (ebook)
ISBN 9781478032977 (paperback)
ISBN 9781478029533 (hardcover)
ISBN 9781478061724 (ebook)
Subjects: LCSH: Social movements—History. | Decolonization. |
Feminist theory. | Critical theory.
Classification: LCC HM881 .B34 2026 (print) | LCC HM881
(ebook) | DDC 303.48/409—dc23/eng/20250617
LC record available at https://lccn.loc.gov/2025021629
LC ebook record available at https://lccn.loc.gov/2025021630

Cover art: Bharati Chaudhuri, *Cosmic Vibe*, 1994. Oil on canvas.
Photo © Superstock / Bridgeman Images.

Contents

Acknowledgments

This book is the fruit of conversations, coexperiences, common projects, and *co-motion* with so many people, groups, and other *beings-becomings* that I fear they cannot all be named. So, I apologize in advance if I fail to account for everyone here.

First, I want to thank the Chochenyo-speaking Ohlone people, your ancestors and future generations. I wrote the bulk of this book on your unceded land, Huichin in Turtle Island, or the place colonizers renamed Berkeley, California, USA. I am grateful to the Tupi-Guarani and Tupinambá people, your ancestors, and progeniture for the use of Mei-embipe and the Tupi-Guarani ancestral lands that the colonizers called Florianopolis, Santa Caterina, and Salvador, Bahia, in the territory they designated as Brazil. In Florianopolis I owe a special debt of gratitude to Miriam Grossi and Carmen Rial. In Salvador I want to thank Felipe Fernandes, Angela Figuieredo, Caterina Rea, Ana Caterina Benefice Barbosa, and Barbara Alves. I also thank the Pataxó people, from the ancestral lands the colonizers called Porto Seguro, for your immense generosity and what you taught me.

I thank my colleagues in the Department of Gender and Women's Studies at the University of California, Berkeley, for providing during these recent years a vibrant, supportive, and intellectually exciting environment for research, writing, teaching, and living: Mel Chen, Patrice D. Douglass, Ianna Hawkins Owen, Minoo Moallem, Courtney Morris, Laura C. Nelson, Leslie Salzinger, Dora Santana, Elora Shehabuddin, Eric Stanley, Trinh T. Minh-ha, Barbara Barnes, and Brooke Lober. Thank you to our brilliant administrative staff: Althea Grannum-Cummings, Gillian Edgelow, and Sandra Richmond.

Many thanks to my friends, sisters, siblings, comrades in my earliest meaningful *co-motion* oriented group Dyketactics!, and in the Dyketactics! community: Chea Villanueva, Sherrie Cohen, Barbara Ruth, the late Cei Bell, Kathy Hogan, Julie Blackwomon, the late Monica Hand, Morgan

Norwood, Sharon Owens, Anita Lam, Arleen Olshan, Anita Cornwell, Laurie Flint, Pauline Miriam, the late Rosalie Davis, Tommi Avicoli Mecca, and T. D. The politics we developed, our care for each other, our ongoing conversations, together leave their trace in my life and work. I remain after all these years fully indebted to Monique Dental of the group Ruptures in Paris, for your personal-political solidarity during my exile that literally changed the conditions of my life.

I thank everyone in the following collective projects: Casa delle donne (Via del Governo Vecchio 39, Rome, Italy); Rifiutare (Rome, Italy); La Maison des Femmes (8 Cité Prost, Paris, France); Archives Recherches Cultures Lesbiennes (Paris, France); Collectif féministe contre le racisme et l'anti-sémitisme (Paris, France); Mouvement contre le racisme (Paris France); the Delhi Group (New Delhi, India); Red Rose Group (New Delhi, India); and Decolonizing Sexualities Network (DSN).

My work on this book was nourished immensely by collective work with friends and colleagues in and with the Decolonizing Sexualities Network, of which I am current codirector. I thank: Sandeep Bakshi, Suhraiya Jivraj, Silvia Posocco, Jin Haritaworn, Fatima El Tayeb, Gee Semmalar, Malek Cheikh, Richard Mar, Sabreen Al Rassace, Tariq Lakhrissi, Walaa Alqaisiya, Haneen Maikey, Huma Dar, Joao Gabriell, Michaëla Danjé, Aruni Kashyap, Alexandre Erre, Ochy Curiel Picardo, Marco Chivalan-Carrillo, Akhil Kang, Dhiren Borisa, Elizabeth Lowe-Hunter, Omi Salas-SantaCruz, Nof Nasser-Edin, Nour Abu-Assab, Santa Khurai, P. J. DiPietro, Roderick Ferguson, Raju Rage, Tala Khanmalek, Living Smile Vidya, Latifa Akay, Tamsila Tauqir, Ghazala Anwar, Mikail Khan, Rima Athar, Daayiee Abdullah, YaSaeen Rahman, Türkan Yildiz, Malissa, Estelle Prudent, Serena Dankwa, Inés Ixierda, Evren Savci, Dawud Bumayé, Judith Gloria Purpre, Kami Xica, Yoann Idiri, Massinissa Garaoun.

For our meaningful conversations, in some cases very extensive over time and in others quite brief, yet that all leave their mark in these pages, I am indebted to: Norma Alarcón, Nawo Crawford, Rabab Abdulhadi, Jalil Bennani, Jules Falquet, Sirma Bilgé, Fuifuilupe Niumeitolu, Nasima Moujoud, Sonia Dayan-Herzbrun, Soraya Tlatli, Louiza Belhamici, Irene Capitelli, the late Lauren Berlant, Donatella D'Angelo, Nelson Maldonaro-Torres, France Winddance Twine, Bishnupriya Ghosh, Roshanak Kheshti, Zakiyyah Iman Jackson, Omi Salas-SantaCruz, Carla M. Trujillo, David Theo Goldberg, Huma Dar, Pratibha Parmar, Shaheen Haq, Ruth Wilson Gilmore, Siké Billé, Sam Bourcier, Leila Ahmed, Sharad Chari, Natalia Brizuela, Marlon Bailey, Che Gossett, Jean Beaman, Leti Volpe, Tinku Ali,

Inderpal Grewal, Lucia Guardi, Maria Lugones, Stefania Pandolfo, Lawrence Rosenthal, Yala Nadia Kisukidi, Elaine Kim, Natalee Kēhaulani, Akila Kizzi, Leece Lee, Gina Dent, Angela Davis, Iman Farag, Laura Fantone, Annie Isabel Fukushima, Veena Das, Soumaya Mestiri, Ritu Menon, Deepak Mehta, Nadine Nabor, the late Dalila Kadri, Angelique Abboud, Susana de Castro, Matt Richardson, Tianna Paschel, Malkia Devich Cyril, Nataša Petrešin-Bachelez, Zahra Ali, Salima Amari, Patricia Hill Collins, Sigrid Vertommen, Soraya El Kahlaoui, Priya Kandaswamy, Sandhya Luther, Meeta Rani Jha, Tiffany Jean Willoughby-Herard, Leti Volpe, Skye Ward, Maria Benedito-Basto, Lawrence Cohen, the late Siddhartha Gautam Gupta, Julie Gorecki, Tanushree Gangopadhayay, Geeta Shah, Amina Mama, Fatima Ait Ben Lmamdani, Wanda Alarcón, Alisa Bierria, Cindi Cruz, Kader Attia, Karl Britto, Sheba Chhachhi, Hatem Bazian, Ingrid Steinmeister, Fatou Sow, Souad Benani, Kathleen Dameron, Caleb Dawson, Diana Eck, Vinicius Kauê Ferreira, Kerby Lynch, Margo Okazawa-Rey, Gayatri Chakravarty Spivak, Rina Nissim, Norma Cantú, Heidi Nast, Alana Lentin, Shireen Hassim, Hanane Karimi, Janet Jacobsen, Bob Lederer, Nikki Jones, Camilla Hawthorne, Patricia Penn Hilden, Thamy Ayouch, Marlon Biley, Lauren Berlant, Dorothy Austin, Randy P. Connor, Houria Bouteldja, Seloua Luste Boulbina, Paul Amar, Maylei Blackwell, Angelika Sifaki, Lucha Corpi, Gaia Maqui Giuliani, Cathy Hannabach, U Aldridge Hansberry, David Hatfield Sparks, Corinna Gould, Caren Kaplan, Anne McClintock, Mame-Fatou Niang, Ewa Alicja Majewska, Nivedita Menon, Geeta Patel, Raka Ray, David Palumbo-Liu, Ochy Curiel Pichardo, Lissell Quiroz, Shailja Patel, Azadeh Kian, AnaLouise Keating, Noémi Michel, Sunaina Maira, Gabriel Rockhill, Jasbir Puar, Gerard Koskovitch, Keo Echeveria, Lisa Dettmer, Alana Lentin, Chia Longman, Azeezah Kanji, Gauri Chowdhary, Anjali Arondekar, Béatriz Rettig, Frances Hasso, Muriel Grenet, Sonia Jabbar, the late Kumari Jayawardena, Bev Ditsie, Ashwini Sukthankar, Ashwini Tambe, Ghiwa Sayegh, Francie Foster, Jayati Lal, Gohar Shanazaryan, Abha Bhaiya, Gayatri Gopinath, Paola Zaccharia, Amina Wadud, Cristina Scheibe Wolf, Paula Barreto Silva, Evelyn Blackwood, Angela Harris, Kathryn Moeller, Nadia Seti, Steven Small, the late Kamla Bhasin, Ben Papadopoulos, Piro Rexhepi, Tanya Golash-Boza, Anna M. Agathangelou, SA Smythe, the late Salim Kidwai, Inès de Luna, Tamar Shirinian, Kanchana Natarajan, Laura Perez, Debarati Sanyal, Jennifer Terry, Maira Kubik Mano, Moon Charania, Fania Noël, Teresa Sacchet, Saida Barkat, Ramon Grossfoguel, Paolo Guerra, Sangita Shroff, Jyoti Puri, Lisbet Tellefsen, Tamar Shirinian, Melissa Thackaway,

Jovita Xixikinha, Laura Wexler, Elena Vasilou, Chela Zimmouri, Caleb Luna, the late Lenn Keller, Margaret Power, Jeanne Scheper, Fouzieyha Towghi, Kath Weston, Howard Winant, Tobaron Waxman, Cha Prieur, Vrushali Patel, Govan Scott Lewis, Jose David Saldivar, Tanika Sarkar, Lok Siu, Zakia Salime, Adrienne Torf, Keo Echeveria, Vitória Silveira, Katharine Trajano, Denize Ribeiro, Adi Morosophe, Pat Purt, Susan Stryker, Dina Siddiqi.

I am grateful to you, my dear nieces and nephews, for being in my life. You are my teachers from whom I continue to learn: Gianna, Chelsa, Nigel, Urias, Tyla, Tavares, Amos, Autumn, Elijah, Ethan, Lily, Steph, and Laila.

Again, many thanks to Angela Figueiredo for everything.

At Duke University Press I am indebted to Ken Wissoker, who from the beginning to the end kindly shepherded this book. I also thank Ryan Kendall, Ihsan Taylor, and Jade Brooks for their extensive help. Thank you to the very many anonymous reviewers at Duke University Press whose comments enhanced the book. Thank you to Ideas on Fire. I am grateful to my generous colleagues and friends who offered to read the entire manuscript and whose thoughtful comments kept me on my toes: Norma Alarcón, Lisa Rofel, Angana Chatterji, Richard Shapiro, and Abdul Janmohammad.

For financial support at various stages I thank: the Fulbright Program; the Andrew W. Mellon Foundation; the University of California Humanities Research Institute; the Al-Falah Program of the Center for Middle Eastern Studies at the University of California, Berkeley; the Office of Research at the University of California, Berkeley; Bear Funds at the University of California, Berkeley; the Vice Chancellor for Research Book Subvention; and the France-Berkeley Fund. Many thanks to the *École des hautes études en sciences sociales* for financing a residency period in Paris. Thank you to the Ministry of Education, Government of Brazil, for a travel grant. For opportunities for exchanges with colleagues, I am grateful to the Center for Race and Gender, and the Townsend Center, both at the University of California, Berkeley; the University of California Humanities Research Institute; and the University of California Center for New Racial Studies. I thank the French Consulate of San Francisco for funding for the international conference on Gender in Multiplicities: Intersectionality, Decoloniality, Assemblages, Co-Formations that I organized at University of California, Berkeley. I am particularly grateful to the French Consulate's cultural attaché, Stéphane Ré.

I also want to thank the cats whose person I am—Maya, Aimée, JazzCat—along with the neighborhood cats who are regulars for breakfast at home—Mr. Boots and Ollie—for insisting that I take breaks from my research and writing to fulfill your many demands: for affection, food, playtime, to break up fights, or to clean up your various messes. Thank you to the free flying birds in the neighborhood, most especially Tara and Tara Ki Saheli of the springtime, for providing beautiful chirpy soundtracks during your stays on our terrace and for continually reminding me how all *beings-becomings* on the planet are centrally important to my life.

INTRODUCTION

Openings

I dream of what it would be to take a collective breath,
to reimagine how we might stop reacting and lean into a
paradigm of our own creation . . .

    Assata Shakur

We are in an epoch of simultaneity.

    Michel Foucault, *Des espaces autres*

Wherever you are is the entry point.

    Kabir

This book speaks to an urgency of our times: the need to come together across the planet massively, to transform relations of power, to preserve and to invent new modes of collective *freedom-life*. It is an invitation to academics, activists, and artivists to rethink where we are, how relations of power operate at present, how to dismantle them, and how to imagine and cocreate elsewheres together. The book aims to induce a pause in time so that—as Assata Shakur, Michel Foucault, and Kabir suggest above—we can "take a collective breath," find other "entry points" for resistance, and construct "a paradigm of our own creation."

    Unfortunately, earlier and present dominant critical theoretical tools in the United States, Western Europe, and sectors in the Global South(s) that reproduce and contribute to them are not fully suitable for such tasks. They have many limitations. Power is constantly reconfiguring its means and manifestations, but the current, most evident theorizations do not necessarily always grasp how power is operating at the moment.

    Historically and today dominant critical theorizations from the Global North(s) remain largely unconcerned with coloniality and further are often *colonialism-and-race-amnesic*. Some confuse questions of decolonization with social justice or civil rights (Tuck and Yang 2012). Many trap us in a binary of *subject-centric* vs. totally subjectless approaches to power. This is the case of a whole range of dominant Global Northern feminist and queer theory, for example. Some dominant critical theorizations confine us to reductive, homogenized, fixed definitions of "the" dominant or "the" subaltern subject, or of "the" Global North and "the" Global South, thereby conveniently erasing an entire range of often deadly relations of power inside and in relation to each ensemble. Unfortunately, dominant critical theorizations cannot clarify our thinking about how alliances fail or thrive.

Below dominant critical theory whole registers of subaltern critical theory in the Global North(s) remain underground, unheard, or inaccurately heard by inattentive, dominant-thinking critical subjects (Sithole 2020). Some of this theory is actually imperceptible in dominant fields of intelligibility. In a parallel mode to dominant critical theory, much of what is currently recognized as subaltern critical theory, too, flows transnationally, unidirectionally from the Global North(s) across the planet. In many sites across the Global South(s) there are university courses and dissertations on subaltern critical theory from the Global North(s) while the subaltern theoretical production in the same Global Southern countries remains marginalized or erased. The theory that streams in this one-way traffic is often used in productive ways, especially when modified, adapted, and transformed *in-context*. Yet we might ask: What are such theories blocking and how?[1] The one-way flow, the enrooting of the categories, logics, presuppositions, and conclusions that it carries, even as they are constructively reimagined *in-context*, can simultaneously lead to inadvertent suppression or obstruction of other possibilities in the site of their arrival. In that sense, albeit with great caution, we can speak of a kind of Global Northern subaltern *epistemic imperialism* that is an effect not of the imperial agency of subaltern theorizing subjects or even of the theory itself, but rather of the flows and blockages produced by transnational relations of power.

This book attempts to open up how we think about relations of power, subjects, and potentialities for alliances across the planet. It tries to suggest new languages as open spaces that can help us to imagine multiple differential sites at once, including in ways that will be incomprehensible outside their context. To do so, the book respectfully engages with both loud and silenced present theorizations even as it labors to reorient us elsewhere. Unfortunately, the work in this book is imperfect, flawed, and sometimes even problematic. It is at every turn capable of inadvertently reproducing everything it opposes and of blocking everything it loves. But we must risk these challenges and more if we are to ever move ourselves into a useful space of possibility. To do so, ultimately, the book proposes some different kinds of critical *theory-assemblages* to think and feel with.

We can think of *theory-assemblages* as ensembles, clusters, or constellations of approaches, theorizations, concepts, logics, sensings, ways of knowing, kinds of knowledge productions, and knowledges. We need new kinds of *theory-assemblages* to open our thought processes, our perception, and modes of meaning making, to comprehend and change our worlds. The *theory-assemblages* I suggest in this book intend to be obsessively attentive to the immediate contexts, lives, perspectives, theorizations, sensings, practices, priorities, and *freedom-exigencies* of the very most extreme subaltern subjects and *beings-becomings* across the planet. Again, this is an impossible task but a necessary aspiration.

I draw the notion of assemblages in *theory-assemblages* from both the English translation of the French term *agencement* and the English definition of the term *assemblages*. In French popular culture and for Gilles Deleuze and Félix Guattari, *agencement* carries the connotation of an action, a doing, or *operability* (Rey and Rey-Debove 1984; Deleuze and Guattari 1980; see below and chapters 3 and 4). Accordingly, the *theory-assemblages* that this book proposes are meant to be dynamic, pliable, reworkable, *in-movement*. They specifically do not constitute a map or program for liberation. They have no set content, boundaries, or plans. They are not meant to be universal or even universalizable. They have no pretention to "applicability" everywhere. For, we are not in the realm of a computer program. Nor are we in sync with colonial progress narratives that unhelpfully presume a "one theory suits all" position with the Global North(s) invariably, oppressively, as the ultimate "freedom" model. Some approaches, concepts, logics, sensings, ways of knowing within these pages will—perhaps fortunately—be absolutely unworkable in some contexts. Others, I hope, will be useful to *freedom-exigent* desires, practices, and movements when reimagined, rerooted, recalibrated, perhaps totally resignified and differently operationalized, or oppositionally frontally rejected in the specifics of given contexts. The concepts, approaches, and orientations in this book are meant as infinitesimal possible points of departure, not arrival.

I understand the notion of theory in *theory-assemblages* as akin to poetry. Such *theory-as-poetry* can be beautiful and loving beyond the words in which it is conveyed. It can disrupt and overcome epistemic barriers. It can unsuppress thought and affect. It can give us other ways of sensing, knowing, critiquing, and constructing. It can produce affect that we cannot yet explain. It can usher in new floods of meaningfulness. It can transport us into other worlds. It can create new times and spaces. It can completely transform our lives. Without *theory-as-poetry* to bring us emotionally, psychically, mentally elsewhere, we risk eternally reproducing the same. *Theories-as-poetry* enact as subjects-agents to move and reorient us elsewhere within, without.

Co-Motion

A pivotal notion in the *theory-assemblages* here is *co-motion*. It is a key term in the book's title, its raison d'être and its main arc. I propose *co-motion* as a large umbrella to include myriad disparate ways that people and social movements come together. *Co-motion* is about unity (*co*) and action (*motion*) together. It also suggests convergent collective affect (*emotion*). Some various kinds of *co-motion* formations are alliances, coalitions, networks, concerted action, unions, associations, unifications, mergings, assemblages, collaborations, solidarities, leagues, collectivities, bonds, convergences, groupings, assemblies, and links. I elaborate the concept of *co-motion* in chapter 2. Here, I want to highlight that for *co-motion* the different terms for coming together are not just semantic. Instead, they entail distinct kinds of subjects, social glue, and projects. *Co-motion* is a large rubric that enables us to discuss them all together.

In these pages I primarily address power and *co-motion*—instead of political or social movement programs—because there are potentially infinite possibilities for getting us to a desirable place for concerted *freedom-exigent transformation* once we more fully understand where we are, in what relations of power we are entrapped, how we are interrelated, and how to move together toward *freedom-life*. Foucault (1981) cautions: "The idea of a program of proposals is dangerous. As soon as a program is presented, it becomes the law, and there's a prohibition against inventing. There ought to be an inventiveness special to a situation like ours." The Invisible Committee (2009, 19) reminds us: "If one knows how to move, the absence of a schema is not an obstacle but a source of opportunity." Thus, this book is an incitement to pause for a moment to radically rethink power and to create *freedom-exigent* solidarities. It hopes to incite a direct assault on the colonial-capitalist-imperialist-racial-gendered-speciesist tactic of divide and rule as we know it today across its many manifestations across the planet.

This book arrives in a period of stunning, confusing paradoxes. Our times are murderous, characterized by the expansion of violent practices of elimination. As I am completing this introduction, Donald Trump has been reelected to the presidency in the United States. This event is part of a broader, rapid rise in extreme right-wing forces, including fascist forces, transnationally. Right-wing leaders, groups, and movements inspire each other and work together. They sometimes share finances, discourses, spaces, strategies, and tactics. Some right wings are brought into state power via "democratic" national elections, as in the United States, India, Brazil, Italy, Turkey, Hungary, Austria, Poland, Japan, Russia, Burma, and Israel. Others are organized into growing oppositional political parties, as in France, Belgium, Switzerland, Sweden, Denmark, and Holland (Bugnon 2022; Durham and Power 2010). Wherever they can, they facilitate, accelerate, or regenerate lethal conditions, whether via proactive enactments, calculated inaction to let die, or apathetic inertia.

Besides the usual recruits, today's right wings are increasingly attracting some queer and trans people and integrating them at high levels. They seduce queer and trans subjects from dominant social sectors by appealing to racialized, ethnic, or religious group privilege and assigning exceptional queerphobia and transphobia to subalternly racialized, ethnicized, or religious Others (Dutta 2023; Bakshi 2022; Bacchetta 2019c, 2004, 1996, 1994; Bacchetta and Power 2002; Sarkar and Butalia 1996). In 2017, a survey by *Institut d'études politiques* (Institute for Political Studies) in France revealed that 38.5 percent of white French gay men voted for the fascist National Front. One white gay man, Florian Phillipot, rose to the party's highest ranks; two others became mayors: Fabien Engelmann and Steve Briois. Milo Yiannopoulos, who is white, British, and gay and infamously calls Trump "Daddy," spent years on US campuses loudly inciting passions against trans people, undocumented people, feminism, affirmative action, and the left. In India, the Hindu extreme right is recruiting some Hindu trans subjects and pitting them against Muslim trans subjects (Dutta 2023; Bakshi 2022). At the same time queer and trans people in these and many other sites are engaged in mutual survival, in oppositional and non-oppositional resistance, and in the creation of spaces of freedom no matter how precarious (see, for example, chapter 5).

I also write at a time when the Israeli state, enabled by the military and financial backing of the US Government, is committing a highly spectacularized, outright genocide in Gaza. Since October 2023, transnational media has been flooded with images of Palestinian bodies of women, children, and men in rubble; bodies wrapped in plastic bags; bodies mutilated and maimed; ruins of entire neighborhoods, homes, hospitals, camps, infrastructure, educational institutions, everything, flattened by Israeli bombing. The enormity and vastness of devastation and suffering in Gaza, along with other ongoing invisibilized genocides (Rohingya, Uyghurs, populations in Sudan, etc.), make this specific moment of the world absolutely horrifying. At the same time, this unspeakable violence is being met with ongoing Palestinian resistance and with extensive solidarity movements across the globe in which anticolonial, anti-imperialist feminists, queers, and trans people are among others playing a crucial role despite intense repression.

The book also comes on the cusp of a period when the world's many preexisting inequities and brutalities of power were aggravated by the COVID-19 pandemic. It had ushered in a murderous triple exposure. First, COVID-19 put into relief the life and death quality of human-to-human interrelationality and of our inseparability from other *beings-becomings* on the planet. Our survival depends on each other. Second, COVID-19 both spectacularized and invisibilized power. The viciousness of colonialism, the forms of racial capitalism that continue colonial logics and practices and that naturalize ongoing imperialist enactments—whether as oppression, repression, exploitation, occupation, dispossession, extraction, appropriation, subjugation, subjectivation, epistemic violence, spiritual obliteration, psychic suffering, incarceration, inequity, or annihilation—are ever more apparent. Across the Global North(s) and South(s), maps of places without access to adequate living conditions, vaccinations and medical care, maps of war and fast or slow military destruction, and maps of extraction and toxification correspond directly to sites of higher rates of infection, illness, and death. While workers are losing jobs, corporate profits are soaring.

At the same time, many merciless inequities remain concealed and the people most subjected to them disregarded. They constitute what earlier HIV activists called the viral underclass, defined not as those infected with a virus (HIV, COVID-19, or other) but rather as those who are "needlessly" exposed to conditions that "shape their lives" such that they are infinitely more susceptible to viral infection (Thrasher 2020). They are subjected to planned deprivations, exclusions, forms of violence, and everything else that leads—as Ruth Wilson Gilmore's (2007) work sustains—to premature death. Third, the pandemic revealed how, for the very most subaltern subjects anywhere, some forms of *co-motion*—such as solidarities, collaborations, bonds, unity—have long been in place as a necessity without which bare survival is foreclosed. This book directly addresses the power that creates and sustains these brutal conditions, as well as modes of coming together to transform them.

Indeed, simultaneously, many kinds of *freedom-exigent* activisms, artivisms, and movements are expanding. They are creating new subjectivities and forms of *co-motion*. Besides the above mentioned examples. In recent years global mass media has amply covered autonomous feminist movements that are flourishing and transnationally converging against sexual violence—whether self-designated as MeToo, *Ni Una Menos* (Not One [Woman] Less), or other. In 2020 Black Lives Matter (BLM) swelled from its US base to become unstoppable across Western Europe and Abya Yala, both places with an infinitely longer history of antiracism theorizations and movements.[2] In 2019, activists in several countries organized massive protest against social and economic injustice, often inspiring each other: in Algeria, Bolivia, Chile, Colombia, Ecuador, Egypt, France, Germany, Guinea, Haiti, Honduras, Hong Kong, India, Indonesia, Iran, Iraq, Lebanon, the Netherlands, Spain, Sudan, the UK, and Zimbabwe. In 2014, solidarity against that year's earlier Israeli massacre in Gaza became visibly planetary. Shortly before all of that, in 2011 spectacular, vast uprisings for dignity and social justice arose globally: Tunisia's "Arab Spring," the *Indignados* (Outraged) in Spain, and Occupy revolts in Africa, Asia, Europe, the United States, and elsewhere. While feminists, queers, and trans activists have long been participants and leaders in broader peoples' movements, in many places they now specifically bring analyses of gender and sexuality to the center.

Today, as dominant media highlight larger scale revolts, many less noticed *freedom-exigent* movements are also unfolding. Since a recent gathering in Chiapas, Mexico, in 2018, Indigenous feminists across Abya Yala, Turtle Island, Aotearoa, the Pacific, and elsewhere have been assembling regularly in global transtribal meetings.[3] In Western Europe, separate movements against Islamophobia, Romaphobia, and anti-Black racism are now uniting. Global Northern queers of color, Global Southern queers, and allies now work together in networks: against colonialism; coloniality; racisms including casteism; capitalism; the multiple kinds of sexist and queerphobic social structures, systems, configurations, and assemblages that I refer to under the rubric of *misogynarchies*; and speciesism (see chapter 4; Bacchetta 2025c, 2017; Bakshi et al. 2016).[4] Present country-specific activisms and moves to link across borders are the fruitful culmination of years of prior revolts, insurgencies, critical art, poetry, music, literature, daily practices of living together otherwise, and transnational solidarities from which we can learn immensely (see chapter 5).

Unfortunately, historically and today, often when we seem to be in revolution, in revolt, or at least in a critical period of hope, the tables quickly turn. In an early example, after the radical 1968 movements in the United States, Richard Nixon came to power. Several recent revolutions in North Africa and the Middle East were followed by dictatorships. In France, after BLM uprisings, the government outlawed autonomous groups of people of color (see chapter 5). Brazil's evolution with social justice was brutally interrupted when in 2016 the right-wing Bolsonaro government took power. Though the extreme right was (barely) defeated in Brazil's 2022 elections, as in the United States' 2020 elections, deep political divides, social damage, the naturalization of right-wing discourses and practices for a broader part of the population, remain. The Trump campaign capitalized on this situation as one among other factors in the 2024 US elections. At present we lack adequate ways of analyzing why such simultaneous openings and closures happen and how to prevent this.

In this contradictory, unsettling planetary context, in the face of the present acceleration of harm, our stakes for understanding power and its operations across scales, and for creating effective *freedom-exigent co-motion* together, could not be higher. This book hopes to make an epistemic and praxis-oriented intervention into these conditions as it proposes *theory-assemblages* precisely for those aims. In doing so, the book is expansive but also has limitations. It does not claim to account for every kind of power, subject, or form of organizing everywhere. That would be impossible and not necessarily fruitful. Instead, this book is primarily concerned with the inseparability of multiplicities of relations of power—colonialism, coloniality, capitalism, imperialism, racism, *misogynarchies*, speciesism—and with *co-motion* that speaks to the conditions and *freedom-exigencies* of extremely subaltern subjects and *beings-becomings*. The book is also limited in space. It addresses mainly four countries: France, Italy, India, and the United States. It refuses to reduce them to passive terrains on which analysis can be imposed. Instead, it engages their theorizations and practices. Each site has different kinds of epistemic, methodological, and empirical contributions and implications (Pandey 1992, 28; Balasurya 1984; Spivak 2003). And, since each is connected to other places by relations of power, many additional locations enter and exit these pages.

Lines of Flight

Four interrelated lines of flight—or axes that try to escape confines, soar, and open up yet other theoretical, affective, praxis-oriented spaces as they move—traverse this book. They are: *freedom-exigent transformation*; power; the constellation *subalternative sensing, perception,* and *intelligibility*; and methodological *operability.*

Freedom-Exigent Transformation

A first moving streak here—that hopefully unseals other apertures ad infinitum—is *freedom-exigent transformation.* It is about creating conditions to become radically free together. The notion of *freedom* in *freedom-exigent* requires the end of colonialism, capitalism, imperialism, racism, all formations of sexism, queerphobias, transphobias, speciesisms, and kinds of rampant destruction of the planet, however they may manifest. *Exigent* in *freedom-exigent* reminds us that freedom is an emergency, a pressing need, a requirement, yet an always unfinished project. We are never already there. It is a continual striving, or what Angela Davis theorizes as "a constant struggle" "without closure" (Davis 2013). To invoke *transformation* with *freedom-exigent* is to make clear that the present order must go. It means a massive uprooting, demolition, and transformation of power. It entails the end of oppression, repression, exploitation, occupation, dispossession, extraction, appropriation, subjugation, subjectivation, epistemic violence, spiritual obliteration, psychic suffering, incarceration, inequity, annihilation. We will need to *sense, perceive,* newly imagine, hallucinate, dream, and envision differently together. It is about alternatively calibrating, assembling, organizing, materializing life for thrive-able relationalities to each other and the planet.

Yet, who and what can constitute *freedom-exigent transformative* forces or not? Not all subjects implicated in *freedom-exigent transformation,* who will change, can so easily become actors of transformation. In these pages it will become clear that the subject-agent of *freedom-exigent co-motion* is vastly beyond the neoliberal, individual, bounded I-subject (see chapter 2). If total *freedom-life* implicates all of life—including its forms that are dominantly not considered to be life at all—then we are in the realm of completely other epistemes, with different sets of categories, logics, presuppositions, and conclusions. The subject of transformation will need to understand some part of oneself in a radically different relationality to other forms of life and to the planet (TallBear 2017; Anzaldúa [1987] 2007).

We will see later that the subjects and *beings-becomings* who/that will be actors of transformation will have to be expansive enough to include sentient life such as a cat, goat, insect, and fish; nonsentient life such as land, minerals, sea, stars, the sun, and air; and entities and subjective states such as ghosts, presences, ancestors, and future descendants. Each is, together we are, all of that. *Freedom-exigent transformation* is about and for all subjects and *beings-becomings* and the planet. It includes freedom for all our dead and as-yet-unborn.

How all this can unfold is a vast area filled with questions. We already know something—far from everything—about what kinds of environments, social formations, mechanisms, and practices must dissolve, be gone. They encompass what Achille Mbembe calls "deathworlds," or the brutal living conditions created by necropolitics that transform people into "living dead" (2019). They include what Orlando Patterson calls conditions of "social death," or the murderous situations of subjects who are not considered fully human (1982). They encompass what Rob Nixon terms "slow violence," or the environmental conditions that, via "incremental and accretive" violence, have harmful-to-lethal effects (2013). They entail what Abdul R. JanMohamed frames as "death-boundedness," or preexisting social orders and settings for eventual death for Black people and other subaltern subjects in the United States (2005). They are about what Ruth Wilson Gilmore highlights as spaces of "pre-mature death," or environments of power that cause Black and other racialized peoples' untimely elimination (2007). This and other kinds of lethal structurings are producing ever more blatantly murderous effects. These are important examples, yet they are not the sum of relations of power or of power's *operability*. The planet is more complex. It is saturated with flagrant power relations: colonialism, capitalism, imperialism, racism, *misogynarchies*, speciesism, and other kinds of local manifestations of power that can and cannot be named. Also, some power remains imperceptible, often with dramatically virulent effects.

To begin to constitute *theory-assemblages* that make *freedom-exigent transformation* central, this book suggests and elaborates concepts such as *freedom-exigency, subjects-in-socialities and another, subaltern-to-dominant continuum, liberation-orientation,* and *situated planetarities.*

Power

A second necessary line of flight here concerns coming to a more multidimensional and comprehensive analysis of power. This book is vitally concerned with rethinking relations of power because currently our lack of understanding is a daunting obstacle to *freedom-life*. Relations of power co-constitute the conditions in which we live. They form and deform us, alienate us from ourselves, each other, and the planet. They block and destroy the will to *freedom-exigency*. They implode, explode, and obliterate *freedom-exigent co-motion*.

This book frontally addresses multiplicities of power and their many kinds of *operabilities*. Most scholarly and activist analyses of power focus on visible power and its apparent effects. That work is extremely important. However, this book equally problematizes imperceptible power that passes under our radar and yet functions intensely. Whether obvious, noticeable, or undetectable at all, relations of power saturate every context across every geopolitical and human scale across the planet. They are part of the very formation of subjects, as Foucault would have it, but also of objects, social and political arrangements, and all of life including its forms that pass for nonlife. It is futile to try to become free without an adequate understanding of the kinds, dimensions, registers, manifestations, silent workings, and effects of power.

I proposed above that a major problem for *freedom-exigent co-motion* is that before it fulfills its promise it gets disrupted, disordered, fragmented, dissolved, even reversed. The most widespread explanation for demise is that powerful actors such as the state, its apparatuses, or other hostile agents act against it. Certainly, across the planet many modes of repression and destruction that attack alliances from their outsides abound. They include targeted assassination, genocide, maiming for incapacitation, incarceration, and slow death of potential insurgents induced by poverty, starvation, (in) toxifications, psychic warfare, isolation, and alienation.

Among states' arsenals for *co-motion* destruction are some particularly insidious modes of co-optation. One such tactic is replacement. For instance, in France in 1985, at the height of the powerful grassroots antiracism movement led by working-class racialized youth, the government stepped in and created its own organization, SOS Racisme (SOS Racism), to derail the earlier movement and substitute its own for it.[5] SOS Racisme was soon everywhere: in schools, universities, the streets. It forced the grassroots movement into the margins where it eventually suffocated. Another state tactic is selective assimilation to split and deradicalize movements. In a recent pre-Trump phase of homotransnationalism, many Global Northern States and right-wing civilian sectors that were previously homo-allergic began to align around newly acceptable models for "national homosexuality" (i.e., of cisgender homonormative queer subjects from dominant sectors) configured against the backdrop of monsterized, racialized, queer, and queered Others (Puar 2007; Bacchetta and Haritaworn 2011). They performed a kind of "murderous inclusion" of some properly disciplined queer subjects in a move that made Global Northern gay rights usable, alongside earlier colonial-racial assertions about women's rights, to judge selective Global Southern states as inherently undemocratic and inegalitarian, to legitimize Northern imperial interventions into the South(s) (Haritaworn et. al. 2013). With the increasing consolidation of extreme-right political power, right-wing-governed countries are shifting backward to pre-homonationalist times. An example is Trump's redefinition in 2018 for Title IX of gender specifically along heterosexist binary lines, as exclusively male or female, a reductive categorization that—as widely flagged across United States and some international media—flies in the face of science (that demonstrates gender and sex flexibilities and spectrums), demonized queer and trans people, and excluded them from the protections against gender discrimination that are guaranteed by Title IX (Green et. al 2018; *Guardian* 2018; Rivas 2018). After a four-year reprieve, on January 20, 2025, a newly elected Trump signed Executive Order 14188, effectively reiterating his 2018 declaration about exclusive binary sex and stipulating the denial of federal funding to "gender ideology" (a right-wing category defined to encompass any scientific or other research and teaching, advocacy, or activisms that question, defy, or bypass the imposed exclusive cisgender hetero sex binary). This example demonstrates how, for some subaltern subjects—here queer and trans people—despite back and forth historical shifts, vulnerability remains a permanent condition.

However, interference by adverse states or other antagonistic forces cannot fully explain the destruction of *freedom-exigent* mobilizations. Unfortunately, all too often the power that saturates the context in which *freedom-exigent* activisms emerge is systematically, albeit unintentionally, reproduced inside them. The reiteration of relations of power inside *co-motion* can fragment and extinguish it. To try to understand how this happens, I draw on Foucault's notion of power as a microphysics that flows, is blocked, melts, crystallizes here and there, disperses, or dissolves, even if I expand on his idea of power and also bring it elsewhere into other realms (Foucault 2001c, 2000a, 1977, 1976). With Foucault in mind, there can be no neat binary between power and resistance. Power contains the potentiality for its own demise; resistance is saturated with power and power gets reproduced within it (see chapters 3, 4, 5). For instance, decolonial activists in France critique French workers' struggles for ignoring the conditions of racialized working-class people, thereby reproducing coloniality and racism; this assessment was part of the rationale for the creation of the Parti des indigènes de la République (Party of the Indigenous of the Republic).[6] At Standing Rock, Native organizers decried some white participants for living off Native generosity, avoiding collective work, and illegitimately speaking for the movement to media, thereby reenacting white settler supremacy (O'Connor 2016). At Occupy Wall Street, some homeless participants highlighted that privileged activists pushed them out to ensure the movement's respectability, ironically based on class; meanwhile, some activists sustained that police sent in ostensibly homeless people to break up the camps (Chen 2011). Women and queer subjects in many insurgencies point to how other activists subject them to sexist and queerphobic violence (Kingsley 2013).

The internal dynamics of power in such mobilizations—as in the daily lives of the people who comprise them—often (not always) unfold without intention. This is because, in the Foucauldian sense, as subject-effects or subjects co-constituted in and by the relations of power that saturate our contexts, we always risk reiterating and reenacting that power, even involuntarily and unknowingly (Foucault 2000b). At times the reproduction of relations of power becomes flagrant and is named in discussions within alliances. Yet, at present, at least some of the power in which we are saturated, in which we are co-constituted as subjects, remains imperceptible even as it performs its devastating operations on us.

One obstacle to understanding how power operates is analytical *subject-centricity*, or making people's agency as wielders of power the center of attention. Nearly all studies of the failures of mobilizations attribute dissolution to actors, whether external or internal to the mobilizations. Yet, *subject-centric* approaches tend to dehistoricize and dematerialize power. They miss many kinds, dimensions, and registers of power, its agencies and operations. They cannot account for how power structures our lives.

Subject-centric analytics also often inadvertently reproduce essentialist assumptions about subjects. They do not necessarily have clarity about what defines people in dominant sectors of society, or an oppressed collectivity or subject. They risk presuming a binary between good allies vs. bad other people who induce, maintain, or intensify harm to subalterns. They frequently imagine the ally as a noble, exceptional, even saintly subject from the dominant social sector in a sea of evil peers (Indigenous Action 2014). This construction can inadvertently place the ally above critique. It also risks reinforcing the idea that the dominant social sector comprises free-willed individuals who can choose to be allies while oppressed subaltern subjects comprise a nonagentic undifferentiated mass (Da Silva 2007). It can problematically presume that the task of ending oppression naturally belongs to those who most suffer from it, instead of to all people. Such presuppositions about responsibility minimalize or erase the commitments, sacrifices, pain, and physical and psychic burdens of subalterns fighting their own (people's) oppression. They can preempt the idea that a subaltern subject can be an ally to other subaltern subjects within and beyond one's own community or social sector. They can unproductively make subaltern subjects judges of privileged allies. In such cases the allies risk getting interpellated as guilty, confessing subjects. Yet, guilt and shame are rarely politically productive affects. Such dynamics can shift the focus away from politics toward moralism, which can drive the now depoliticized dominant ally toward individualized self-help and self-improvement. These mechanisms and ostensible solutions can substitute for actual work to change material conditions that are harmful, even deadly. A *subject-centric* approach often keeps dominant subjects, now in the form of exceptions as allies, at the epicenter of analysis and action, thereby reinforcing the relations of power that *freedom-exigent co-motion* aims to work to end. *Subject-centricity*—which diverts attention away from power's operations and toward its effects on subjects—also risks homogenizing complex entities deemed as enemies, such as the state or global capitalism, and unhelpfully locating power in subjects and institutions as their possession (see chapter 3).

Thus, this book tries to open up how we think about power and its *operability*. It is especially interested in understanding the kinds of power that we cannot yet perceive or identify. For these aims it suggests and expands on concepts such as *situated planetarities, co-formations, co-productions, scattered hegemonies, saturations,* and *dilutions of power, et cetera; x; and (in) articulations* (see chapters 2, 3, 4, 5).

Subalternative Sensing, Perception, and Intelligibility

A third, related line of flight is the dynamic constellation comprised of *subalternative sensing, perception,* and *intelligibility*. This ensemble aims to free us and propel us out of habits of knowing and meaning making that keep us in chains. *Subalternative sensing, perception,* and *intelligibility* is about affirming, developing, or creating radical sensibilities and understandings beyond dominant epistemes and even beyond some normative subaltern epistemes. Everything, everyone at present is saturated *in-coloniality, in-global-racial-capitalism, in-racialization, in-misogynarchies*. Thus, no current episteme is completely free from the dominant episteme's effects or threats of effects. In this contaminated world, the cluster *subalternative sensing, perception*, and *intelligibility* incites us to further affirm, expand, and/or create disallowed forms of knowledge and knowledge production. Some already exist in various Native and other Global Southern epistemologies. They are also present in many kinds of nonlinear kinds of reasoning, dreams, deliria, hallucinations, trance states, and visions (see also Bénani et. al. 2025; Bennani 2022; Di Pietro 2020a; Pérez 2019, 2007; Anzaldúa 2009a). This cluster invites us to seek yet other ways of knowing altogether with other subjects and *beings-becomings*. For example, what can I learn about power, subjects, and alliances from a tree, a bird, or a snake beyond those thematics? The constellation *subalternative sensing, perception*, and *intelligibility* is useful to constructing *freedom-exigent theory-assemblages* that speak to what in chapter 4 I call *situated planetarities*.

But what exactly do the components in *subalternative sensing, perception*, and *intelligibility* signify and how do they work? First, let us distinguish *subalternative* from *subaltern* and *subalternist*. I discuss *subaltern* in some detail in chapter 2. Here, I will briefly invoke Antonio Gramsci's use of *subaltern* to mean any subordinated subjects *in-relationality* to any dominant subjects. For Gramsci, there are many kinds of subalterns: working-class peoples (vs. factory owners), prisoners (vs. the state and the nonincarcerated), peasants (vs. rural elites and urban dwellers), but also rural elites of inferiorized regions (vs. urban elites in dominant regions). The example of rural elites demonstrates how a same group can be dominant in some relations and subordinate in others. For Gramsci, the subaltern subject cannot stand alone, is never fixed or homogenous. The subaltern is always relative. The above examples suggest how for Gramsci many criteria can define the subaltern: economic, cultural, linguistic, geographic, etc.

To consider the *in-relationality* of subalterns and to account for how multiple kinds of power operate to form subaltern subjects and their interrelations, in chapter 2 I draw specifically on Gramsci to suggest considering subalterns along a dynamic *subaltern-to-dominant continuum*. The notion of a continuum puts into relief not only that there are many kinds of subaltern subjects but moreover that there are many degrees of subalterneity and dominance. Given the real or potential instability of the social realm, the subaltern and the positionality that a subaltern (collectivity or individual) may occupy at any given point can change. It can all be in flux. In the Gramscian sense, and with Foucault, there is no such thing as an absolute, fixed, forever subaltern.

Occupying a subaltern positionality does not make of the subaltern an inherently resistant subject. There is no natural correspondence between a subaltern social location and a critical political stance. This idea is complicit with some classical decolonial theorizations and some US feminist, lesbian, and queer of color theorizations that attest to how knowledge and ways of knowing are socially situated while refusing a reductionist, essentialist correlation between the subject, the subject's social location, analysis, and political conduct (Fanon 1952; Memmi 1973; Combahee River Collective 1977; Anzaldúa [1987] 2007; Lugones and Spelman 1983; Haraway 1988; Collins 1991). One of power's deadly operations for its own perpetuation is to alienate subaltern subjects from themselves so they will serve the dominant's interests. Among subalterns there is an array not only of different positionalities but also of mindsets.

In contrast, *subalternist* involves a sensibility and a stance oriented for the subaltern in the subaltern's interest. The speaking subject of a subalternist stance is most often the subaltern but can also be allies. A subalternist agenda is a program that is concerned with remedying the subaltern's conditions, via equality, equity or liberation. Unfortunately, a subalternist agenda does not necessarily strive to understand and terminate all oppression, repression, exploitation, occupation, dispossession, extraction, appropriation, subjugation, subjectivation, epistemic violence, spiritual obliteration, psychic suffering, incarceration, inequity, and annihilation. A *subalternist* project can advance the interests of some subalterns while leaving in place social structures and value systems that are murderous for others. Historically some anticolonial national movements worked for "the people's" liberation but left queerphobia intact. To build supportive life spaces for themselves, some Global Northern gentrifying white gay subjects displace people of color—including queers of color—from their homes (Haritaworn 2015a; Hanhardt 2013). Some Global Southern queers reiterate hierarchies of religion, class, and caste in queer movements (Bakshi 2022). Thus, any subaltern might do well to understand that there is always someone more subaltern than thou.

Finally, *subalternative*, as I mobilize the concept, is something entirely different. The term, proposed in the scholarly work of the sociologist Nacira Guénif-Souilamas and operationalized in some grassroots movements in France, signals a radical, critical subaltern politics far beyond identitarian affirmations, equality aims, or any partial liberation. Inspired by these renderings, herein I use *subalternative* in its sense of an alternative, an opening, a nonrepetition, an escape from reductive oppositionality. I also understand it as beyond the binary comprised of the presumed-to-be internally homogenized, bounded terms *subaltern* vs. *dominant*. The alternative that *subalternative* signifies can be oriented around the lives of, and in the interests of, the very most subaltern subjects. This way of thinking about *subalternative* is concerned with the *freedom-exigencies* of all, including those who are positioned in and outside the social fabric beneath the subjects who are perceived in dominant fields of intelligibility to be subaltern. A *subalternative* politics requires the freedom of the most extreme subalternized subjects *in-context* everywhere. It has no use for reforming presently murderous relations of power, such as equal rights for just some subalterns in coloniality, capitalism, imperialism, racism, and *misogynarchies*. Instead, a *subalternative* political project would demolish and transform relations of power, unleash floods of creativity, and invent thrive-able modes of life for all people, *beings-becomings*, and the planet. In keeping with a Gramscian notion of the subaltern as a subject *in-relationality* across many kinds of relations of power, *subalternative* describes *freedom-exigent* thought, feeling, enactments, practices, action, in any and all registers: economic, cultural, symbolic, psychic, energetic. *Subalternative* is fully incompatible with dominant assemblages of power. It is a frontal attack on them. And it is elsewhere from them.

What of the grouping *sensing, perception*, and *intelligibility* in the term *subalternative sensing, perception*, and *intelligibility*? Why is this cluster necessary to *freedom-exigent theory-assemblages*? How can we use it in analyses and activisms?

A different kind of *sensing, perception*, and *intelligibility*—one that is *subalternative*—is vital to comprehend the world, to make sense of it otherwise, to radically change it. At present we are saturated in dominant epistemes and fields of intelligibility (Fanon 1952; Appadurai 1984; Maldonaro-Torres 2008). They impose categories, presuppositions, logics, assumptions, conclusions, and common sense (Foucault 2000c). They limit our understanding and our capacities to imagine *freedom-exigent* elsewheres for the present and future. They act on our thought processes in destructive ways but also manifest, crystallize, self-perpetuate, reorganize themselves, in economies, institutions, culture, the body, the psyche. They occupy every dimension. They induce habits of thought, corporeality, affect, dispositions, tendencies. They cause numbness, forgetting, erasure.

Everywhere they enact epistemicide. And with it they induce what Trinh T. Minh-ha (2016) calls *lovecide* (death of love) and more broadly *affecticide*, or the obliteration of many kinds of *feeling, sensing,* and *perception.* Across vast parts of the planet, we now no longer know who we would have been, what and how we could have thought or felt, what kind of world we might have created had this lethal sensory and epistemic violence not occurred.

In this entrapment, the cluster *subalternative sensing, perception,* and *intelligibility* gives us hope. It reminds us how—even if we are formed in and caught in relations of power—we can escape. *Subalternative sensing, perception,* and *intelligibility* opens an exit, a line of flight, in dominant epistemes. Some of its methods are dreaming, hallucinating, trancing, states of spirit possession, and envisionings otherwise.

Some phenomena related to *subalternative sensing, perception,* and *intelligibility* already coexist beside or below dominant epistemes. One area is subaltern knowledges and knowledge production. It is happening across the Global North(s) and South(s). For example, Gramsci (1991) refers to nondominant knowledges and ways of knowing in Italy's impoverished southern provinces and islands as "popular" or "subaltern" knowledges. He describes them as amalgams formed by constantly selecting, integrating, and reframing dominant cultural elements into popular culture. Foucault writes of "subjugated knowledges," defined as either past dominant knowledges that are now disqualified or present nondominant knowledges that were not universalized (Foucault 1969, 2003). For Foucault we can reanimate "subjugated knowledges" by excavating their "genealogical fragments" and putting them "in circulation with each other," even if they risk getting "recoded in the dominant grid of intelligibility" (Foucault 2003, 10–11). Deleuze and Guattari (1975) invoke "minor knowledges" developed by populations that are sociological (not necessarily numerical) minorities. For them, "minor knowledges" sustain the populations' life and have implications for political resistance.

Some subaltern-generated theories, concepts, and approaches are actually closer than near, in fact already within, the realm of *subalternative sensing, perception,* and *intelligibility.* An example is Gloria Anzaldúa's theory of *la facultad,* a "survival tactic" that permits perception that is different from the dominant's expectations (Anzaldúa [1987] 2007). *La facultad* opens up alternate consciousness so the subject can intuit danger at the surface and the "soul" in the depth (Anzaldúa [1987] 2007). It is about instant sensing beyond the rational, a perception in surface realities of deeper realities. *La facultad* makes knowledge available to the subject through corporeal sensation. A related Anzaldúan notion is her queer elaboration of *ne-planta*, an Aztec concept to describe a transitional state in which humans "cross the border into other subjective levels of awareness," becoming "a tree, a coyote" or "another person" (Anzaldúa 2009a, 182). There is also the work of the Bolivian Native Aymara lesbian Julieta Paredas. She offers a conceptualization of knowing and *being-becoming* through a kind of fleshy human oneness that subverts coloniality, neoliberal individualism, the capitalist privatization of corporeality, and misogyny all at once. Paredas remarks: "We are flesh, we are people, we are not enemies, we are one. I am your body, you are my body."[7] Finally, an example of a subaltern practice of *subalternative sensing, perception,* and *intelligibility* is when queers in queerphobic societies develop "gaydar," or the capacity to *sense, perceive,* and render *intelligible* other queers even when the latter, generally for survival, are enacting heterosexual cisgender drag.

Many current forms of subaltern-inspired approaches to knowledge production reject dominant reason altogether because they associate it with colonialism, Eurocentric enlightenment, and racialized, gendered, speciesist classification and typologization schemes based in selected biological, climatic, or cultural criteria. *Subalternative sensing, perception,* and *intelligibility* is fully complicit with this anticolonial stance and yet, at the same time, can find value in some forms of dominant reason. Indeed, opposition to dominant reason is not inherently incompatible with power; it can even be lethally aligned with it. For example, in the United States and Brazil, evangelism—which claims "spiritual" ways of knowing against Western science—bolsters Trump and Bolsonaro (Amar 2013). In Uganda, Pentecostal divine knowledge is used to argue for the death penalty for homosexuals (Ekine and Abbas 2013).

The constellation *subalternative sensing, perception,* and *intelligibility* is intuitively aware of and has an aversion to dominant epistemes. It is allied with the below and the outside of dominant sociality. It can induce clarity about dominant knowledges, ways of knowing, and ways of life with which it is *co-present.*

Such a relation of *co-presence,* of dominant and *subalternative sensing, perception,* and *intelligibility* coexisting in a same time and space, can be read through the city of Paris. Dominant (white) French people can feel entitled to the space of Paris as an effect of their co-constitution as subjects in French nationalism and northern European supremacy. Yet, racialized French people who are massively concentrated in the "new colonial space" of the banlieues (racialized working-class suburbs) often have a troubled, doubled relation to Paris (Bancel and Blanchard 2002, 81). On the one hand, Paris has some familiar, hospitable neighborhoods with concentrations of racialized people and ethnic small businesses: Barbès, Belleville, la Goutte-d'Or, Ménilmontant. White supremacist elites generally avoid these areas unless out for an entertaining evening of cultural consumption, or to perform the (culinary and other) gesture that bell hooks calls "eating the other" (1992). Paris also has fluid sites of safety such as central Chatelet where the density of transnational tourists from across the globe and across classes can allow for anonymity (Bacchetta 2009a). On the other hand, for working-class racialized people much of Paris can feel distant, closed, foreign, domi-nating, wealthy, white supremacist. It has many intense anxiety zones.

One such disconcerting spot for many French racialized people is the Latin Quarter. Among relatively dominant subjects, the Latin Quarter is famous for its bourgeois cafés, universities, theaters, and restaurants. It is a favorite hub for elite and middle-class foreign tourists. However, a closer consideration of the place with subaltern interrelationality in mind reveals a world of distress. To understand this, only one temporal-spatiality there need be invoked: the massacre of Algerian nationalist demonstrators on October 17, 1961. This event indelibly marked Algerian descendants in France and has repercussions for other racialized people, too. The success of the 2005 film *Caché* (Hidden) by Michael Haneke suggests that the ef-fects of the psychic and political repression of October 17, 1961, on white French subjects who are directly entwined with its history can also be con-siderable (Chekkat and Mokaddem 2013).

October 17, 1961, began as an anticolonial demonstration in Paris (Lambert 2021). It was organized by the Algerian National Liberation Front against French colonialism and for Algerian independence. Be-tween twenty and thirty thousand Algerians—mainly adults but also some children—from Paris and its outskirts planned to converge in three areas in Paris. Before they reached their destinations, the French police attacked them with batons and guns. At Saint-Michel and Saint-Germain in the Latin Quarter police opened fire with live bullets. Many demonstrators were assassinated right there. Others, to avoid getting shot, jumped off the Saint Michel Bridge into the river Seine and drowned. Witnesses saw police throw dead bodies into the Seine throughout the night. Today the number of deaths is still under dispute. Over 10,000 demonstrators were arrested. Officially 260 were wounded.

The temporal-spatiality of October 17, 1961, is alive in the Latin Quar-ter today and in the hearts and corporeal experience of many subalternly racialized subjects. The massacre's ghostly insistence is probably most intensely present for survivors and direct descendants of the martyrs and survivors. It is also far from forgotten by other Algerians, Maghrebians, francophone racialized people and allies. For instance, on October 17, 2016, the massacre was publicly recommemorated when the artist Kader Attia opened a restaurant-café-cum-meeting-place called La Colonie (the Colony, with a bar through the letters). In 2022, the fictional film *Ossekine* in four episodes, which portrays the racist police murder of the Algerian-French student Malik Ossekine the night of December 5 to 6, 1986, in the Latin Quarter, additionally invokes October 17, 1961. In sum, for many, earlier and today to walk through the Latin Quarter is to feel the massacre's haunting. It is to *sense* a special anxiety in the body: a rapid pulse, blood rushing into the head, short gasps, vacillations of anger and numbness, an all-too-present bond, and a disconnect. In contrast, the state, most white French subjects, and unknowing tourists continue to felicitously romanticize that site. Colonial-racial privilege enables them to not know or to unremember October 17, 1961. They sense nothing about it. The blind spot left from its obliteration blocks their *sensing* and *perception* of the parallel, differential experience of immediate subalterns. That experience becomes for dominant subjects inaccessible, unintelligible.

Dominant ignorance about and forgetting of October 17, 1961, is further reinforced in dissimilar receptions of sporadic subaltern repoliticizations of the massacre's space. Throughout the years, the Latin Quarter has been re-marked as a setting of protest, from demonstrations for immigrant rights to the bombing of the San Michel subway station. Dominant subjects do not usually *perceive* these actions as related to October 17, 1961. Instead, they imagine (every time) that uprisings by racialized people suddenly come out of nowhere, take place anywhere, thereby confirming colonial narratives about the colonized's unprovoked, essentialized aggression.

The blind spot that the massacre has been made to occupy in the French hegemonic field of intelligibility is all the more disturbing in light of a long-held Parisian consensus, left to right, about the political signification of city space. Space was at the center of post-Letterist and post-Situationist *détournement* (turning around, derailment) and *récuperation* (recuperation, reappropriation, and resignification) practices. Today a sort of spatial agreement is apparent in any mass demonstration in Paris when activists of any political persuasion rename streets after their ideals. Habitually they make placards, bring ladders, and cover official street signs with their own. A popular rename for the left, now recuperated by the right, is

Rue de la Liberté (Freedom Street). Of course, the right defines freedom very differently. Anyway, with this and October 17, 1961, in mind we can understand how human subjects inhabit, *perceive*, make *sense* of, feel, and act in different *co-present temporal-spatialities* in profoundly incommensurate ways. No *freedom-exigent* solidarity is possible without *sensing* and undoing that gap.

To shift our attention to *subalternative sensing, perception*, and *intelligibility* can induce clarity about power through its effects. On the one hand, confrontation with power can provoke corporal-somatic sensations, conditions, and states of *being-becoming*. We can learn much from the uncomfortable feeling of bodily (im)balance, temporal acceleration or deceleration, the pull of gravity, awareness of the weight of bodily parts, the spine giving way, rising or falling temperature, pain, the sudden feeling of aging, rapid heartbeat, gushing of stomach juices, blood speedily flowing, ghostly presence, visitations by ancestors, simultaneous disparate psychic states. On the other hand, the radically *freedom-exigent* solidarities that the ensemble *subalternative sensing, perception*, and *intelligibility* has the potential to induce go beyond simply adopting a common political platform. This knowing together can—like the force of love—set in motion a total realignment of every cell in our bodies. It can seed new kinds of intersubjectivities, collectivities, and kin. It can incite us to create other forms of life together.

Operability

The fourth axis here is the Foucauldian-Deleuzian notion of *operability*. It is an approach to understanding power, subjects, and *co-motion*. *Operability* shifts attention away from the habitual question of *why* anyone or anything comes about, falls apart, or flourishes to *how* phenomena occur. *Operability* was developed by Foucault in dialogue with Deleuze decades ago but has hardly been noticed by scholars anywhere (Deleuze 1986; Deleuze and Guattari 1972; Foucault 2001e). *Operability* does not appear in any Foucauldian or Deleuzian dictionaries in French or English. It has not been the sustained object of any scholarship. Yet, this book suggests that *operability* has enormously productive consequences for analysis. *Operability* brings into focus the actual workings of power, subjects, and *co-motion* in contextual conditions at different geopolitical and human scales.

Operability moves against the grain of most dominant approaches to *co-motion* today. Generally, dominant approaches underscore causality or the *why* of origins and of cause-effect, goals, programs, or actors. They focus on subjects, movements, and agency. They generally confine analysis to theoretical contributions drawn solely from Global Northern contexts.

Some classic causality examples are the social psychological works of Gustave Le Bon on crowds and Robert Gurr on frustration-aggression. Causality also animates sociological focuses on disequilibrium inspired by Talcott Parsons. It informs interest-group-conflict theories from Charles Tilly to Samuel Huntington. Today many disparate social scientists study causal rationale for political alliances. Some examples are Alberto Melucci's theory of how submerged networks of subjects precede new social movements and help them to gel; rational choice paradigms according to which people make rational decisions; and Theda Skocpol's important work on multiregister conflicts involving state, elite, and working-class actors simultaneously. *Causal* concerns are also prominent in activisms across the political spectrum. The pamphlet *Indignez-vous!* (Get Outraged!) by Stefan Hessel that incited recent anticapitalist movements in France, Spain, and elsewhere highlights the affect *indignation* (outrage) as the "motive" for action (2010, 14, 16, 11). All of these works provide important reflections. *Operability* does not seek to eliminate questions of why or what. It is not in a binary oppositional relation to the why or what. Instead, *operability* highlights the how, to "present these questions in a different way," to include a different "complex configuration of realities" in the analysis (Foucault 2000b, 336–37).

Goal-centric approaches—defined as those that make social movement aims, objectives, or programs the focal point—are both useful and limited. They guide us on our path. However, they can also block, invisibilize, or ignore social movements' current and future potential innovations. Above I referenced Foucault's idea that goal fixations are dangerous and prohibit invention. I pointed to The Invisible Committee's sense that objectives are easily co-opted. Instead, to highlight *operability* is to recognize the "invention of modes of life, of modes of desire" as a necessary dimension to what I call *freedom-exigent transformation* (Benasayag and Sztulwarl 2009, 151).

Subject-centric analyses that make social actors pivotal, too, bring us both insights and problems. They unfortunately rely on dominant notions of the subject, agency, and collective action. This leads them to fail to historicize and contextualize the relations of power in which subjects are formed and operate. *Subject-centric* analytics end up negating many subaltern subjects and *beings-becomings* and blocking *subalternative* understandings (see chapters 1, 2). This book suggests that the kinds of social movements and individual or collective subjects that are currently intelligible in dominant fields of intelligibility, while certainly important, are not the sole or even main agents in *co-motion* today. The present is a time of many differential subject, intersubjectivity, and collective formations, stages, intensities, and densities of *co-motion* (see chapter 5).

Most academic and activist approaches to *co-motion*—in the Global North(s) and often in the South(s)—are saturated in dominant *Global-Northern-centricity* (Western-Euro-centricity and US-centricity together). The bulk of dominant Western European and US knowledge production today prolongs earlier theories born from those contexts' empirics and fields of intelligibility. *Operability* can help bring into relief that which is hidden inside and outside those contexts. It can uncover and highlight that which is under erasure.

However, *operability* is not about infinite additions of kinds of relations of power and subjects that have been previously unnoticed. It is not additive. *Operability* moves away from encyclopedism or claims to exhaustively identify and record. *Operability* also takes leave of comparative approaches that rely on standardized, universalized dominant criteria through which to perceive and judge. Dominant criteria tend to render imperceptible any relation of power, any subject, that does not fit the grid or to assign minor status to whatever fails to conform to dominant models. Instead, *operability* clarifies how relations of power, subjects, and *co-motion* are composed, splintered, fused, amalgamated with, and work with other messy fragments within and beyond the borders that ostensibly define them. This shift in perspective ensures that relations of power, subjects, and *co-motion* are understood as agentic multiplicities.

Archival Encounters and Critical Conceptual Wanderings

This book brings together for analysis several kinds of sources primarily from France, India, Italy, and the United States from the 1970s to present. These are all places where I have lived, including in political exile (mainly Paris, also Rome) and post-exile, been intellectually engaged, studied, and/or taught. Most importantly, I have been intensely active in social movements, in universities, and sometimes in artivisms (as a musician and a writer of poetry) in all of them. I continue a strong relationship with each one, with its history, theoretical inventions, and activist and artivist creations. Each of the four sites—and especially people, ideas, and actions in each—is a permanent part of my most intimate relational, intellectual, activist, and human formation, across my past and present and in how I envision my futurity. As a queer subject from and in a multiply racially, culturally mixed family that encompasses both working-class and middle-class subjects, across the locations of this study and more broadly in the world the brownness of my body is variably positioned and my experiences shift. This situation continually incites and nourishes my thinking. In this book it kindles some of the concepts I suggest and develop, such as *subaltern-to-dominant continuum*; *situated planetarity*; *sensing, perception*, and *intelligibility*; and *reductive evidence*.

The book takes seriously theory produced inside but also beyond the genres that are generally recognized as valid for theory-production in academies across the Global North(s) and South(s). Some such major theoretical sources here include activist, artivist, and social movement analytical materials: tracts, leaflets, pamphlets, banners, posters, art exhibits, graffiti, poetry, slam, music, theater performances, comic books, political cartoons, film, and words and illustrations sent across social media including Facebook, YouTube, blogs, Instagram and X. I also draw on my own participant-observation in academic spaces and in social movement actions and events in each of these sites. I make use of my own reflections on my different kinds of *sensings in-context*. Some actions and events herein are temporally-spatially brief: demonstrations, sit-ins, graffiti zaps, music concerts, jam sessions, film showings, poetry slams, art exhibits, and group meetings. Others are more extensive: long boycotts, experience in musical groups, and life in squats or communal homes. The sources additionally encompass *testimonio* and personal narratives of an array of activists and artivists. They range from long-term dialogues to collective polylogues of varying lengths to extremely brief interactions. They include elements outside general consideration such as various forms of gossip. The book operationalizes governmental reports and dominant and alternative media such as films, TV interviews, and journalists' accounts. I reflect with an array of kinds of critical thought produced in each site studied here.

I engage the sources in their original languages: French, Italian, English, (oral) Hindi, and sometimes Spanish. Many vital primary sources here are previously unpublished. Some are in print with limited circulation. All translations unless otherwise indicated are my own. Many of the subjects and collectivities who created the archival items are unknown outside their immediate contexts. This book brings sources from several languages into conversation with each other and makes some formerly untranslated feminist and queer materials accessible to English-language audiences for the first time.

The book deeply interacts with knowledge and ways of knowledge production in each site. France, India, Italy, and the United States are not simply places that provide data to analyze. They are all locations where critical theorizations are produced. Instead of performing *imperial white-out* by using dominant critical theory and dominant categories from the United States or continental Western Europe to understand empirics elsewhere, a move that erases contextuality, distortedly reframes and resignifies data and performs epistemic violence, this book connects with both theorizations and empirics from each site. It is in conversation with sets of critical dominant, subaltern, subalternist, and *subalternative* analytics *in-context*. I have learned immensely from living extensively inside and deeply engaging with theoretical and activist productions in each of these spaces even if I rather consistently reposition my inquiry. Often their insights enable such reorientations.

Importantly, the book's focus on France, Italy, India, and the United States has conceptual, practical, and activist implications. Each place has different relations to knowledge production and activism. In several of them there is much more fluidity between the academy, theory, and activism than in the United States. For example, in Italy there is no real split between academic critiques and what Kath Weston (1991) calls "street theory." The knowledge produced inside and outside the university is an integral part of collective practice (Suárez-Krabbe 2011). In India, too, there is academic-activist dialogue and fusion, mainly around class analysis but also sometimes around analytics of gender, colonialism, capitalism, casteism, and religion. Second, each site in this ensemble is formed through distinct assemblages of power in a planetary context of power. To work with the four places is to unfix our conceptual and activist concerns from the confines of any one location.

However, this expansive conceptual and activist engagement also presents problems. A major challenge is to avoid plucking theories, concepts, and practices out of any given context and expecting them to be operational elsewhere. Instead, here I suggest a deep historical contextualization. Within each country there are dominant and subaltern epistemes, each with their distinct presuppositions, categories, logics, likely conclusions, and habits of meaning making. There are also disparate practices of *co-motion*. It is imminently helpful to think about how theories, concepts, and practices emerge, in which historical periods they became salient, what work they do or cannot do *in-context*. I have found it useful to reflect on how they travel, where they can and cannot go and why, and in sites of arrival what they mean for the most extremely subaltern subjects.

To be mindful of these challenges this book tries to enact what I call *critical conceptual wandering*. In his classic essay "Travelling Theory," Edward Said warns that the movement of theory from person to person, place to place, or from one historical moment to another can result in misreadings, reductions, reframings, and institutionalizations into new dogmas (1983). One current example is the racist use in France of US critiques of US racism to construct France by comparison as exceptional, as without racism (Soumaharo 2020; Guinhut 2020). This same tendency to imagine racism as not-here but rather as concentrated elsewhere—generally in the United States alone—exists more widely across Western Europe (El-Tayeb 2011). Another example is the popularity in the US academy of postcolonial theory that attacks British colonialism as compared to the quasi-total lack of US interest in US Native studies analyses of US settler colonialism (Byrd and Rothberg 2011; Cheyfitz 2002).

Said, this time in his "Travelling Theory Revisited," also suggests that such unfortunate receptions and redomestications of theory can be an effect of elements that exist—or are missing—in the original theory (2001). His observation should incite us to be attentive to possible nefarious uses of our *theory-assemblages* and to proactively prevent that by building incompatibility with power into the theory itself. For example, theory in the Black radical tradition that engages with planetary relations of power such as colonialism, globalized raciality, and (planetary) racial capitalism is much less susceptible to recuperation. Said additionally points out that at times a theory's geographical extension can result in enhanced critical potential. Accordingly, US Black liberation forces used Frantz Fanon's work on Blackness and on Algeria to better understand US racism and to connect US Black liberation with much of the colonized world.

With this in mind, the aim of *critical conceptual wandering* is to contribute to *theory-assemblages* that preempt unhelpful interpretations and redomestications, and instead try diligently to ensure radical critical potentiality both *in-context* and beyond. This book invites the reader directly into this messy process. A litmus test is to ask, How is this or that theory compatible or not with relations of power in its context and across the planet? How does it engage or not colonialism, coloniality, imperialism, capitalism, racism, *misogynarchies*, speciesism, the destruction of the planet? What is its use to the most subaltern subjects *in-context* and beyond?

A consideration of any theory's relation to power is complicated by the fact that every relation of power has many disparate contextual manifestations, dimensions, registers, and extents (see chapters 3, 4). Let us take coloniality as an example. Each colonizing country herein engages in several kinds of colonization (Bacchetta 2023). The United States is a genocidal settler colony on stolen Native land, an invading colonizer of other lands and an imperial power that intervenes militarily and economically across the Global South(s) officially and unofficially (Lee-Oliver 2019; Churchill 2004; Back and Solomos 2000; Stember 1976). France is an administrative colonizer (Senegal, Morocco), a former settler colonizer (Algeria), a neo-colonizer (the DOM-TOM), and in some countries a necropolitical imperial power, as in its drone interventions in Syria and elsewhere (Mbembe 2019, 2001; Khiari 2006). India is a commercial and administrative postcolony that won political independence from Britain in 1947 and now dominates in its region. India has internal colonies (Kashmir) and arguably a colonial relation to some internal social sectors: Dalits, Bahujans, Adivasis, Muslims, and other religious minorities. Like many other postcolonies, India remains structured by colonial state apparatus models such as the British parliamentary, and educational and juridical systems. It officially adopted some colonial categories to describe internal subalterns, such as "backward caste" or "tribe." Italy, a place that—like other parts of Europe—has always been home to Italians of color of many shades, including racially mixed Italians, in this case since the Roman Empire, is also multiply colonial (El Tayeb 2011). It is a colonizer first of its own internal south and islands, and then under fascism as it tried to dominate in East Africa, failed, and left lasting, devastating damage in its path (Lombardi-Diop and Romeo 2012; Ben-Ghiat and Fuller 2005; Gramsci 1995, 1992). Historically, Italy's impoverished southern areas were drained by massive peasant and worker population out-migrations. Today its south is a site of substantial in-migrations from war torn and devastated areas of Eastern Europe, Africa, and the Middle East (Hawthorne 2022; Paolos and Maglio 2015; Schneider 1998; Patterson 1982, vii). Currently people of color in Italy are organized into social movements that reimagine borders, citizenship, and belonging (Giglioli et al. 2017). In sum, no relation of power is a monolith. This book directly addresses these complexities.

Yet another factor is that each country discussed in this book has its own historical political movements and priorities that bear on the critical theory that authors located there produce. For example, unlike in the United States, both Italy and France have recent histories of successful labor movements. Scholars, activists, and artivists there, regardless of the issue or movement in question, continue to make capitalism, labor politics, and class central to their work. They are variously integral to other social movement analytics and practices too: against racism, antiwar, proimmigration, feminist, queer, and trans.

Presently there are important shifts in scholarship and social movements in the four countries of this book. In India subaltern knowledge production—by Dalits, Bhajunas, and Adivasis—after erasure for centuries is now increasingly unignorable. In France, where colonialism is dominantly dismissed, postcolonial subjects—citizens, legal residents, or undocumented—who remain marginalized and largely spatially segregated, can no longer be totally discounted. They are a political force. Everywhere powers are resisting these conceptual shifts. For instance, in May 2017, the French government officially banned a conference in Paris on intersectionality in education. It was only partially reinstated after much protest.

Another aspect of *critical conceptual wandering* is limitations carried by language. In this book I bring everything into English translation. This is not a neutral transition. English is saturated in colonial-racial planetary relations of power. It is the most widely spoken language in the world. Out of the world's 7.8 billion people, largely as an effect of colonialism and insertion into capitalism, approximately 1.35 billion speak English. It has created widespread murderous linguistic and epistemic violence across the planet. Yet, it is not the only dominant language of this book's archive and not the only one to have done extensive damage.

To consider creating a feminist, queer, decolonial translation into English is to encounter what I call the *pre-translation* elements of othered languages that precede it, that it absorbs, marginalizes, silences, works to eliminate but cannot fully suppress (Bacchetta 2022). I think about *pre-translation* elements as the *co-presence* in the translated text, here in English, of traces from those languages and of the lives of their speaking subjects (Bacchetta 2025b). *Pre-translation* languages are generally (not always) subalternized in relation to a dominant one. For example, depending on an author's mother tongue or prior languages, Kashmiri, Urdu, or Gujarati may be *pre-translation* languages in English texts, as may be Amazigh, Arabic, or Wolof in French texts. Further, Kashmiri, Manipuri, and other languages may be *pre-translation* elements in Hindi. *Pre-translation* languages may manifest in the dominant language or in the translated text via sporadic untranslated terms, or logics, repetitions, rhythms, or silences. They may be highly hearable in some dominant languages, such as in English spoken in India or Nigeria. In other cases, they may be fully present but less noticeable, as in the difference in Italy between standard Italian (which evolved out of Tuscany's language) and subalternized southern regional languages. Finally, as I have suggested elsewhere, we get into a world of complexities when we translate from one dominant language (herein French, Italian, English as used India, each with their own *pre-translation* traces) into another dominant language (here English as used in the United States, again with its own prior *pre-translation* manifestations).

Yet another problem is that a term in English can mean something different in the same context depending on the speaking subject. When I call myself a dyke it is different from some random queerphobe calling me a dyke. When Corinna Gould, leader and spokesperson for the Ohlone people, pronounces the term *land* she means something entirely distinct from its English language dictionary definition. Also, theorizations from different periods in the same site may use an identical term variably. The term *gay* is a case in point. Today in the United States, *gay* most often invokes an idea of cisgender homonormative white gay men. Yet historically, *gay* signified a variety of queers, including lesbians and trans people. For instance, *gay* is found as such in early in texts by the 1970s collective Dyketactics! and is a self-designation by trans activists in film interviews at the 1966 Compton's Cafeteria rebellion (Dyketactics! Archive; Silverman and Stryker 2005). The Althusserian linguist Michel Pêcheux reminds us how temporal-spatial contexts matter: "Words, expressions, propositions" do not have inherent significations but instead are effects of their construction in "social-historical" processes (1975, 144). My *critical conceptual wandering* work with *theory-assemblages* tries to be attentive to such complexities.

Structure, Flow

This book is organized not around but rather to surface the four main lines of flight explained above. In keeping with its focus on reimagining power and *co-motion*, and on creating useful *theory-assemblages*, the chapters are not arranged into cases or situations but instead according to conceptual constellations.

Chapter 1, "Co-Motion at Present," provides historical groundings for the rest of the book. It critically engages with a broad legacy of intersectional and decolonial feminist, queer, trans and other subaltern theories and practices of *co-motion* from the 1970s until today in the main four focal sites of this book. It differs from the other chapters in that it serves as an entry point to open up other directions and registers for what follows. However, readers who are impatient with history and are eager to get to the more creative solution-oriented parts of the book may want to skip it and possibly return later. In sum, chapter 1 asks: What can we learn from limitations and closures, or from openings and potentialities, of prior *co-motion* that is useful to think with today? How is power reproduced or not in *co-motion* at present? What exactly are the problems that we need to solve, escape from, or circumvent? For the purposes of discussion, the chapter is structured into clusters of disparate kinds of *co-motion*. It shows how differences among them matter. It proposes that to avoid reproducing destructive relations of power inside *co-motion*, and to prevent obliteration from without, we need to think and speak about power and subjects very differently.

Chapter 2, "Imaginings Otherwise," is designed to begin to overcome some of the conceptual and lexical constraints that chapter 1 identifies. It suggests some new concepts to think with: *co-motion* (again, a large rubric for ways of coming together, including solidarity, union, coalition, network, association, etc.); *subjects-in-sociality-and-another* (a way to consider how subjects come into being with each other [*in-sociality*] and to take account of the most subaltern subjects that are otherwise erased [the *and another*]); *subaltern-to-dominant continuum* (drawing on Gramsci, the recognition of multiple kinds of subalterns and of dominants, the range of their locations in power and the importance of context); *liberation-orientation* (a tendency, yearning, desire to stay alive, inhabit the world differently, invent new forms of life); *freedom-exigency* (a refusal of compromise with any relations of power, an urgency and requirement for *freedom-life* now).

Chapter 3, "Co-Formations, Co-Productions," continues the attempt that chapter 2 began of proposing other ways of thinking and articulating, here specifically about multiplicities of power and their inseparable *operabilities*. Chapter 3 engages with prior *dominant-to-subaltern* theorizations of power before suggesting two new concepts for rethinking power for our times: *co-formations* and *co-productions*. With *co-formations* we can consider small scale assemblages of power such as gender, sexuality, race, caste, and class together. With *co-productions* we can reflect on power as manifested across large-scale temporal-spatialities such as coloniality, coloniality, capitalism, slavery, imperialism, *misogynarchies*, and speciesism.

Chapter 4, "Situated Planetarities," again takes up the work of rethinking power for our times. Its key contribution is *situated planetarities*, an approach to power, subjects, and *co-motion* based in a relatively small geographical or human scale with at the same time the entire planet in mind. Our analysis and praxis become situated in a specific site and planetary at once. Another feature of this chapter is its proposal of additional concepts with which to think about situated planetaries. An example is the range of *political amnesias*.

Chapter 5, "Other Sensings in Praxes, "shifts our discussion to provide a living example of how some concepts from the book's *theory-assemblages* can operate in analyses and in actions, and also how a specific context might spark yet other conceptual tools. The chapter focuses on one place—Paris, France—and on the immensely productive political and affective work by one set of subalternized subjects: racialized queers+, trans+, and dykes+ and allies.[8] The focus on the microscale context enables a detailed analysis. It begins with a *situated planetarities* perspective to explain the site and its relation to the world especially via colonialism, capitalism, enslavement, and immigration. The chapter suggests a *backwards-sideways* method, or a genealogical and horizontally relational orientation. It explains how the present *co-motion* is informed by a related history and concurrent unfolding of racialized queer+, trans+, and dyke+ and allied analytics, experiences, practices, and actions. It affirms the possibility of creating a *freedom-exigent* present and futurity. The chapter's concluding remarks wrap up both the chapter and the book.

I thank in advance readers who will be attentive to the book's voicings and silences, who will pursue despite its inadequacies and limitations. Wherever you are, I hope you might find in the book something useful—in complicity, oppositionally, or elsewhere—toward the *freedom-exigent co-motion* that we urgently need to imagine and enact now.

An army of lovers can not fail.

    chant and slogan, 1970s US radical queer movements

We are family. I got all my sistas with me.

    Sister Sledge, "We Are Family"

We are family. Brothers and my sisters with me. And yours truly.

    We Are Family: A Musical Message for All

You don't go into coalition because you *like* it. The only reason you would consider trying to team up with somebody who could possibly kill you, is because that's the only way you can figure you can stay alive.

    Bernice Johnson Reagon, "Coalition Politics"

Where are we now with *co-motion*? What can we learn from the challenges and accomplishments but also the limitations and failures of collective organizing, practices, and actions? What are the problems and how can we avoid them? How can we reimagine and craft *co-motion* to open up a *freedom-exigent* present and futurity?

    This chapter delineates and discusses different kinds of *co-motion* from the 1970s to present. Across the chapter, across its spatial and temporal frames, I suggest that one continual difficulty is our inability to identify and critically engage with a full spectrum of relations of power. Instead, unfortunately, in any *co-motion* formation some relations of power get left intact and are reiterated and reenacted inside the *co-motion*, destroying it from within. Such reproductions and reinforcements of power are sometimes intentional. But, generally they happen inadvertently, precisely as an effect of power. Herein, I elucidate some of power's damaging operations. The chapter is meant to clarify why we need alternative ways of thinking about and speaking about power, subjects, and *co-motion*. Thus, the critical overview here is an absolutely necessary starting point for the rest of the book.

France, India, Italy, and the United States all have an immense range of conceptions and enactments of *co-motion* from the 1970s to present. I draw from all of them. I do not arrange the *co-motion* formations by country or in chronological order. Instead, to make sense of the ensemble, I demarcate clusters. I organize them according to these questions: What kind of social glue maintains unity? How is it envisioned and practiced? (As familial relations? Friendship? Self-interest?) What is the scale and kind of action? (Large or small social movements? Collective living? Artistic expression?) What is the social and political orientation? (Decolonial? Anticapitalist? Intersectional? For reformist social justice? Revolutionary? How?) What kinds of subjects are inside or excluded from the *co-motion*? What are the limitations that disrupt unity?

This ensemble may look like quite a mess. Yet, I purposefully gather the clusters around multiple kinds of criteria to avoid categorizing them according to any one standard. The single standard classificatory method recalls reductive colonial-racializing procedures and incites comparisons that reproduce unhelpful hierarchizations and colonial-racial progress narratives. Instead, in this chapter each criterion is a sort of pole of attraction around which a cluster takes shape.

Many of the *co-motion* formations in any given cluster could belong to more than one cluster. However, they are where they are to emphasize an aspect of the alliance that illustrates something about the ensemble it is in. The groupings are not meant to be pure, bounded classifications. Like other theoretical categorizations to sort out social thought, the demarcations among clusters here are porous (Omi and Winant [1994] 2015). The ensembles here are akin to Wittgensteinian colors: They could fuse or blend here and there; they could expand or contract; they could pull toward one another, amalgamate; or they could push away, separating (Wittgenstein 1984). The first three clusters are defined mainly around human relationalities, and the last three primarily around relations to power. I dedicate differential space to delineating, describing, and analyzing the clusters because some are more heterogeneous while others seem easier to render intelligible and require less explanation.

Affective Alliances

The first cluster, *affective alliances*, is defined via solidarities forged around friendship, love, or the erotic. *Affective alliances* are specifically outside *sanguinal-familial* (blood family) arrangements (see below). We might think of June Jordan's point: "It's always the love . . . that will carry the action into positive new places" (2002, 269). Here, affect includes emotion, subjects' "bodily capacities to affect" others "and be affected" by them, intensities, and forces and actions (Clough 2007, 2; Ahmed 2006, 2004; Deleuze and Guattari 2005, 1980). Affect entails sensations and perceptions that can alter dominant and subaltern knowledge, history, and memory. Relatedly, Sarah Ihmoud (2023) demonstrates, with the alchemy dimension of an archive of letters to incarcerated Palestinian prisoners at the center of analysis, how the affect decolonial love is invoked, created, and materialized in/as resistance in Palestine. For Ryan M. Lescure (2023), points of invisibilization and nonintelligibility in dominant perspectives on queer relationality can be brought out of erasure and studied with a focus on sensory information such as scent, appearance, and feeling. With *co-motion* in mind we can consider how affect can unite or divide subjects and collectivities.

Thinking about some (not all) forms of *affective alliances* has a long genealogy in Eurocentric and US-centric philosophy that is currently hegemonic across the planet. Jacques Derrida helpfully points to an early dominant Global Northern divide between the ancient Greek notion of friendship, or a voluntary bond between people, and the Roman idea of ethnos, defined as a people with common blood descent and culture (Derrida 1994). This friendship-ethnos binary is historically reiterated in myriad ways. It reappears in differential criteria for citizenship. Some nation-states, such as the United States, base citizenship in jus soli (the right derived from birth in a state's territory, by association). Others, such as Germany, ground citizenship in jus sanguinis (blood right). This territorial-associational vs. blood divide also surfaces in many forms in social science theories of intrasocietal solidarities. For instance, Gregg Lambert underscores Marx's notion of communism as a universal society of friendship of the proletariat (2008, 45). Derrida points to the sanguinal in right-wing formations such as monarchy, ethnic rule, or fascism (1994). The friendship-ethnos binary manifests amply and it shifts historically. In Eurocentric contexts, at a certain point friendship gets reimagined in relation to the figure of the enemy. Lambert highlights how the Greeks first conceptualized friendship outside war, but today "the friend'" incorporates an "opposition between 'the friend' and 'the enemy.'" Traces of this polarization exist widely, including in the Marxian notion of the comrade that combines the social concept of friend with that of the ally in war (2008, 44–45).

Many feminist, queer of color, and allied scholars across the Global North(s) and South(s) have proposed that politics can productively be based on friendship across difference. For example, Niharika Banerjea et al. (2022) argue not only that friendship can helpfully accompany social justice activism but that actually friendship can comprise social justice activism. For them, friendship has to do with social movement activities such as survival, repair, healing, creating alternative socialities, imagining other ways of life, and dreaming other kinds of worlds.

Banerjea et al.'s reflections resonate with and add to work on affect from an earlier period, too. Relatedly, M. Jacqui Alexander foregrounds mutual recognition, unlearning mythologies about each other and becoming "fluent in each other's histories" (2002, 91). Chela Sandoval elaborates "revolutionary love" and "reverse interpellations" (2000). Bell hooks highlights the "transformative power of love" (2000, xvii–xxix). María Lugones suggests that we "learn to love each other by learning to travel in each other's 'worlds'" to become "fully subjects to each other" (2003, 8, 97). Janet Jakobsen advises us not to naturalize the "we" that presupposes a stated or unstated "they" but rather to investigate "how we create ourselves as allies" ethically (1998, 3). In a study of the US academy, Aimee Carrillo Rowe centers "intimacy," "love," and "belonging" (2008, 3). For her, bonds are "power lines" or "webs" that "connect us . . . across time and space," allowing us "to build community" (26–27, 38, 176, 178). Carrillo Rowe finds that white women ally with higher-status white individuals as fictive kin (father, mother, or elder sister) who bring them up (i.e., nurture and help rise) in the hierarchy, while women of color consider as allies all those who simply do not block their path.

Yet another constellation of *affective alliances* centers queer affect in ostensibly nonerotic friendship. This is the case for Leela Gandhi's (2006) research on the solidarity between Edward Carpenter—the British out homosexual, socialist animal-rights advocate, prison reformer, and anti-imperialist—and Mahatma Gandhi in India under colonialism. For her, Carpenter "arrives at his anti-imperial sympathies" after deciding that homosexuality is "first and foremost" a "capacity for radical kinship" (36). Carpenter's "homosexual politics" are not about sex but rather "a radical reconfiguration of association, alliance, relationality, community"

(36). Through a Global Northern lens Carpenter might seem sexphobic. Yet Leela Gandhi, carefully considering Carpenter's context, suggests that "his sexual evasiveness" is "a condition of possibility for an occluded politics of homosexual exceptionalism" (39). She connects Carpenter's anti-imperialism and friendship with Mahatma Gandhi to Carpenter's consciousness that as a homosexual he was positioned near "the nonwestern savage," outside what British colonizers considered as "civilized sociality" (61; see also Hoad 2000).

Some important historical queer of color theorizations in the United States emphasize erotic affect in alliances even while resignifying it. For Audre Lorde, the erotic is not primarily about sex but rather is a force. Lorde argues that women's erotic potential has been suppressed precisely because it has subversive uses. She states: "As a Black lesbian feminist, I have a particular feeling, knowledge, and understanding for those sisters with whom I have danced hard, played, or even fought"; this "has often been the forerunner for joint concerted actions not possible before" ([1978] 1993, 343). For Lorde, when women unleash their erotic power and come together, they create a formidable political capacity. Some parts of Lorde's reflections are commensurate with some nonfeminist new social movement theories. For instance, during the same period, Alberto Melucci, writing on "submerged networks," argues that affective bonds precede and reinforce larger scale social movements (1991).

In the United States, both sexuality and the erotic have been historically central to queer alliances. An example is the 1970s lesbian, queer, anticolonial, anti-imperialism, antiracism group Dyketactics! in Philadelphia. Its members were from multiple colonial, racialized, religious, and class legacies and were simultaneously active in many social movements: decolonial (for Native American land and sovereignty); anti-imperialist (for Puerto Rican independence); anticapitalist; for Black liberation; antiracism; for labor; antiwar (Bacchetta 2019a; 2009b). Dyketactics! members lived collectively, primarily in two houses. They saw every dimension of social and intimate interrelations as political. Dyketactics! highlighted nonmonogamy as a desirable mode of intersubjectivity around which forms of collective life and politics could be organized. The group critiqued binary (lesbian, gay, bisexual) coupledom as an offshoot of heteronormative marriage with its genealogy in (white) patriarchy and capitalism.

In figure 1.1, a Dyketactics! poster in a demonstration against queer oppression on December 4, 1975, in Philadelphia's City Hall illustrates something of the group's view on affect as social glue: "An Army of Lovers

1.1 Dyketactics! at the demonstration against Bill 1275, December 4, 1975, City Hall, Philadelphia, PA (Greenberg 2023).

Shall Not Fail." During that demonstration—attended by many in the queer community—the armed Civil Disobedience Squad in plain clothes zeroed in on and brutally attacked and beat up Dyketactics! members. When they recovered from the hospital, six members—myself included—filed charges in what became the case of *Dyketactics! v. The City of Philadelphia, Mayor Frank Rizzo, and named and unnamed members of the Civil Disobedience Squad for Excessive Force* (1975 to 1976). Our case was the first in the United States (and possibly the world) of queers taking police to court for police brutalities committed against queers. The motivational affect was far beyond desires for juridical equity and way outside of carceral logic. Instead, we were incited by accumulated indignation, anger toward the brutalities of queerphobia, and a desire to call out state queerphobic actors on the State's own terrain—here, its courts. Most important for the Dyketactics! Six was an uncompromising, shared commitment to radical justice, our love for each other, and our mutual solidarity.

In practice, Dyketactics!'s internal political-affective arrangements took many forms. The "lovers" in "An Army of Lovers Shall Not Fail" could designate subjects in sexual and nonsexual *alter-kinship* relationalities (see below). Still the idea of sexuality as glue was made manifest in many

Dyketactics! actions. For instance, it appears in the song "Powers" (cowritten by members Barbara Ruth and myself), which Dyketactics! sisters and siblings sang during many actions including while walking to and from the courtroom during the 1976 trial:

Powers

Powers
are around
when women make love
together.

We evoke
spirits
that could shake the earth
if we only knew
how to harness them.
     The women's revolution
     will not be waged in bed,
but that may be the source
of its strongest
weaponry.

Affective alliances have many useful features (and I happily discuss some below). But lest we overzealously idealize them, it is important to recognize their constraints, too. A major limitation is that they can veil the fact that friendship, the erotic, and love are never politically neutral. Affect itself is always already a historical construction in relations of power (Berlant 2008, 2012; Ahmed 2004).

Relatedly, in some cases *affective alliances* risk making concerted political action so *subject-centric* that the allies' relations are in danger of becoming an end unto themselves. They thereby can have a depoliticizing and limiting effect. *Affective alliances* often unfold primarily across small-scale face-to-face connections and risk marginalizing other scales. They can become exclusive, for they tend to incorporate only subjects who are mutually intelligible to each other. However, intelligibility is not neutral. It is an effect of relations of power. Leela Gandhi frames Carpenter and Gandhi's solidarity as "the co-belonging of nonidentical singularities" (2006, 26). Yet, let us recall that for all their differences the two men also share much: the English language, British education, class status, age, professional position, and formation in their respective societies' (economic, cultural, racialized, and, in India, caste) dominant social sectors.

Another aspect is that *affective alliances* can easily ignore violent kinds of social glue involved as people come together. Sara Ahmed underscores that the imperative to love is "a humanistic fantasy" (2004, 140). Many other emotions can bind people. The composer, musician, and activist Bernice Johnson Reagon, founder of the Black feminist vocal group Sweet Honey in the Rock, suggests in a quote that begins this chapter that to ally sometimes subjects must suppress, overcome, or work around affects instead of celebrating them. Some examples of such affects are outrage, disgust, hatred, fear, and helplessness.

Friendship, eroticism, and sex have enormous potential for *freedom-exigent co-motion*. But the affects they invoke can also sometimes depoliticize alliances. They can shift attention away from, romanticize, and directly help to reproduce, intensify, and expand relations of power. This is clear in the highly publicized 2010 US national controversy involving Henry Louis Gates, professor and chair of African American Studies at Harvard University. One day Professor Gates, who is Black, arrived home from an international trip without his keys and tried to pry open his front door. A white female neighbor presumed he was a burglar and called the police. They arrived. Under the command of Sergeant James Crowly, a white male, the police allegedly bullied and arrested Gates. The story made headlines. Soon, prompted by a journalist, President Obama remarked that he knows Gates, the cop acted "stupidly," and "racial profiling" is still prevalent. The US mainstream media went into racial panic and constructed Gates as out of line for calling out Crowly's racism.[1] Many accused the President of hating white people. Though Crowly was clearly the offender, blame was assigned to both Black men. President Obama tried to publicly explain his reaction, to no avail. Finally, Obama invited Crowly and Gates for a beer on the White House lawn. Soon the media circulated images of the three relaxing together as "friends." President Obama was then reconstructed as a racial conciliator. And in the process the question of racial profiling and of the psychic violence done to Gates (and by extension all other Black subjects) was made to disappear.

Another problem with *affective alliances* is the potential proximity between the category friendship and the normative heterosexual family in hegemonic Eurocentric and US-centric conceptions. Derrida highlights that (nonsanguinal) friendship is haunted by sanguinal relations as its unstated model (1994, 159). For him, "the figure of the friend, so regularly coming back on stage with the features of the brother, seems spontaneously to belong to a familial, fraternalist and thus androcentric configuration of politics" (12–13). Luce Irigaray argues that in dominant political discourse there are no women friends. Women do not exist as subjects; the universal political subject (as friend or enemy) is always male. She calls political alliances "hom(m)osocial," using the *(m)* to highlight the combination of *man-Man-Human* (in French *homme-Homme-Homme*) (1977, 167–85; 1984).

In dominant discourses and practice, affect is often arranged in binary oppositions and wielded as an arm against colonized, racialized, gendered, sexed subalterns. In colonial discourse there are divides between the subaltern's ostensibly inappropriate emotion and the colonizer's reason (Vaughan 1991; Fabian 2000). Affect also underlies the (colonial-racial-class-gendered) partitioning of madness from sanity and of anormative from normative sexualities (Foucault 1972, 1976).

But feminist and queer *affective alliances* have many potentially fruitful aspects too. Foucault remarks that to introduce "love where the law, the rule or custom" otherwise would be, can radically transform power. For him, "homosexual" is not defined in terms of biological, psychic, or sexual traits but rather is a "historic occasion" to reinvent "friendship as a mode of life" (1981).

Foregrounding friendship, love, the erotic, and sexuality in alliances can sometimes usefully remind us of their place in the co-constitution of subjects and intersubjectivities, which are agentic forces in alliances. Affect can helpfully destabilize notions of fixed subjects. Giorgio Agamben does so by rethinking friendship through the concept of "con-sentir" (2007, 34). It literally signifies *to consent* (in Italian *consentire*, and in French *consentir*). Yet Agamben's hyphen (*con-sentir*), which separates and links the *co* (*con* in both Italian and French) with *feel* (*sentire* in Italian and *sentir* in French), evokes *co-feel* or *feeling together*. For Agamben, consenting and feeling together "dislocates and deports toward the friend, toward the other same. Friendship is this desubjectivation in the very heart of the most intimate feeling of the self" (2007, 34). Relatedly, Egyptian writer Ahdaf Soueif highlights how in the 2011 revolution in Tahrir Square, Cairo, anonymous others became friends while experiencing desubjectivation and resubjectivation in concert (Khan 2011).

Finally, centering affect can help uncover how relations of power operate to unite or divide in stylistics of address, recognition, and reception in differential settings. Bell hooks mentions a highly theoretical lecture on "De-centering Europe: The Crisis of Contemporary Culture" that Professor Cornel West of Princeton University presented to a Black audience in a "sermon mode popular in Black communities" where it signals "depth and seriousness" (hooks 1990, 21). She reminds us that this same stylistic in US white contexts gets disqualified because it is equated with "a lack of substance," "spectacle," or simply "entertainment . . . precisely because it moves people" (21–22). Here affect makes us notice "moving people," who gets moved to come together, and how.

Sanguinal-Familial Alliances

In the cluster *sanguinal-familial* alliances, subjects, and relations are based on actual, presumed, and intended blood kinship arrangements. They involve biological kin and fictive kin (i.e., formal or informal adoption or fostering). They include figures such as siblings, parents, children, aunts, uncles, and cousins. While the subjects of *affective alliances* depend on affect, the ethnos subjects of the *sanguinal-familial* are united around identity. Unlike the subjects of *affective alliances*, the subjects in *sanguinal-familial alliances* have supposed commonalities such as morphology, history, heritage, geography, or culture. Their links span the face-to-face (family, community) to transnational scale. Yet, *sanguinal-familial alliances* have definite limits. They never encompass the whole planet because they always require an Other, an outsider, as a backdrop for their self-definition.

A typical political unit of the *sanguinal-familial* is the nation form. A host of feminists have long pointed out how the nation form is distinctly modeled on the cisgender heteronormative family and simultaneously upholds the latter as the primary and sometimes exclusive modality of social organization (Naterstad 2023; Peterson 2000; McClintock 1995). In fact, we can observe that a scaled relation between cisgender heteronormative familial and political structures exists in all the languages of this study. The French term *alliance* can literally signify marriage. In English, *alliance* signals the bond between two families forged in the matrimony of a partner from each. In Italian, *allianza* is a political concept but also carries Old Testament traces of the union between God and men. Some of its synonyms have simultaneous familial and political relational connotations. Examples are *unione* (union) or *sposare una causa* (to marry a political cause). Hindi has many terms for political connections. Some are literal: *sambandhana, maitrīpūrṇa sambandha, vaivāhika sambandha*. Others are interchangeable with familialities: *gaṭhabandhana* (which carries the sense of marriage) or *nātā* (connection, kin). Still others include political alliance among other meanings: *sandhi* (pact, treaty), *samajhautā* (agreement). The Hindu right uses the term *sangh parivar* ("family" of the *sangh*, that is, of the organization called Rashtriya Swayamsevak Sangh [RSS], or National Self-Worker Organization) as an umbrella term for the RSS's two hundred organizations, each designed to recruit a different sector of society (e.g., women, teachers, factory workers, agricultural workers, Dalits, Adivasis, etc.). In contrast, most useful on the left is *ēktā*, which translates as "oneness," "concurrence," or "unison." It is used by Indian social movements to signal unity against the Hindu right. Craig Calhoun aptly suggests that kinship, ethnicity, and nation are "three distinct forms of social solidarity" that "may overlap—or articulate with each other—to varying degrees in specific situations" (1997, 29). In *sanguinal-familial* models they are often fused.

A central feature of *sanguinal-familial alliances* is the dominantly positioned blood family as a model for all associational modes. Across the planet, kinship systems differ immensely. It is far beyond this book's objectives or capacities to take account of every version. Yet, a reasonably detailed engagement with some relevant literatures reveals how familial structures are historical-contextual constructions. They are powerful fictions-with-effects. Many historians have traced the genealogies of relations of power that have produced them (Uberoi 1994; Shorter 1977; Ariés 1960). Notwithstanding this, today in the Global North(s) the idea that the prevailing dominant cisgender heteronormative family structure is natural and permanent remains hegemonic. So, it is not surprising that subjects there, regardless of their positionalities or capacity for reflexivity, get caught up in interpellations to reproduce it.

Sanguinal-familial arrangements have been critiqued from many directions. For Marxists, and French materialist and differentialist feminists alike, the blood family is where wives and children are made the private property of husbands or fathers, daughters function as objects of exchange between men, and unmarried women become the collective property of all men (Engels 2010; Delphy and Leonard 1992; Irigaray 1984, 1977). Women are expected to perform both biological and cultural reproduction (Federici 2004; McClintock 1995). In postcolonial and decolonial feminist scholarship, the dominant cisgender heterosexual family is a micro-unit of disparate large-scale sexist-racist configurations that we can arrange under the rubric of *misogynarchies*, such as patriarchy, *fraternarchy*, or *filiarchy* (Bacchetta 2025c, 2004).[2] In some European critical theory the dominant cisgender heteronormative family is also the site of oedipalization, wherein the child is made into a docile, capitalism-desiring worker and consumer

(Deleuze and Guattari 1972). In scholarship on fascism this dominant family-writ-large is the central unit on which "murderous exclusion" is argued and enacted (Haritaworn et al. 2013; Bacchetta and Power 2002; Theweleit 1989, 1987).

Yet such theorizations have limitations if we consider the cisgender heteronormative blood family in relation to the most subaltern subjects in heterogeneous contexts of power. As Christina Sharpe argues, in the United States the dominant idea of kinship cannot be separated from whiteness as "a political project." The hegemonic notion of kinship is inscribed in white supremacy, and white supremacy deploys kinship metaphors to sustain itself—for example, in claims such as "for our families" or "for our children" (2016). In the United States and much of Central and South America, Indigenous families have been continually destroyed as part of the logic and practice of genocidal elimination (Kauanui 2016; Wolfe 2006). In the United States, it has manifested in outright assassination, theft of living space, privatization of lands, division into plots, reduction to patriarchal nuclear familial structures, stealing Native children and placing them into boarding schools, imprisonment, impoverishment, and more. Historically, the kinship of enslaved African subjects was violently disrupted through forced transport across the Atlantic, division of new kinships, and their treatment as property (Morgan 2021). There are myriad continuities (and discontinuities) in the destruction of the US Black family from slavery, including through to contemporary incarceration (Davis et al. 2022; Gilmore 2007; Davis 2005, 2003). Tiffany Willoughby-Herard (2016) points out that imprisonment often results in loss of parental rights, but moreover it teaches incarcerated families and their kin in violent, brutal ways that "their primary relation of belonging is to the State as its property."

In studies of the nation, the *sanguinal-familial* looms large in the classical Global Northern distinction between primordialist and constructivist, or essentialist and constructivist approaches (Calhoun 1997, 29–50; Bacchetta 1996; Anderson 1994; Brass 1992; Hobsbawm 1990; Hobsbawm and Ranger 1983; Gellner 1983). Primordialism-essentialism explains national cohesion through naturalized criteria such as blood kin, ethnicity, or heritage. For constructivists, such elements that dominate in national imaginings are generated and congeal historically.

There is currently much insightful feminist, queer, and critical race scholarship on the (heterosexual) *family-to-nation* configuration from which we can learn immensely. Some of it owes a debt to the earlier work of Wilhelm Reich (2015), Erich Fromm (1941), George L. Mosse (1985), and others who first analyzed sexualities with nationalism. Unfortunately, the early European theorists generally ignored colonialism, racism, capitalism, women, gender, and speciesism. Andrew Hewitt (1996, 38–78) shows how some prior theorists queerphobically linked fascist nationalism to homosexuality by positing fascists as repressed homosexuals. Later scholarship changed the debates considerably. Foucault's (1976) critique of Reich's "repressive hypothesis," or the notion that authoritarian patriarchal-familial sexual repression induced fascism, provides a blow to the queerphobic impetus. Frantz Fanon's work unerases colonialism and race and makes them central to the *family-to-nation* configuration. For Fanon (1952, 121), the dominant, white family "presages a more vast institution: the social group or the nation," wherein white paternal authority is linked to state authoritarianism. These entities fantasize the figure of white men as father and elder brother, Black men as eternal children, white women as mothers, wives and daughters whom young Black males threaten to rape, and Black women as white men's sexual property (127–28, 134, 114–16, 51–66, 35–52). Ashis Nandy extends Fanon to consider how the colonial British construed themselves as protective, disciplining parents, and Indian males as too childish for independence. This was exemplified in colonial-racist representations of Mahatma Gandhi in his dhoti (a classical wrapped cloth worn by adult Hindu males) as a baby in diapers (1983).

Anne McClintock, drawing on Fanon, reconceptualizes the colonial nation specifically as "the white family of man" writ large (1995, 232–57). She highlights the genealogy of the notion of the nation in *natio* (to be born), that territoriality has parental associations (motherland, fatherland) and that nations are "symbolically figured as domestic genealogies" (357). In them, people of color are represented as children—backward, savages, primitives—who threaten the white nation with disease, contagion, and degeneration (46–52). Heidi Nast, reflecting on the contemporary United States, identifies the "racist oedipalization" of the *family-to-nation* (2004). She rethinks the Freudian oedipal triad as actually a quadrat thus comprised: (white) Mother-Father-Son, and Repressed-Bestial (racialized other). All of these *sanguinal-familial* subjects and solidarities depend on constructions of negative Others.

In other strands of *family-to-nation* scholarship, figures of women and queers loom large. Nira Yuval-Davis argues that (presumably white) women are positioned in the nation variously as biological and cultural reproducers, citizens, military actors, antiwar activists, and potential internal threats (1997). V. Spike Peterson highlights the nation's heterosexism. Therein (dominant) women function as biological reproducers of citizens, social reproducers of citizens and cultural forms, signifiers of heterosexist group identities, agents and victims in political conflict, and citizens themselves (2000, 64–74). The gendered relational language of *sanguinal-familiality* sometimes expressly and sometimes inadvertently excludes queers even in contexts such as homonationalism or homotransnatonalism, wherein models for what we can call the proper *homo-citizen* are proposed (Puar 2013, 2007; Bacchetta and Haritaworn 2011). For example, the gendered appeal to "sisters" and "brothers" (in struggle) or "daughters" and "sons" (of this or that territory) to invoke social glue can sometimes operate in queerphobic ways to dismiss nonbinary people, agender-identified folk, and other queers.

Many scholars underscore that the dominant *family-to-nation* requires that (internal or external) others be excluded (Anderson 1994). Toni Morrison (1993, 47) remarks that to become American, immigrants of all colors are interpellated to internalize racism against African Americans. In an analysis of post-9/11 Islamophobia, Angela Davis (2005, 120) argues that no community of color is immune from reproducing racism against another. Contextually, exclusion may be blatant or veneered. In India many internal subalterns (e.g., Dalits, Bahujans, Adivasis) are left outside hegemonic Indian *family-to-nation* imaginings even if, paradoxically, like others in face-to-face relations, they may be called (by dominant subjects) by normative *sanguinal-familial* designations (e.g., in Hindi, *bhai* [brother] or *behn* [sister]). In contrast, Kim TallBear (2018) highlights the anti-Other character of the dominant settler Global Northern family, as opposed to Native notions of kinship that include all beings and natural forces across the planet.

The dominant *family-to-nation* configuration leaves three principal avenues of action for excluded subalterns: integration, insertion, and subalternist (re)inventions of yet other nations. Integration reinforces the dominant nation. Insertion can transform it. To create yet other nations is to opt out of the dominant nation for an elsewhere.

In integration, the excluded other must be purged of otherness to assimilate into the dominant nation. Two methods are forced forgetting and inducing the subaltern's assimilation desire. Yet not all subalterns are candidates for assimilation. Some nations, such as Nazi Germany, depend on total exclusions and obliterations. In many contexts, integration entails shifts in social borders by splitting, separating, and partially incorporating. Rey Chow demonstrates how the United States increasingly absorbs "subject x" or any previously excluded subject while keeping the hierarchal self/other binary intact (2002). In Jasbir Puar's conception of homonationalism, the "national recognition and inclusion" of some queer subjects "is contingent upon the segregation and disqualification of racial and sexual others from the national imaginary" (2007, 2; 2013). For Puar, writing in 2002, the extreme figure of queer deviance was no longer solely the extravagant (gendered and sexed) queer subject but equally—in the aftermath of September 11, 2001—this position was assigned to the figure of the racialized (Muslim) terrorist as queer. At that time, in the pre-Trump era, to become a proper assimilated queer citizen, thus a *homo-citizen*, a subject had to align with homonormativity and homonationalism, and disavow, ignore, or find irrelevant the prevailing relations of power (Duggan 2003; Puar 2007). After Trump's second election and his accelerated war on "gender ideology," of course, this schema changed to exclude any virtuous or even acceptable position for queers, homonormative or not.

In contrast, in insertion othered subjects enter the dominant nation in ways that could transform it. Contextually, insertion is polysemic. In the 1980s in France, insertion was largely defined in economic terms. It had a positive connotation for many racialized people. The *beur* (Arab) youth movement demanded insertion because it signaled a livable life with paid employment and social belonging on one's own terms. For racialized workers who came in a first large wave in the 1970s (see chapter 5) the 1980s demand for insertion meant a job and bearable working conditions, thus survival and dignity. These imaginings required reconceptualizing France as a multiethnic, pluricultural, socialist society. Such a vision defies the dominant governmental notion of French monocultural universalism. For the French Government, insertion signified making racialized people workers instead of so-called freeloaders on the welfare state. In sum, there was a large gap between disparate kinds of claims around insertion, and between claims and practices. A popular chant at immigrants' rights demonstrations expressed it well: *Ils nous parlent d'insertion, ils preparent l'expulsion* (They talk to us about insertion while preparing deportation).

By the 1990s, in French state discourses insertion was replaced by integration. The disappearing act was made possible and supported by state and societal Islamophobia. The media was flooded with queerphobic-xenophobic constructions of racialized men as sexually out of control (Bacchetta 2013; Guénif-Souilamas and Macé 2004). The French state self-identified as feminist and proposed to "save brown women from brown men" (Spivak 1988). By 2000, integration was inseparable from cultural assimilation. The integration-assimilation pairing got reified in legal decisions. In 2004 the now infamous law banning the hijab and other Islamic head coverings from public schools was passed. In a high-profile case in 2011, an otherwise qualifying Algerian male was spectacularly, pedagogically refused French nationality ostensibly for oppressing his wife. The official argument was that "his idea of sexual equality is not that of the Republic." French Interior Minister Claude Guéant stated that constitutional nationality refusal for "lack of integration" could (now) be interpreted to include failure to culturally "assimilate" (Willsher 2011).

Insofar as perceptive and interpretive habits are conditioned by power, today some insurgent formations are misread as integration-assimilationist when they are actually about radical insertion. An example is the coalition the Campaign for Lesbian Rights (CALERI) in India. It began as a small lesbian activist formation and expanded to include over forty lesbian, queer, women's, trade union, left, civil rights, and anti-Islamophobia groups, and many artists, actors, and filmmakers. CALERI congealed in 1998 in Delhi in response to Hindu nationalist attacks on cinemas showing *Fire*, Deepa Mehta's 1996 award-winning feature film that depicts two sisters-in-law in love (CALERI 1999). The initial CALERI collective organized demonstrations, vigils, and press conferences around a call for lesbian existence and rights (Patel 2002). Those who read CALERI solely through this issue as a *monofocal* phenomena erroneously reduce the struggle to a demand for lesbian integration (Bacchetta 2002). However, this was never the case. *Fire* was only the tip of an iceberg. The initial CALERI lesbian collective was composed of long-term activists and intellectuals from many radical, critical movements (CALERI 1999; Sukthankar 1999). Their vision had long been the total transformation of India for all.[3] They posed the question of lesbianism in broad terms around the question of what kind of society Indians desired: a closed ethnos, sexist, queerphobic, right-wing Hindu nationalist one, or an open, free one in which all subjects can thrive? This analysis and articulation opened space for an expansive coalition.

A third possibility for subjects who are excluded from or subalternly positioned within dominant cisgender heteronormative *family-to-nation* configurations is to construct their own *subalternative sanguinal-familial* nation, either internal or external to the dominant nation. In the internal-nation option, a sector of subjects inside the dominant nation space create *family-to-nation*-like alternatives within it. An example is subaltern families invented by urban working class and employment deprived African Americans under racist conditions. They include "fictive kin" such as "othermothers" (Collins 2005, 1991). There are also the fractional, nuclearized families postcolonial immigrant workers re-created in the 1970s in France's banlieues following the French state's (heterosexual) family-regrouping laws designed to stabilize the workforce and clear urban streets of single racialized men. How to interpret these vital entities is a subject of much debate.

Another variant of the internal subaltern *family-to-nation* is the horizontal subaltern *family-to-nation*. It can take the form of an alternate societal organization. An example is 1970s US territorial and nonterritorial lesbian nation projects invoked in Jill Johnston's book *Lesbian Nation* (Rankin 2000; Atkinson 1984).[4] The thousands of 1970s lesbian-only rural settlements constitute such an alternative territorial nation. The lesbians built houses, farmed the land, sometimes held part-time jobs nearby, and linked with lesbian and left alternative infrastructures: food co-ops, clothing exchanges, and collective recycling and use. Today approximately one hundred lesbian nation–project-based communities still exist (Kershaw 2009). In contrast, a nonterritorial lesbian nation project is the Van Dykes. They were nomadic dykes who lived and traveled in vans. They conceptualized each other in familial terms as sisters. Many legally dropped their patrilineal (father's) names and adopted the surname Van Dyke. Some retain the name today. They thus reiterated normative *sanguinal-familial* relations only to subvert them. These territorial and nonterritorial projects were connected. The Van Dykes often stopped to rest in lesbian settlements or converged at mass lesbian events such as the Michigan Womyn's Music Festival.

External nations are projects established outside the dominant nation space by subjects from its internal sectors. They may or may not result in actual nation-states. A nonstate example is the Gay Homeland Foundation and Gay Parallel Republic. A full-blown nation-state example is the Back to Africa movement that created Liberia. To date there is only one independent queer nation-state, albeit not recognized by other states: The Gay and Lesbian Kingdom of the Coral Sea Islands. Some wealthy white gay men founded it in Australia's ostensibly uninhabited Cato Islands in 2004 after a pro–gay marriage bill failed.

The Lesbian Nation and the Kingdom have much in common. They both entail sharp inclusions and exclusions. The Lesbian Nation projects leave out nonlesbians. Some (not all) additionally reject trans lesbians. The Kingdom bans straight people. They both affirm members' collective history of oppression: for the lesbians, life under heteropatriarchy; for the gays, life under heteronormativity. The members are predominantly white. They propose a common heritage of struggle. The Lesbian Nation has its amazons, (s)heroes, and goddesses. The Kingdom has its shared continuum of (white) gay male existence. They each rework and reinvent language. The lesbians tried to purge English of sexism and lesbophobia and invented *lesbian-centric* terms such as *womyn* and *wimmin*. The Kingdom gays resignified drag expression (king, queen, etc.) and incorporated them in their political structure (i.e., emperor and court).

The *sanguinal-familial* cluster has several important political limitations around contextuality and form. Contextually, the *sanguinal-familial* territorial projects in settler colonies such as the United States and Australia uncritically participate in settler coloniality by forgetting that their projects are on stolen Native land. They inadvertently reenact the "logic of genocide" according to which Native peoples are either gone or must always be disappearing, thereby justifying the settlers' sense of entitlement to the land (Lee-Oliver 2019; Kauanui 2016; Wolfe 2006). In the San Francisco Bay Area of Turtle Island, the Ohlone people, whom the state of California and the US state refuse to recognize and who are thus without tribal lands, suggest as a gesture toward land justice that non-Native residents on Ohlone ancestral lands give *shumi* (in Chochenyo, "gift") or a financial contribution to the tribe so it can purchase its own land. In terms of form, both territorial and nonterritorial *sanguinal-familial* projects tend to assume an already constituted unitary, gender and sexually neutral subject. They do not necessarily address other relations of power—coloniality, capitalism, imperialism, racism, the range of *misogynarchies*, speciesism—and thereby inadvertently risk reproducing them. It should not be surprising then that the most subaltern subjects and the most *freedom-exigent* subjects tend to avoid *sanguinal-familial* alliances.

The poet Julie Blackwomon, a Dyketactics! member, radically clarifies some *sanguinal-familial* limitations in her poem "Revolutionary Blues" (Dyketactics! Archive). It invokes two separate sisterly erasures: one by Black men "in leopard dashikis whose roots entwine with mine in Africa"; the other by "my angry white sisters, my lesbian feminist sisters, whose chains still mesh with mine" (1976). She remarks that her Black brothers say about sexism and lesbophobia, and her white sisters say about racism: "Yes, but what has that to do with our revolution?" Her poem's last lines insightfully dissect the deadly stakes in separating relations of power:

> I expect to be shot in the back.
> I expect to be shot in the back.
> By someone who calls me
> "sister."

Accordingly, the aspects of the Gay and Lesbian Kingdom that draw inspiration from heteronormative settler colonies inadvertently reproduce some dimensions of their colonial violence. The Kingdom's national imaginary includes the settler colonial fantasy of a "land without a people." It bases citizenship on Israel's colonial "right of return" policy: all lesbians and gays across the globe are potential citizens. The Kingdom is both autonomous and separatist: only lesbians and gays can visit. In its constitutional monarchy all emperors have been white gay males. Its constitution is modeled on the US Constitution, including sexist terminology such as "all men are created equal."

Another potential difficulty with the *sanguinal-familial* is that it can reroute queer affective potentialities into normative prescribed familial conduct. The positionalities and relationalities it offers tend to be reductive. The rhetorics and models of brotherhood and sisterhood or of "sons of" and "daughters of" this or that entity are heteronormatively gendered. They exclude or subalternize nonbinary people. Through projections, introjections, and psychic transfers the members of entities modeled on the *sanguinal-familial* can get pulled into prescribed relations with others as familial subject-figures—siblings, children, and parents. Above I mention that Derrida (1994) suggests that fraternity can naturalize friendship that would otherwise be open to other becomings. With its unitary in-group criteria and otherness as a required backdrop, *sanguinal-familial* relations can block innovations.

Yet, the *sanguinal-familial* cluster also has useful features for *co-motion*. Under neoliberal conditions of forced individualization and isolation, the mutual construction of solidarities can end imposed separation, produce new subjects, and open alternate socialities and phases of struggle. For many US queer people of color the term *family* usefully signals in-group recognition and survival. In contrast, white queer acknowledgment often manifests through references to nonfamilial relations such as "friend of Dorothy" (a reference to *The Wizard of Oz*).

Lest reiteration (here, of hetero-familial relations) always be conceptualized as an obstacle to change, let us consider Luce Irigaray's suggestion that some kinds of mimicking can seriously undermine relations of power. She posits *mimésis* (mimesis) as a strategy for altering signification. *Mimésis* entails "deliberate resubmission" to a norm "so as to make visible by an effect of playful repetition what was supposed to remain invisible" (1977, 73–74). Women's expertise at miming indicates they are not fully absorbed into the dominant function; they remain elsewhere (74).

For Irigaray, *mimésis* "unanchors" and breaks down the system of subordination (75–77).

With all its potential challenges, some aspects of the Gay and Lesbian Kingdom enact *mimésis*. The Kingdom adopts a right-wing form, constitutional monarchy, but rewrites it queerly. While other national anthems celebrate war, the Kingdom's anthem is the iconic (white) gay bar song "I Am What I Am." Its lyrics affirm a (white) self-determining queer subject in a queer world:

> I am what I am
> I am my own special creation
> So come take a look
> Give me the hook or the ovation
> It's my world that I want to have a little pride in
> My world
> And it's not a place I have to hide in
> Life's not worth a damn
> Till you can say I am what I am.

Some scholars point out that the phrase "I am what I am" is "marketing's latest offering to the world" entangled in neoliberalism's "mass personalization" and military maneuvers (Invisible Committee 2009, 29). Certainly, the idea that "I am my own special creation" seems constructed through the neoliberal idea of the individualized subject with absolutist agency, with "choice" (Grewal 2005; see also chapter 2). At the same time, the Kingdom has largely opted out of the dominant market and it has no military. It might have potential to exceed its (racialized and class) dominant confines, to create something else. It is possible that the Kingdom's *mimésis* capacities are, beyond *sanguinal-familial* structuration, a subversive effect of the convergence of anormative (queer) bodies of affect in a same time-space.

Alter-Kinship Alliances

Alter-kinship is an alternative to *sanguinal-familial* alliances that draws on some of the latter's characteristics but is totally distinct from it in many ways. Mainly, unlike the *sanguinal-familial*, *alter-kinship* formations need not claim a common heritage, culture, or anything. Their sociality does not require or even tend to produce excluded Others. They are generally (not always) about solidarities across differences. And they can be based in multiple kinds of temporalities at once. Unlike the *sanguinal-familial*, they do not make unity dependent on shared blood inside cisgender heteronormative familiality. *Alter-kinship alliances* differ also from *affective alliances* because their social glue entails actual kinds of alternative kinship configurations as opposed to friendship.

There is a long literature in the field of Indigenous studies—produced by Indigenous scholars and allies—that addresses epistemes beyond the dominant Global North(s), with their own presuppositions, categories, logics, and possible conclusions. This work is instructive for *alter-kinship* as it speaks to the broad range of distinct kinds of categories such as kin, subject, and agency that are variably inclusive of the nonhuman, and how they survive despite colonial epistemic violence that works to erase them. For example, Caissa Revilla-Minaya (2023), who specifically warns against the reduction, homogenization, and fixing of Indigeneity, points to how for the Matsigenka of Amazonian Peru a broad array of subjects are considered human (e.g., the moon) or ex-human. In Huichin, or what is now the San Francisco Bay Area, where I live, the Ohlone people refer to salmon as relatives. Importantly, Indigenous perspectives and practices long precede all the academic knowledges on this topic and the latter are indebted to the former even if not acknowledged as such.

Additionally, a quote at the beginning of this chapter helps us to understand a more recent history of spectrums, shifts, and expansions of what we can consider to be *alter-kinship* and its coexistence within a dominant episteme and specifically within popular culture: "We are family / I got all my sistas with me." These words come from the earliest rendition of a 1979 Sister Sledge hit song that has many incarnations in US popular culture. The 1979 version invokes Black women's solidarities in female sibling intersubjectivities based in semblance:

> We are family
> I got all my sistas with me
> we are family
> get up everybody and sing
> everyone can see we're together
> as we walk on by
> and we flock just like birds of a feather
> I will tell no lie . . .

In each subsequent rendition of the song the lyrics are modified to expand, including more subjects. At first, the added subjects are familial-based figures. The British Spice Girls' and the US drag queen group The Goldman Girls' versions retain the "sistas" intact (as in "I got all my sistas with me"). But they allude to including "women" as men-identified persons in female drag. A cartoon variant by The Chipmunks includes alternately "sistas" and "brothers" (as in "I got all my . . . with me"). Finally, a Jordon Pruit adaptation shifts out of familiality and erases gender constructions with the comprehensive and all-gendered "I got everybody with me." The song also appears in several films and has been adopted by a (men's) football team. These earliest renditions of the song border on *sanguinal familiality*, but later ones push away from it and thereby clarify how the relations the song invokes are within *alter-kinship alliances*.

For this cluster, two later filmic versions of the song are especially important. They both became objects of right-wing outcry precisely because of the radical *alter-kinship* they propose. One is a realist interpretation by the We Are Family Foundation by the song's coauthor Nile Rodgers. His film *We are Family: By All Stars*, directed by Spike Lee (2001–2), brought together two hundred celebrities and musicians. The context was after September 11, 2001. The US government was promoting exclusive nationalist pluralism. This was exemplified spectacularly in state-sponsored TV ads wherein people with visibly distinct skin tones and from disparate racial-ethnic communities proclaimed: "I am an American." In contrast to the ads' attempt to drum up internally, racially pluralist nationalism, Rodgers's film evokes a planetary human family without Others and without national borders. No wonder it irritated right-wing groups for which national unity requires an enemy Other.

A particularly striking next rendition of the song appears in a 2005 cartoon video, created this time by Rodgers himself, with the title *We are Family: A Musical Message for All* (figure 1.2). Here the "for all" signals potential total inclusivity, thus distinguishing this version from earlier varieties. This 2005 video featuring the song was mass produced on DVD, colorfully packaged, and sent to 58,000 US elementary schools and 3,000 National Head Start Association centers. The 2005 cartoon video presents an immense and fully inclusive *alter-family*. Its cast of about one hundred features animal cartoon characters from TV series such as *Bear in the Big Blue House*, *Sesame Street*, and *The Muppets*, alongside human stars such as Diana Ross, Whoopi Goldberg, and Bill Cosby. Its new lyrics commence not with "We are family" but rather with this interpellation: "People,

1.2 The 2005 cartoon "We Are Family: A Musical Message for All" by the We Are Family Foundation ("We Are Family: A Musical Message for All," n.d.).

monsters, lions, bears, dinosaurs, mice, chicken, aardvarks, all coming together. Let's sing together." Here, the subjects of this *alter-kinship* formation come from different species and disparate temporal-spatialities. By including the monster (Mitter 1997; Vergès 1999)—a figure that variously symbolizes colonized others, racialized bodies, revolutionaries, and miscegenation in colonial and dominant Global Northern academic disciplines and popular entertainment such as universal exhibitions or "human zoos" (Bancel et al. 2004)—it radically defies colonialism and racism. Next in the video, the humans, animals, and monsters sing together: "We are family / brothers and my sisters and me." This plural "and me" invokes life beyond gender and species binaries. Then, the tiger sings "and yours truly," thereby reinforcing the *co-presence* of nonhuman subjects and of all previously unacknowledged subjects.

The video's visuals, too, present the "we" as "family" as potentially encompassing all life-forms. Floating rainbow-colored hearts abound. The image and auditory scapes suggest queer otherness. A middle-aged male character with lavender skin speaks US English with an accent. There are many animal and bird languages and sounds. This version was vigorously denounced by right-wing groups specifically for its queer representations. Indeed, the multiple incarnations of "We Are Family" demonstrate the dynamics of *alter-kinship* and how it subverts and undoes the *sanguinal-familial* by making it include subjects it is meant to exclude.

Another destabilizing version of the *alter-kinship* alliance is the Italian feminist practice of *affidamento*. As a form of political connectivity, *affidamento* tries to reinvent assigned-female familial intersubjectivities to create new women subjects. The term *affidamento* has multiple meanings and translations. When referring to humans, *affidamento* signifies custody, care, dependency, or charge of children. In reference to the nonhuman, it means "consignment" or "keeping." Of all its English translations, "entrustment" seems most accurate, for it accentuates relations of disparately positioned subjects based in trust (*feducia*) without losing other potential meanings such as relations among persons and of persons to things (Cicognia and de Lauretis 1990).

Historically, *affidamento* was elaborated in a 1987 book by activist members of the Libreria delle donne di Milano (Milan Women's Bookstore).[5] It was also theorized by philosopher Luisa Muraro, a member of Colletivo Diotima (Demeter Collective) in Milan and by feminist lawyers (Campari et al. 1985). In all its incarnations, *affidamento* draws from Irigaray's notorious claim that in misogynous contexts women do not exist as subjects, for their *subject-becoming* is blocked by the lack of a Third, or symbolic dimension, to mediate their interrelations (Irigaray 1986, 1984, 1981, 1977). The mother-daughter relation is the site of the most damage. It is also a potentially "explosive kernel" that could, if differentially enacted, make patriarchy crumble (1981, 86). In *affidamento* two disparately positioned women work to reconstitute themselves as subjects by creating an ideal mother-daughter relation together. *Affidamento* thus requires pairs of women divided by inequities such as education, class, employment, age, symbolic capital, etc. The most dominantly positioned woman enacts the mother and the most vulnerable the daughter. Unfortunately, to date, theorizations of *affidamento* do not consider coloniality, race, national origin, religion, and more.

In brief, *affidamento* is conceptualized as a relation of power that gets transformed into a relation of trust. The more vulnerable woman, the daughter, consigns herself to a more powerful one, the mother, who takes on this responsibility. They attempt to speak together outside of sexist, dominant masculine references, re-creating language between themselves as a mediating Third. To do so, for example, they use historical and divine feminine figures as sources in conversation. Teresa de Lauretis highlights that "the function of female symbolic mediation that one woman performs for the other is achieved not in spite, but rather because, of the power differential between them, contrary to the egalitarian feminist belief that women's mutual trust is incompatible with unequal power" (Milan Women's Bookstore 1990, 9). For Maria Grazia Campari et al. (1985), *affidamento* ensures the visibility and eventually the hearability of women (to other women) who otherwise are only audible in the public space if they speak as men, such as in the courtroom as lawyers. All proponents of *affidamento* claim that women making woman subjects together would spell the fall of Western civilization.

A current form of *alter-kinship* alliances with a very long history is that composed of self-organized transgender subjects across South Asia for many centuries: *Hijras, Chakka, Khusra, Kojja, Aravanis, Nupi Maanbi*, etc. Across the continent and across the divides of national borders, some groups (not all) live together collectively in joint family-based structures. While they are often homogenized, including by well-meaning allies, they are a heterogeneous ensemble. Disparate subjects variably identify as women, third gender, neither, or both. They may be homosexual, heterosexual, bisexual, pansexual, or asexual. Each specific community has its own genealogy.

At this time, *Hijras* are the most well-known group across northern South Asia. The term *Hijra*, their own self-designation, itself evokes departure from normative kinship, for in Urdu it is derived from the Arabic *hjr*, or "leaving one's tribe." While Urdu was formed only during the Delhi Sultanate (1206–1527), trans existence in South Asia is a much earlier phenomenon. Trans subjects who go by other names appear across Hindu sacred texts such as the *Kama Sutra* (ca. second century BCE) and the epics *Ramayana* (ca. fourth century BCE) and *Mahabharata* (ca. ninth century BCE).

Today, *Hijras* live in households that often encompass fifteen to fifty persons in urban or rural space. Many members are often (not always) exiled from their *sanguinal-familial* homes or run away to escape abuse. *Hijras* address each other by normative female kinship terms based on age status: elder or younger sister, mother, second mother, mother's sister, maternal grandmother, etc. Nearly everywhere relationships between older and younger members are structured through the *guru-shishya* (teacher-student or mentor-mentee) relation. *Hijras* come from all religious, class, caste, and national backgrounds. While the Indian and Pakistani governments (not peoples) are often at declared or undeclared war, *Hijras* living in these countries do not necessarily accept these divides. Historically their identity and existence do not depend on any anti-Other discourse or practice.

A related, albeit much newer *alter-kinship* formation is US ballroom culture. It was first created by trans and queer Black and Latinx subjects in cities in the United States but which has now spread across parts of the Global North(s) and South(s) such as to Brazil (Wong 2024; Bailey 2021, 2013). Today the number of ballroom events and gatherings seems to have spiked as an aftereffect of the economic- and COVID-related increasing closure of gay bars (Ghaziani 2024).

Importantly for the *alter-kinship* cluster, in the United States, ballroom culture is organized into houses, each with a house mother (and/or father) and many children. The members' statuses do not depend on age; some children may be older than mothers. Members are bound together by affection, loyalty, and bonds of nurturing (Bailey 2021, 2013; Arnold and Bailey 2009). Like the Van Dykes mentioned above, house members often legally adopt their house name as their surname, thereby breaking the patrilineal mold. Houses are often linked to queer activisms. Ballroom differs from Lesbian Nation configurations in that ballroom has no nation aspirations.

Alter-kinship alliances have much to offer. But, lest they be romanticized, it is important to understand their limitations. Like *affective*-friendship alliances, *alter-kinship* alliances risk reiterating relations of dominant *sanguinal-familiality*. Saidiya Hartman, while discussing her connection as an African American to Africa in *Lose Your Mother*, remarks that the search for a "proxy" to relationships "severed long ago" is not necessarily a solution, and "fictive kinship" is "too close to the heart of slavery's violence for" her "comfort" (2007, 199). Hartman helps us consider how collectivity formation unfolds within relations of power and can thereby unwittingly reproduce them. This is a valuable, rarely explored dimension of *alter-kinship*. To add to her insights, we might also consider scholarship that highlights another dimension: how African American *nonsanguinal* kinship formation—with its "othermothers," sisters, or brothers—has ensured Black survival (Collins 1991). For Patricia Hill Collins, nonblood attachments need not supersede wounds created by accumulations of violence effects from historically brutally severed ties. Instead, they can work to heal them. Finally, *alter-kinship* alliances sometimes reiterate a "we" vs. "they" binary that othered the alter-subject in the first place.

A major strength of *alter-kinship* alliances is their potential to invent deep solidarities and fulfilling lives for subaltern subjects without necessarily requiring an enemy Other. *Affidamento* proposes no human or other enemy. Its agent of oppression and repression is a patriarchal system in which humans are imagined as unfixed and capable of change. *Hijras* and ballroom subjects, too, designate no static Other. The subjects of *affidamento*, *Hijra* life, and ballroom communities all play with identitary statuses to collectively reinvent themselves, their relationalities, and their worlds.

Hard Interest Alliances

Yet another kind of *co-motion* is *hard interest alliances*. Their defining criteria is the narrowly, subjectively self-identified interests of disparate members. They generally come together around only one issue. Unlike *affective, sanguinal*, and *alter-kinship alliances*, the affect, the relational statuses, and the social glue of the subjects of *hard interest alliances* are irrelevant. The main thing that holds *hard interest alliances* together is a shared, usually temporary, always limited political objective. Often their convergence for a common cause (and notably "cause" is habitually in the singular) is a necessity for survival. Bernice Johnson Reagon sums this up well in the quote at the beginning of this chapter: "You don't go into coalition because you like it. The only reason you would consider trying to team up with somebody who could possibly kill you, is because that's the only way you can figure you can stay alive." Unlike *common conditionalities alliances* (see below), the parties to *hard interest alliances* need not share anything about their social location in relations of power. The subjects of *hard interest alliances* may be from vastly different, even antagonistic, social sectors. And finally, unlike *common political desires alliances* (again, see below) *hard interest alliances* are transient and short-lived, have an extremely restricted focus (most often one issue), and are very far from *freedom-exigency*.

Hard interest alliances span structuralist and poststructuralist tendencies, political divisions of right and left, and political objectives. They have been theorized in the Global North(s) and South(s) over centuries—for example, in Machiavelli's *The Prince* and Lao Tsu's *The Art of War*. Currently, *hard interest* has a dominating presence in the form of rational choice in the social sciences in the United States (and not necessarily elsewhere). It also has several subaltern incarnations.

Scholarship about coalitions between Indigenous people and settlers, groups that otherwise are at odds around notions of the land and water (often the former conceptualize land as mother or grandmother, while for the latter land is property), provides a case in point for understanding *hard interest alliances* and especially their immense limitations. An example is temporary coalitions between Indigenous people in the United States and right-wing Christian evangelicals to combat the immediate toxicity of their (unequally) shared environment. Andrea Smith (2008) points out that these kinds of "unlikely alliances" disrupt logics about who counts as a potential ally. She explains that Native Americans often do not have the luxury of choosing with whom they work. She draws on Angela Davis's notion of "dis-articulation" to argue that Native Americans "re-articulate" or reframe struggles to "garner broader support" (Smith 2008, xiv; Davis 2003). Their strategy is not to find common ground but rather to create it. For example, in South Dakota, a predominantly Republican state, Native peoples and white farmers are both faced with large corporations that would take their water or land to create a resort that would change the local economy and way of life. In that case, for survival Native subjects "re-articulate" the struggle not in terms of treaty violations with Natives but instead more broadly as a question of the corporate effect on everyone's water and land.

As vital as they can be in some lethal situations, a major limitation of *hard interest alliances* is that they can only work around one or a few issues. After that gets resolved, they generally dissolve. *Hard interest alliances* are nearly always directly oppositional. They fight against some aspect or dimension of oppressive-to-deadly laws or practices. They are not about transformation. However, there are exceptions. Some very radical groups may work toward "non-reformist reforms" for survival (Davis 2003; Smith 2008, 203). And some collectivities that begin with reform can with momentum vastly exceed their initial focus.

Another potential problem for me, specifically with "re-articulation," is that the turn toward unitary so called universal concerns could seriously harm extremely subaltern subjects for whom multiple issues are inseparable. For example, for queer and trans Natives, their tribe's solidarity with queerphobic and transphobic right-wing groups can constitute intense violence.

Hard interest alliances also may have many potential uses. They are nearly always an immediate remedy to dramatically oppressive situations. They can help us question simplistic notions of subjects, politics, and strategies. They can undo the idea of static, essentialist, undetachable sets of interests. Sometimes separating issues, rethinking them through other frames, can denaturalize them and reveal their political genealogies (Hall 1988, 167). When rearticulation moves subjects to create a common language, or a Third as Irigaray (1979) would call it, it can also help co-constitute new subjects and intersubjectivities.

Common Conditions Alliances

A form of *co-motion* that may be outside dominant-informed perception is *common conditions alliances*. They are solidarities that subjects create based on their mindfulness about how they are situated in identical or analogous kinds of relations of power. An example is alliances for trans liberation among young working-class trans subjects of Moroccan heritage in the banlieues of Paris or Marseille that are happening right now (Danjé 2021). The subjects in question understand that they are similarly located in relation to colonialism, coloniality, capitalism, racism, and *misogynarchies*, including racialized transphobia.

However, obviously, all similarly situated subjects do not make *common conditions alliances*. There is no natural link between how subjects are situated in relations of power and the alliances they make. A great many factors enter to muddy consciousness and to divide and rule. As Foucault (2001e) continually reminds us, all subjects are formed in power and thus power is integral to the subject itself. The power of our formation can induce us to act against our own interests and instead in the interests of the dominant. In our attempts to unite, relations of power intervene as divide and rule. This means that if we are ever to create effective *freedom-exigent co-motion*, we need to better understand power and its operations.

Common conditions alliances differ starkly from the former kinds of *co-motion* in this chapter. The subjects who unite in *common conditions alliances* may or may not be family, friends, or nonsanguinal relatives as in *affective, sanguinal-familial*, and *alter-kinship alliances*. The defining feature of *common conditions alliances* has nothing to do with those kinds of social relations. Instead, the primary common characteristic is the subjects' consciousness about their shared social positionalities. Unlike *hard interest alliances*, the subjects of *common conditions alliances* may not have a unified political stance or even intentionality to come together across differences around a limited single issue. Instead, in *common conditions alliances* the crucial trait is subjects' understanding of how they are similarly situated and exposed in conditions of power and their will to oppose or transform that power together.

Some historical, now classical, queer discussions of "situatedness" can help clarify our definition of *common conditions alliances*. For instance, in Black queer studies the question of who is a queer subject and who is in a similar positionality to queers has an extensive genealogy (Johnson and Henderson 2005). Cathy J. Cohen pinpoints obstacles that Black queers face in uniting with white queers when she remarks that the historical shift from earlier queer civil rights discourses to (white) queer theory did not end white queer racism but rather produced a new "single-oppression framework that continues to marginalize queers of color" (2005, 25). For Cohen, coalitions can usefully be forged "around a more intersectional analysis of who and what the enemy is" (21). Specifically, Black queer coalitionality can include subjects who are nonidentically yet somewhat similarly positioned in relations of power—that is, "punks, bulldaggers and welfare queens" (43). While recognizing commonalities of Black subjects constructed with anormativized sexuality, Marlon M. Bailey highlights some complexities by suggesting that familial and institutional queerphobia are obstacles to such coalitionality (2013). In sum, to think with *common conditionalities* can open potentials for obvious as well as seemingly unlikely alliances.

An interesting theorization of some manifestations of *common conditions alliances* can be found in what Francoise Lionnet and Shu-mei Shih, drawing on Deleuze and Guattari's notion of the minor, call "minor transnationalism" (Lionnet and Shih 2005). Global-South(s)-to-South(s) interconnections have most often been mediated by the North(s). In contrast, "minor transnationalism" signals critical horizontal solidarities from below, within, and across the Global South(s) and North(s). It is the subaltern underside of hegemonic transnationalism from above—that is, among powerful capitalist sectors.

A present Global-South(s)-to-South(s) *common conditions alliances* example is the linkage among queers under occupation in Palestine, Kurdistan, Kashmir, and under settler colonialism in Turtle Island and Abya Yala. This *co-motion* comprises subjects who have all worked for decades in their own sites against occupation and colonialism. Many define their antioccupation, anticolonial politics in totally *freedom-exigent* ways. It is about transforming every relation of power, including sexism and queerphobia. For example, in 2017 the Decolonizing Sexualities Network organized a first panel in Paris during Queer Week that brought together antioccupation activists from Palestine, Kurdistan, and Kashmir for dialogue (see chapter 5). In 2021, at the organization's massive transnational online conference called Decolonial Café, the opening panel was on Queers Combatting Settler Colonialism with speakers from Palestine, Kashmir, Turtle Island, and Abya Yala.[6] Today, Ohlone, Palestinian, and Kashmiri activists in the San Francisco Bay Area are forging links. Unlike in *hard interest alliances* (above) and in *political desires alliances* (see below), these movements are in a relation of mutual understanding, dialogue, and solidarity without claims to a common agenda.

While the *common conditions alliances* cluster is assembled around situatedness, certainly no two groups' positionings in relation to power are identical and their differences matter. Their distinctness can bear on *co-motion*. Subalternized peoples *in-coloniality* across the planet have been variably, not identically, subjected to colonial violence, genocide, land theft, cultural decimations, psychic violence, and epistemicide. They are also often divided by intragroup or intranational inequities. In India, Mahatma Jyotirao Phule (1827–90), the renowned Dalit leader, wrote that Dalits' main enemy was not colonialism but rather Hindu caste and gender oppression. Today, as critical analyses by Dalit, Bahujan, Adivasi, and Muslim feminist and queer intellectuals—such as Thenmozhi Sundararajan, Akhil Kang, Huma Dar, Shaista Patel, and many others—make perfectly clear, stark class-, caste-, and religion-based oppressions are reproduced in dominant Indian feminist and queer movements.

Another aspect of *common conditions alliances* is that awareness of conditions may lead to spontaneous solidarities based on identifications and disidentifications. Such consciousness did not drop from the sky; it has a long genealogy. It was the guiding light of the April 15, 1955, Bandung conference composed of representatives from twenty-nine African and Asian governments against (neo)colonialism. It was central to the (peoples,' not governments') Bandung of the North organized in Paris in May 2018. It manifested in the words of the African American comedian Chris Rock when after 9/11 a kind of docile US patriotism with Islamophobia as social glue became hegemonic in the public space. Rock understood the politics of forced identifications and disidentifications and refused belonging based on violently othering Muslims. He remarked: "I'm not afraid of Al Qaida; I'm afraid of Al Cracker."[7]

The alliances in the *common conditions alliances* cluster also entail potential problems even if the examples mentioned above (Cohen, Lionnet and Shih, queers under occupation and settler colonialism, Dalit feminists and queers, the Bandungs, Chris Rock) avoid them. Political agendas based on more or less *common conditions* risk homogenizing, essentializing, or romanticizing minor positionalities and arranging them into an unhelpful victimhood vs. heroism binary. They can forget how minor sectors may be split internally by relations of power and reproduce them therein. They may ignore that some subalterns will play into divide-and-rule practices and dis-ally from other subalterns to join dominant forces (see chapter 2).

In *common conditions alliances* the definition of "common," too, can present challenges. "Common" is often a function of power and scale, but these can have extreme differentials. We now have several decades of scholarship that highlights how power can get erased in the all too broad notions of "colonial" and "postcolonial" (Bacchetta 2022; McClintock 1995). Argentina, with its strong economy, European-descended population, and history of genocide against Native peoples, is not "postcolonial" in the same way as Bangladesh. In India, caste and class have produced internal "cultures of servitude"; the relations of power on which they are based can get reproduced in broader social movements (Bakshi 2022; Ray and Qayum 2009). In Abya Yala, historically African-descended and Native subjects have critiqued the Eurocentrism of the so-called unifying term *Latinidad* and some have suggested alternatives. For example, the Black and Indigenous Brazilian feminist scholar Lélia Gonzalez proposed *Amefricanidad*, which unerases Native and African descended subjects across the continent (Gonzalez 2020, 1988; Gonzalez and Hasenbalg 1982). Decades later, today in Turtle Island these critiques are not taken up as *Latinidad* is continually reiterated. Finally, after a history of exposing racism within queer and trans communities and transphobia in cisgender heteronormative subalternly racialized communities, many scholars and activists are now opening up discussions about how trans subjects of color dodge entrapment, express creativity, and thrive in the intra-trans solidarity they invent (Danjé 2021; Di Pietro 2020a, 2020b, 2016a, 2016b). These examples demonstrate how the idea of "common" in *common conditions* can invisibilize some relations of power and the most subaltern subjects, but also how "common" can serve as a basis for subaltern lines of flight.

Convergent Political Desires Alliances

A last *co-motion* form here is *convergent political desires alliances*. Unlike *hard interest alliances*, which are temporary, oppositional, organized around one or a few objectives, and can involve parties with extremely conflicting political perspectives on many other issues, *convergent political desires alliances* entail common kinds of perceptual, sensual, and political orientations. Unlike *affective, sanguinal-familial,* and *alter-kinship alliances*, these do not require that the allied subjects have any particular relation to and social glue with each other. Unlike *common conditions alliances,* the participants in *convergent political desires alliances* do not need to be from same or similar conditions. Angela Davis expresses this point extremely well as she advocates "basing the identity on politics rather than the politics on identity" (1997, 318).

A historical example of this kind of shared political project among diversely positioned subjects is the Italian left feminist practice of transversality. It proposes that disparate social locations (especially class) provide dissimilar perspectives and that to have a more complete view subjects need each other. Transversality seeks to move beyond the universalism vs. relativism binary and beyond essentialism by proposing equity in critical nonhierarchical difference. Transversality also distinguishes between "positioning, identity and values." No one can represent their community unless elected. Subjects located anywhere can advocate for a different community if they practice "rooting" (acknowledgement of their social location) and "shifting" (putting themselves in other's shoes) (Yuval-Davis 1999).

A present example of *convergent political desires* is the transformation in 2020 of the annual queer Pride march in Los Angeles, California, into a (rather queer) Black Lives Matter march. It was announced in June 2020 during massive global demonstrations against police violence, sparked by the publicity around the murder of George Floyd in Minnesota. Like the other uprisings I discuss (see chapter 5), this one too did not drop from the sky but instead is a culmination of a longer history of struggles and critiques. Many prior moments are *co-present* in the 2020 decision. For example, there is the fallout from the 2008 passage of the California statewide ballot proposition against gay marriage. Some white queers and their allies used the ballot to blame Black voters for exceptional queerphobia. Yet the Black population is not numerous enough to have swayed the vote. (White) evangelists massively financed and coordinated the campaign. Some Black queers and other queers of color and allies had critiqued the sexist, racist, and class logic of gay marriage in the first place (Bailey et al. 2004; Mecca 2008; see also the multiple articles on the website of the group Against Equality founded by Yasmin Nair and Ray Conrad). Some critiques drew on earlier feminist analytics to highlight that all marriage is grounded in capitalist sexist relations of property and extends the realm of privatization by the capitalist state. Gay marriage would bestow rights such as inheritance from which only queers with financial resources would benefit. It would further marginalize and demonize queers outside coupledom. Another strand in the 2020 Pride decision is the merging of movements against racist and queerphobic police brutality, including murders. Black Lives Matter, founded in Oakland, California, in 2013 by three out queer-identified Black women—Patrisse Cullors, Alicia Garza, and Opal Tometi—took a strong stance against police murders of all Black people, including women and all trans people, from day one. California is also home to Critical Resistance, the (antipolice) abolitionist organization created by Black and other feminists and/or queers of color including Angela Davis, Ruth Gilmore, and Alicia Bierra. The LA Pride March decision is about *convergent political desires* insofar as it is about foregrounding a broader, uncompromising intersectional analysis and practice.

Ernesto Laclau and Chantal Mouffe usefully highlight a Gramscian distinction that can help us father clarify *convergent political desires alliances*. There are on the one hand convergences based on sectorial interests in which participating entities retain their separate identities (such as class alliances) and on the other those based in "ideas and values" shared "by many sectors" that produce "a collective will" that becomes the "cement" for a "historic block" ([1985] 1999, 66–67). The latter mutual orientation "defines a new series of relations among groups" that "baffles their structural location" (67). Accordingly, the *convergent political desires* cluster implicates associational modes beyond the allies' structural positioning (thus, beyond the defining feature of *conditional alliances*). Unlike *hard interest alliances* in which unity is based on vigorous, calculated self-interest, *convergent political desires alliances* involve affect and bodily sensations, such as yearning, longing, and craving, for a vision for which subjects mutually strive. *Convergent political desires alliances* often (not always) come closer than other kinds of alliances to *freedom-exigent co-motion.*

While the unifying cement in this cluster comprises a political analysis and ideals, it is bolstered by affect and identifications. The affect in *convergent political desires alliances* may even consist of a collective disappearance of affect.

A relatively large-scale historical example of *convergent political desires alliances* is the 2011 Tunisian revolution. The turning point for it is most often named as the protest by self-immolation by Mohamed Bouazizi. That moment, however, could become a spark because it was preceded by years of public critique by musicians, artists, and bloggers. Ba'adia Bouhrizi sang about the Ben Ali regime's brutality in Redeyef in 2008. The rapper El Général (Hamada Ben Amor) articulated the people's sentiments in "Malesh" (Why?), "Sidi Rais" (Mr. President), and later "Rais LeBled," which became an anthem for the Tunisian and Egyptian revolutions (Morgan 2011; El Général 2011). Blogger Slim Amamou, too, voiced discontent. The terrain was ripe when Bouazizi's martyrdom downed "the wall of fear" (Colla 2011). Commentators remarked that Bouazizi's self-immolation spectacularly conjoined "material deprivation" with emotional "distress" about "non-recognition of wrong" and unleashed a "process of collective subjectivation" (Benslama 2011). It provoked a "rupture in normality," a "brutal acceleration of political temporalities" and a "tearing apart of history" (Khiari and Hibou 2011, 23). Disenfranchised sectors led the revolution. Electronic media helped to connect elites, intellectuals, and artists to it (El Forkani 2011; Tlatli 2011; Miladi 2011). Pro–Ben Ali officials publicly and reductively called demonstrators a "fanaticized hoard," a point magnified by its reproduction on Tunisie TV Replay. In Egypt, too, a prior "history of revolution, a history of poets" helped to enable the revolution (Colla 2011). Atef Shahat Said rightly points to "lived contingencies" or fragilities and unpredictabilities of what such a *convergence* of *political desires* can produce, how it may manifest, and what it may or may not become (2024). Importantly, in both Tunisia and Egypt, notwithstanding all other factors, *convergent political desires* superseded potential divides, permitting new subjects to reclaim and reinvent life itself, even if only briefly, even if stopping short.

Sometimes *convergent political desires alliances* can in struggle expand and intensify. This happened in March 2020 when the refugee and immigration association Cittadini del Mondo (Citizens of the World), based in Rome, organized an evening of fairy tale readings for children by drag queens inside the multilingual library the organization founded.[8] Cittadini del Mondo, created by the feminist medical doctor Donatella D'Angelo, who remains its president and spokesperson, has many activities. It works within a squat, *Palazzo Selam* (Peace Palace), where about nine hundred refugees mainly from northeast Africa—but also Bangladesh, Syria, and elsewhere—reside. D'Angelo created a free medical clinic with volunteer doctors and medical students—including herself and her son—inside *Palazzo Selam*. Cittadini del Mondo provides information about documentation, employment, social benefits, etc. to squat residents. It agitates for change in Italian and European refugee and immigrant policy. Its *Biblioteca Interculturale* (Intercultural Library) has books in over forty languages, free language classes, a speakers' series, professional formation, film showings, bingo night, day care, and children's events.

As soon as the drag queen fairy-tale reading event was publicly announced, right-wing groups began to attack it. D'Angelo was placed in a position of explaining to the public that the organization—albeit visibly mobilized around refugee and immigrant conditions—actively opposes all oppression, including all queerphobias.

The event and the right-wing attack have a deep genealogy in prior struggles. D'Angelo has been an activist against capitalism, on feminist issues, and around immigration since the late 1970s. Paolo Guera, the *Biblioteca Interculturale's* manager, cofounded the radical left organization *Autonomia Operai* (Worker's Autonomy) in Rome in the 1970s. In the 1980s Guera was imprisoned on false charges and only liberated when a broad movement demanded his release. The Italian right has attacked the pro-refugee, proimmigrant, and queer movements from their inception. The drag queen fairy-tale event suddenly spectacularized the potential merging of otherwise separate movements and in so doing sent the right into a tailspin that continued for months. In the meantime, the event spurred some radical sectors of both queer and refugee-immigrant movements to enter into new dialogue and alliance with each other.

Convergent political desires alliances present both challenges and openings. On the side of difficulties, constructing a common political orientation can produce erasures of subaltern conditions and subjects further below. Thus, not all demonstrators for Black lives feel that trans life matters. Not all drag queens and their allies are in solidarity with refugees and immigrants, and vice versa. For convergent political desires there needs to be consensus that all forms of oppression must be dismantled. This re-quires continually questioning the potential exclusion mechanisms of the political-affective "we" that gets constituted in political projects including those with "revolutionary" goals (Singer 1991, 126). On the side of openings, *convergent political desires alliances* can create new perspectives on political objectives and new political subjects and intersubjectivities.

Toward Freedom-Exigent Co-Motion

We can draw three conclusions from the above discussion.

First, obviously, there are many very distinct ways of coming together. The terms that currently describe them—whether alliance, convergence, solidarity, network, or other—have different meanings. The broader term *co-motion* can encompass them all and enable us to discuss them together without erasing their distinctions. *Co-motion* also opens up space for reimag-ining and rearticulating coming together in ways we have not yet imagined.

Second, this chapter shows how various kinds of current and his-torical *co-motion* formations have limitations. They risk leaving in place, reproducing, expanding, or producing anew at least some relations of power. We saw in several clusters—and perhaps most clearly in *hard in-terest alliances*—how power can operate to render its own workings and the most subaltern subjects imperceptible. We understood from some other clusters—perhaps most strikingly for *sanguinal alliances*—how so-cial glue can require a negative Other as backdrop. Clearly the remedy to these problems is not additive. It is not to simply include more subaltern subjects or more critiques of conditions of power in analyses, practices, and activisms. Inclusion doesn't necessarily change structures, configura-tions, or assemblages of power. Additive logic can operate as "murderous inclusion" (Haritaworn et al. 2013). Whoever, whatever, is brought into *co-motion* additively can be subjected to forced assimilation or get placed in the margins and get neutralized there.

Finally, this chapter can help us understand the need to shift entirely, to move to what Assata Shakur (in the quote at the beginning of this book's introduction) calls "a paradigm of our own making." For me, it is about imagining different sets of *theory-assemblages* for effective *freedom-exigent co-motion* for our times. The next chapter begins to propose some concepts toward those ends.

The master's tools will never dismantle the master's house.

    Audre Lorde

A concept is like a brick. It can be used to build a court-house of reason. Or it can be thrown through a window.

    Brian Massumi, translator's foreword to Deleuze
    and Guattari, *A Thousand Plateaus*

Rupture means ceasing to live in the enemy's world.

    Jacques Rancière

If chapter 1 exposed how power reappears, is reproduced, and therefore is reinforced inside *co-motion,* this chapter aims to break with that cycle and to open up lines of flight to an *elsewhere-present* and an *elsewhere-futurity.* It desires to escape from the "master's house," to throw a "brick" through the dominant episteme, to enact a "rupture." It hopes to contribute to *theory-assemblages* that can generate other worlds. It honors and works with present subaltern theorizings. However awkwardly, it also proposes some *subalternative* concepts to think with about power, subjects, and *freedom-exigent co-motion.*

    The concepts suggested here (and throughout this book) are not meant to be elements for a universalized—or even a particular localized—map for the present or future. They are not parts of an ultimate uniform solution for all. By definition whatever is *subalternative* is concerned with the most minute infinitesimal questions of subalterneity anywhere. Such concerns differ from one context to another, and even from one temporal-spatiality to another in a same context. Instead, the *subalternative* notions here strive to operate a halting, to induce disorientation, to open up a different *sensing, perception,* and *intelligibility* in the present dominant order. For in the end, effective and persistent *freedom-exigency* may need to be preceded by a productive collective vertigo.

Some of the concepts discussed here have already emerged briefly in these pages. Others are as yet unheard, only now materializing.

Co-Motion

I mentioned *co-motion* in the introduction and in chapter 1 as an umbrella term to include different ways of coming together: alliances, solidarities, networks, associations, convergences, community, unions, coalition, and more. But *co-motion* has a wider spectrum of meanings and dimensions too.

One of its aspects is this: *co-motion* is a synthesis of *co* and *motion*. The *co* refers to simultaneity, to *co-presence*. It is about convergence, coalescence, coming together, cohabiting, cohering, and comingling, concurrently in a common moment. *Co-motion* implicates human and nonhuman *beings-becomings* in a same collectivity, as kin. The *co* in *co-motion* is close to the idea of *co-present temporal-spatialities* that is invoked throughout this book.

The *co* in *co-motion* is also about multiplicities of *subjects-in-socialities and another* (see below). The comings together of subjects in any kind of *co-motion* and how they are thought are not abstractable or otherwise detachable from the relations of power in which they are co-constituted as subjects and operate. The *co* of coming together in *co-motion* might be differentially induced, animated, or blocked depending on contextual configurations and techniques of power. In some conditions, the co in *co-motion* can relocate, align, realign, reposition, shift, and morph. In others, the *co* in *co-motion* may be disparately immune to, or vulnerable to, premature dissolution.

Co combined with *motion* invokes dynamism—motion together. The motion in *co-motion* reminds us how everything *freedom-exigent* moves. It urges us to be attentive to what is moving or not and how. But importantly, it helps us to redefine moving. Rosa Luxemburg remarks that "those who do not move do not notice their chains." Yet, there are many kinds of moving and of moving together. Moving can entail gentle stirrings or frantic action. It can also encompass movement-in-complete-immobility. It can be about playing statue. A digging in of heels. Or otherwise remaining still. We might consider the in-place *co-motion* of some mobility-challenged disabled activist subjects.

Some *freedom-exigent* action entails refusing to move physically and instead maintaining, expanding, improving life where you are. This kind of refusal is exemplified by peoples under colonial occupation who are subjected to lethal conditions designed to remove them, such as via geno-cide or relocation: Palestinians, Kashmiris, Kurds, Native peoples in Turtle Island, Abya Yala, and elsewhere, or queer people of color under condi-tions of gentrification (Alasah 2023; Nabulsi 2023; Gould and Montalvo 2020; Lavie 2011). Even when brutally forced out of place they create move-ments for their right to return. Tianna Bruno (2023) provides an extremely thoughtful set of considerations—beyond dying-living and oppression-resistance thematics—about how US Black subjects construct and live life in place, in relation to space and the environment. Not budging is also a tactic, albeit differently, of some of the most subaltern subjects among squatters, and of many unhoused people, from Paris to Rome to Delhi to Mumbai. In sum, the *motion* in *co-motion* implicates many worlds of (im) motion.

Co-motion is also never far from commotion. It can be a smashing of walls, a shattering of windows, in the house of Order that relations of power make. It can be a hullabaloo, a ruckus, a pandemonium. *Co-motion* as commotion can burn down anything in its path. It can be loud, a scream, the confusions of multiple musics blasting at once. But the *co* in commo-tion can also entail the turmoil of silent survival in deadly contexts. It can be a tumultuous refusal to disappear. It can be about a frenzied insistence on thriving.

Co-motion is also about emotion together or what we might call *co-emotion*. It is about being moved by and with. The work of thinking affect as an imminent force of the political has an expansive genealogy (Reich 2015; Berlant 2012; Clough 2007; Ahmed 2004; Lorde [1978] 1993; Anzaldúa [1987] 2007; Mosse 1985; Fromm 1941). It entails sentiment, feeling, sensi-tivities, intensities, passions, corporeality, the psyche. Chapter 1 disclosed some different kinds of affect (love, friendship, solidarity, hatred, disgust, fear), disparate sites of affective *operability*, its place in various relation-alities, its different qualities and concentrations, and some of its distinct meanings contextually for *co-motion*.

Beyond affect, *co-motion* entails yet other dimensions: the sensual-corporeal, including everything surface-fleshy, everything deeply cellular; blood and bones; the energetic dimension including spirit(s), the ghostly, *beings-becomings* that are unseen, unfelt, or even not yet here; states of awareness and unawareness; the transient and the permanent; and the imperceptible.

Subjects-in-Sociality and Another

The concept of *subjects-in-socialities and another* refers to humans and all other sentient and nonsentient *beings-becomings*. They are the actors of *freedom-exigent co-motion* and/or one of its main concerns. Briefly, the *in-sociality* in *subjects-in-socialities and another* signals that each subject is co-constituted in historical-contextual relations of power inseparably with other subjects. We are all part of each other's coming into being. The idea of *and another* in *subjects-in-socialities and another* recognizes, flags, and provides space for whatever subject or *being-becoming* is imagined in dominant discourses to be outside of the *in-socialities* at any point in time. In chapter 1 we saw how some *co-motion* formations required or allowed for the exclusion of distinct kinds of subjects—such as *sanguinal alliances* or *hard interest alliances*—while other *co-motion*—such as *alter-kinship co-motion*—remained ever open to include a vast range of subjects and *beings-becomings*. More in line with yet not identical to the latter, the *and another* in *subjects-in-socialities and another* helps us to recognize the full subject status of everyone and everything that power marginalizes, hides, or deletes from *co-presence in-socialities*. The *and another* in *subjects-in-socialities and another* can include human or nonhuman sentient or other forms of existence altogether. The concept-term *and another* is part of an ensemble with *subjects-in-sociality* precisely to emphasize the inseparability of the *and another* in that configuration. The awkwardness of the term *subjects-in-sociality and another*, and the fact that it challenges conventions of syntax, grammar, and logic in English, puts into relief the limits of the English language to convey *subaltern*, *subalternative*, and *freedom-exigent* ways of thinking. The term *subjects-in-socialities and another* is also meant to induce a pause wherein we might reflect on what disrupting, disregarding, and disobeying those very constraints might open up.

The notion of *subjects* in *subjects-in-socialities and another* does not claim full allegiance to any particular theory of The Subject, the subject, The Subjects, or the subjects. It has no loyalty to any component analytic of the assemblage that I call *The S/subject(s)*. *Subjects-in-socialities and another* is very far from dominant, colonial-racialized, Global Northern notions of the subject. It specifically resists the idea of the subject that is presumed in *particular-universalized* dominant and critical Global Northern thought. The latter theorizations have helpfully been critiqued for presupposing the subject as a bounded, individualized, ideally internally homogenized and coherent, autonomous entity that is different and separate from other subjects (Di Pietro 2020a, 2016; Bharati 1985). That model is perhaps best exemplified in Eurocentric and US-centric psychoanalysis. But it gets reiterated in many kinds of critical structuralist and poststructuralist thought, including dominant feminist and queer theory. In the dominant colonial-racialized epistemic context, the subject is imagined as a closed, individualized entity, as a foundation who then in interaction with others can get productively or unproductively changed in some way. This assumes as given a bounded individual capable of entering into relationalities including *co-motion*. Instead, the notion of *subjects-in-socialities and another* signals that human and nonhuman subjects as well as the sentient and nonsentient subjects who/that we can call *beings-becomings* are always already inseparably co-constituted, saturated in, and operating in relationalities that are part of their very existence and that continually alter them and vice versa.

Subjects in *subjects-in-socialities and another* also resists and circumvents the dominant uncritical and critical Global Northern idea of the subject's becoming in relation to time. Indeed, there are many other ways of subject-becoming. For example, P. J. Di Pietro (2020b) demonstrates how in Argentina, Native subject-becoming is marked by time but is also conceptualized in relationality to a sacred animal, the dog. Another example is the subject-becoming invoked by Gloria Anzaldúa ([1987] 2007) in her interpretation of the Nahuatl concept of *nagualismo*, or a kind of shapeshifting. These forms of theorizing subjects and subject-becoming coexist with dominant Global Northern uncritical and critical thought but are totally marginalized by them.

Foucault is often engaged by scholars who presume the bounded individualized human *subject-with-agency* of Global Northern theorizations. But his work can also be mobilized differently to open a way out of this bind. For Foucault, of course, subjects are formations in specific configurations of discourses, institutions, and practices that saturate the subject's context. As such they risk reproducing the power with which they are formed, including while struggling for social change. For Foucault, effective resistance requires (among other things) desubjectivation, or the taking apart of oneself, and resubjectivation, or the construction of "new forms of subjectivity" (Foucault 1976; Foucault 2001d, 2001e, 2001c). Martin Jay articulates this desubjectivation as "tearing the subject from itself in such a way that it is no longer the subject as such, or that it is completely other than itself so that it may arrive at its annihilation, its dissociation" (Foucault qtd. in Jay 1993, 158).

Across his work, Foucault radically de-essentializes the dominant Global Northern notion of the subject, highlighting its historical emergence and contingency. Yet, he also presumes the universality of a definition of the subject that is particularist (in relation to the planetary), that is situated in dominant thought in the Global North(s). Unfortunately, Foucault's work on subject formation is not informed by awareness of colonialism, coloniality, capitalism, imperialism, racism, *misogynarchies*, or speciesism. He inadvertently reproduces the dominant Global Northern model of the subject as presumably white, male, and middle class (Sithole 2020; Irigaray 1984, 1977). He does not imagine other conceptualizations that would include as subjects all humans and sentient and nonsentient *beings-becomings*. Yet across the planet many other notions abound. For instance, for the Wayuu people who are native to the places that colonizers call Venezuela and Columbia there is no inherent Other at all. There is only *alijuna*, a category of the estranged, defined as "the one who comes to destroy," thus characterized by conduct alone. In sum, if we consider subject co-constitution as situated within all relations of power we will understand subjects, subjectivation, desubjectivation, and resubjectivation completely differently.

Many other situated ways of conceptualizing *The S/subject(s)* across the planet point us in this direction and yet do not necessarily go there. At present there is a small but emerging literature on notions of the subject beyond Global Northern hegemonic thought including in the context of decolonial theory (Bhatia and Priya 2021; Hardman 2020; Bhatia 2020). It comes on the heels of much earlier inquiry into the topic. In chapter 1, I mentioned that in some ancient Brahminical Hindu texts (which are dominant in India) and in some critical Indian anthropology, the subject is ideally not an individual but instead a "dividual" who normatively is comprised of internal multiplicities and contradictions. The subject, from the moment of its coming into being, is inseparably merged with other subjects horizontally in the present with family and community, and vertically across time with ancestors to progenitors (Bharati 1985). The subject's Others (by caste, class, gender, sexuality) are also an integral part of the subject's formation. Yet another, albeit related, example of *in-context* dominant conceptualizations outside the Global North(s) is provided by the three-volume set of books entitled *Indian Psychology*, produced by Jadunath Sinha (1986). Together these works present vastly different registers for imagining the self. Each volume engages many different concepts of the subject across hundreds of ancient Sanskrit texts. Beyond the *in-context* hegemonic reach of these former notions, many Othered conceptualizations of the self—such as in Dalit, Bahujan, Adivasi, Muslim, and other cosmologies—abound. The point here is that the Global Northern presumption of the universality of the basic presuppositions that serve as foundations of its critical theory are particularist and self-universalized.

Interestingly, the dominant Global Northern conception of the subject does not have universal linguistic support either, whether in other dominant or in subaltern languages. In English the individual, bounded self is signaled via the singular *I* and you. In French the familiar you (*tu*) is singular, but the respectful singular you is plural (*vous*). In Italian the respectful you can be a third person feminine singular (*lei*) or a third person plural (*voi*). In both Italian cases, this you is considered "neutral" and is thus masculine as Irigaray would have it (Irigaray 1985, 1977). In Hindi and Urdu, *ham* signals the I-we. Each of these different linguistic realities has its own particularistic assumptions, logics, and terms around what constitutes a subject.

Another aspect of dominant Global Northern analytics of *The S/ subject(s)* is their shared *human-centric* tendency. It can manifest even in theories that self-proclaim antihumanism or that suggest nonhumanism. It can take the form of presuppositions of a common human grain in *S/ subject(s)*. Thus, for Walter Benjamin and Emmanuel Levinas all human subjects share vulnerability; for Benjamin and Jean-Luc Nancy they have in common the inevitability of death. Yet, we can ask, What is the political function of foregrounding characteristics constructed as universals as opposed to highlighting deadly power relations among humans, or between humans, nonhuman sentient, and nonsentient *beings-becomings*? How might underscoring commonalities abstracted from the context of power reinforce the power of dominant subjects? What are its effects on subalterns?

Presuppositions about commonalities do not only concern *The S/ subject*. They saturate both dominant and *subaltern-complicit* theorizations of collective human *S/subject(s)*. They are found in theoretical models of classes (with supposed common interests), singularities (with potential common interests), and multitudes (with definite common interests). They are present in the notion that subjects in workers' unions have exploitation in common. They exist in the idea that subjects in social movements have common interests whether for recognition (such as of identity or dignity) or redistribution (of resources, employment, etc.) or both. Yet, presuppositions about commonalities often problematically recognize only some relations of power while erasing others. For instance, unions bring into relief capitalist class relations while dominant feminist movements make sexism visible, but neither necessarily understands these as interrelated.

To take seriously the context in which theorizations emerge and the relations of power that (in)form them opens perception to a complex world of infinite *subaltern-to-dominant-complicit* ways of thinking about *The S/subject(s)*. Thus, some subjects, including some dominant subjects, in the Global North(s) work against the grain of the totalized universalized subject, even if they forget some (other) relations of power. A tormented Walt Whitman counters internal homogenizations thus: "Do I contradict myself? Very well I contradict myself. I am large. I contain multitudes." For James Joyce the subject is fractional and plural. Drawing on Joyce's work, Hélène Cixous posits that the categories *woman* and *women* are internally multiple (Cixous 1979). Jean-Luc Nancy usefully undoes the Eurocentric self/other binary as he proposes the "singular-plural" subject (Nancy 1996). The Deleuzian-Guattarian notion of the subject as an *agencement* (generally translated as "assemblage" in English) comprised of messy, moving, conjoined parts also refuses reduction to internal consistency (Deleuze and Guattari 1972; see chapter 3). However, these theories still presuppose an individual bounded self. They risk presuming for the subject an arbitrary set of pluralities abstracted from the subject's co-constitution in relations of power.

Some fruitful instances of more full attention to multiplicities of power can be found in US feminist and queer of color analytics. Two major sites are intersectionality theory, developed by Black feminist and queer scholars, and the kinds of theories of multiplicities elaborated in Chicanx feminist and queer thought (see chapter 3). Kimberlé Crenshaw's work on intersectionality brings together race, class, and gender in subject formation (Crenshaw 1989, 1991; Nash 2018). Gloria Anzaldúa makes present colonialism, race, class, gender, and sexuality and imagines an internally heterogeneous, culturally plural, manifold-dimensional subject (2002, [1987] 2007). Norma Alarcón proposes a multiply-voiced subject who is formed inseparably in coloniality, racism, class, and misogyny (1990; 2013). María Lugones underscores gender, race, and class in (de)coloniality and proposes an internally plural "subject-at-play" (2003, 57). These theorizations inform the notion of *subjects-in-socialities and another*. They put into relief subjects' pluralities, as well as registers of the ancestral, spirit, and ghostly that are systematically absent in dominant Global Northern theories of *The S/subject(s)*.

Many scholars observe that US feminist and queer of color theorizations have come under attack in academic publications, conference presentations, and other discussions, by scholars of *monofocal colonialism-and-race-amnesic* feminist theory over several decades (Bacchetta 2020; Pérez 2007; Hong 2006; Alarcón 1990; Moraga and Anzaldúa 1984). The critiques claim feminist and queer of color theorizations are outdated, essentialist, and stuck in identity politics. They thereby mistake feminist and queer of color theorizations for expressions of the very dominant notion of subjects and subjectivities that such theorizations are actually countering. Feminist and queer of color theorizing has unfolded in academic genres such as professional journal articles and university press books. But it has often been unhearable, unintelligible as theory there. It is also expressed in nonacademic creative genres such as essays, novels, poetry, photography, art, film, and more. The theory's dual inscription inside and beyond the academy is sometimes mobilized as a pretext for its dominant depoliticization and reduction to amusing personal narratives. Grace Kyungwon Hong argues that such misinterpretations and dismissals of feminist and queer of color theory are themselves a function of neoliberalism's technologies of perpetuation against theories that threaten its continued operations (2006). Yet, there should be nothing a priori contentious about the ability of any genre to express theorizing. Mikhail Bakhtin highlights that every genre is a chronotope, or a time-space, that permits or excludes a certain type of content (1981, 1980). For Aristotle, poetry opens up potentialities for what can be thought and said. Derrida points to genres' impossible borders, their intertextualities and mergings (1980). If we take epistemicide and epistemic violence seriously, we will read feminist and queer of color theory and its dominant interpretations with relations of power ever in mind.

I want to put into relief that the violence articulated against feminist and queer of color theorizing mirrors the violence enacted against feminist and queer of color subjects. The dominant positions both the theorizing and the theorizing-subjects in her/his/their own past. In this way, a whole range of critical analytical contributions can be reduced to zero, transformed into mere entertainment for the dominant.

With this in mind, let us listen differently, in complicity, to yet other openings for thinking *subjects-in-socialities and another*. A stunning theoretical contribution is in this line of a long poem by the poet-academic June Jordan: "I was born a Black woman / and now I am become a Palestinian" (1982). Here a subaltern subject becomes another other while remaining herself. Black woman and Palestinian here cannot be reduced to identity politics; they are primarily about subject formation and solidarities in conditions of power.

Or we can turn to a 1984 poem by Native American (Potawatomi), Jewish, disabled dyke Barbara Ruth (1986, 41), a member of the group Dyketactics! She writes:

Untitled

The Eskimos
Make 60 names for snow.
The Balinese
Have words
For fifteen separate
Degrees of trance.
I have spent my life
Searching for the words, the names
To tell you who I am.
I am the eleventh trance.
Which comes within
The 27th kind of snow.
I am the note between the ivories
If you play them both together
That is not it.
I am the color between navy blue and black
If you mix them both together
That is not it.
I am the smell you have no words for

You say	You like it.
You say	You don't like it
I ask you:	Do you know its name?

I believe every lesbian Indian Jew
Is exactly like me.
And I believe in dreams of snow
In the nights of Bali.

Here, Ruth's poem-as-subject remains untitled because there is no adequate name, again no possible reduction to identity politics. Ruth challenges the listener to suggest a designation ("I ask you: || Do you know its name?") but ends up with none. For Ruth the subject is a plurality telling itself through reference to *co-present* worlds of altered states (trance), sensations of intensities (cold or hot), sightings of disparate colors-textures in what appears—in the dominant field of intelligibility—as one color-texture (snow) or not (black and blue), hearings of simultaneous fractional notes, or scentings. Ruth invokes situated multidimensionalities across disparate contexts: lesbian Indian Jew with references such as Eskimo (subjects), Balinese (nights), Europe (piano), etc. Her subject is aware of its own hybridity but also its unfinalizability or inability to be fully known (Bakhtin 1984). There is always something more. Ruth invokes collectivity, seriality, fusion, and impossible identifications (the "I believe every lesbian Indian Jew / Is exactly like me," which is undone by the "dreams of snow" with their sixty names), even as the speaking subject's kaleidoscopic multidimensionalities disallow its dominant reframing and fixity in the identitarian register. Ruth's speaking subject is elsewhere.

Ruth's refusal that her subject be reduced to anything is reinforced in yet another poem: "Poem to My Straight Sisters." There she writes with sarcasm: "If I tell you I am a lesbian, you will think that I have told you who I am" (1976). Importantly the *and another* of *subjects-in-sociality and another* moves frontally against and beyond such reductionism. The *and another* refuses *plural-singularization*, or the reduction of many subjects, or the multiplicity of any one subject, to a single representation. It also resists *singular-pluralization*, or the practice of making one stand in for a whole. Both these operations entail oppressive compression, essentialization, universalization, obliteration.

Several concepts in prior analytics move how I think about *and another* in relation to the *in-sociality*, but do not define it exactly. Let us consider these notions: masses (Marx); publics (Habermas or, further back, Tarde); crowd (Canetti, Debord); The People (of nationalism theorizations that homogenize); the people (where homogeneity fades into the background); the co-belonging coming community (Agamben 2001); singularities together (Nancy); or the multitude (Hardt and Negri, Virilio). They all designate different kinds of political groupings. But *and another* is elsewhere. It is about infinity plus one or more. It rejects the politics of lack and excess in any social body. It insists on the *co-present in-socialities* of whomever/whatever can or cannot yet manifest as a subject or *being-becoming* therein.

And another is a placeholder for subjects and *beings-becomings* who/ that in dominant discourses are imagined as various kinds of *not-fully-subjects* or who/that are made imperceptible and forgotten. The *and another* asserts their full subject status and their integral place *in-sociality*. How subjects are made less-than, or in-excess-of, or marginal or disappeared, and their consequences, are topics of much important ongoing research and reflection (da Silva 2017). For instance, Silvia Wynter's work suggests that dominant discourses define the Human as Man—and his other—in relation to animals, in two phases: Man1 and Man2. Dominant discourses delineate Man1 in early colonialism around the criteria of Christianity in relation to Natives whom they construct as savages, irrational, a form of life between Human and animal. Man1 is True Christian Self vs. the Native as Untrue Christian Other (Wynter 2003; see also Jackson 2020). Wynter remarks that here Black people are assimilated to the category of Native. Then, dominant discourses describe Man2 in a second phase during the rise of scientific racism with its classificatory obsession where the principle binary criteria is biology. Here, for Wynter, the dominant referent-we as Human is constructed against the backdrop of Black Africans and other darker skinned peoples, who become the model for the Other positioned between Man and animal. Alexander Weheliye (2014) takes up Wynter's analysis, the Deleuzian notion of "assemblages" and Stuart Hall's interpretation of Marxian "articulation" (see chapter 3) to propose the idea of "racializing assemblages." For Weheliye, "racializing assemblages" is a way to think about race in terms of sociopolitical and fleshy constituents that together divide Humanity into human (whites), not-quite-human (Blacks and other people of color) and nonhuman. Wynter and Weheliye provide two of many helpful analyses of the construction of others inside relations of power. *And another* is a way to recognize the violence done to the Other's full subject status and to restore and reinstate it.

In some cases, a subject can shift from an *and another* positionality into *subject-in-sociality* status. An example is Sarah Hagazi (1989–2020), a writer, an anticapitalist activist in the 2017 Egyptian revolution, and an out lesbian. In 2017 she was arrested for unfolding a rainbow flag at a concert in Cairo by the Lebanese group a *Mashrou' Leila*, and was sentenced to three months in prison where she was tortured. Upon her release, Hagazi was granted asylum to Canada. She lived there with post-traumatic stress disorder and yet remained active in anticapitalist and lesbian movements. In June 2020, at the height of social movement activisms, Sarah Hegazi ended her own life. Like many queer subjects, Sarah Hegazi is an *and another* that movements would not necessarily know existed in their ranks. As we remember her, she shifts out of the obscurities that define the *and another* position and into the light as a contextually recognizable *subject-in-sociality*. This kind of belated postdeath bestowal of subject status onto *and anothers* has been vehemently denounced especially in trans of color movements. Instead they demand that the subject be considered with full subject status during life.

And another is not about add x and stir (here into the *in-sociality*). Nor does *and another* aspire to the inclusion mechanism that Charlotte Bunch critically calls "add women and stir," or the politically toxic notion that inserting women into misogynist institutions (such as the US Congress or the US military) will lead to liberation. *And another* does not seek to operate as what Rey Chow (2002) identifies as increasing absorption, or what we can call neoliberal multiculturalism's *expansion-by-inclusion* imperative. Chow demonstrates how subject x, or previously excluded subjects, become serially integrated into dominant society without altering the society's structure and often rebolstering it. *And another* is equally distant from add-x-and-stir forms of "murderous inclusions" that reinforce oppression, obliterate the included subjects, and create symbolic borders for yet other exclusions (Haritaworn et al. 2013). Bergozza et al. (2024) demonstrate how the *inclusion-enthusiastic* group Gays for Trump relies on and buttresses white supremacy, imperialism, and forms of fervent patriotism that ultimately work against most queers. Indeed, add-x-and-stir inclusivity is predicated on a binary division of subjects into acceptable and unacceptable. Whenever some are murderously absorbed, yet others are murderously further demonized and excluded (Haritaworn et al. 2013).

In contrast, the subject of *and another* is never an Other but rather simply another. The notion of the subject of *and another* refuses the Subject-Other binary. For regardless of how elastic or vulnerable to disruptions it may be, the binary only stretches to remain in place. One interesting instance of potential disturbance is the stranger as O/other that Shane Phelan (2001, 4–5) deems "a figure of ambivalence" located between or beyond the "us" vs. "them" division. Puar insightfully remarks that the stranger can never be one but always many, for strangers are constructed and positioned differentially through gender, race, and class (2007, 48). Yet, *and another*—which is elsewhere from the Other—should allow for different ways of thinking about otherness in dominant discourses and practices precisely by contrast.

Across the four sites of this study, three common criteria for constructions of otherness dominate: spatial relativities, relations to the plural subject-we, and qualities assigned to the subject itself. In France, India, Italy, and the United States, an important dominant mode of framing otherness is via spatialized positionalities. Others are defined in terms of inside, outside, proximity, and distance. Such spatializing relies on what, after Henri Lefebvre, geographers call abstract space, or space imagined in essentialist terms as a given, as immutable materiality or dimensions. The notion of abstract space underlies the conception and practice of dominant spaces such as the *misogynarchic* household or nation, and spatial strategies and technologies such as colonizing (see chapter 4).

Abstract space informs the dominant construction of fixed subject-positionalities that depend on social fragmentation, such as *near-internal-others, distant-internal-others, near-external-others*, or *distant-external-others*. In Hindi some of these spatialized subject-positionalities are named thus: *garhwali* (person from the same household); *desi* (from the same country); or *firinghi* (foreigner, from outside the country). In French we find the *intime* (intimate person*)*; *prochain* (nearby person); *voisin* (neighbor); or *étranger* (foreigner but also alien, stranger, outsider, and sometimes—more rarely—intruder) (Bertrand 2007). Further back, there are the Nietzschean notions of the *prochain* (next or nearby person) and the *lointain* (far away person). For Nietzsche, interestingly, the relation to the *prochain* is inferior because constructed by a self that does not really love itself, that is afraid, while the relation to the *lointain* can be of friendship across difference (Nietzsche 2006).

Others are also represented in dominant discourses via qualities assigned to the not-self other in relation to the self. In many dominant Global Northern imaginings the (large-scale) we-collectivity is represented on the model of the (small-scale) individual, narcissistic, internally homogenous, bounded dominant subject. A dramatic instance is the fascist nation. It has strict binary delineations: an aggregate of we-subjects is defined against its paranoid exclusions. However, a version of this model also holds in relatively porous Eurocentric national contexts such as in France. Fascism and social democracy both posit otherness around the quality that Freud called the narcissism of small differences, or deviations from The Same and the same. In French, this is expressed via categories such as: *Autre* (The Other); *autre* (the other); *Altrui* (An Other); or *autrui* (an other but not quite *another)*. *Autre* (capital *A*) evokes a subject who is different from The Same, while *altrui* signals a subject who is part, like oneself, of a series of The Same. *Autre* (lowercase a) is somewhat between the two (*Autre* and *altrui)*.

In dominant Western European conceptualizations of relations of the subject to an Other, dense metaphors of specific, isolated body parts loom large. Here there is a face (Levinas); there a hand (Maurice Merleau-Ponty).

For generations of white Western Europeans, these have seemed like just neutral corporeal parts. But for othered subjects—in Europe or beyond—they can be sites of intense historically accumulated trauma. They can only be held up as points of connection with the humanity of the *Autre*, *autre*, or *altrui* if their place in deadly relations of power is forgotten. Operations of *colonialism-racism-misogynarchies-amnesia* allow selective body parts to stand in for whole subjects. We also find reliance on the symbolism of hands in dominant (state and other) US attempts to call for unity. For example, in chapter 1 I mentioned that after 9/11 the image of four hands—each of a differently racialized subject—became repeated iconography to signify the multicultural nation. However, by relying on four distinct shades of skin color it references and reiterates, thereby reinforcing, the chromaticism criteria of eighteenth- and nineteenth-century scientific racist theory. The so-called humanity and relationality signification of such hands was famously mobilized in the May 25, 1986, Hands Across America project with the aim of combating homelessness and hunger. The latter of course solved little as it offered no critique of colonial-racial-capitalist production of impoverishment. Instead it reproduced *colonialism-racism-misogynarchies-amnesia*.

Yet, there is nothing neutral about reiterating the face and hand in abstraction from a critique of relations of power. To propose body parts as signs of humanity is to forget their place in constructing murderous categories of otherness: skin color, tones, shades; racialized facial measurements; form and contour of features; and more (Fanon 1952, 1964; Guillaumin 1972; Stember 1976; Balibar 1991; Gilman 1991). Such imaginings erase deadly colonial-sexual-racialized fixations on lips, spaces between eyes, nose shapes, or skull dimensions. They disappear a spectrum of current subaltern practices animated by internalized power such as skin bleaching, "corrective" eye surgery, and vaginoplasty.[1] In these cases the subaltern is induced by power to erase its difference from dominant models. At the same time, the subaltern is called on to forget disparities that are clearly an effect of power. We are supposed to unfeel, to not feel, to unsee and to not see calloused, broken, painful hands. We should not ask: What type of hands do Bill Gates or Donald Trump have? And their gardeners? Construction workers? How do descendants of owners of enslaved people in the United States or France hear the intensities and densities of generations of accumulated pain, love, and resistance in Stevie Wonder's song "Grandma's Hands"? Barely at all, of course. Whole societies are haunted by such erasures.

There are many interesting attempts across the planet to subvert the Subject vs. Other binary and its negation. Georgio Agamben proposes the figure of *essere qualunque* (2001). That term is generally translated from Italian into English as "whatever subject." But, with a nonessentialist Deleuzian ontological concept of being that is always a becoming in mind, *essere qualunque* can also be thought as *being-becoming whatever*. Another attempt to exit from the narcissistic Subject vs. Other trap is Leela Gandhi's concept of "nonidentical singularities" (2006). Furthermore, in many non-Eurocentric contexts no exit is necessary because an Other never is one but instead is a fusional part of the self-we. Laura Pérez contributes to opening up ideas about the self as she invokes the Mayan expression "You are my other self" (2007, 144). In India, some Dalit scholarly readings of Dalit notions of the self frontally dethrone Global Northern universalizing claims about the self but also defy presuppositions about the Hindu self (see, for example, Madhu 2024).

To better understand *and another* let us reflect with Jorge Luis Borges's celebrated essay on classificatory gestures in the "analytical language" of John Wilkins (1614–72) (Borges 1965). Borges claims that, in line with Descartes's suggestion that all the ideas of the world can be summarized in a "general language," Wilkins sought to create a language that would be a "universal key" to all meaning and a "secret encyclopedia." Everything would have its place in this totalized world. As his essay unfolds, Borges presents an English translation of some paragraphs of a Chinese encyclopedia entitled *The Celestial Emporium of Benevolent Knowledge* (hereafter TCEBK) in which the (anonymous) author tries to classify all animals. The TCEBK list, of course, is now renowned since Foucault reproduced it, following Borges, in his preface to *Les mots et les choses* (1966) to illustrate incompatible classificatory logics across distinct epistemes. Interestingly, the entries on the TCEBK list are arranged not in hierarchical order or even randomly but instead in alphabetical order, presumably in Mandarin. Besides animals, the list includes two entries that function as gaps and placeholders, and that could illuminate *and another*. They are the *etcétera* (et cetera); and the *incluidos en esta clasificación* (included in this classification).

The Borgesian-TCEBK's *etcétera*, as Maria E. Maciel notes, is not, as might be expected, the *etc.* generally found at the end of lists (2006, 48).[2] It is not merely additive, not a sign of yet more in a series. It is not even placed at the end of the list. Instead, it is entered at the letter L in the alphabetical itemization and is followed by two more terms. As such, this *etcétera* moves us out of the logic of *additive-seriality*. Moreover, the status of whatever this *etcétera* stands for is not inferior to the animal terms recorded; it does not signal animals that are considered not important enough to be named. The Borgesian-TCEBK's *etcétera* is positioned on equal ground among named terms. It is also not a sign for what is already understood and yet not deemed necessary to name. Maciel rightly notes that the *etcétera* designates the unclassifiable (2006, 48). For Randi Gressgård, it signals the excluded from every category (2008). Drawing on Maciel and Gressgård we can observe that in the first capacity the *etcétera* marks the limits of classificatory logics and in the second it signals the limits of classificatory totalism. Because *etcétera* is positioned in alphabetical horizontality, here the unclassifiable and excluded are assigned a strong presence. We could extend this to think the *etcétera* in relation to what Gilles Deleuze calls the glimmering or shadowed contents that do not appear in the (full) light of any temporal-spatiality (1986). That is, the *etcétera* is not someone or something known (as is the Global Northern etc.) but instead is a placeholder for the *unknown-knowable* (see also chapter 3).

We can also read *incluidos en esta clasificación* in relation to this *etcétera*. If *incluidos en esta clasificación* is itself a category, then we can presume that the classifying gesture aims to incorporate that which is not named but only signaled in the *etcétera*. The *etcétera* then becomes a macrocategory (of that which is *incluidos en esta clasificación*) that can in turn be contained in the classification. Here we are working with scales within scales. The point is the escape route constituted by *etcétera*. It marks and operates a rupture with both the animal list and its own incorporation into another category. Like the *etcétera*, the *and another*, too, is always an outside even when it is made present inside by being listed or *incluidos en esta clasificación*.

How might *and another* become manifest in relations among humans and other *beings-becomings*? A translation by Kanchana Natarajan of C. S. Lakshmi Ambai's (2000) queer Tamil short story entitled "One Person and Another" provides a relevant opening (Vanita and Kidwai 2000, 352–55). In it, Matthew Nathan, a painter and racially mixed gay man, moves to an Indian mountain town where in a crowded party he encounters a particular resident, Arulan. They become friends and lovers. Arulan begins to live with Matthew. They often speak of death. Matthew discloses that he does not want to die alone. Arulan reveals that he desires to die like a bird with "no one to look after me, no one to nurse me, without any plan, suddenly, without anyone to remember me" (354). The two have differential approaches to relations and to life and death. Eventually Matthew falls ill and Arulan takes care of him. One night, Matthew dies in his sleep beside Arulan. Soon thereafter Arulan climbs to a mountain top. He opens his arms "like a bird," soars, plummets onto a rock, dies instantly.

With Matthew and Arulan we can consider subjects who across disparate positionalities are not fully intelligible to each other and yet are for each other an *and another*. They are far beyond the form of a Same, same, Other, or other. They live in sync as *co-presences* attached in love. They are about intensities, conjointment, nearness. They bring to mind embodiments and relationalities beyond human-centricity. We can note Arulan's becoming-bird before leaving corporeality altogether. But also *and another* opens up serialities and metonymies that highlight other living, nearly dead, or passed-on *beings-becomings* who/that in dominant discourses are signified in opposition to the normative human: the bird unfolding into animals, plants, fish, reptiles, insects, rock, water, or earth. With Matthew and Arulan, we are in the realm of morphing forms, affects, intensities, vibrationings, stillness, speeds, excess.

In sum, these are all so many dances and melodies around subjects and relations who/that cannot be precisely named, pinned down, forced into the Subject vs. Other binary. The *and another* remain—like Ruth's poem—unfixed, unidentified, untitled. Accordingly, the idea of *subjects-in-sociality and another* reminds us that we lack adequate ways of thinking about all the subjects of the vast assemblage that *freedom-exigent co-motion* requires (see chapters 4, 5).

Subaltern-to-Dominant Continuum

The notion of *subaltern-to-dominant continuum* is a way of thinking about subjects in relations of power. It brings together several strands of thought about subjects and power, and reorients them for our times. It unites an expanded Gramscian idea of the subaltern, an extended Foucauldian understanding of (all) subject co-constitution, and a rethinking of relations of power beyond binaries, either/or, and *monofocality*. Instead, the idea of *subaltern-to-dominant continuum* engages multiplicities of *co-present, operative* relations of power. *Subaltern-to-dominant continuum* is a way to bring greater attention to a spectrum ranging from the most imperceptible to the most flagrantly evident relations of power and how they co-constitute subjects. It is a move against the kind of identitary purity that, as we saw in chapter 1, most especially in *sanguinal alliances*, can define who is inside or outside *co-motion*.

To understand the *subaltern-to-dominant continuum,* let us first consider the concept of subaltern therein. My point of departure is Antonio Gramsci's broad conceptualization of subaltern subjects. Two of Gramsci's texts are pivotal: *Quaderno del Carcere 25: Ai margini della storia: Storia dei gruppi sociali subalterni* (1934; hereafter QC 25); and *Letteratura e vita nazionale* (1991; hereafter LVN). As mentioned in the introduction, for Gramsci—and for me—the subaltern is not The Subaltern, not a singular subject or generic type, but rather always multiple. Gramsci defined subaltern subjects in historical-contextual relationality to other subjects in relations of power. I highlighted that for him subalterns included peasants, urban workers, but also all the various class sectors of the population of Italy's marginalized non-northern regions (see LVN). Gramsci referred to subalterns variously as subordinates, instrumentals, the popular classes, the commoners (*poplin*), and—in specific reference to the Roman Empire and across racialized positionalities—enslaved people.

With Gramsci, I think of subaltern subjects as a large internally differentiated multiplicity comprised of all humans and *beings-becomings* that are part of disparate kinds of subordinated collectivities. They are constructed and positioned as such in relations of power that morph, reconstitute themselves, shift, assemble, and disassemble, that exert themselves to keep oppression continuous or that, as in the case of revolution, are forced to open up, to transform.

To understand Gramsci's ideas about subalterns and their co-constitution in power let us briefly turn to Gramsci's life. According to his own definitions of the subaltern, he is one. Those who read him as impatient with the subaltern (for example, with the subaltern's dimension of subjective self-alienation) might revisit his trajectory with this in mind. Gramsci was born in 1891 in a financially struggling, rather outcast family in Ares, a small village on the Italian island of Sardinia. He remained there until age fourteen when he shifted to Cagliari, Sardinia's capital, to live with his brother. The languages in these sites in Sardinia (and across the Mezzogiorno) are considered just dialects and are sometimes deemed barbaric by mother tongue dominant Italian speaking subjects. Gramsci left Sardinia only at age twenty for studies in Turin, Italy's major industrial center. How could this move not provoke cultural, including linguistic, shocks? Gramsci's observations about peasants (the most numerous subalterns of rural Sardinia) and workers (the most numerous subalterns of urban Turin) unfold in succession and in parallel. In Turin he maintained contact with Sardinian culture and subjects. He did not imagine the futurity of subalterneity in terms of progress or civilizing mission narratives. He did not become fully *unsubaltern* through access to dominant culture, knowledge, modes of articulation, and intelligibility. Instead, in Gramsci's conception and in his personal experience components of the subalterneity that is part of a subject's very co-constitution remain with the subject regardless of where the subject may go. Gramsci's idea of the organic intellectual relies on this presupposition. Similarly, much of the privilege of subjects who are co-constituted as dominant in their contexts, regardless of their repositionings elsewhere, such as in diasporas, remain with the subjects. That explains why postcolonial subjects with class and/or caste privilege and cultural capital in their original contexts are more likely to reproduce their class status and acquire new cultural capital in diaspora than those without such privilege from the start.

While Gramsci's notion of the subaltern is about humans alone, I extend his insights to include as subaltern subjects all human, nonhuman sentient, and nonsentient *beings-becomings*. This expansion is not merely decorative. It is not simply additive. It changes everything. I do not think it possible to imagine and enact effective *freedom-exigent co-motion* until all these subjects and *beings-becomings* become central to analysis and praxis.

Veena Das's work clarifies how subalterns are not predetermined "morphological categories" but rather subjects with potential to "represent a perspective" that they may or may not come to have (1989). Often—but not always—perspectives for the subaltern are also from the subaltern. Yet, Das warns against essentializing subalterns. All subjects risk reproducing the power that is part of their very co-constitution. The perspective of any given subaltern is not necessarily *subalternative* or even *subalternist* (see introduction). Some subalterns become *dominant-complicit*, or even *functionally-dominant*—that is, they think and act in the interests of the dominant to varying degrees. Inversely, some dominant subjects dis-ally with the power of their co-constitution, their positionality and social sector's interests, to become radically *subaltern-complicit* (see chapter 5).

In critical literatures, *subaltern*—as a noun and adjective—has been overwhelmingly associated with subjects and fruitfully so. But *subaltern* is equally useful to consider conditions, temporal-spatialities, enactments, objects, epistemes, relations, and fields of intelligibility. *Subaltern conditions* refer to contexts of relations of power that produce, saturate, and act on subaltern subjects, statuses, situations, states of being, and experiences. Attention to *subaltern conditions* can shed light on processes of *subalternization*, or procedures for making (anyone, anything) subaltern. *Subaltern* temporal-spatialities are those that are of and for subaltern subjects. They are generally invisibilized, repressed, or suppressed by power. They may operate as animating forces in the subaltern. *Subaltern* temporal-spatialities coexist within a *hegemonic temporal-spatiality*. I invoked an example in the introduction: Paris's Latin Quarter. Subaltern enactments are materializations of the agentic capacity of subaltern subjects, activists, artivists, or movements. They include action and *inaction-as-enactment*. Such moves may be oppositionally or nonoppositionally resistant to, or complicit with and reproductive of, conditions of hegemony *in-context*. Subaltern objects are things such as art, film, a poem, a banner, or a photo that—because of their relation to the subaltern—are positioned as inferior in relation to dominant objects. *Subaltern fields of intelligibility* are comprised of devalued or submerged knowledge, knowledge production, categories, logics, presuppositions, perspectives.

My notion of *continuum* within the *subaltern-to-dominant continuum* takes inspiration from several different innovative uses of Gramsci's subaltern-as-subject. One productive point of departure is in subaltern studies, created by Indian historians. In an early phase, they primarily defined the subaltern subject in terms of its assigned lack of history. This subaltern-made-to-be-lacking (by power) had its first incarnation in the work of Ranajit Guha, a founding scholar of subaltern studies, in the figure of peasants whose rebellions were erased in British colonial, Indian elite and Indian nationalist historiographies. As other subaltern studies scholars developed it, subaltern came to signal many more sorts of oppressed Others, defined as without a history, or with only a fragmentary history, or without the means of representation, or in a condition of inaccessibility, always in relation to the dominant: workers, women, etc. I find many contributions of subaltern studies extremely salient for reflecting on what I envision as distinct points across the larger *continuum* of subalterns. They also help us to consider that there can be many different criteria for defining kinds of subalterns.

A fruitful example is Gayatri Spivak's now classic category of the subaltern subject. She defines the subaltern in terms of "not-speaking-ness," or rather the dominant's inability to hear—i.e., make sense of—the subject's speech (1988, 25; 1996). Here, the subaltern is characterized by what we might call a double-sided lack (comprising the subaltern as a *not-speaking subject* and the dominant as a not-hearing subject) inside the dominant field of intelligibility. Spivak mentions that she thinks only briefly with Gramsci and instead primarily with the work of the Subaltern Studies

Group (1995, 208). That genealogical distinction is important. In a lecture entitled "The Trajectory of the Subaltern in My Work," Spivak further clarifies that, for her, the subaltern is above all a positionality-formation occupied by an inaccessible other (2004). Thus, her subaltern is an impossible subject in the dominant field of intelligibility. Her subaltern remains unheard on her/his-their own terms or imperceptible altogether.

I would like to expand Spivak's important epistemic criteria to consider an array of silenced and unhearable subaltern *subjects-in-socialities and another*. For me, the criteria that Spivak invokes can describe an instance that, with the *subaltern-to-dominant continuum* in mind, we can call the *human-subaltern-in-extremis*. But, I suggest, there may be multiple kinds of silences and unhearabilities in any context. Let us recall US queers chanting, "We're here. We're queer. Get used to it." These are speaking subjects imposing some form of self-articulation into a dominant field of intelligibility that otherwise habitually silences and ignores them. They intervene in the dominant frame in a mode that Spivak's *subaltern-in-extremis* cannot. For Spivak the subaltern is defined in terms of not (ever) being heard in the dominant field. The only hearing in this case is Spivak's speaking not for but rather "nearby" (Trinh 1989).

However, the *subaltern-in-extremis* is not the ultimate subaltern. (Of course, Spivak herself does not claim such status for the subaltern she discusses.) In fact, there is no such purity or last instance, but only infinite relationality. Let us recall that Spivak's *not-speaking subaltern* is objectively positioned as a Brahmin, that is in the top 3 percent highest caste, and in a very privileged class. Let us consider that all of this is unfolding in India, a context where Dalit, Bahujan, and Adivasi scholars have been critiquing caste, class, and other relations of power for centuries. Only if we abstract Spivak's subaltern from the multiplicity of contextual relations of power could we imagine her as emblematic of "the" subaltern. In fact, the same subject is not subaltern in relation to an unhearable Dalit woman in poverty in Calcutta who is murdered, commits suicide, or starves to death. No hearable subject is speaking "nearby" this latter subject (Trinh 1989). Relations of power do not disappear with death; they are structural. The uppercaste, upperclass subaltern's positionality as *in-extremis* is further relativized if we consider the forms of life that masses of both dominant and subaltern humans regard as inferior to humans, such as animals, reptiles, insects, plants, rocks, and the ocean.

Today, in English the notion of subaltern has many messy deployments and thus one may wonder why I wish to reawaken it at all. It is because, notwithstanding its limitations, I know of no other concept-term that has such continuous potential critical force for the four contexts I study. Still, let us briefly consider some alternatives.

First, minoritarian. I mentioned in chapter 1 that *minoritarian* appears fruitfully in some English-language theorizations such as by Françoise Lionnet and Shu-mei Shih. But, further back, *minoritarian* was formed in France as a subset within French *national-normative* universalism, within social-democratic neoliberalism, and carries that weight. Dominant sociologies have erased minoritarian's tracks in the numerical (as in small numbers) to make it signify simply the Underdog. Yet, minoritarian remains difficult to free from such measurements. Minoritarian appears in various forms in colonial savior and progress discourses designed to infantilize, to make minor, colonial subjects (Nandy 1983). Minoritarian designates a smaller quantity in ways that can reinforce injury, death-boundedness, and genocide. For instance, for Native Americans and Alaska Natives who—postgenocide—now constitute about 2.9 percent of the US population, "minority status" in "democracy" can function as a "weapon of mass destruction" and produce statistical elimination (Grande 2004, 31–32; Willmott 2023).

Another possible concept-term is precarious subject or precarity as a condition. Precarious arrives in English both in neoliberalism and on the left. But in continental Europe it has a life across political leanings, including on the right. In France and Italy, precarious and precarity surfaced in 1980s and 1990s labor movements. Scholars and activists used the terms to describe nefarious economic and psychic effects of neoliberalism on working class employed and unemployed people. But precarious and *precarity* were soon critiqued as insufficient. They were sometimes called complicit with capitalism, racism, and colonialism.

With reference to the Italian context, Laura Fantone clarifies that precarious in its earlier incarnation served "as an umbrella concept in order to give voice to a variety of new life conditions" (2007, 7). It then "shifted over time, to the point where it has actually become humorous, even trendy" (7). Today its deployment has "many ambiguous consequences" (7). It functions as "a paradoxical term, capable of hiding old inequalities and new forms of exploitation," including especially those "introduced by flexible work contracts" (7, 10). Fantone points to how in southern Italy precarity has long been a normative condition, especially for women. It is characterized by labor without safety, stability, or rights. This includes labor in black markets, labor without contract, illegal economies, and both productive and reproductive exploitation within families (10). In contrast, as Fantone highlights, in Italy the new precarity is primarily associated with "the unexpected loss . . . of recently acquired privileges" by "relatively wealthy sectors of the population" (11). Precarity, thus, has differential effects according to "income differences and family support" (11). Working-class women in provincial towns or working-class suburbs of cities have no alternative to precarious work. But for "middle-class, educated women, living in urban areas, precarity" is associated with flexibility (11). It "can become a life choice, a reclaimed space of temporary freedom from family ties and a boring job in the local service sector" (11). Fantone distinguishes thus between what we can call (working-class) precarity-as-obligatory-condition and (middle-class) precarity-as-choice. Importantly, both depend on and reinforce the dominant Global Northern gender binary and heterosexist-familial unit.

In France, too, there is nothing inherently critical about the notions of precarity and precarious. They appear in discourses of the state, institutions, mainstream media, analyses, and slogans by political parties and in social movements on the left and right. Again, precarious designates multiple conditions and subjects. In France, and increasingly in Italy, precarity carries dominant racialized (white) connotations. In France, precarity can signal temporary, transitional, correctable deprivation of presumably entitled (white) working or unemployed poor people in need of a brief welfare-ist intervention. Racialized working or unemployed poor people are not necessarily considered precarious, for they are not automatically presumed to be entitled to anything more than permanent conditions of deprivation. Precarity is often connected to the idea of social solidarity, but racialized people are not habitually conceptualized as subjects of the social realm (Sithole 2020; Jackson 2020; Weheliye 2014; Bancel et al. 2004; Wynter 2003; Patterson 1982).

While neoliberal Western European states happily deploy terms such as minoritarian and precarious, not a single one speaks of subalterns. Albeit imperfect, the Gramscian notion of subaltern was born in and continues to evoke a radical critique of capitalism and other relations of power such as regionalism. I find it easy to extend subaltern to take account of a full spectrum of power and the complexities of different kinds of subjects, subjectivities, and subjectivations that power coproduces. In contrast, minoritarian and precarious are not incompatible with colonialism, capitalism, racism, misogynarchies, speciesism, and other relations of power. Minoritarian risks inscribing everything in the binary majority vs. minority. Moreover, not all the oppressed are minorities (e.g., women) and not all minorities are oppressed (e.g., whites in South Africa). Precarious, as Fantone's discussion illuminates, evokes a soft critique of capitalism that does not necessarily go anywhere. It can put into relief a temporary difficult situation based in a "choice" of flexibility by privileged subjects. In contrast, subaltern invokes a radically critical political relation to any, and potentially to all, configurations of power. Subaltern can account for all subaltern conditions, fields of intelligibility, *subjects-in-sociality and another*, and more.

Liberation-Orientation

Liberation-orientation is related to but distinct from a concept that I briefly suggest in the introduction and in chapter 1 and that I explain below: *freedom-exigency*. *Liberation-orientation* is about a tendency, a yearning, a desire. It can induce in the subject ways of *sensing, perception*, thinking, and enacting beyond the modernist project of an end-game political program that presupposes identical conditions and phases everywhere. *Liberation-orientation* can incite us to try to understand where precisely we are, in what kinds of relations of power we are caught. It can induce aspirations to create a *freedom-exigent elsewhere-present* and an *elsewhere-futurity* now. In how I am thinking about these terms, *liberation-orientation* is primarily oppositional, while *freedom-exigent* is both oppositional and nonoppositional (see below).

Liberation-orientation is about the desire to stay alive, to inhabit the world differently, to invent other forms of life. It is a social and psychic opening, an enticement, a leaning, a slant, a twisting, a pull or push here or there, an inclination or disorientation in any subaltern subject or ally. *Liberation-orientation* maintains breath. It engenders trust in life. It can be a prelude to transformation.

Several prior analytics and notions inspire the idea of *liberation-orientation*, without actually defining it. A major area is sets of ideas that refine our understanding of *liberation-orientation* via considerations of *subjects-in-society and another* vis-à-vis life and death. An example is Patrick Wolfe's now classical concept of the logic of elimination and especially its elaboration in the work of feminist Native studies scholars (Wolfe 2006; Lee-Oliver 2019; Barker 2017; Kauanui 2016). The logic of elimination refers to how in the aftermath of the massive colonial genocide in Turtle Island and Abya Yala, today Indigenous life is still discounted, imagined to no longer exist or to be continually disappearing. It is about settler logic to justify the original and continued usurpation of Indigenous land, but also of bodies, culture, spirituality, everything. The logic of elimination enables settlers to turn a blind eye toward corporate or governmental mass annihilation that is enacted through action or inaction. In spring 2020, while the Navajo nation suffered a genocidal percentage of COVID-19 deaths, the US Government did nothing. In the same period in Brazil, there were serial murders of Indigenous leaders and governmental privatization of Amazonian Indigenous lands, combined with its inaction as COVID-19 spread among Indigenous communities. From north to south, the "Americas" are built and maintained on the dead, presumed-to-be-dead, *repeatedly-in-the-process-of-making-dead,* and left-to-die bodies of Indigenous peoples. In these conditions, *liberation-orientation* is the subaltern's yearning and action on the side of life itself. It is about the subaltern's desire to live and thrive. It is also the ally's recognition of horrifying conditions and the aspiration to directly oppose them.

Orientation in *liberation-orientation* draws on Sarah Ahmed's concept of orientation and its implication in disorientation (Ahmed 2006; see also Egan 2023). Ahmed organizes her ideas about orientation around the notions of sexual orientation and the "Orient." She is concerned with ruptures with social and political normativity that manifest as unequal distributions of power, forms of capital, exploitation, oppression, and repression. She asks about the place of desire, corporeality, spatial proximity, and distance in the labor required to reproduce and congeal the normative (92, 23). For Ahmed, orientation happens through repetition over time. She revisits Louis Althusser's classic scene of subject formation through hailing by an authority, to ask "which way one turns" when hailed; for, depending on one's spatial orientation, "different worlds might come into view" (15). The normative subject becomes so by "'lining up' with lines that are already given" and that the subject reproduces and extends (13). Thus, normativity is "a direction" that is "produced over time" by following "a straight line," by "not deviating at any point" (16). Drawing on the Indo-European etymology of queer, Ahmed posits queer as that which is "twisted," refuses to line up or repeat (67). Diversion from the norm implies a body that becomes "queer in its sensitivity 'to all the rest'" (67). The becoming in question is through desire, for "desire is, after all, what moves us closer to bodies" (103). Thus, lesbian desire "can be rethought as a space for action, a way of extending differently into space through tending toward other women" (102). With Ahmed's reflections in mind, we can better intuit the place of *in-sociality* and of *and another* in how a subject can begin to sense itself as disoriented, out of sync, *in-context*.

Ahmed's Althusserian elaboration-diversion can be fruitfully read with E. Patrick Johnson's work. For Johnson, specific subaltern subjects turn, or turn away, differently when hailed precisely because of the relations of power that produce the norm. Johnson highlights circumstances in which for Black men subject interpellation is articulated primarily through race and gender. Literally, "hailing" by police is about racial targeting and harassment. Black men cannot successfully "hail" a taxi because the taxi driver, having internalized racialized fantasies about Black male criminality, refuses to stop (2004, 64). We have here quite a different orientation for resilience, for survival, and further, for thrival (Jolivette 2015).

In my conception, however, regardless of the subject's sexual orientation(s), in the very co-constitution of the subject of *liberation-orientation* something queer (twisted, bent, and crooked) is always unfolding. It is there in the undoings, recompositions, congealings, dissipations. The *liberation-oriented* subject never is one or One. Such a subject is co-constituted with a multiplicity of generative relations of power, *in-sociality*, that can induce many tendencies. That subject may be incited at any point to become-together suddenly "queer in its sensitivity to all the rest" (Ahmed 2006, 67).

For Ahmed, desire provokes the formation of diverted, disoriented, reoriented subjects. In my conception of *liberation-orientation*, too, desire is present. Yet, many other impulses, drives, affects, states of being, registers, dimensions, or their disappearance, are operative as well: loathing, shame, paranoia, joy, excitement, the assertion of ancestors and ghosts, the arrival of trance, the refusal to reproduce power, etc. Several scholars of the Tunisian revolution highlight that Mohamed Bouazizi's self-immolation on December 18, 2010—an event I mentioned earlier—sparked massive collective action because it incited people to abandon fear in sync. Bouazizi's courage became suddenly triggering, contagious. There was something in his slant, the leaning away, the rejection of repetition, that opened a space. Newly unbarred, unblocked, reoriented, suddenly undaunted subjects moved together, risked death. In this collective *liberation-orientation* enactment, a situation of no return unfolded. It became part of an accumulation that compounded in 2018 with the uprising around economic issues and dignity.

Yet another ensemble of works helps us reflect on how subjects can move out of the caughtness of subjectivation in relations of power and collectively set themselves in motion for *liberation-orientation*. Agamben's

(1999) engagement with *potentiality* in Aristotle can serve as a point of departure. Agamben underscores in Aristotle two binary oppositions: One is potentiality (*dynamis* in Greek) vs. actuality (*energeia*); the other is the (precise) knowledgeable subject who has the potentiality to use or not use their acquisitions (such as the poet who may or may not write) vs. the "generic subject" who "must suffer an alteration (a becoming other) through learning" (177, 179). For Aristotle, potentiality is a "faculty" of the subject, such as "vision" or "speech," that exists in terms of "the possibility of privation," as "the presence of an absence," as something like "a combustible object that does not burn" (Agamben 1999, 178, 181, 197). For me, *liberation-orientation* steers away from the essentialist Aristotelian conception of liberation strivings as a faculty inherent in a subject and, as mentioned above, away from the idea of the subject as an individual. I think of *liberation-orientation* as a potentiality, a capacity, created in subjects in the context of their ongoing co-constitution as a subject *in-collectivity, in-sociality*, in relations of power.

Agamben is interested in potentiality as "can." This perspective is legible in his reflections on a passage from Anna Akhmatova's "Instead of a Preface," from her collection of poems *Requiem*.[3] Agamben notes that Akhmatova describes waiting in line "for months and months . . . outside the prison of Leningrad" for news of her son, a political prisoner, when one day a woman, also waiting, asks: "Can you speak of this?" (Agamben 1999, 177).[4] Agamben remarks: "Akhmatova was silent for a moment and then, without knowing how or why, found an answer to the question: 'Yes,' she replied, 'I can.'" For Agamben, this response marks "the experience of potentiality" (177–78).

If we return to Agamben's initial referent, Akhmatova's first person telling, we might further clarify his thinking:

> In the terrible years of the Yezhov terror, I spent seventeen months in the prison lines of Leningrad. Once someone "recognized" me. Then a woman with bluish lips standing behind me, who, of course, had never heard me called by name before, woke up from the stupor to which everyone had succumbed and whispered in my ear (everyone spoke in whispers there):
> "Can you describe this?"
> And I answered: "Yes I can."
> Then something that looked like a smile passed over what had once been her face. (April 1, 1957, Leningrad) (Akhmatova 2000, 384)

For our purposes, two points here are particularly noteworthy. First, for Agamben the question is addressed to Akhmatova in her quality as a particular subject of potentiality: the poet. Agamben remembers the question as "Can *you* speak of this?" (Italics mine). Akhmatova did mentioned that "someone 'recognized'" her and called her by name. Second, Agamben is not concerned with the effect of the interaction on the woman posing the question. He omits the last line altogether, in which her reaction is expressed. In contrast, for me Akhmatova's subjectivity and the interaction are key (see below).

Yet another return, this time to the context of "Instead of a Preface," can help bring into relief a relation between Agamben, Akhmatova, and *liberation-orientation*. The "Preface" is preceded by a short poem titled "Requiem" (1957):

No, not under the vault of alien skies.
And not under the shelter of alien wings.
I was with my people then,
There, where my people, unfortunately were. (2000, 384)

In "Requiem," Akhmatova presents herself as fully merged in "my people." She is an Aristotelian "generic subject" in an "unfortunate" collectivity. She remains in fusion thus through the beginning of "Instead of a Preface." She describes herself as one in a series of anonymous suffering women ("of course, had never heard me called by name before"). Only after an extended repetitive indistinction in "my people" does any differentiation occur. Suddenly Akhmatova notices another anonymous subject in line, "a woman with bluish lips," with a voice. Her "Can you describe this?" resounds as a provocation-evocation, or a Third in the sense of Irigaray (1979, 1981; see the discussion of *afidamento* in chapter 1). It brings Akhmatova in touch with her own potentialities. In Agamben's discussion of Akhmatova, and in Akhmatova's prose, the woman in line "with bluish lips" summons some strand not only of Akhmatova's "faculty" and potentialities but also of her co-constitution as a subject. She is made anew.

Though Agamben does not mention this (for certainly it exceeds his theoretical objectives) significantly for Akhmatova the triggering event is a whisper. It is an almost-nothing-more-than-breathing. It is an almost-nothing-more-than-being-alive. And yet, it is multiply productive. Akhmatova makes clear that her "Yes, I can" induces a return. An effect materializes in the body of the woman "with bluish lips." It is visible in her facial expression. But her altered face is more than a sign. If "something like a smile passed over what had once been her face," then with the smile "her face" is no longer "her face." The woman is suddenly someone else. Thus, in the moment of interpellation-response the two women come into being together as altered subjectivities. This event depends on the *in-sociality*, the capacity to *sense* and *make sense* of a sentence, the *perception* of the face of an *and another* who is not an Other.

For *liberation-orientation*, the most important aspect here is inter- and intrasubjective chemistry. It is what animates *liberation-orientation*. This might be clarified via the relationality implicated in the *Ni Una Menos* (Not One [Woman] More) movement mentioned in the introduction. It began with a massive demonstration in Argentina in 2015 to mark the misogynist murder of fourteen-year-old Chiara Paez. It soon spread elsewhere and is now a transnational movement. The phrase *ni una menos* is drawn from a line—"*ni una muerta más*" (not one more [woman] dead)—in a 1995 poem by feminist activist and poet Susana Chávez to denounce sexist murders of women in her city, Ciudad Juárez, Mexico. *Ni una menos* became a chant of the antifeminicide movement after Chávez herself was murdered in 2011. It has an intense genealogy in the combat against misogyny, terrifying suffering, and ultimately annihilation (Gago 2019).

In this situation, we can think of Chávez as a "generic subject," merged in a potential "my people" comprised of feminist and queer subjects that had not yet gelled as such. Her murder induced an accumulation of rage. It fueled initial actions that then expanded and intensified into demonstrations, strikes, and from 2020 energetic collective street performances in Chile of a song "Un violador en tu camino" (A rapist in your path). Thanks to social media, the song traveled transnationally and was translated. Feminists performed it on every continent. In Turkey—while street demonstrations were outlawed—women members of Parliament, who have immunity, sang it inside Parliament. Here, in reverse seriality from Akhmatova's becoming, *Ni Una Menos* incited spectacular corporeal revolts that repeatedly announced a "Yes, I can" that then resounded *in-sociality* as a "Can you?" In so doing it transformed subjects who had "previously been just a face" (anonymous) into a "my people" of new subjects of feminist and queer revolution. They became authors of futurity itself. Alongside *Ni Una Menos*, misogynist murders could and do continue. However, for many women and queers everywhere, the movement is already in a place where there is no turning back.

In sum, *liberation-orientation* is a tendency, a desire, and a potentiality for subjects together and for the collectivities they create. It is not an essentialist characteristic. It is rather a (heretofore often crushed) (im)possibility within the subject's co-constitution in relations of power. *Liberation-orientation* is a strand of subjectivity that is open to provocation. Any transformation in its becoming might make way for other affects, states of being, registers, dimensions, to overtake it, take over, in turn producing their own effects. One never knows for sure where *liberation-oriention* will go. One of the places it might (or might not) go is to *freedom-exigency*.

Freedom-Exigency

Freedom-exigency is about an urgency, a demand, a recognizable need, a requirement, for *freedom-life* now. It translates into practice as a continual effort to combat and transform every and all conditions of power, and to create something else. It is always an unfinished project, a potentiality, a process, or in Angela Davis's words a "constant struggle" (2013). It is about keeping the most flagrant, subtle, and imperceptible relations of power, and the most subaltern *and another* of *subjects-in-sociality and another*, in mind. *Freedom-exigency* is both oppositional and nonoppositional. It is adamant about attacking, transforming, and dissolving the relations of power that otherwise all too often are left intact and thereby get continually reproduced and reinforced. In chapter 1 we saw what kind of damage relations of power can do to destroy different kinds of *co-motion* from within. In contrast, *freedom-exigency* is a stance of total refusal of any compromise with any relations of power. It includes the will to uncover and engage ever more imperceptible relations of power. It is about creating an *elsewhere-present* and *elsewhere-futurity* together.

We can learn much that is useful for *freedom-exigency* from an ensemble of zero-concession approaches in many kinds of extremely subaltern theorizations. An example is the analytic and practice of the group Dyketactics! that I mentioned in chapter 1. The collective developed a queer perspective that was expressly anticolonial, anticapitalism, anti-imperialism, antiracism, against *misogynarchies* and speciesism, all along. This analysis was explicit in Dyketactics!'s writing, collective life, and political actions. Dyketactics! enacted concrete solidarity to a whole range of social and political independence-bound movements. It is a microscale example of a radical, expansive interconnectivity within lesbian, queer, and trans movements, and across movements. Here the microscale, far from confinement to a very local set of concerns and political work, is actually an opening, a point of departure for thinking singularities and pluralities across the planet. Indeed Dyketactics! and its members came under attack from the state and its policing apparatus precisely because the collective had developed a broad, stubborn, unaccommodating, radically uncompromising *freedom-exigent* political orientation and was engaged in very extensive alliances with others across similarly exigent social movements.

From the small example of Dyketactics! we can understand how an extremely subaltern singularity can open the potentiality to take seriously the distinctive historical and present conditions of any other subaltern human collectivities. Chapters 3 and 4 explain how it is unhelpful to homogenize, universalize, and essentialize forms of oppression, repression, exploitation, occupation, dispossession, extraction, appropriation, subjugation, subjectivation, epistemic violence, spiritual obliteration, psychic suffering, incarceration, inequity, and annihilation. They do not operate identically everywhere, across time and for all. When their multiple forces and manifestations get collapsed, relations of power and subaltern subjects outside the dominant field of intelligibility get erased. To recognize the singularity of any subaltern collectivity is far from applauding identity politics or reenacting the oppression olympics, two gestures that free no one. Instead, they can reinforce entrapment in the confines of colonial, capitalist, imperialist, racial, *misogynarchic*, and speciesist divide-and-rule. They refuse to acknowledge relations of power within the singular collectivity itself. They preclude coming together across different collectivities in *freedom-exigent co-motion* for the planet.

Freedom-exigency is primarily a radicalization in perspective and action, a point of no return. It is not the culmination of *liberation-orientation*. Not all *liberation-oriented* subjects or *co-motion* are or will become *freedom-exigent*. While *liberation-orientation* is a tendency, *freedom-exigency* is a requirement, a prerequisite, an essential precondition for analysis, praxis, and life. *Freedom-exigency* entails addressing the most flagrant to the most minute details about relations of power. It is ready to dispose of anything incompatible with the possibility of creating *freedom-life*. The *freedom-exigent* subject can come from any point on the *subaltern-to-dominant continuum*. It is about what Zakiyyah Iman Jackson (2020) calls a subject's fruitful disordering of being that opens the subject to other kinds of becoming. It is about what Anzaldúa ([1987] 2007), drawing from Aztec philosophy and theology, (re)calls as *Coatlicue* (in Nahuatl, "Serpent Skirt"), which—for her—is symbolic of the state of dominant discourses and subaltern desires colliding within. *Freedom-exigency* is about different kinds of *sensings, perceptions*, and modes of *intelligibility* that carry subjects into yet other forms of knowing, states of being, and enacting in the world.

Freedom-exigency is both a burden and a beautiful way of life. It can set into motion personal and social disarticulation, chaos, a halting altogether, a radical alteration of affect, of corporeality, of intersociality. It has the potential to induce a total reconfiguration of every cell in our bodies, of every minute component of every *in-sociality*, of all of life.

Concluding Remarks

This chapter introduced some ways of breaking with presuppositions, logics, and conclusions that were operative in the *co-motion* clusters in chapter 1. It suggested that we cease to confuse and homogenize different kinds of coming together. It developed the umbrella rubric *co-motion* to accommodate their differences and to make space for yet other kinds of coming together that are not yet imagined. It offered *subalternative* ways of envisioning who and what count or are discounted in dominant fields of intelligibility as subjects. It suggested how we can bring to the center of our concerns all subjects otherwise, including subjects made absent—that is, the *and another*. The chapter proposed the idea of *subaltern-to-dominant continuum* to consider the dynamics of how subjects are co-constituted and complexly assigned positionalities in relations of power and in relation to each other. A same subject can be multiply located across the *continuum* depending on the contextual interrelationality in question. The chapter suggested *liberation-orientation* to consider desire brought about by awakenings of the mind, psyche, body, and spirit beyond total entrapment in and by power. It put forth *freedom-exigency* as the uncompromising demand for a total break with caughtness in power, for the creation of *freedom-life*.

All the elements of this chapter are meant to open diagonals, lines of flight, in dominant fields of intelligibility and to incite yet more imaginings for *subalternative theory-assemblages* for our times. But the discussion here only begins this work. Ultimately *freedom-exigent co-motion* necessitates a radical reconceptualization of power. The next two chapters focus on rethinking power precisely to move us toward that end.

Doesn't this difficulty, our confusion and trouble (*embarrass*) finding adequate forms of struggle come from what we still don't know about power?

　　Foucault, *Dits et écrits* I

You can be deaf and nonetheless hear sounds thanks to the vibrations of the acoustic medium, you can be blind and intuit colors thanks to the magic of words; I wonder how thought can stop in its tracks and notice the unthought that is happening to it.

　　Luisa Muraro, *The Italian Difference*

Extending the discussion in the previous chapter, this chapter suggests *co-formations* and *co-productions* as entryways toward a more precise small-context to planetary understanding of relations of power and their *operability*, so as to better imagine how to transform them here and now. With this in mind, this chapter asks: What can be done about the "confusion and trouble" that comes from "what we don't yet know about power"? How can we "stop in our tracks" to "notice" the kinds and *operations* of power that are hidden, "unthought," even unfelt?

　　Here I suggest two concept-terms, *co-formations* and *co-productions*, to help open up our collective *subalternative sensing, perception,* and *intelligibility* about power. They are not ends unto themselves. They are not a master theory to explain all kinds of power and its *operability* everywhere. Their aim is not to bulldoze and replace salient contextual theorizations of power. In this journey *co-formations* and *co-productions* can fruitfully function as "theoretically polyvalent" signposts—alongside, below, or merged with other concepts and approaches (Canguilhem 1988, 6). They are not intended for solely additive ends. Their usefulness is not limited to simply outing and compiling ever more aspects of power for analysis. In fact, while often revealing unthought power is helpful to struggle, in some situations, in some dimensions and registers of power, for some of the most subaltern subjects, relations of power are sometimes better transformed when left unaddressed (Foucault 2001a; see chapter 5). Instead, *co-formations* and *co-productions* are meant to incite us to think differently about power and its *operability*. They hope to provide an exit out of fixed, repetitious, current analytical confines in which we are entrapped that constrict our capacity to understand power and therefore our potentiality to invent effective *freedom-exigent co-motion*. The desire here is that *co-formations* and *co-productions* will help us—as Luisa Muraro's quote above suggests—to retune our senses to as yet unnoticed "vibrations" of power, to yet other "intuitions," to the "unthought that is happening" to us and the world.

In what follows, I first speak to the notion of power that seems most useful for our times. Next, I discuss, respectively, *co-formations*, *co-productions*, and some related concept-terms that can help us to understand the different dimensions, registers, extents, and limitations of *co-formations* and *co-productions*. Finally, I engage with how *co-formations* and *co-productions operate* together.

Power

Every theory about relations of power presupposes some kind of notion of power itself, and of power's *operabilities* via tactics, strategies, techniques, or stylistics, even when these are not named. The idea of power that is most relevant herein draws on Foucault's "revolutionary" conception of power as a dynamic microphysics (Deleuze 1986). For Foucault, power is capillary, flowing at different speeds, densities, and intensities throughout the social body. It has "no single focus, concentration, or center (*foyer*) from which all relations of power would emanate" (Foucault 2001b, 379). Power saturates the entire social realm, in different distributions and concentrations.

Foucault notoriously departs from preceding dominant conceptualizations to understand power as productive, sustaining, transformative, and destructive. Power is an agent in the formation of structures, materialities, techniques, discourses, subjects, identities, relations, objects, conduct, events, techniques of power, and more. Prior to Foucault, power was imagined as a thing that dominant subjects possess and wield over powerless Others, and/or as permanently concentrated within political entities such as the state and its apparatuses. When presupposed as a possession, power's function was thought to be essentially repressive. Yet, the power-as-repressive idea is extremely narrow. It relates to only one aspect of power. It is also human-centric (see introduction). It reduces power to a commodity that can be disputed or exchanged in ways that reflect—and reproduce elements of—capitalist hegemony, even when scholars using it fervently oppose capitalism.

While Foucault highlights power's productive capacity, he also understands power's agency more broadly. For Foucault, power can accumulate, converge, congeal—and dissolve—in states, their apparatuses, institutions, economies, material and immaterial objects, the body. Contrary to what some who read him only in English translations imagine, Foucault does not dispute power's congealments and its mobilizations in oppression, repression, exploitation, occupation, dispossession, extraction, appropriation, subjugation, subjectivation, epistemic violence, spiritual obliteration, psychic suffering, incarceration, inequity, or annihilation. He addresses this point in untranslated works, including on "states of domination" that, for him, are no longer power relations but rather about complete stasis (2001c). While prior theorists make power-as-thing's deployment exclusive, for Foucault, power's use-ability constitutes only a fraction of its capacity. He advises us to pay attention to what is happening "above the conduct of the powerful and below the tempest of resistance" (2009, 268). Ultimately, with the exception of "states of domination," power remains "something that circulates" (2003, 30). For Foucault, power cannot be fully equally redistributed in social structures because power is everywhere, flowing through "dominant and dominated" forces, subjects, and entities (Deleuze 1986, 35).

The pre-Foucauldian idea of power-as-thing problematically assumes that power is *operative* only by subjects and only where it is visible. The effect of this inadvertently ableist ocular-centric, human-centric approach is to reduce *subaltern-to-dominant* subjects to the binary subaltern vs. dominant and lock them in it (see chapter 2). It leaves subalterns without viable options for *freedom-exigency*. Even their *liberation-orientation* gets harnessed into limited action, such as in substitutionalism (i.e., the subaltern becomes dominant as in Marx's dictatorship of the proletariat); reversal (inequity remains even as positions in it shift as the subaltern seizes power and wields it over the dominant); appropriation and redistribution (in the "equality" versions of these, the overarching oppressive system remains intact even as the subaltern takes power in some domains and spreads it among a [sub]set of subalterns, while in the more "revolutionary" versions power is distributed among subalterns who are recognized as subjects while un-recognized subjects and *beings-becomings* remain excluded); separatism (the subaltern leaves the dominant's context to create something else, such as the *alter-nations* discussed in chapter 1); or, albeit rarely, elimination (of the dominant). While subaltern responses counter, invert, or try to escape from apparent aspects of power's entrapments, ultimately, they risk leaving in place some aspects of relations of power.

The pre-Foucauldian idea that power is permanently resting in political and economic structures and entities is equally constrained. It means that subjects desiring change can only propose a less inequitable redistribution of power that is perceptible inside those configurations. Certainly, real-locations are vital to alleviate deadly and injurious conditions. Yet, they do not necessarily alter power's concentrations and functions. Thus, the US Supreme Court's 2020 passage of a federal ban on gender and sexual discrimination in employment eased important forms of queer and trans suffering but did not usher in a nonqueerphobic, nontransphobic, non-*misogynarchic*, decolonial, postcapitalist, nonracist, noncasteist, nonspecie-sist, nonableist, or postwar society. Because such reforms leave dimensions of gender, sexuality, and other relations of power in place, there is no guar-antee that they will not prolong or even further exacerbate the deadly dimensions of power's operations. Moreover, as we see with the Trump government in 2025, such reforms can be fully open to reversal.

Deleuze and Guattari, in dialogue with Foucault, helpfully bring into relief qualities of power such as densities, intensities, and affect (Rajchman 1998; Jay 1993; Deleuze 1986; Deleuze and Guattari 1980). They also suggest non-ocular-centric ways of sensing power: the auditory, tactile, olfactory, etc. For example, in the Global North(s), rarely do wealthy, powerful people have to live near loud noise or unpleasant smells. Rarely do they have to use prod-ucts that would injure their skin: cheap detergents, plastic fabrics, etc. Rarely do they even imagine that their sensory environment is protected from sen-sory onslaught in ways that the environments of subalterns are not. This area of sensing power can be brought into conversation with some feminist and queer of color understandings of the powerful agencies of ancestral, ghostly, spiritual presences that act on the world (see below and chapter 4). Together all these dimensions, registers, and modes of enactment can be thought in relation to attunement to the *unsensed* and "the unthought" that "acts upon thought" as invoked in Luisa Muraro's quote above.

With this in mind, let us consider relations of power and their *operability*.

Co-Formations

Co-formations is a way to think about multiplicities of relations of power that are simultaneous, *co-present,* and about their *operability* in relatively brief, smaller-scale contexts. I posited and developed this concept, along with the notion of *co-productions,* over time (Bacchetta 2009a, 2015, 2020). Here, I specifically place *co-formations in-contextuality* with a more elaborated *theory-assemblage* and more intensely *in-relationality* with *co-productions.*

In some places, the most obvious *co-formations* may be race-racialization-racism, class, gender, sexuality, or disability; in others class, caste, religion, rurality, etc. *Co-formations* signals that each relation of power (gender, racism, class, etc.) is not separate or homogeneous; instead, it is the effect of its co-constitution by and with other relations of power together. Everywhere *co-formations* involve some relations of power that are imperceptible.

In the introduction I mentioned that *co-formations* is not a synonym for the broad term relations of power. Here I would like to elaborate their differences. In standard dictionaries, relation signifies "the state or condition of being related or the manner in which things are related; the position, association, connection, or status of one person or thing with regard to another or others; an association between ordered pairs of objects, numbers, etc., such as . . . is greater than" (*Collins English Dictionary* [2003], under "relation"). These points all have structuralist connotations. In contrast, a formation is "the act of giving or taking form, shape, or existence; something that is formed; the manner in which something is formed or arranged; a formal arrangement" (*Collins English Dictionary* [2009], under "formation"). In the specialized *American Heritage Stedman's Medical Dictionary* (2002), formation signifies "the act or process of forming something or of taking form; something formed." The *American Heritage Dictionary of the English Language* (2009) adds that formation means "the manner or style in which something is formed." In sum, while the notion of relation primarily evokes states of being, positions and associations, the concept of formation mainly signals an activity, a coming into (and out of) existence, a process, a dynamics, a style, a manner in which something becomes arranged and an arrangement that is always in flux. Formation is most clearly located in poststructuralism.

Formation in *co-formations* can be distinguished from prior (structuralist) theorizations of formations. In Marx's *A Contribution to the Critique of Political Economy* and *Capital*, formation appears as "social formation" to signal a specific kind of society with its own empirical assemblage, such as capitalist or feudal (Marx [1859] 1970, [1867] 1967). However, a *co-formation* is not a Marxian (social) formation. Instead, *co-formations* are one of the constituents or *co-formants* of *co-productions* such as feudalism or capitalism, and vice versa (see below).

Co-formations is also not simply another word for many relations of power or even many formations of power together. Instead, *co-formations* entails a different way of thinking about power, relations of power, and the work they do. *Co-formations* is an invitation to reconceptualize any relation of power that seems singular or discrete as instead dynamically *co*-constituted by and *operative* through multiplicities in different scales and temporal-spatialities. Thus, I do not consider gender as a (monofocal) formation as in dominant *colonialism-race-class-caste-amnesic* feminist and queer theory. Instead, I think of gender as a *co-formation* that is always already co-generated, co-composed by, and functioning with multiple localized perceptible and imperceptible relations of power with their various dimensions and registers—racism, caste, class, sexuality, disability, among others—and by and with *co-productions* (defined below) such as colonialism, coloniality, capitalism, slavery, *misogynarchies*, and speciesism, at once. *Co-formations* is inspired by Michael Omi and Howard Winant's ([1994] 2015) historical materialist theorization of race as a formation. However, like gender, to rethink race as a *co-formation* is to understand it as co-constituted by and with other *co-formations* and *co-productions*. In sum, *co-formations* highlights how any relation of power that is imagined to be singular—gender, race, or other—never is so.

With a Foucauldian notion of power in mind, we can think of *co-formations* and their fractal components as agentic forces with multiple capacities. *Co-formations* produce, maintain, reproduce, mutate, transform, undo, or dissolve economic and cultural conditions, temporal-spatialities, subjects, *beings-becomings*, etc. For example, there is no such thing as a neutral lesbian subject; she-they are always already co-constituted in relations of power that may be racism, class, caste, or other.

Each *co-formation* has its own densities, intensities, fractures, and openings. *Co-formations* co-constitute, saturate, disperse, or congeal in every dimension and register: economic, epistemic, cultural, juridical, symbolic, psychic, corporeal, affective, energetic. *Co-formations* shifts how we think about power and its *operability*.

Co-formations is inspired by and in conversation with many analytics of multiplicities of relations of power, such as intersectionality, assemblages, articulations, and matrix. Though *co-formations* differs from each of these, they all provide inspiration for distinct aspects, dimensions, and registers of *co-formations*. I will engage with them one by one before arriving at some concluding remarks on their relation to *co-formations*.

Intersectionality

Intersectionality is a main cluster within multiplicities theories that inform *co-formations*. Analytics that think of race, gender, and class together have a long genealogy in US Black feminist and queer thought, as well as in other feminist and queer of color thought, that precedes intersectionality (May 2024; Johnson and Henderson 2005; Guy-Sheftall 1995; Connor 2010; Bacchetta et. al. 2012). However, intersectionality as we know it today was specifically theorized and named as a concept-term by Black feminist legal scholar Kimberlé Crenshaw in her 1989 article on Black women's absence in labor law. Crenshaw (1989) argued that US law only recognizes white women as subjects of sexism and Black men as subjects of racism, yet Black women cannot be accounted for by adding these two parts. Race and gender do not act independently of each other; instead they intersect. Thus, from its inception, intersectionality was tied to subjects under erasure in power. Intersectionality remains an extremely dynamic site of continual theoretical innovation on subjects and power, including by Crenshaw herself. For example, in 1991, Crenshaw distinguished between "structural intersectionality" or conditions of power, and "political intersectionality," or multiple relations of power in resistance. Today Crenshaw envisions "categories" of power as "always permeated . . . , fluid and changing, always in the process of creating and being created by dynamics of power" (Crenshaw 2020; Cho et. al. 2013, 795).

At this time, intersectionality is a very complex mode of theorization spanning structuralism and poststructuralism (Davis and Lutz 2024; Nash 2018; Collins and Bilge 2016; May 2015). It is infinitely more useful to *freedom-exigent* theorizations and political projects than prior, concurrent, and even later monofocal (dominant) feminist and queer analytics of gender and sexuality that by definition reproduce *colonialism-race-class-caste-amnesia*.

While many intersectionality theorizations contribute centrally to *co-formations* (and *co-productions*), this vast field includes less useful theorizations too. To delineate this ensemble of intersectionality theory, the following criteria are useful: the specific intersectionality theory's definitions of relations of power, its understanding of how relations of power *operate* together, its blind spots or dimensions of intersectionality's (in) action, and its critiques of other notions and uses of intersectionality.

I would like to suggest that a major distinction in intersectionality theorizations is whether relations of power are conceptualized in linear, nonlinear, or other terms. Notwithstanding this delineation, it is not uncommon for several or all of these distinct notions to be a part of a same author's discussion, or of a common conversation among several authors (see, for example, Davis and Lutz 2024, where many different concepts and logics are used to illuminate intersectionality). Importantly, the problem is not that this or that author or group of authors are inadequate. Instead, the problem is with our shared vocabulary that restricts how and what we think. I am interested in understanding the lexical and content limitations so as to open up possibilities for solutions.

To explain further: in linear conceptions, gender, race, and class are variously regarded as "lines," "vectors," "axes," or "axes of differentiation" that intersect here and there (for some classical work, see Brah and Phoenix 2004, 1; Mohanty 1991,14). A drawback of linear intersectionality is that it can leave many points nonintersected: between, upon, outside, or elsewhere from lines. Thus, vast areas, dimensions, and kinds of relations of power are excluded. Linearity presupposes relations of power in monofocal or unitary terms and often imagines intersectionality as additive or accumulative, a vision that many intersectionality scholars—including those who might deploy linearity terminologies—critique.

In nonlinear intersectionality analytics, gender, sexuality, race, and class are understood variably beyond lines as "systems," "structures," "stratifications," "antagonisms," or "classifications" (Combahee 1997). Nonlinearity, too, has limits. For instance, "systems" does not tell us about intensities, densities, extents of relations of power, how they operate together, or whether all power must be organized into a recognized system to count. Indeed, disability is generally not considered a "system" and thus risks exclusion from nonlinear intersectionality.

It is not always clear in nonlinear intersectionality what exactly is intersecting: relations of power, discourses, cultures, identities, or all of these. For example, "systems" appears in the early writing of the Combahee River Collective (1997) as "systems of oppression." In contrast, Dean Spade (2011, 25) highlights "systems of meaning and control." In France, Danièle Kergoat (2004) uses a Marxian-inspired structuralist notion of "systems" to describe convergences of gender and class (without race) as "consubstantial systems" (for an important critique, see Moujoud 2025). In H. Edward Ransford's theory of multiple jeopardy, the term "category" substitutes for "structure" (1980).

Generally, conceptualizations beyond linearity and nonlinearity consider multiplicities of relations of power as one entity. Thus, Cathy Cohen's analytic, which I mentioned in chapter 1, focuses on the relation between intersectionality, the norm, and anormativity (Cohen 2005, 21–51). For Cohen, US Black heterosexual subjects are positioned outside (white) sexual normativity and thus as a variant of queer. Cohen productively shifts concern from queer identity to the power-effects of sexuality and race on subject-positions. But, here the subject, not power, seems central.

The distinctions I draw between linearity, nonlinearity, and beyond linearity have implications for how relations of power are thought together, albeit not determinatively. Some differences are semantic, others conceptual. Many authors deploy linear and nonlinear terms interchangeably. For instance, Susanne V. Knudson uses the nonlinear term "categories" but then iterates linearity, explaining that "the word intersection means that one line cuts through another line, and can be used about streets crossing each other" (2007). Tavia Nyong'o usefully argues that "it is not enough to take up the simultaneity of race, class, gender and sexuality" and then invokes intersection as a "meeting place of two streets" that becomes "a place of particular hazard for the pedestrian" (2005). Some scholars also interchangeably deploy nonlinearities ("systems," "categories") and, in a same text, posit relations of power operating like lines crossing (Eng et. al 2005, 1; Mohanty 1991, 14; Crenshaw 1989). Intersectionality is sometimes expressed in related, analogous linearity terms such as "switchpoints" or "crisscrossings" (Stockton 2006, 5). Different authors disparately consider how relations of power interact: as "interlocking," as multiple "social antagonisms" together, as "entanglements," as "consubstantialities," in "intra-actions," as "mutually transforming one another," or as "interanimating" each other (Combahee 1997; Eng et al. 2005; Glenn 1999; Kergoat 2004; Lykke 2005; Yuval-Davis 2006; Johnson and Henderson 2005, 1). We can see through these examples that it might be very helpful if we could all clarify our conceptions and language around intersectionality.

Another differentiation across intersectionality theories is whether relations of power in intersectionality are conceptualized as separate or inseparable. When thought to be separate, or what I call atomized or separation intersectionality, they get imagined variously as analogous, parallel, cumulative-additive, compounded, overlapping, or—more rarely—as differential, parallel but conjoined. Atomized or separation intersectionality notions can be highly complex. Avtar Brah and Ann Phoenix describe social class (separately) as simultaneously subjective, structural, about social positionality and everyday practices (2004). When relations of power are imagined as separate yet analogous, they unhelpfully risk intrahomogenization and interhomogenization. Calvin Warren (2017) points to how an analysis can get totally skewed by imagining "equivalence" among differential relations of power. An example from my own work is how, in France, analyses of anti-Muslim racism that take anti-Semitism as their model and equate the two as anti-Other stances problematically invisibilize colonialism and orientalism that are essential to understanding Islamophobia.

In turn, the idea that relations of power are inseparable, or what we can call inseparability intersectionality, spans many conceptualizations. In some, relations of power are merged from the start (Yuval-Davis 2006, 200). In others, relations of power are first imagined as separate, then fuse in the construction of social conditions or subjects. But inseparability can obscure conditions and subjects, too. For example, in the United States the dominant discursive collapsing operation that makes class and race identical reinforces the idea of correspondence, such that subalternly racialized subjects (people of color) are presumed to be uniformly subalternly classed (working class or impoverished) and vice versa. This unhelpfully erases complexities such as whites in poverty or wealthy elites of color.

Intersectionality can also be understood through its zones and modes of action. Intersectionality generally pertains to smaller scales (Knapp 2005). Vrushali Patil demonstrates that English-language intersectionality studies focus mainly on the Global North(s) (85 percent), especially the United States (65 percent), and the intranational scale (75 percent) and not the regional or transnational scales (2011). Patil calls this "domestic intersectionality" (Patil 2011). Some scholars differentiate between whether intersectionality operates universally (identically everywhere) or is contextually contingent. Irene Browne and Joya Misra call this division "ubiquity vs. contingency" and argue that most studies are ubiquitous (2003).

Disparate authors consider intersectionality's reach diversely. Chela Sandoval speaks at once of "social classifications" and "differing oppositional ideologies" (2000, 42.3, 44.5). For Evelyn Nakano Glenn, "The social construction of race/gender is a matter of both social structure and cultural representation" (1999, 11). For Brah and Phoenix, intersectionality flags "complex, irreducible, varied, and variable effects which ensue when multiple axes of differentiation—economic, political, cultural, psychic, subjective and experiential—intersect in historically specific contexts"; they propose that "different dimensions of social life cannot be separated out into discrete and pure strands" (2004, 1–2).

Authors also differ on what work they think intersectionality does. For most, it describes the construction of subjects, for some it explains social conditions, and for others it does both. Grace Kyungwon Hong, bringing yet other dimensions into the discussion, argues that intersectionality is primarily an epistemology (2006).

Scholars outside and inside the field of intersectionality have offered a range of kinds of critiques of the literatures. For Devon Carbado (2013) the critiques of intersectionality problematically, variably, reduce intersectionality to being: only about Black women, or only about race and gender; identitarian; static, incapable of capturing dynamism; overly subject-centric; or limited, with nothing more to teach us. Carbado argues that intersectionality is imagined as eternally inadequate, as requiring substitution or supplementation.

For the Black feminist theoretician Jennifer Nash, who did a thorough book-length study that analyzes critiques of intersectionality and critiques of the critiques, the act of constructively but critically engaging intersectionality has become contentious in ways that are unproductive for Black feminism. Nash mentions a talk by Patricia Hill Collins in which Collins compares intersectionality to a holy object and to Columbus's origin story on which adherents are obsessively fixated (cited in Nash 2018, 41–42). Nash ultimately argues that loving Black feminism might mean "letting go" of "the lure of territoriality" and putting "the visionary genius of black feminism to work otherwise" so it can continue to be "a practice of freedom" (130, 138). For Nash, "policing intersectionality's uses and circulations" is unproductive for intersectionality and it limits theoretical creativity in and with Black feminist theory more broadly. Nash suggests that intersectionality is highly useful when it can freely circulate, is open to elaboration, and is placed *in-relationality* with other concepts. The notion of *co-formations* is inspired by, indebted to, complicit with, and always *in-relationality* to intersectionality, for it is intersectionality that in the first place opens up the possibility of developing yet other dimensions and registers about power and its *operability*.

In another internal problematization, specifically concerned with power, some scholars think of intersectionality as not inherently anticapitalist and as risking supporting the "commodification" and "institutionalization of difference" common to neoliberal multiculturalism (Ferguson 2012, 213). Other scholars feel that intersectionality is ocular-centric, engaged solely with visible relations of power. Yet others have tried to develop intersectionality into different directions or dimensions and this has been sometimes interpreted as critique instead of complicity. Some examples are works that highlight intersectionality's affirmation of multiplicities beyond the visible, such as Anna Marie Smith's (1994) intersectional work on "nodal points," Evelyn Nakano Glenn's (2002, 14) "anchor points," and Valerie Purdie-Vaughns and Richard Eibach's (2008) "intersectional invisibility."

One main external critique—that is now ancient but continually revived—is that intersectionality is reductively focused on identity and has fragmented (presumably white) feminism. This idea, which is found in *colonialism-race-class-caste-amnesic* feminisms, problematically presupposes that (white) feminism came first and was harmonious until women of color arrived. This claim inadvertently reenacts the disciplining power of white supremacy (Alarcón 1990; Jayawardena 1986).

There are also transnational critiques. Importantly, Nivedita Menon questions why a concept forged in the United States should be relevant in India (2015). Huma Dar argues that some *savarna* (upper caste Hindu) feminists call intersectionality imperialist, yet uncritically use dominant (white) US feminist concepts of gender (2015). Many Dalit feminist and queer scholars currently mobilize intersectionality to analyze caste, class, and gender together (Patni and Khan 2024). Yet, others see intersectionality as a *savarna* import to "police, oops theorize, gendered violence that goes down in Dalit communities" but not in their own (S. 2017). They call on *savarna* feminists to analyze their own communities in intersectional terms, thus to recognize caste privilege (S. 2017). Relatedly, Nasima Moujoud and Fatima Ait Ben Lmadani explain how, in France, white feminists engage US intersectionality texts but exclude the thought of racialized French feminist intellectuals (Ait Ben Lmadani 2025; Ait Ben Lmadani and Moujoud 2012). Sirma Bilge highlights racism's disappearance in dominant European intersectionality scholarship, a process she calls the "whitening of intersectionality" (Collins and Bilge 2016; Bilge 2013). Additionally, scholars in Europe who initially forget about racism sometimes reintegrate it, but often in ways that do not correspond accurately to racialized relations of power in their contexts. An example is the notion of *consubstantialité* that I mentioned earlier. Initially, it aimed to account solely for class and gender relations of power while ignoring race. But later, drawing on Angela Davis's early theorizations and on Kimberlé Crenshaw's early work on intersectionality in translation—and not on the analyses of racialized feminists in France—*consubstantialité* was expanded to consider questions of race (Kergoat 1978, 2004; Galerand and Kergoat 2014). At that point, some proponents of *consubstantialité* wrote that the concept was distinguishable from intersectionality because it emerged from the French context and from materialist feminist and sociological notions of power. While context is certainly vital to think with, in much of this literature intersectionality is unfortunately misread as failing to account for dynamism in relations of power.

In sum, *co-formations* (and *co-productions*) are deeply indebted to Crenshaw's theorizations and to intersectionality literatures that focus on analytics of dynamic multiplicities, energetic inseparabilities, active mutual co-constitutions of power, and—specifically with Collins, Glenn, and others—on power's vibrant investments and capacities across all dimensions and registers. *Co-formations* might be considered a deeply intersectionality-complicit, specifically poststructuralist, variant of intersectionality.

However, unlike prior intersectionality theorizations, *co-formations* (and *co-productions*) begin with a Foucauldian notion of power. For *co-formations* any relation of power—gender, sexuality, class, race, etc.—is always already co-constituted with other relations of power *in-context*. *Co-formations* have no fixed shape, contours, or modes of configuration. They are neither linear nor nonlinear. *Co-formations* are about power that is constantly in circulation, in process, *in-co-formation*. For *co-formations* (and *co-productions*), how power seems to manifest or not at any point in time and space is a function of *sensing, perception,* and *intelligibility,* and power's own agentic work of circulation, congealment, revelation, or concealment. Whereas intersectionality is often centered on the present, for *co-formations* the present is always already the *co-present* that includes genealogies, futurities, and many other temporal-spatialities.

Matrix

A next valuable notion for *co-formations* is matrix. A Foucauldian notion, it sometimes appears in monofocal *colonialism-race-class-caste-amnesic* feminist and queer analytics. However, more importantly, matrix is also fruitfully developed in some multiplicities theorizations. Thus, in some of her most classical work, Collins (1991, 225) proposes "matrix of domination" and sometimes, interchangeably, "matrix of oppression." She explains that she draws matrix from a 1989 text by Black feminist theoretician Johnella

Butler. For Collins, "matrix" helps clarify intersectionality. For her, many scholars reduce intersectionality to discourse and imagine gender and race as additive (225; 1998a). Instead, for Collins intersectionality should foreground power and consider "axes" of power as "mutually constructing" (1991, 226). Intersectionality should focus on social groups and not individuals to avoid reproducing a major tenet of neoliberalism (Collins 1997; 1998c, 203–5, 206–7). In Collins's view, intersectionality scholars sometimes assume equivalencies of oppression across groups, and this view potentially benefits some groups more than others. For her, different "axes" within intersectionality (race, class, gender, etc.) have different weights. Thus, "most African American women would identify race as more determinative than gender" (1998c, 208).

Collins proposes "matrix of domination" to describe the overall organization of power and the place of groups and individuals therein. She proposes that intersectionality is just one of its features. For her, "race, class and gender" are historical constructions that "constitute axes of oppression that characterize Black women's experiences within a more generalized matrix of domination" (1991, 226). The axes are organized through four sites of power—structural, disciplinary, hegemonic and interpersonal—and three "levels of domination": the personal, the cultural, and the institutional (1991, 227). In the "matrix of domination" power relations operate in three scales: the micro, the meso, and the macro.

In turn, for Vivian May, intersectionality is always already "matrix thinking" (2015, 21). She is interested in what work intersectionality as matrix thought can do (18). For her, matrix thinking dispenses with the additive view of distinct oppressions that accumulate; instead, it allows for "enmeshed multiplicities" (22). She also highlights that matrix thinking incites us to consider how, insofar as everyone is located within the same matrix, the relations of power within that matrix affect not only the subaltern subject but also the dominant, albeit differently (23–26).

Collins's focus on relations of power and their co-constitution in her matrix theorization, and May's insights about intersectionality as matrix thinking and thus its very broad usefulness for analysis (of differently positioned subjects, objects, etc.), directly inspire *co-formations* and its possible analytical *operabilities*. Together, Collins and May helpfully make material-economic conditions, culture, the symbolic, the epistemic, and the psychic central at once.

Yet *co-formations* and matrix differ, too. One dissimilarity is that matrix emphasizes effects of power that produce the present, while for *co-formations* genealogies and the plural temporal-spatialities that they imply are always *co-present* within a hegemonic temporal-spatiality (see below). Another distinction is that while matrix describes an overall context of power, *co-formations* (and *co-productions*) highlight(s) any context's internal differential densities, intensities, and saturations of power and the dynamism of power's continual reconfigurations at disparate speeds.

A related multiplicities notion of matrix that differs from Collins's and May's is "crosscutting matrices." Donald S. Moore (1997, 93) proposes this but without elaboration. It perhaps can be taken to mean separate matrices for gender, race, class, et cetera, and colonialism, which may either intersect or be fused. In both cases, "crosscutting matrices" would be additively monofocal and multiply unitary. While meant to take into account multiplicities of relations of power, "crosscutting matrices" does so differently from *co-formations*.

Articulations

Another multiplicities notion that contributes to *co-formations* (and *co-productions*) is articulation (Bacchetta 2009). It exists across structuralist and poststructuralist literatures, and across disciplines.

Current feminist uses of articulation in the four sites of this study can be grouped into Marxist-Althusserian, Marxist-Gramscian, and finally Gramscian-Hallian (i.e., of Stuart Hall). They all owe to Marx the initial notion of articulation (*Gliederung*), defined as how elements from disparate periods are carried into, coexist in, and are hierarchically ordered within a same historical social formation. Louis Althusser and Étienne Balibar point out that Marx delineates social formation in two ways: as an empirical concept designating a concrete existence, such as France in 1870, and as an abstract concept replacing the ideological notion of society (1977, 207). Marx's elaboration was focused on the mode of production. He attempted to explain how economic systems of prior and concurrent moments converge into an ordered, stratified assemblage in a same period. Though not his intention, Marx's perspective on simultaneity, and what I call *co-presence*, move counter to the Eurocentric "common sense" idea of homogenous linear historical time comprised of a separate past and present (1977, 99). It directly informs the *co* in both *co-formations* and *co-productions*. After Marx, theorizations of articulations often highlight how different components come together, or what of this amassment becomes expressed or manifested (articulated).

Gramsci makes an important contribution by analyzing articulations in what he considers to be the base (economy) and superstructure (ideology and culture) separately, and their interworkings. His empirical focus, Italy, is notoriously "brutally marked" by "massive industrial development to the north" and "massive underdevelopment" in the subaltern "south" (Hall 2002, 54). Gramsci identified Italy's simultaneous "different modes of production (capitalist and feudal)" and dissimilar "social orders" (Hall 2002). His notion of separate complex registers (economy, culture) and strata within registers (sedimentations, convergences, antagonisms) operating disjointedly or in unison directly inform the *co* in *co-formations*. To consider ideologies, Gramsci shifts away from the Marxian idea of "false consciousness" to reflect on how "common sense" is constituted and becomes hegemonic for both the dominant and subaltern classes. For Gramsci, hegemony is an effect of the dominant class's selection and coordination of cultural, ideological, and affective components that produce acquiescence-to-consent in subaltern groups (Mathieu 1985).[1] These reflections help us to understand how subaltern culture, a complex assemblage, is not necessarily *subalternist* or *subalternative*.

Gramsci (1991) provides a pertinent example in *Letteratura e vita nazionale* where he explains folklore. First, the Italian dominant class, including its intelligentsia, reads foreign literature in translation, worships foreign culture, "is subjected to, undergoes, is affected by," or "suffers" (all significations of the Italian *subisce*) "the intellectual and moral hegemony of foreign intellectuals" (124–25). Together Italian and foreign components constitute the dominant class's "common sense." The Italian subaltern class's culture, ideology, and "common sense" are composed of some same and disparate sets of "diverse strata" that get marginalized in the dominant class's consensus process (263). The strata are comprised of elements that are "fossilized" and "reflect conditions of past life" (263). They get characterized as "conservative and reactionary" but also encompass "innovations" that are "often creative and progressive, spontaneous determinants of forms and conditions of life in the process of development" (263). These "innovations" are assigned extraneity in the dominant "culture, ideology and common sense" (264). Here, Gramsci theorizes assemblages of cultural heterogeneity, layers of compositions, and hierarchical arrangements across disparate class formations and within a same nation, all notions that incite my attention to genealogies and scale in *co-formations*.

Gramsci's analysis of culture and ideology influenced Althusser's work on articulation. In Althusser's *For Marx* (1965) and in *Reading Capital*

(1977) with Étienne Balibar, articulation is a synchronic principle. Every social formation is heterogeneous. It has many "levels" of prior modes of production, legal systems, and superstructure. Each "level" has "a peculiar time" that is "relatively autonomous and hence relatively independent, even in its dependence, of the times of the other levels" (Althusser and Balibar 1977, 99–100). Althusser and Balibar ask us to reflect on both "the visible and measurable times" and the "invisible" including "invisible rhythms and punctuations concealed beneath the surface of each visible time" (101). Their intuitions on time and invisibility inform how I conceptualize temporal-spatialities, *co-presence*, and power's *operability* in *co-formations* (and *co-productions*).

Shortly thereafter, Ernesto Laclau attempts to develop articulation through discourse analysis (1977). His work draws on a Marxist-Gramscian vision of multiple discourses coexisting in a same time-space, Gramsci's hegemony, and Althusser's interpellation. For Laclau, the dominant class rearticulates its ideology to interpellate dominant and subaltern classes, to deter subaltern revolt by absorbing and neutralizing subaltern resistant "ideological contents" (161). Signifiers such as *freedom*, *equality*, etc. have no fixed signification or class affiliation. They can be incorporated into disparate discourses. Laclau calls this process "double articulation." Yet, especially in the planetary context, given the potential multiplicity of the signifieds, signifiers, and subjects in question it seems to me that perhaps *pluri-articulation* is more accurate than "double articulation." Laclau's insights inspire *co-formation*'s insistence on the *co-presence* of multiple discursive elements from many temporal periods. Indeed, for *co-formations*, any given present moment is dense with multiple disparate *co-present temporal-spatialities*.

Stuart Hall's pivotal work on race usefully expands articulations analytics. He identifies two "tendencies" in "the study of racially structured social formations": the economic and the sociological (2002, 38–39). For Hall, "One must start . . . from the concrete historical 'work' which racism accomplishes under specific historical conditions—as a set of economic, political, and ideological practices, of a distinctive kind, concretely articulated with other practices in a social formation" that "fix and ascribe" but also "legitimate" its arrangement of "different social groups in relation to each other" (59). These "are practices which secure the hegemony of a dominant group over" subalterns and "over the whole social formation" (59).

Hall clarifies that he is not proposing a uniform theory of racism nor any determinism. For instance, for him (contra some notions of racial capitalism), "Racism is not necessary to the concrete functioning of all capitalisms" (59). Instead, "How and why racism has been specifically over determined by and articulated with certain capitalisms at different stages of their development" is something that "needs to be shown," not merely assumed (59). We should identify what "form," "logic," and "necessary stages" are at work in racism and demonstrate racism's "articulation with the different structures of the social formation" (59). Hall asks us to analyze the how, or what I rethink in terms of Foucauldian-Deleuzian *operability*, of "race"-racialization-racism's emergence, manifestations, and functions contextually. I find this part of Hall's work very useful for distinguishing between specific, small-scale *co-formations* and larger-scale *co-productions* (see below).

The feminist geographer Gillian Hart helpfully clarifies three distinct notions of articulation in South Africa with implications far beyond that geopolitical space (2007). The first signification of articulation, introduced by Harold Wolpe (1980), draws on the Althusserian interpretation of coexistent modes of production. It uses articulation to analyze the conjoining of precapitalist and capitalist modes of production and the corresponding racial forms of the apartheid racial capitalist order. Hart associates the second meaning of articulation with Stuart Hall (discussed above). The third idea of articulation that she identifies is in Laclau and Chantal Mouffe's ([1985] 1999) work, which, she suggests, "renovates . . . liberalism in the name of 'radical democracy' and post-Marxism" (Hart 2007, 86, 91). For Hart, Laclau abandoned "any conception of determination" and produced an "impoverished concept of articulation that cannot account for many questions that are central to capitalism," including "material conditions, forms of power and processes of subject formation" (91).

Hart proposes, instead, to reconsider articulation by rereading Gramsci, with sensitivity to race, class, and gender (89). Michael Ekers, Stefan Kipfer, and Alex Loftus (2020) put into relief two of Hart's major contributions to literatures on articulation. Hart clarifies how contradictory, autonomous relations and processes get conjoined in a particular historical moment, and illuminates the place of language and culture in articulation. This enables Hart to better understand the elements that converge within a political conjuncture and the complexity of how language works in articulation. For example, in one of her studies, Hart posits that South African President Jacob Zuma mobilizes "official articulations of nationalism" such as "national struggle, suffering for freedom, racial oppression and dispossession" to successfully represent himself as the "rightful heir" of the liberation struggle (2007, 94). Zuma unites "often contradictory meanings into a complex unity that appeals powerfully to 'common sense' across a broad spectrum" (97). He can be read as "a man of the left," a "traditionalist in leopard skins," and an "anti-elitist" who is "not educated" but "extremely smart" (98). He functions as "a point of condensation for multiple, pre-existing tensions, angers, and discontents" (98). Hart's focus on understanding convergences of distinct and even conflicting elements inspires how I think about *co-presences* in *co-formations* (and *co-productions*).

Anne McClintock, too, engages articulation and/as a multiplicities theorization. She draws on intersectionality, critical race theory, postcolonial theory, and "feminism, Marxism and psychoanalysis" (1995, 8). For her, "Race, gender and class are not distinct realms of experience" but rather "come into existence in and through relation to each other" "in contradictory and conflictual ways" (5). As such, "Gender, race and class can be called articulated categories" (5). McClintock highlights subaltern conditions and subjects but also dominant formations: privilege, cisgender men, heterosexuality, white people. McClintock's articulation includes everything economic, institutional, discursive, symbolic, cultural, and representational at once. For her, understanding imperialism requires "a theory of gender power" for "gender dynamics were, from the outset, fundamental to . . . the imperial enterprise" and remain so today (6–7). McClintock's notion of how some fragments of relations of power get articulated with and through each other leads me to consider how other *co-present* fragments are muted or made *inarticulate* as part of power's *operations* in *co-formations* (and *co-productions*).

Agencements/Assemblages

Another important cluster is *agencements*/assemblages. The most relevant for *co-formations* (and *co-productions*) are Gilles Deleuze and Félix Guattari's theorization of *agencements*, generally translated as assemblages in English, and Jasbir Puar's conceptualization of "assemblages" that draws on their work.

Importantly, *agencement* exists in everyday French and only becomes a philosophical concept with Deleuze and Guattari's elaboration.[2] It is a masculine noun with a verb form. As a noun, *agencement* signifies "an action, a manner of acting" (*agencer*); "an arrangement resulting from a combination," "laying out" (*aménagement*); "disposition, ordering or arrangement; organization" (*Le petit Robert* [1984], under "*agencement*"). *Agencement* shares a same root with *agent* and *agency*. In fact, *agencements* in French are dynamic arrangements that have agency, capacity, potentiality to act, do, perform, produce effects. The verb form, *agencer*, among other significations, includes to "arrange, organize, or place by combining elements" and to "adjust, arrange, order" (*Le petit Robert* [1984], under "*agencer*").

Assemblage, too, exists in French but Deleuze and Guattari do not use it. It is a masculine noun, signifying "the act of assembling (elements) to create a whole, an object"; "assembling the pieces of a machine"; "*montage*" or "means by which to assemble"; "reunion of assembled things"; "structure" or "construction"; "collection" or "ensemble"; "assortment of heterogeneous elements": "mixture"; in math "a succession of signs"; antonym: "disjunction, separation" (*Le petit Robert* [1984], under "*assemblage*"). Unlike *agencements*, in French *assemblage* has no verb form.

Deleuze and Guattari theorize *agencement* in *Kafka* (1975) and *Milles plateaux* (1980), and Deleuze does so alone in *Foucault* (1986). *Agencement* responds oppositionally to French structuralist totalizing theories characterized by interiority, in which a whole (i.e., a society) is imagined as a self-contained sum of its parts whose internal relations explain the whole. *Agencement* is a theory of exteriority that posits disparate components as bits in processes of connection and disconnection within, across, and outside constellations that they induce, produce, or dissolve. For *agencement*, whatever appears as a whole is a temporary ensemble of moving parts that can be detached and reinserted somewhere else. While dominant political analytics are constructed around rationality and confine political affect to psychoanalytic theorizations, *agencement* makes affect, intensity, and energies together central. An *agencement* is always an excess, exceeding the forces that comprise it. Also, while universalism dominates in France, *agencements* are about contingency.

Deleuze and Guattari are primarily interested in the *operability* of *agencements*, or *how* they function and what they do (1980). *Operability* helps clarify how *agencement* works simultaneously as a noun (a thing) and a verb (a doing, producer of effects), thus in continuity with *agencement*'s French popular usage. For Deleuze and Guattari an *agencement* has three main axes: (1) a material or content to expressive horizontal axis; (2) a territorial to deterritorial vertical axis; and (3) a coding to decoding diagonal axis. In its material or content dimension the *agencement* is a mechanic assemblage of bodies, actions, and passions that interact together. In its expressive dimension it is a collection of enunciations, acts, statements, and incorporeal transformations. In a scene composed of ("bodies" of) a cat, her human, and a chair, the material or content comprises the cat, human, and chair that interrelate, each of which is yet another complex *agencement*. The expressive components are those that operate as catalysts producing effects, such as the scent by which the cat recognizes her human. Second, an *agencement* involves territorialization that stabilizes parts and deterritorialization that disrupts, dislocates, or dissipates parts along a vertical axis. Finally, processes of coding consolidate the *agencement* into an identity, while decoding inhibits or undoes such congealment. *Agencements* have fragile, unstable identities that are open to decomposition, recomposition, dispersal.

Another aspect of *agencements* is their arrangements, transformations, and disintegrations across what Deleuze and Guattari (1980) call the "molecular" and "molar." For them, molecular and molar do not designate fixed scales. Instead, they are about dynamic relations. Molecular refers to parts and molar to whole *agencements*. So, "What is molecular at any scale is that which plays the role of the component or part, while the molar is the statistical result of the molecular populations at any given level of scale" (DeLanda 2006, 252). A molar element can function as a molecular (component) of another *agencement* (see below).

Puar pushes Deleuze and Guattari's *agencements* into interesting directions. Her reflections appear primarily in *Terrorist Assemblages: Homonationalism in Queer Times* (2007) and "'I Would Rather Be a Cyborg Than a Goddess': Becoming-Intersectional in Assemblage Theory" (2012). The latter title is the last sentence in a Donna Haraway article critiquing intersectionality theorizations of identities. Puar problematizes intersectionality so as to contribute to it by "supplementing" and possibly "complicating" it through "assemblages" (2012, 50).

Puar's critique centers on subjects and power. On subjects, she finds intersectionality too focused on representation, the ocular, and signification, a problem it shares with many nonintersectionality (US) feminist and queer theories (2007, 187–89). She argues that "intersectionality privileges naming, visuality, epistemology, representation, and meaning, while assemblage underscores tactility, ontology, affect, and information" (215). For Puar, the representation focus—in intersectionality and nonintersectionality theorizations—enables the construction of "women of color" as an "Other who must invariably be shown to be resistant, subversive, or articulating a grievance," as "a prosthetic capacity to white women" and "an alibi for the recentering of white liberal feminists" (2012, 52). Puar also recognizes intersectionality theorizings beyond identity, such as Audre Lorde's "dynamic, affectively resonant postulation of lived intersectional subjectivities" (52).

On power, Puar argues that intersectionality cannot account for shifts in disciplinary and bio power in the post-9/11 United States because "sexuality, nation, religion, age and disability" on which intersectionality depends are "identitary categories" based in "modernist colonial agendas and regimes of epistemic violence" (54). She critiques intersectionality's "hermeneutic of positionality that seeks to account for locality, specificity, placement, junctions" (2007, 212). For her, "taxonomies" such as race "categories" are a "tool of diversity management" and a "mantra of liberal multiculturalism" that "colludes with the disciplinary apparatus of the state" (212). Drawing on Brian Massumi's work, Puar considers intersections as effects of "attempts to still and quell the perpetual motion of assemblages" to produce "gridlock," to depoliticize assemblages and control them (212–13).

Puar's critique seems to be based on a part of (early) intersectionality literatures inscribed in *nonlinearity* ("taxonomies," "categories"), the humanities, and structuralism, with an exclusive focus on subjects. It leaves aside poststructuralist intersectionality theorizations and intersectionality analytics of power by social scientists such as Collins and Glenn.

For Puar, "assemblage" can solve some of what she identifies as intersectionality's limitations. She invokes *agencements*, clarifying that she considers "assemblage" an "awkward translation" or "'mis' translation" (2012, 57). Drawing from English-language sources, she defines *agencements* as "design, layout, organization, arrangement, and relations—the focus being not on content but on relations, relations of patterns" (57). Here, Puar presupposes *agencements*' noun aspect, not its verb aspect, thereby aligning her notion of "assemblage" closer to the English term assemblage.

For Puar, "assemblage" usefully allows us to conceptualize the human body as not a bounded, discrete organic thing with an identity (2012). "Assemblage" de-exceptionalizes the human body so that many forms—water, cities, etc.—can be bodies (57). In "assemblage" theorizations matter is an actor, a doing. "Assemblage" analytics displace representation and signification, and de-emphasizes language (65). In "assemblage"—unlike in intersectionality—gender, race, and class are "events, actions and encounters, between bodies, rather than simply entities and attributes of subjects" (65). "Assemblage" makes us "more attuned to" relations of power as "interwoven forces that merge and dissipate time, space, and body" (Puar 2007, 212). These points converge with the Deleuzian-Guattarian idea that *agencements* are agentic multiplicities, in continual interaction.

Puar provides several illuminating examples of the theoretical work that her conception of "assemblage" does. In the most elaborated of these, she proposes that we not understand a Sikh man wearing a turban in the hegemonic normative way—that is, within a narrow visual, ocular-centric economy of identity as a man with an appendage (2007). The turbaned Sikh is a complex representation in the first place. There are many different kinds of turbans and Sikhs are of disparate classes, regions, and sects. Dominant epistemic knowings about this figure are often reductive. Instead, Puar asks us to understand the turbaned Sikh figure within an affective economy of "assemblage" that foregrounds affect, intensities, and forces. The Sikh becomes after 9/11 that to which an array of affect is stuck: fear, victimology, religiosity, dignity, cultural continuity. The difference here is felt before it is seen.

Co-formations draws on important elements of both (Deleuzian-Guattarian) agencements and (Puar's) "assemblages," as I explain below. However, co-formations reorients the discussion. It tries to bypass some of the problems that agencements carries. For example, for agencements, temporal-spatialities—with the histories and cultures that they imply—are detachable and reattachable, like objects in a collage. Thus, the notion of agencements risks reproducing colonialism-race-class-caste-amnesia by fragmenting, only partially acknowledging, and sometimes eradicating subaltern genealogies. Deleuze and Guattari have no investment in decolonial and noncolonial ways of knowing. Their anti-identity stance in agencements arrives during a dynamic period of anticolonial and immigrant rights uprisings in France. Unfortunately, instead of thinking in complicity with the insurgent subjects, Deleuze and Guattari focus on (white) subjects, positing them as "becoming-minor" (1976). At times their notion of agencements seems to reiterate the unitary universalized (white) subject, albeit with qualities, intensities, and speeds attached (see chapter 2). Agencements risks ignoring power and subjects that are outside the perceiver's awareness of the dynamic bits that seem co-present (in a still dominant field of intelligibility) through affect, tactility, scent, etc. Yet, to presume that affect, tactility, and scent are neutral modes of perception is to universalize and essentialize dominant modes of sensing, perception, and intelligibility. Finally, Deleuze and Guattari's language of levels and layers of geological space reinscribes "abstract" space that, as I explain in chapter 4, is the notion of space on which the colonial-racial depends.

However, co-formations (and co-productions) amply draw(s) from Deleuze and Guattari's idea, via agencements, of relations of power as nonbinary, dynamic, shifting, molecular and molar compositions, decompositions, and recompositions with affect, intensities, and energies. Co-formations is also inspired by Puar's important call to rethink power for our times and by her creative notion of subjects as complex, multidimensional, dynamic configurations that must be understood far beyond gridlocked identitary categories, as events, actions, encounters, doings, and catalysts.

Co-Productions

Co-productions are a way to consider multiplicities of relations of power that operate across vast *co-present temporal-spatialities*. Above, I mention some *co-productions* that are at work today: colonialism, coloniality, capitalism, effects of slavery, *misogynarchies*, speciesism. *Co-productions* comprise every dimension and register that *co-formations* do. A major difference is this: *Co-formations* manifest and function at relatively small localized scales, while *co-productions* are about arcs that operate across immense temporal-spatialities across the planet. *Co-productions* generally seem relatively static, stable, and dense, and yet they are always in motion, in composition and decomposition. They entail circulations of power at all densities and intensities, with effects in all dimensions and registers.

As for *co-formations*, a *co-production* is not an entity composed of compounded separate productions. It is not an additive aggregation, such as the Marxist mode of production plus the sexist mode of production that Colette Guillaumin and Christine Delphy call "sexage" (Guillaumin 1978a, 1978b; Delphy 1975). Instead, each *co-production* is co-constituted by many other relations of power. Global capitalism as a *co-production* is not reducible to class relations but rather is co-composed of other *co-productions* such as colonialism, coloniality, capitalism, slavery, imperialism, *misogynarchies*, speciesism, and of *co-formations* such as gender, sexuality, racism, class, religious difference, and disability. A *co-production* includes all the dimensions, registers, stages, states of being, and *co-present temporal-spatialities* of all its co-constituents.

The notion of *co-productions* is especially indebted to postcolonial and decolonial theorizing. It draws on yet differs from the concept-term coproduction in postcolonial theory. Therein, coproduction helpfully signals that colonialism is not simply enactments done to (presumably passive) colonized subjects and space by (presumably active) colonizers. Instead, as a coproduction colonialism is a relationship that produces both colonized and colonizing subjects and spaces, a notion first elaborated by Frantz Fanon, then others. Foucault partially reiterates it when he invokes the "boomerang effect" of "colonial practice" on the "juridico-political structures of the

West" even if, contrary to Fanon, Foucault problematically reproduces the binary active colonizer vs. passive colonized (2003, 103).

Postcolonial theory's concept of coproduction has fruitful aspects for *co-productions* but also presents challenges. Coproductions generally presumes an *exclusive* colonizer vs. colonized binary—for example, Britain vs. India, or France vs. Algeria. But, as Minoo Moallem demonstrates, coloniality operates beyond the binary, too, in countries such as Iran that are orientalized and demonized and yet were never formally colonized (2005). Moreover, the colonizer vs. colonized binary in postcolonial theory's coproduction obscures many kinds and dimensions of power and subjects, on the side of both colonizers and colonized and in their interrelations. Some erasures are flagrant. Queerphobia and queer subjects rarely appear in postcolonial scholarship on coproductions. Leela Gandhi highlights that the colonizer vs. colonized lens renders anticolonial and decolonial resistance unintelligible beyond "action performed solely by the putative non-West upon the putative West" that is organized either oppositionally (e.g., as culturalism, nativism, or "fundamentalism") or by infiltration (e.g., via hybridity, mimicry, reactive interpellation, or "the journey in") (2006, 1). Importantly, the binary presumption fails to make perceptible the complexities of multiple colonizers in a same space (e.g., Portuguese, French, and English in India), of colonizers' interrelations with each other from rivalries to cooperation, or the plethora of kinds of relations that colonized peoples have to colonialisms in a same space (Bacchetta 2023).

In contrast, *co-productions* herein is nonbinary. It considers the dynamism of a plurality of power and subjects in colonialism and coloniality across the planet in vast temporal-spatialities. For example, *co-productions* induces us to understand mathematics, astronomy, medicine, literature, architecture, music, and philosophy in the "West" as effects of centuries of multidirectional, multidimensional planetary interactions across the Global South(s) and North(s), a genealogy occluded in the East-West binary (Hunke 1997).

Another approach that informs *co-productions* herein is decolonial theory. A central feminist theorist here is María Lugones. She brings Kimberlé Crenshaw's intersectionality into conversation with Aníbal Quijano's "coloniality of power" to propose the "coloniality of gender" (Lugones 2020, 2008). For Lugones, intersectionality helpfully makes invisibilized subjects visible but also problematically proposes a limited "logic of categorical separation" (2008). This reading of intersectionality seems to only consider *nonlinear* ("categorical") *separability* analytics. Lugones rightly remarks that—at the time of her writing—intersectionality does not inherently include a critique of coloniality.

Lugones comments that for Quijano, race and gender are organized through two large structural axes of power through which he theorizes "global, eurocentered capitalist power"; the "coloniality of power"; and modernity. The "coloniality of power," or simply "coloniality," includes colonialism and its continuing effects by some same and other means—e.g., economic, cultural, institutional, etc.—after political independence. Quijano defines gender/sex in terms of "sexual access, its resources and products" (Lugones 2008). For Lugones, Quijano helpfully theorizes gender/sex as inseparable from other relations of power. But unfortunately he also reduces sex to a biological (not social) category, imagines gender through it, and reiterates a Eurocentric feminist notion of gender that erases precolonial gender and (post)colonized gendered subjects.

In contrast, in Lugones's view in the "colonial/modern gender system" gender/sex has a "light side" that pertains to sexual bimorphism and colonizing women, and a "dark side" that is about colonial impositions of gender and sexuality, and (post)colonized women (2008). For Lugones, Quijano's "coloniality of power" exclusively addresses the "light side." To elaborate the "dark side" Lugones draws on feminist scholarship that demonstrates how colonialism invents gender or freezes, destroys, or reorders precolonial gender relations and imposes the Eurocentic gender/sex binary and queerphobia.

Co-formations and *co-productions* are indebted to Lugones's attempt to theorize the co-constitution of gender and sex with coloniality and modernity with differential consequences for colonizer and colonized women. Yet, these two concepts depart from Lugones, too. While the notion of system in the "colonial gender/sex system" aligns it with structuralism, *co-formations* and *co-productions* are poststructuralist. Lugones's idea of "light" vs. "dark" calls to mind the colonizer vs. colonized binary, thereby risking excluding from analysis some kinds and dimensions of power and subjects. Instead, *co-formations* and *co-productions* foreground a range of subalterneities and consider dynamic multiplicities and continuums of power and subjects. For example, in India the conditions of Dalit, Bahujan, Adivasi, Muslim, Christian, and upper-caste Hindu women and queers—all on the "dark side" of the colonial binary—are vastly disparate (Rege 1998; Bacchetta 1996; Omvedt 1993; Ballhatchet 1980). The same is true in France for variably subalternized subjects: Black African, Black Caribbean, Arab, Muslim, white working class, Jewish, etc. Importantly, Lugones calls for more detailed studies of the "dark side." Thus, to consider "dark" (and "light") through *co-formations* and *co-productions* (and the *subaltern-to-dominant continuum*) can respectfully extend Lugones's very valuable work. As mentioned in the introduction to this book, however, to push (with Lugones) beyond the universalization of patriarchy, to consider multiple gender and sexuality formations, and yet further to extend beyond binarism, to consider broad assemblages, crystallizations, and structurations of gender and sexuality in their specific kinds of (co-constitutive and other) relationality with all other relations of power, to account for their *operability* across all registers (social, psychic, economic, cultural, spiritual, institutional, political), I think with the broad rubric *misogynarchies* (a concept I explain in some detail in chapter 4). It is a *co-production* with many disparate manifestations at the scale of *co-formations*.

Co-Formations, Co-Productions Together

At first encounter it may seem that the relation between *co-formations* and *co-productions* is micro to macro. However, those terms are often imagined as distinct, self-contained categories. Instead, I think about the relation between *co-formations* and *co-productions* as akin to the Deleuzian-Guattarian conception of molecular to molar (Deleuze and Guattari 1972, 1980). Like the molecular to molar relation, *co-formations* are co-constituents of *co-productions*, and vice versa. But *co-formations* are also components of yet other *co-formations*, and *co-productions* are parts of yet other *co-productions*. Both *co-formations* and *co-productions* are multiplicities. They are dynamic, constantly in co-constitution. They are without essences, transcendent principles, fixed shapes, or properties. To consider their capacities together, several other concept-terms are useful: *scattered hegemonies, distributions of dilution*, and *(im)perceptibilities*.

Scattered Hegemonies

Scattered hegemonies can help us understand localized concentrations and dilutions of power across the planet. I draw *scattered hegemonies* from the 1994 volume *Scattered Hegemonies*, coedited by Inderpal Grewal and Caren Kaplan. They do not provide a precise definition as this is not their book's objective. Yet, this much is clear: Grewal and Kaplan usefully extend Gramscian hegemony to conceptualize the world not in terms of *linear* or *nonlinear* configurations but rather as a distribution of disparate "hot spots" of power (see also Grewal and Kaplan 2002).

Building on their insights, I think about *scattered hegemonies* in terms of sites of intense concentrations of *co-formations, co-productions,* and hegemonic temporal-spatialities across the planet. *Scattered hegemonies* involve convergences and accumulations, flows and blockages, across many strata. They include those suggested by Arjun Appadurai (1984)—"financescape," "technoscape," "ideoscape," "ethnoscape," and "mediascape"—along with many possible others such as a(n) *(in)securityscape, warscape,* and *theological-politicalscape* (Eriksen 2018; Amar 2013; Maldonaro-Torres 2008). *Scattered hegemonies* produce their own spatialities: transnational clusters, regionalisms, nation-states, cities, gated neighborhoods, slums, bodies, corpses. They construct some subjects as subjects, others as objects, and yet Others as nonexistent.

Scattered hegemonies implicate distributions of power at different intensities and densities, across what I call a *concentration-dispersion continuum.* To consider the *co-productions* colonialism, coloniality, capitalism, slavery, *misogynarchies,* and speciesism across the planet through *scattered hegemonies* and the *concentration-dispersion continuum* is to bring into relief an array of geographical points. Some hegemonies and dilutions of power are not attached to spatialities but instead accrue to subjects. For example, globally women do 66 percent of the world's work, receive only 11 percent of its income, own only 1 percent of its land, and comprise 66 percent of illiterate adults. Of course, the category "women" is complex and fragmented by other relations of power across the *subaltern-to-dominant continuum*: colonialism, coloniality, capitalism, imperialism, racism, *misogynarchies,* speciesism, etc. "Women" has its own *co-formational* and *co-productional* concentrations and dilutions of power that produce many disparities within and beyond these statistics.

Imperceptibilities

Another dimension of *co-formations* and *co-productions* is that they include some highly operative *imperceptibilities* of power. By *imperceptibilities* I mean invisibilities, blind spots, erasures, effacements, nonapparitions, unnoticeabilities, shadowed content. Generally relative dominants can remain oblivious to relations of power that for subalterns loom large every day (Alcoff 2024). For example, most non-Indigenous people in the United States don't perceive that they are on stolen Indigenous land (Tuck and Yang 2012). They often imagine Indigenous people to have disappeared (Wolfe 2006). In France, most dominant subjects have little understanding of the murderous violence of colonialism but instead imbibe the state's claims that colonialism is beneficial to the colonized (see chapter 5). In both examples, not only colonialism but also many aspects of the whole array of relations of power that co-constitute colonialism (capitalism, imperialism, racism, *misogynarchies*, speciesism) and their many effects slip under the radar.

The different undetectable co-constituents have variable kinds of (in)accessibility, reasons for nonapparition, intensities, and effects. To understand them, some additional concepts are helpful: *etcétera*, *x*, *articulationinarticulation continuum*, and *political amnesias*.

ETCÉTERA AND X

The *etcétera* theorized by Borges (see chapter 2), when reconsidered in relation to power, can highlight that some *known* and *unknown-knowable* relations, dimensions, and registers of power are not named in an analysis. *Unknown-knowable* elements, as represented by the *etcétera*, are contextual *absent-presences*, exterior to an analysis but that can eventually enter. For instance, speciesism is an *unknown-knowable* in dominant French feminist analytics. It is absent from nearly all related activisms, artivisms, and movements, and yet is *knowable* as it does exist in feminist analytics elsewhere.

In contrast, to account for power that is beyond human perception in current fields of intelligibility, I propose the concept-term *x*. This is not Rey Chow's important "x" that I discussed in chapter 2. Instead, this *x* represents *unknown-unknowable* relations, dimensions, and registers of power. It designates *unknown-unknowable absent-absences* that keep an analysis forever incomplete. This *x* marks an intuition that some relations of power are concealed everywhere, yet may be intensely active (Deleuze and Guattari 1980). They may be in a currently unrecognizable dimensionality in any *co-present temporal-spatiality*.

Like the *etcétera*, also discussed in chapter 2, the *x*, too, in analytics of power is not the habitual *etc.* that appears in some multiplicities theorizations following a list, as in "gender, sexualities, racism, etc." Scholars use this latter *etc.* for disparate reasons. It can be a placeholder for relations of power that are *known* but excluded from the analytic, whether to avoid unhelpfully complicating it or compromising depth for breadth, or to remind us that all analytics of power are incomplete. Some scholars problematize *etc.* as a superfluous addendum that invokes the existence of additional relations of power without taking them seriously. Some liken *etc.* to a meaningless laundry list. Whatever that *etc.*'s function, *etcétera* and *x* differ radically from it.

Etcétera and *x* can be clarified through two notions that Michel Pêcheux and Catherine Fuchs formulate with respect to Freud's first topology:

"Forgetting 2" and "Forgetting 1" (Pêcheux and Fuchs 1975; Pêcheux 1975, 159). Forgetting 2, somewhat like *etcetera*, concerns absent content that can be recalled with effort. It is associated with Freud's consciousness and preconsciousness. Forgetting 1, like *x*, is about what the subject cannot ever remember. It is attached to Freud's unconsciousness and associated with content excluded from the preconscious-conscious via unconscious repression.

Following Borges's advice for his *etcétera*, in a list of relations of power *etcétera* and *x* should be placed among other terms instead of at the end (Borges 1965). This signals that the status of disparate kinds of relations of power outside the analysis—that *etcétera* and *x* differentially represent—is equal to that of whatever is named. In sum, *etcétera* and *x* do much more than briefly remind us that something is included, excluded, or intrinsically forever absent.

ARTICULATION-INARTICULATION CONTINUUM

The *articulation-inarticulation continuum* refers to degrees to which in any field of intelligibility disparately formed subjects are able to *sense* and make sense of some relations of power (that are *articulated*) but not others (*inarticulated*). Where other concepts of articulation presume that all power is knowable, the *articulation-inarticulation continuum* that I suggest here presupposes that only some power is knowable. The *articulation-inarticulation continuum* has a direct relation to *etcétera* and *x*. An *etcétera* can eventually become articulated, while an *x* is too far beyond perceptibility to ever be articulated.

Articulation and *inarticulation* are generally paired. Some known relations of power can seem fully *articulated* even when they are only partially so. An ethical vegan who, recognizing animal abuse, prefers plastic shoes over leather ones may not think about how plastic destroys the ocean, marine life, and other *beings-becomings*. Here, veganism as an enactment against one part of the *species-murder-industrial-complex* might bolster an (as yet *inarticulated*) other part.

Articulations and *inarticulations* can be unplanned or by design. One unplanned form is *reproductive articulation-inarticulation*. Here, an *articulation-inarticulation* from an earlier temporal-spatiality takes hold in the *co-present* and is reinforced as a co-constituent in a new temporal-spatiality. For instance, colonial, racist, speciesist discourses that liken colonized people to animals presently *operate* to produce indifference toward massive refugee drownings in the Mediterranean (Hawthorne 2022).

There is also *generated articulation-inarticulation*. Therein a previously acknowledged relation of power becomes undetectable for many audiences as *co-formations* and *co-productions* reassemble in a new dominant temporal-spatiality. An example is when, during the age of homonationalism, some US laws for queer rights got deployed as what, elsewhere, I call *reductive evidence*, or the selective identification, magnification, generalization, and extension of any item to stand in for, and in fact to collapse and substitute for, a heterogeneity (Bacchetta 2020; 2025d). Here queer rights laws were mobilized as *reductive evidence* to imagine the United States as a postqueerphobic society even as its daily deadly queerphobic violence lived on. Today, with the second Trump election, we are in a different, post-homonationalist phase that we have yet to fully understand.

Another form of *articulation-inarticulation* is *disarticulation*. In *disarticulation*, a fraction of a more complex *articulation* or *inarticulation* surfaces distortedly, keeping important aspects of power hidden. An example is the February 23, 2005, French law (no. 2005–158) on teaching colonialism in French state schools (see also chapter 5). Its article 4 stipulates that instruction about French colonialism must "acknowledge and recognize . . . the positive role of the French presence abroad, especially in North Africa." French decolonial activists and allies denounced it as colonial. Some (mainly white) French historians opposed it as censorship. The historian protest predominated. Here *disarticulation* involved invisibilizing colonialism to articulate what is dominantly understood as unacceptable: censorship.

There is also *inadvertent ex-inarticulation*. It is an effect of a mistake, a slipup, a fissure. It can reveal a world of power. An example is former French President Nicolas Sarkozy's exposure of the gap between dominant French "raceless" universalism and republicanism during the Mohammed Merah affair. Merah, aged twenty-three, a French-born citizen of Maghrebian Muslim origin, murdered four racialized people and four white Jews in March 2012, ostensibly as retribution for war in Afghanistan and Iraq and France's support of Israel. Merah was assassinated in a shootout with police. Subsequent psychiatric reports officially categorized him as insane.[3] Journalists highlighted that Merah was raised after September 11, 2001, by a single mother in a banlieue of Toulouse with an unemployment rate at 30 percent, in a national context of anti-Muslim rhetoric.

The right strategically mobilized Merah as *reductive evidence* to blame all Maghrebian Muslims for all violence in France. In a radio interview on March 26, 2012, President Sarkozy dismissed that interpretation, stating that two of Merah's victims, French soldiers, were "Muslims, at least in appearance, because one was Catholic, but in appearance, as they say, visible diversity" (Tasvuhein 2012). A public controversy ensued. The connection of "appearance" to "race" assailed France's dominant national particularist universalism according to which morphological "race" categories are nonexistent. The positing of Catholic as normative and Muslim as "visible diversity" defies French notions of France as *laic* (secular). Colette Guillaumin critiques these dominant presumptions in her classic article "*Le Racisme avec ou sans race*" (Racism with or without race) (1972).

Sarkozy's phrase "Muslims in appearance" soon became the object of jokes beyond the Merah affair. The humor they provoked relied on disrupting the dominant French willful unseeing and unspeaking of race, the French state's longstanding public suppression of the signifier race, a national *calculated inarticulation* of race, and its spontaneous presidential transformation into an *inadvertent ex-inarticulation* of race that, inadvertently, in effect actually produced a *rearticulation* of race. Here race functions as a prior *etcétera* that was historically deleted, but not an *x*.

Indeed, Sarkozy's blundering *rearticulation* of morphological race disrobes the state's "integration" discourse that attributes responsibility for racialized people's conditions to their supposed personal failings instead of to conditions of power including practices of "discrimination" (Mazouz 2017). Yet, surveys (such as by the state's *Observatoire des Discriminations* [Observatory of discriminations]) indicate that racialized embodiment, non-Franco-French names and banlieue residence negatively influence hiring, firing, and housing and educational access. Here, to understand racism as a *co-formation* would disclose the present *operability* of racism's genealogical and convergent strands such as colonialism, slavery, historical scientific race constructions, and present continued colonial spatial practices.

The *articulation-inarticulation continuum* is also useful to understand the *co-formation* of disparate subjects and *beings-becomings*. Depending on the field of intelligibility, some are made perceptible, others imperceptible. In a hegemonic field of intelligibility, generally dominant subjects are more visible. However, parts of that subject, too, will be disappeared (see below).

POLITICAL AMNESIAS

One of many functions of *inarticulations* is to create, maintain, and represent states of *political amnesia*. They can be thought through anesthesias, a notion derived from the Greek *αν-* (*an-*, "without") and from *αἴσθησις* (*aisthēsis*, "sensation"). Anesthesia signifies a situation of total loss or incremental decrease of all or part of a subject's mental, emotional, and corporeal awareness. Anasthesia is about amnesia (from the Greek Ἀμνησία) and analgesia (derived from Greek *αναλγησία*, combining *an-*, "without," and *algos-*, "pain") that are induced or activated by certain conditions and that are potentially reversible and/or transformable.

Several postcolonial and decolonial theorists have done useful work on related phenomenon. An example is the cluster around aphasia, meaning "without speech" in ancient Greek. For Ann Laura Stoler, French historiography is aphasic, defined as a "political disorder" characterized by many "tiny, fragmented regions" that are "unconnected islets" (2011). In a different usage of the term, Assia Djebar identifies her mother as aphasic and develops anamnesis to resist speechlessness for herself as daughter via biographical writing based in memory (1999). In turn, Jodi A. Byrd proposes to understand agnosia, or the loss of ability to process sensory information, as a manifestation of colonial aporia, or puzzlement, in which dominant (US white settler) subjects are unable to understand settler colonialism (2011). Manu Vimalassery, Juliana Hu Pegues, and Alyosha Goldstein suggest colonial agnosia as "a social construction, formed and informed through racialized and gendered normativities" (2016; Grech and Soldatic 2015). Omi Salas-SantaCruz proposes the notion of "colonial dysphoria" to consider the specific kinds of distress and alienation that colonial discourses about binary gender and trans of color people produce in the lives of trans of color subjects, which are relevant to the discussion here (2025; 2023). For Salas-SantaCruz, to analyze these discourses and their effects on trans of color subjects requires, among other things, deconstructing and displacing the now universalized colonial-racial dominant Global Northern model for the subject and subject formation, to make room for other ways of thinking (2025; 2023). Tasha Williams (2018) lends insights into how racist police murders of Black individuals reverberate as trauma throughout Black communities.

Such reflections, drawing on medical, analytical, and lived phenomena, provide insights for considering subject-effects of political, psychic, and corporeal violence across the *subaltern-to-dominant continuum*. However, some disability scholars point out that by identifying all neurological differences as political effects they risk invisibilizing people with the actual physical disability (Vimalassery et. al. 2016). This critique helpfully urges us to be cautious about how we use medical terms. While colonialism and racism definitely produce manifold psychic and corporeal damaging effects (mental confusion, stress related physical disease, etc.), the problem is when colonial destruction is shifted to metaphorization that then takes over lived experiences.

Yet, some clinical amnesia categories may in fact help us think about concrete effects of political events and relations of power. They include post-traumatic amnesia (induced by a traumatic event such as genocide); lacunar amnesia (about one specific event, idea, or sentiment at a time, such as a colonial rape or a massacre); dissociative amnesia (as in fugue state and repressed memory state, as when a population is forced to forget its language and learn the colonizer's language); developmental amnesia (occurring in unfoldings of time albeit usually referring to childhood, as in forgetting earlier anticolonial rebellions); memory distrust syndrome (the subject lacks faith in her/his/ their memory, as when one's history has been erased and rewritten by the dominant); blackout phenomena (total loss of memory for a period, as when a population loses intergenerational transmission of its culture); transient global amnesia (which is full but temporary, as when a population forgets it was ever anything but colonized); source amnesia (recall of information but not its source, as when stereotypes and controlling images become "common sense"); and again, the extreme distress of colonial dysphoria (Salas-SantaCruz 2025). All of these are effects of brutally violent colonial discursive and materialized procedures and are extremely damaging to those subjected to them.

Another helpful concept-term is analgesia, signifying being without pain. It can be considered a state of suppressed affect, sentiment, ways of knowing, and knowledge with potential to reemerge. This is not an "opium of the people" frame or a "repressive hypothesis" analytic (Foucault 1976). Instead, (political) analgesia is about how states of (political) painlessness (ἀναλγησία) are constituted and how states of (political) heightened awareness are weakened or annulled.

Subjects who are co-constituted with *political amnesias* can be continually lured by their context into states of subjectivity in sync with hegemonic relations of power. The *inarticulations* that these processes entail have differential intensities of suppression of sensation, memory, and pain. They can cause fractures in the subject, culture, and history (Donaday 1999). Subjects have varied capacities and blockages for sensing *inarticulations* and for waking from anesthesia, amnesia, and analgesia. Across the *subaltern-to-dominant continuum*, subjects risk reproducing, with varying degrees of indifference to enthusiasm, the very relations of power that entrap them. Accordingly, the cartoon in figure 3.1 spectacularizes how in the United States dominant-subalterns (white working-class people) vote against their own interests and for the interests of the (white) wealthy (Metzl 2019). Indeed, here they adamantly reproduce one contextual *co-formational*

3.1 Cartoon, working-class white people articulating views against their own interests (Mitchell 2020).

strand (white supremacy) in ways that reinforce yet another co-constituent (class), resulting in extremely detrimental effects on vital aspects of life (health care, labor conditions, clean food, water, air, and more).

Correspondingly, in the 2016 elections in the United States, 56 percent of white women voters supported Trump, who openly sexually harasses women. In 2024, that number dropped to 45 percent, still remarkably high since by that time Trump had actually been convicted of sexual abuse. These supporters acted on the dominant discourse that holds people of color, especially immigrants from Mexico—instead of capitalism, uneven wealth distribution, and of course sexism—responsible for all ills. Their *political amnesia* masked their own relative subalterneity in relation to the *co-productions* capitalism and *misogynarchies*, and the *co-formations* class and gender. This *political amnesia* depends on a *monofocal* notion of race, class, and gender. Kimberlé Crenshaw rightly described the 2016 election of Trump as an "intersectional failure" (2020). For me, additionally, it is a situation wherein *political amnesia* conceals what *co-productions* and *co-formations* aim to reveal: that white subaltern collusion with racism boomerangs as it amplifies white subaltern class and gender subordination.

Several theorists have worked meaningfully on post-amnesic recovery. For Lionnet, anamemnis is an anticolonial device to resist colonial-induced amnesia (1989). Marianne Hirsch invokes "postmemory" to consider how the "generation after" deals with "personal, collective and cultural trauma" (2012). These works provide valuable insights about grappling with confusing information and affective overload, forgetting, and repression. Infinitely more research in these areas would be fruitful. There are many kinds of *political amnesias* and they may require disparate political solutions for de-alienation.

Concluding Remarks

This chapter proposed some points of departure for rethinking complexities of relations of power and their *operability* at different scales. The next chapter continues the work of opening lines of flight with attention to precise analytical approaches and procedures that consider power *in-context* from the small to the planetary scale.

To continue in the direction of our prior reflections, this chapter proposes the notion of *situated planetarities* as a sensibility, a theoretical disposition, and an approach to analyses, creative inventing, and enactments regarding power, subjects, and *co-motion*. *Situated planetarities* reminds us that wherever we are, we are at the same time part of the entire earth. It is a way to think with *co-formations*, *co-productions*, and related concepts from within one's specific small-scale context—not in isolation but instead in connection with the whole world. Keeping in mind the molecular to molar relationality of *co-formations* and *co-productions* (explained in chapter 3), *situated planetarities* signals that in whatever smaller place we are located, planetary relations of power are *co-present* there and vice versa. *Situated planetarities* is about *sensing, perception*, and, with this awareness, rendering *intelligible* power—its multiplicities, its dimensions and agencies, its densities and intensities, and its *operabilities*.

Situated planetarities is an effect of a dynamic encounter, not a fixed cementing, between the adjective situated and the noun planetarities. It totally disrupts, deconstructs, and takes leave of the local vs. global binary. Situated and planetarities are theoretically and in praxis elsewhere. To conjoin them is to produce a third term that resignifies each component part and the whole. *Situated planetarities* aims to put into relief that placing flagrant, invisibilized, and imperceptible power and vibrant, dynamic, extremely subaltern *subjects-in-sociality and another* at the center of our concerns is a necessary precondition for inventing effective *freedom-exigent co-motion*.

In what follows, I address *situated*, then *planetarities*, and then the conjoined concept *situated planetarities* and the work it can do for our analytics and practices.

Situated

Situated, specifically as I mobilize it in *situated planetarities*, differs from many other ways of thinking about situated. For instance, the *situated* in *situated planetarities* is not about an essentialist rootedness or fixity within a social structure, configuration, or assemblage (e.g., via family, race, ethnicity, community, nation, region, etc.). Instead, this *situated* can encompass contextual caughtness, dynamic movement, and/or escape at once wherever we are at a relatively small human or geopolitical scale. *Situated* in *situated planetarities* can entail any of the above mentioned spaces, or even a city, a street, a village, a neighborhood, an event in any of those sites, a human body. *Situated* is relational. It is about a small scale in a dynamic constellation or assemblage of scalar relationalities. The point is this: As Kabir suggests in a quote at the beginning of this book's introduction, in the chaos of the world there are many entry points and wherever one is located can be such a point. Any small-scale temporal-spatial context is a possible site of departure for rethinking power, subjects, and *freedom exigent co-motion in-context* with concerns for the *freedom-life* of the entire planet.

In *situated planetarities*, *situated* has several other genealogical strands and dimensions, each emerging in distinct literatures and practices. One of the meanings of *situated* herein is akin to the Deleuzian-Guattarian notion of "rhizome," or the horizontal expanse that they oppose to the hegemonic, vertical idea of "roots" that by definition entails hierarchy (Deleuze and Guattari 1980). Deleuze and Guattari remark that the tree with its roots and branches is a symbol for much dominant thought that is caught in and contributes to stabilizing internal classificatory rankings: biology, zoology, psychoanalysis, etc. For them, instead, "rhizome" brings us away from notions of origin, cause and effect, and the perpetual fixity of power. "Rhizome" glides us into the realm of *operabilities*. Deleuze and Guattari write this about "rhizome": "It is not made of units, but of dimensions or rather of moving directions. There is no beginning or end, but always a middle or environment (*milieu*) through which it grows and overflows. It constitutes multiplicities" (1980, 31). Similarly, we can understand the *situated* in *situated planetarities* not in reference to eternally fixed units or points but rather in connection with specific environments that relations of power variably create and saturate—with different densities and intensities—at many scales. Each such context consists of a multitude of *co-present temporal-spatialities*, dimensions, registers, thicknesses, thinnesses, speeds, and (im)mobilities. They co-constitute, inundate and animate a spectrum of *subjects-in-socialities and another* across the *subaltern-to-dominant continuum*.

There are many ways of understanding the extent, expanse, depth, and concentrations or dilutions of power within and across the scales that the idea of *situated* in *situated planetarities* implies. Some of its elements are materialized in worldviews whose very existence moves against the grain of hegemonic ones. An instance of disconnect between dominant and subaltern notions of the space or site of *situated* in *situated planetarities* can be found in the Pacific Islands. Through a dominant Global Northern lens informed by coloniality (with its "primitive" vs. "advanced" humans binary), capitalism (relations of property, reification, instrumentalization, commodification), imperialism (appropriation, extractivism), and geopolitical perspective (about habitation, relations to the environment), the Pacific Islands are small and thus insignificant landmasses. However, historically Pacific Islanders understand their living space as a vast, vibrant entity encompassing the entire Pacific Ocean, the sky, the islands, and all the sentient and nonsentient inhabitants therein (Niumeitolu 2019, 2015; Hau'ofa 1993). It spans one-third of the globe. This is not about a simple disagreement on size and measurements. It is about disparate epistemic fields. The dominant relies on the notion of abstract space that always already is evaluated in the normative terms that the dominant articulates. Pacific Islanders are inside a different epistemic realm, with its own distinct understanding of space. To comprehend disparate epistemic fields and their dissimilar categories (here, living space) requires context-sensitive *subalternative sensing, perception*, and *intelligibility*.

Elsewhere across the world, notions of situated that help to elucidate *situated planetarity* appear in various subaltern, and sometimes in contextually dominant, critiques of the presumed naturalness of the so-called natural world. They mutually undo ideas about stable materiality and fixity. Indeed, situated can be in deep flux. An example of situated in a subaltern critique is alive in many Indigenous philosophical systems in Abya Yala that consider earthly life as a divine creation wherein spirit takes provisional forms and will return to a nonform state—that is, to the underlying permanent state of spirit being. An example of situated in a relatively dominant discourse is the upper-caste Hindu notion of maya in India. Therein, maya signifies that the material world that seems permanent and concrete—land, bodies, trees, etc.—is impermanent, illusory. Here the concept of *subaltern-to-dominant continuum* helps us to understand how *situated* operates in relation to contextuality. In India upper-caste Hindus are highly privileged in relation to people from subaltern castes and religions. However, at the planetary scale the power of upper-caste Hindus can be modified by Global Northern imperialism and racism.

An important dimension of *situated* can be found in early Global Northern critical scholarship that directly interrogates the contextual hegemonic presumption of scientific neutrality. A historical precursor is Giambattista Vico's *Scienza nuova* (1725), a text that postcolonial theorist Edward Said (1978) cites repeatedly in his *Orientalism*, most notably while tracing Vico's influence on twentieth-century scholarship out of Germany. Vico established the foundations of the sociology of knowledge in the Global North by highlighting how knowledge is historically and socially constructed. Remarkably, Vico and many subsequent relatively dominant yet critical Global Northern authors who write about how society, subjects, and ways of seeing are social constructs—Marx in *The German Ideology*, Karl Mannheim, Émile Durkheim, Marcel Mauss, Peter L. Berger, Thomas Luckmann, and more—still presuppose the "natural world" as a given. Foucault leads us away from this idea in discussions not about nature but rather about the human body. During the same period as Foucault, both Monique Wittig and Colette Guillaumin most radically deconstruct what Guillaumin calls "the idea of nature" for lesbian, women's, racialized, and even dominant human bodies (Wittig 1992; Guillaumin 1978a, 1978b).

Some dimensions of *situated*, though not the term itself, are also historically theorized in feminist, lesbian, trans, gay, and other queer of color feminisms that highlight the inseparability and simultaneity of a plurality of relations of power (colonialism, capitalism, imperialism, racism, *misogynarchies*, speciesism) and the struggles of subalternized subjects who are located at their nexus. In the United States this insight is inscribed in 1970s and 1980s publications: *The Combahee River Statement* (1974–1980); the many writings by Dyketactics! published in feminist, lesbian, and queer newspapers (1974–1977); the anthologies *This Bridge Called My Back* (Moraga and Anzaldúa 1981) and *Home Girls: A Black Feminist Anthology* (Smith 1983); and more. Some individual authors, too, elaborate it. Gloria Anzaldúa proposes *auto-historía* (one's own history) against the grain of hegemonic historiographies, and *testimonio* (witnessing) as both a singular and collective potentiality (Anzaldúa [1987] 2007). This work often directly moves against neoliberal individualism when, as Patricia Hill Collins points out, it specifically references historically shared kinds of experiences and not a neoliberal conception of additive individual ones (1991). Donna Haraway, drawing inspiration from women of color feminism, exposes the nonneutrality of dominant scientific discourse and proposes feminist partiality through embodied vision (1988). Haraway's reflections join those of Jeanne Favret-Saada in France who argues that "the conditions for objectivity are subjectivity" (1985).

A certain register of *situated* appears broadly elsewhere, too, in many guises to account for different sites of subaltern enunciation in relation to power. Postcolonial theorist Gyanendra Pandey invokes the "fragment" to signal multiple subalternly positioned narratives within an ensemble (1992; see also chapter 5). Queer anthropologist Kath Weston speaks of "street theory" produced in venues outside acceptable academic genres, such as lesbian activist discourse that critiques dominant discourses and/or provides alternatives (1991).

Some other aspects of *situated* in *situated planetarities* are theorized and practiced in critical analytics of colonialism and coloniality, in postcolonial and decolonial theory, and in epistemologies of the Global South(s). In a version of Southern epistemologies that preexists the theoretical tendency's naming, the early 1980s situated analytics of sociologists from Delhi School of Economics and associated with the journal *Contributions to Indian Sociology*—Veena Das, Asis Nandy, Jit Uberoi, etc.—took apart established Global Northern theories and concepts, exposed their nonneutrality, demonstrated their limits for understanding Indian realities, and proposed other concepts to do so. This kind of critique and creativity is also found elsewhere in the Global South(s), such as in the work of Lélia Gonzalez or Silvia Rivera Cusicanqui in Abya Yala. Yet, as Ramón Grosfoguel points out, what passes for knowledge globally (i.e., dominant knowledge) remains the particularist creation of only 6 percent of the world's population—that is, white men from the Global North(s) (2013). Unfortunately, many kinds of hegemonic critical theory from the Global North(s), too, are similarly characterized by self-universalized dominant particularisms and exclusions.

Currently, there is an increasing dominant audience for situated decolonial, anticapitalist feminist, and queer of color analytics from subaltern speaking subjects transnationally from within their smaller scale environments (Bakshi et al. 2020). While the dominant openness to some sets of othered voices can produce interesting effects, there are also risks and dangers. They include tokenism and essentialization, wherein specific kinds of subaltern speaking subjects are made to represent entire entities (e.g., communities, nations, regions) that did not elect them to do so. Moreover, subaltern enunciations when heard through dominant epistemes can get reordered and resignified in distortionary ways and subsequently mobilized in dominant productions of ignorant certainties.

Whatever the case, if we were to reduce the *situated* of *situated planetarities* to just a locus of enunciation, many problems would arise. We might end up in bulldozing circumstances for the *and another* who is yet unhearable in the entity of speaking subaltern subjects. For example, an enunciation-dependent definition of situated would both include and exclude what in chapter 2 I called the Spivakian *subaltern-in-extremis* defined in terms of "nonspeakingness." Articulations by one set of subjects *in-context* can render others *in-context* inaudible (Mohammed 2022). It is generally the most privileged—among subalterns or not—who are hearable inside the dominant episteme. Further, to imagine situated only as a site of enunciation is violently human-centric for it discounts nonhuman *beings-becomings* who/that have no inclination to express themselves or who "speak" in ways that are not intelligible to humans. If this kind of situated manages to encompass nonhuman *beings-becomings* at all, it still amounts to imposing the human-centric criteria of subject-of-enunciation on them.

Instead, the *situated* in *situated planetarities* must be able to consider subjects, *beings-becomings*, and relationalities far beyond the human and enunciation realms. It may ask: How and what does a peacock perceive? What are the modes of communication among leopards, between leopards and birds? How and what does an elephant feel? What tree sensibilities do we not imagine? How does a buffalo make sense of her world? What fields of affect belong to the sea? What are the agencies and capacities of our dead, of spirits, ghosts, ancestors, future progenitors? In what dimensions do they manifest or not? How does power operate to guide answers to these questions in ways that keep humans as the central referent? How does power induce human awareness or numbness to power's own saturations *in-context, in-scales*, its apparent and *imperceptible* manifestations, its evident and indiscernible *operabilities* on itself and on all subjects, *beings-becomings*, and *co-motion*?

Planetarities

The notion of *planetarities* in *situated planetarities* is a way of reimagining the entire earth and the *operabilities* of power that co-constitute, traverse, and saturate it. *Planetarities* is about an expansive scale that includes myriad other scales, dimensions, registers, intensities, densities.

My main point of departure for thinking about *planetarities* is the work of the Sri Lankan philosopher and theologian Tissa Balasurya. He writes as a highly educated person inside the context of a subalternalized Christian minority of a Sri Lanka whose official religion is Buddhism and whose national life was dominated by Tamils and Buddhists at war from 1983 to 2009. Christian presence in Sri Lanka dates from AD 52. Christians make up only 7.4 percent of the population. My path to Balasurya was first opened by Gayatri Spivak's (2003) very thoughtful, albeit brief, discussion of his work. Balasurya contributed "planetarity" (in the singular) to critique current imaginings of global power. He wished to propose a "systemic analysis at the level of the whole planet earth, together with historical dimensioning" so as "to understand how particular sectors and events in the world relate to each other" (1984, 17). For him, the unfolding of any event or action is shaped by forces both near and far, with planned and unforeseen reverberations in proximity and across distance.

Balasurya's notions of interconnections, scales, and multiple agencies and capacities are vital to how I think about *planetarities* in *situated planetarities*. Balasurya's (1984) "planetarity," however, becomes for me *planetarities* (in the plural) to highlight many *co-present* worlds, scales, dimensions, registers, temporal-spatialities, *subjects-in-sociality and another*, and fields of intelligibility within and across what he calls "the whole planet earth" (Balasurya 1984). *Planetarities* announces earth itself as a living plurality, a *being-becoming* in motion.

Planetarities differs from other concepts of the earth as an enormous scale that abound at present. For the purposes of clarity here I will distinguish *planetarities* from related concepts that are currently in extensive use: global, transnational, international, translocal, and transversal.

Global

Today, global is a hegemonic category that stands for the world scale. It is used on the right and left, within the Global North(s) and parts of the South(s). Global belongs primarily to the vocabulary of governments, international institutions, economists, social scientists, humanists, and university projects around global studies, but also to projects for counterglobalization and alter-globalization studies, activisms, and artivisms (Eriksen 2018). In discussions about power and the world, global is primarily linked to the idea of capitalist globalization.

A strong point of consensus across many constituencies is that globalization constitutes a postinternational moment wherein capitalism is not merely expanded across national borders (as in internationalism) but is functionally integrated across them (Dicken 2000, 316). The traditional center right imagines capitalist globalization as useful to "develop" the world. The extreme right thinks of it often in overtly xenophobic terms primarily in function of the national scale. The left understands capitalist globalization as an extension of economic exploitation and neoliberal values. A third heterogeneous cluster—comprising Indigenous peoples, other colonized and postcolonial subjects, and allies—emphasizes capitalist globalization's damaging effects to life, the lifeworld, and epistemes. These different broad groups disagree, often fruitfully, on what globalization entails, when it appeared, and what it does.

Currently, scholars disparately identify three large-scale heterogeneous periods as the genealogy of globalization: the twentieth century, the third millennium BC, or over five hundred years ago. According to the position that dominates in the Global North(s), globalization began in the twentieth century. Here, scholars claim that globalization—and the spread of the term itself—began in the 1940s when they assume that US economic and military power was at its (first) height. Others date globalization slightly later, in the 1960s, when Marshall McLuhan proposed the idea of the global village to describe effects of new communications technologies on human life (Dicken 2000, 315). For yet others, globalization commenced in the 1970s when governments, international institutions, critical activists, and others began to recognize the worldwide integration of capitalism. For a second group of scholars, economic globalization has been a feature of human societies for millennium. It far preexists capitalist expansion. The third set of scholars locate globalization's beginning over five hundred years ago, specifically with colonialism. Across the three stances, many agree that globalization is manifested today in flows and blockages in (global) registers, including the established ones cited in chapter 3—Arjun Appadurai's financescape, technoscape, ideoscape, ethnoscape, and mediascape—and possible others such as the (in)securityscape, warscape, and theological-politicalscape (Appadurai 1984; Eriksen 2018; Maldonado-Torres 2008; Amar 2013).

The disparate analytics rather consistently, albeit variously, elaborate global and globalization in relation to capitalism. An important *subalternist* perspective is the African American scholar Cedric Robinson's insight on global capitalism as racial capitalism (Nowak 2024; Kelley 2017; Robinson [1983] 1999). For most Marxists, capitalism constitutes a break with the past. Robinson demonstrates that instead it evolved out of European feudal society. Therein European subalternized subjects were racialized and internally colonized: Roma, southern Italians, Jews, Slavs, the Irish. Violent practices of appropriation, extractivism, and commodification are always already racial. For Robinson, the first proletariat, however, was not in England but instead on the colonial plantation. To think with Robinson's contributions is to understand oppression, repression, exploitation, occupation, dispossession, extraction, appropriation, subjugation, subjectivation, epistemic violence, spiritual obliteration, psychic suffering, incarceration, inequity, and annihilation as part of a long continuum. All current racist practices carry the intensity of accumulations of the forms of violence that precede them—earlier phases of colonial genocide, racial slavery, what I call *segregationality* (see below), etc. (Sithole 2020; Kelley 2017; Leong 2013).

In India, Dalit intellectuals, artivists, activists, and their allies have proposed particularly insightful critiques of global capitalism and especially of its place in the consolidation of racialized caste and class power (Maitland 2019; Omvedt 2016; Teltumbde 2011). For instance, the Dalit Sahitya Akademi has created important analytics for over four decades even if they have been ignored outside Dalit intellectual circles. There are also critiques by radical queers of color and allies. For example, Rahul Rao proposes the notion of "homocapitalism" to put into relief an operational yet quasi-invisibilized arrangement of power that entails the absorption of homonormative cisgender lesbian and gay subjects into homotransnationist agendas while "murderously excluding" and devastating the rest (Rao 2015; Haritaworn et al. 2013; Bacchetta and Haritaworn 2011; Puar 2007; Duggan 2003). Native scholars, activists, and allies have long assessed how settler-colonial capitalism appropriates, privatizes, and destroys the environment, and the complexity of Native relations to that process (Mihesuah and Hoover 2019; TallBear 2017; Coulthard 2010; Andersen 2009). Salar Mameni (2023) offers an important decolonial, anticapitalist perspective of the idea of the global and how in dominant Eurocentric scientific imaginings it implies the reduction of earth to functionality. Dominant scholarship and social movements against global capitalism rarely incorporate anything about subaltern critiques. Yet, articulated subaltern critiques are only the tip of the forgotten iceberg. What of those subaltern critiques that are inaccessible to outside audiences? And further, beyond the human, how is global colonial-racial capitalism perceived, experienced, endured, and combatted or not by sentient and nonsentient nonhuman *beings-becomings*?

Some geographers across the political spectrum consider global as an accurate way to describe how processes of time-space compression—or the annihilation of space by time under capitalism—requires refocusing analysis on the entire world and de-emphasizing smaller scales such as region, nation, or community (Eriksen 2018; Harvey 1989). In contrast, Lucia Tomassini and Elena Cavagnaro (2020), who studied scale in the COVID-19 crisis, draw on the classical work of the feminist geographer Doreen Massey (1991) to affirm that de-emphasizing the local can problematically presume that place—or small-scale settings in which social relations are formed, enacted, and felt—does not matter anymore, even as we are currently seeing that it looms large. For me, to reflect on this ensemble of scholarship is to see problems in privileging one scale over another wherever located across the spectrum from enormous to infinitely small. The either/or approach risks concealing relations of power both inside and outside the analyst's view. As discussed in chapter 3, hidden power is very often, as Foucault would have it, most dangerous. Relatedly, epistemic limitations or the dismissal of whatever is beyond dominant perception—or even simply outside dominant categories—threatens to obscure the most subaltern subjects, *beings-becomings*, and *co-present temporal-spatialities* within and elsewhere from the perceiver's view.

Another drawback to global is what global presupposes about the planet's space and spatial segmentations. The idea of global corresponds primarily to the category of space that I briefly invoked in chapters 2 and 3: abstract or Euclidean space, space as a fixed, stagnant, lifeless, timeless object in a binary relation to human agency. Abstract space presumes space as nature within a nature vs. culture binary. Therein the earth is an inert mass just waiting to be invaded, conquered, occupied, possessed, mapped, managed, partitioned, parceled, appropriated, commodified, exploited, and ultimately depleted. For J. K. Gibson-Graham, abstract space metaphorically enacts a (heterosexual) rape script in which an immobile earth-body is available for nonreciprocal and unwanted penetration (2002). Luce Irigaray reminds us that the (Global Northern) heterosexist, misogynist gender binary entails collating women-nature-space-passivity and placing these in opposition to men-culture-time-activity, an arrangement made to legitimize women's totalized subjugation in the name of sexual difference (1974, 1977). In sum, abstract space underlies a range of terrifying discourses and practices: colonialism, capitalism, racism, imperialism, and in relation to the body sexism, lesbophobia, transphobia, homophobia, and other queerphobias.

In fact, many critical cultural geographers mark three basic approaches to space of which abstract space is only one. They define abstract space as an essentialist conception of space as a given, an empty grid of points, a docile ground on which subjects and objects exist and events occur (Smith 1984). A second conception, relative space, a structuralist notion, posits that space is not completely passive but rather exists in a dynamic, interactive relation to subjects and the social realm. Yet, both abstract space and relative space ultimately rely on the problematic notion of space as ground. In a third and different conception proposed by Henri Lefebvre, a Marxist precursor to poststructuralism, space or spatiality is a production in relations of power. Lefebvre emphasizes class relations, the rural-urban divide, culture, and the symbolic in the production of space (1974). Doreen Massey extends Lefebvre to think about spatiality as a turbulent field, a "power geometry" that is formed and transformed through gendered practices and performances (Massey 1999, 1994, 1993). Giancarlo Iazzolino (2020), in a study of a Kenyan refugee camp for Somalis, extends Massey's work to highlight how power is reproduced and even amplified through daily spatial practices.

In brief, while global relies on abstract space, the idea of *planetarities* in *situated planetarities* is inspired primarily by Native notions of the earth as a living *being-becoming*, and by Lefebvre's and Massey's concepts of the production of space in relations of power. With *co-formations* and *co-productions* (see chapter 3) in mind, *planetarities* can unveil what global invisibilizes: that all scales are simultaneously co-constituted in, saturated with, and productive of relations of power such as colonialism, capitalism, imperialism, racism, *misogynarchies*, and speciesism.

Moreover, everything that informs the reified notion of global (abstract space, the passive vs. active binary, etc.) is also *operative* in the category local when local is constructed and arranged in a global vs. local binary. In dominant discourses, the local is represented as a small-scale bit of abstract space with limited horizons. In relation to the global, the local is assigned backwardness, particularism, weakness, manipulability, but also unruliness requiring management and control. The local becomes that which is available for colonization, "development," and insertion into (the underside of) global capitalism. In recent years, agency at the so-called local scale has become difficult to ignore and thus has been reframed in dominant discourses not as a quality of local dynamics but rather as effects of the global on the local.

Currently concepts such as glocal try to account for how local sites make the global their own. The idea of glocal thereby attributes some agency to the local, albeit still dependent on interaction with the global. Glocal first appeared in Japanese commerce when *dochakuka*—or the localization of the global—was used to describe how dominant agricultural techniques adapt to local conditions. Scholars subsequently brought this idea into German and later it entered English as glocal. Today, critical cultural geographers use glocal differently. They push against the procapitalist agenda by imagining the local as small-scale spatial formations that are subjected to trans-scalar flows and blockages but that moreover also contribute to them.

In contrast to global and glocal, *situated planetarities* considers spatialities (in the plural) as inseparable from temporalities (in the plural) in an ongoing process of co-constitution. *Situated planetarities* is concerned with the many kinds of *co-present temporal-spatialities* that co-construct, invest, and saturate all scales. *Situated planetarities* recognizes *co-present temporal-spatialities* as effects and as co-components that make, sustain, and dissolve different contexts at many scales across the planet. Here, the pluralization of spatiality and temporality and their attachment together is not simply additive. Instead, *spatialities* in *co-present temporal-spatialities* flags a plethora of kinds of spatial formations that come into existence inseparably with temporalities, with and by multiplicities of relations of power across scales.

This reconception of the planetary scale in relation to *co-formations, co-productions*, and *co-present temporal-spatialities* induces us to rethink some related familiar terms. An example is segregation. It is generally defined as a racial and class division of space-with-subjects into separated dominant and subaltern segments. But if we rethink segregation through *planetarities*, it opens us to consider racial and class segmentation more broadly. We can reimagine this separation, subdivision and compartmentalization as *segregationality*, defined as multiple effects of historical-contextual processes of uneven partitioning that implicate but exceed spatial, economic, material, physical, psychic, and energetic-spiritual dimensions (Bacchetta 2016; see also chapter 5). *Segregationality*, if thought through US empirics, entails ongoing *co-present* effects of murderous colonial-racial-sexual violence, including genocide, slavery, Jim Crow, economic exploitation, targeted slaughter, incapacitation, incarceration, etc. *Segregationality* helps clarify why, as suggested in chapter 2, the idea of precarity falls short of describing the entire lethal configuration of relations of power that characterize the conditions of subalternized subjects.

Another issue with global is its reduction of space in some quarters to materiality, to its economic dimension and to the present. Jacques Derrida remarks that global invokes the globe as a ball without history or memory (2002). In fact, such contraction and presentism are typical of abstract space. Derrida argues that global is more popular today because of the hegemonic status of the English language. Instead of global and globalization, he prefers the French terms *mondial* (worldly) and *mondialisation* (world-ization) because they include history, the social dimension, and relations of power (2002). For Derrida, both global and *mondial* belong to a Christian European field of intelligibility. Yet, he suggests, *mondial* is "autoimmune" insofar as it has the potential to interrupt its own Eurocentricity, to contest Europe from within, and to open up sites of unforeseeability, or what he calls "events" (2002; see also chapter 5). Like *mondial*, *situated planetarities* resists economic reductionism. But *situated planetarities* also urges us to refuse human-centricity. It asks us to recognize and respect all forms of life. It does not primarily move oppositionally against the Eurocentric field of intelligibility but instead invites us to exit those confines. It hopes to reorient our imaginings altogether (and all together).

Global, problematically, has a totalizing, homogenizing tendency. It calls to mind the earth as a broad container of enormous-scale formations that extend everywhere, and/or it evokes neutrality or abstraction from relations of power. Global affirms a positivistic and empiricist model of the world (Grewal 2005, 21–22; Duggan 2003, 11; Spivak 2003, 72–73). An example of global's problematic totalism is how, when attached to patriarchy as in the notion of global patriarchy, it gets mobilized to identify and explain all sexism everywhere. Yet the idea of global patriarchy is very limited. It does not necessarily acknowledge lesbophobia, transphobia, homophobia, and other queerphobias. M. Jacqui Alexander and Chandra Talpade Mohanty highlight how "the" global patriarchy is presumed to be transhistorical and transgeographical, as is the corresponding idea of global sisterhood. Global patriarchy and global sisterhood "assign Third World women the burden of difference in the name of inclusivity" (1997, viii-xx). The notion of global patriarchy erases histories, contexts, and relations of colonialism, capitalism, imperialism, racism, speciesism, and the many different ways that sexism, lesbophobia, transphobia, homophobia, and other queerphobias are configured, systematized, structured, or assembled inseparably with other relations of power. It presupposes dominant Global

Northern norms as a valid standard for measuring sexism and feminist and queer liberation everywhere.

To think about gender and sexuality through the notion of global risks closing off our capacity to recognize contextual constructions whose *operabilities* are far from stable in time and space (Lugones 2020). To judge a subaltern society's ideas, manifestations, and practices of gender and sexuality by the dominant's hegemonic standards is an imperialist gesture in continuity with the colonial imposition of gender and sexual norms. It is unsurprising then that the idea of global patriarchy ignores many conditions of the most subaltern women and queers everywhere. It erases histories of colonialism, enslavement, human trafficking, dehumanization, and imperialism in which not only dominant men but also dominant women are actors. It cannot account for the racist ungendering of enslaved women and men (Spiller et al. 2007; Spiller 1987). It overlooks gender and sexual violence that is forced on different subalternized collectivities across the *subaltern-to-dominant continuum* via colonialism and capitalism. It says nothing about the colonial imposition of colonial gender, reconfigurations of kinship structures, the criminalization and pathologization of queered genders and sexualities, or the sexual objectification and consumption of racialized bodies and their "murderous inclusion" as permanently othered and marginalized (Bacchetta 2020, 2016; Haritaworn et al. 2013; Lugones 2008; Stoler 2002; Oyěwùmí 1997).

The idea of global patriarchy can invisibilize highly *operative* singular and combined systems, structures, *dispositifs*, and assemblages of sexism, queerphobia, and transphobia to which in any context the most subaltern women and other subalternly gendered people are subjected. Everywhere it has the capacity to efface lesbians, trans, nonbinary and intersex people, gay men, and other queers. In India, Dalit feminists have avoided global patriarchy's erasures by proposing the concept of "Brahminical patriarchy" to speak to their conditions (Dhanaraj 2018). Some Palestinian queers simply circumvent global patriarchy when they highlight the centrality of occupation, apartheid, and genocide—each with its own mobilization of colonial sexism and queerphobia—along with the necessity of "weaving" queer into the struggle for decolonization (Alqaisiya 2022). In Black feminist theorizations in France—such as by Maboula Soumahoro (2022, 2020), Rokhaya Diallo (2014), or Mame-Fatou Niang (Niang and Nielsen 2016)—not global patriarchy but instead the notion of "misogynoir" enables analytics of the structural sexism and queerphobia to which Black women and Black queers are subjected. In my prior work I found that Hindu nationalists in India conceptualize themselves as sons of the soil, thus a symbolic filiarchy, but also as brothers, thus as *fraternarchy* (Bacchetta 2019a, 1996). Disparately situated sexisms, queerphobias, transphobias—even when still called patriarchy—have long been theorized in Indigenous and Black feminist and queer scholarship and activism (Cabnal 2010; Collins 1991; Davis 1981). Moreover, global patriarchy does not account for differential assemblages of colonial and colonized misogynist systems together. It says nothing about the specifics of sexism, queerphobia, and transphobia in various gendered social relations such as matriliny, matrifocality, patriliny, patrifocality, or combinations thereof. Nor can global patriarchy encompass as yet unnamed compositions of misogynist power beyond what is currently recognizable as such. Indeed, global patriarchy, with its forms of reduction, totalization, and homogenization, risks obscuring every other kind of system, structure, dispositive, and assemblage of misogyny in the Global North(s) and South(s) that does not conform to its contours.

Norma Alarcón points out that global, when attached to feminisms, reductively (re)presents the most dominant subaltern subject (here US white, cisgender, straight women) as the universal subject of emancipation theorizings (Bacchetta 2018; Alarcón 1990). Inderpal Grewal and Caren Kaplan refer to this imposition as "a kind of western imperialism" (2002, 17). Similarly, with the notion of global, the normative subject of queer becomes a white cisgender Global Northern gay male, a model against which all—North and South—are measured (Bacchetta 2018; Bacchetta and Haritaworn 2011).

With Alarcón in mind, we might also wonder whether, in democracies across the Global North(s) and South(s), patriarchy is entirely accurate. While many feminists imagine Global Northern democracies as patriarchal, none are ruled by a king or other paternal figure. In fact, democracy is historically conceptualized as a *fraternarchy* wherein the ruling class of men are in a position of brother to each other. In that sense, Europe's transition from monarchy to democracy marks a transmutation from predominantly (white) patriarchal to (white) fraternarchal political power. In the Global Northern democratic nation model, the highest political offices are, historically and presently, primarily occupied by (white) cisgender heterosexual men together, thus a collectivity of brothers or *fraternarchy*. Indeed, at a time when only 4 percent were women members, prior to the gendered power-sharing policy called *parité*, the Moroccan feminist scholar and writer Fatema Mernissi called the French National Assembly a harem of men (Mernissi 2003; Ait Ben Lmadani 2025). In relation to this model, Britain with its monarchy might be said to have a mixed *patriarchal-fraternarchal* assemblage.

In the Global North(s) when global patriarchy is mobilized to consider the kinship register, here too it unhelpfully upholds the Global Northern white middle-class heteronormative family as the norm. It does not necessarily consider the kinds of *alter-familial* forms that we saw in chapter 1. With growing numbers of single people in dominant social sectors (by "choice" and/or divorce) in the Global North(s), white heterosexual middle-class women may now be conceptualized through a sexist, queerphobic lens as less the private property of individual white heterosexual patriarchs and more the public property of the collectivity of fraternarchs. For the Global South(s), the idea of global patriarchy obfuscates the colonial imposition of colonial kinship models in colonized spaces, the disruption of Indigenous kinship, the creative reconfiguration of kinship by colonized and enslaved peoples, and many kinds of colonial sexual violence that target subalternized women and queers.

My point here is this: It is neither accurate nor useful to reduce all gendered and sexed configurations of power across the planet to global patriarchy. It is imprecise. It universalizes dominant particularist *colonialism-and-race-amnesic*, monofocal feminisms and erases everyone and everything else (Abdulhadi et al. 2021). Far from uniting, the idea of global patriarchy obscures or dismisses many relations of sexist, queerphobic and transphobic power thereby enabling their intensification and expansion. Global patriarchy cannot take into account the many different kinds of relationalities and subjects that exist. To impose global patriarchy as a global standard eliminates a *co-formational, co-productional* understanding of how gender, sexuality, sexism, queerphobia and transphobia *operate* inseparably with the entire array of other relations of power. Global patriarchy also conceals resistance that is elsewhere from direct oppositionality to the presupposed standard.

For the above reasons, as an alternative I prefer to think in terms of *misogynarchies* (in the plural), a notion I briefly invoked in the introduction and chapter 3 (see also Bacchetta 2025c). *Misogynarchies* is a broad umbrella term that can include an infinite number of situated, distinct kinds of systems, structures, *dispositifs*, and assemblages of sexism, queerphobia, transphobia, and other misogynist configurations that are *co-formative* and *operative* inseparably, disparately, with other relations of power (colonialism, racism, capitalism, imperialism) at different scales instead of collapsing them into one (e.g., into global patriarchy). *Misogynarchies*, a large, extensive overall rubric, opens our perception to any kind of *misogynarchic* system, structure, *dispositif*, or assemblage. It works to keep present not only women but all subalternly gendered and sexed people, including those who as yet have no name or who in their contexts simply do not need to be named. To think with *misogynarchies* is to deuniversalize, decentralize, and parochialize patriarchy, to open a space to consider many other kinds of formations and assemblages.

Yet, *misogynarchies* does not aim to erase patriarchy or any other local notions of how multiple distinct sexisms, queerphobias, and transphobias operate. Instead it includes them all. *Misogynarchies* can also encompass variabilities inside each *co-formational* rubric. An example is what Rita Segato (2015) categorizes as either "low intensity" or "high intensity" patriarchy (see also Segato and Monque 2021). If we think through *misogynarchies* with Segato about the societies that she arranges under the two variants of patriarchy, we can open our perception beyond patriarchy. We might then retain Segato's very useful insights about "low" and "high" intensity sexist systematizations but, further, additionally consider how Indigenous and colonial gender and sexuality might be differently organized from the start, and then reflect upon the impact of the latter on the former. To think with *misogynarchies* is to open the possibility that Indigenous society may be organized around gender and sexuality axes that do not line up with patriarchy, that may better be described under a different name altogether. It is to consider the possibility that, in any particular case, even if we end up identifying both systems as patriarchy, the imposition of colonial patriarchy, gender, and sexuality onto a colonized society may result in more than an increase in the specific Indigenous patriarchy's intensity. It in fact might produce a *co-present* third distinct sexist, queerphobic, transphobic kind of system altogether.

In sum, *misogynarchies* has many possible theoretical uses and implications for praxis. It can help to identify specificities of sexist, queerphobic, and transphobic systematizations in any given site, so as to oppose and transform them. It can aid in creating solidarities without requiring equivalence. It can recognize distinct relations of power within and across sites in the hope of avoiding reproducing them. It can take a detailed account of a whole array of differential conditions of both dominant and subaltern *subjects-in-sociality and another.*

Transnational

A next related concept is transnational. It too has many constituencies. Transnational appears on the right as transnationalism-from-above in pro-capitalist agendas to mark a shift from the multinational corporation, which is administratively and commercially headquartered in one nation-state with operations in others, to the so-called transnational corporation, which is decentered with its administration and operations spread across several nation-states (Lionnet and Shih 2005). Besides spatial variations, a major difference is that transnational corporations employ postcolonial bilingual elites at relatively high levels in their administration (Anderson 1994).

Relatedly, many scholars point to the historical development of multinationals in colonialism. Companies based in the colonizing Global North(s) expanded by extracting natural resources, redirecting the colonized economy and transport systems, creating a working class to exploit, and eventually imposing a colonial market. A pertinent example is the British East India Company. Today, anticorporate researchers, activists, and artivists highlight that transnational corporations continue the harm of multinationals through some same and some different means. They establish themselves in colonized or postcolonial nation-states where they can appropriate natural resources and manipulate workers with relatively little hindrance from protective laws (Gómez-Barris 2017). In the United States, corporations now have the legal status of persons with all the rights therein endowed (and more insofar as they do not have human limitations such as death) in a country and world where so many persons are dispossessed. Joel Bakan argues that if corporations were human persons they could be classified as psychopaths who exhibit antisocial personality disorder (2005). Unfortunately, this formulation can, of course, be read as insensitive to human disability. However, Bakan's observation that corporations normatively exploit people, threaten their safety, commit murder, refuse to pay damages, and disrespect the law, for profit and without guilt, is accurate. Anticorporate actors propose various solutions such as greater state regulation within capitalism, or socialism, or the total displacement of corporate entities and the creation of small-scale economies everywhere.

In contrast, the term *transnational* in its feminist and queer incarnations is often used differently, to signify transnationalism-from-below (Lionnet and Shih 2005). It speaks to planetary interconnectivities and to feminist and queer solidarities beyond the reiteration of power that global feminism and international feminism imply. Transnational feminist and queer theory has a lively genealogy in postcolonial, decolonial, and feminist and queer of color theories (Bakshi et al. 2020). It brings to analysis multiplicities of power—colonialism, capitalism, imperialism, racism, *misogynarchies*, speciesism. Inderpal Grewal, Caren Kaplan, M. Jacqui Alexander, and Chandra Mohanty argue that while international relies on the idea of the nation-state, transnational seeks to undermine it (Grewal and Kaplan 2002, 2001; Alexander and Mohanty 1997). Indeed, many insights from transnational feminist and queer theory inform the idea of *situated planetarities*.

A main limitation of transnational, which it shares with international (see below), is that it always references the nation and eventually the nation-state even if only oppositionally. Yet, the nation is an intraplanetary political-social category grounded in abstract space and requiring processes of othering. The nation form connotes a normative, bounded, homogenized unit (a space, a sociality) in opposition to other such entities. The entire world has been divided into nations and regions by colonialism. In chapter 1, I discussed how the dominant nation-idea is a large-scale version of the heteronormative Global Northern nuclear family. The nation-idea also resonates with a smaller scale that I mentioned in chapter 2: the normative Global Northern conception of the subject, exemplified in the figure of the white, cisgender male individual who is imagined as bounded, internally coherent, separated from other subjects. This is not to say that all nationalisms actively choose to reproduce this model. Under murderous conditions of colonialism, anticolonial nationalism is often the only viable tactic for survival.

International

Yet another major related geopolitical category today is international. It looms large in the language of governments, international organizations, and international nongovernmental organizations. In the Global North(s), international has the merit of considering life beyond the belly buttons of neoliberal individualist dominant subjects.

However, a difficulty with international is that it reproduces the nation-state and *national-normativity* as the privileged framework across our *planet-in-coloniality*. In the context of international as lens, only subjects who are intelligible as proper citizen-subjects within national norms are recognized as subjects. Like all the above categories the most subaltern subjects in any nation are constructed in terms of lack or erased. A category that cannot account for Dalits, Bahujans, or Adivasis in India or Native peoples in any settler colony has very limited use for *freedom-exigency*. International suggests a world carved into nation-states, each with borders, a unique history, memory, and culture, its own "imagined community," and whose interests are different from and/or oppositional to those of other nation-states (Anderson 1994). In procapitalist interventionist agendas, international allows for sites whose economies, cultures, languages, and theologies are disarticulated as an effect of colonialism, to be arranged along a colonial-racialized developmental continuum (i.e., underdeveloped, developing, developed) with the Global North(s) as the apex, a model that parallels and resembles the colonial-racial division of humanity (Sithole 2020; Wynter 2003; Bhavnani et al. 2003; Shanin 1997). International risks problematically situating colonized sites—as "backward," "primitive," "underdeveloped," or "developing"—in the past of the Global North(s)' present (Ramirez et al. 2023; Fabian 1983).

Translocal

The concept of translocal has interesting possibilities but also limitations. When imagined with the planetary scale, translocal can fruitfully bring into relief analogous and disparate conditions and subjects across countries or regions. It can highlight commonalities among different subalterns such as Adivasis in India and Native peoples in the United States. When thought in intranational terms, translocal can make perceptible scattered resistance such as revolts in individual prisons across the United States and/or the world.

Unfortunately, translocal problematically depends on the notion of a global-local binary. This binary tends to line up with the West vs. the Rest. Rarely are hot sites of power, such as the United States or Western Europe, or even major cities therein, imagined as local. When such powerful places are framed as potentially local, as in calls to "provincialize Europe," they are unfortunately often presumed in homogenous terms without racialized subaltern intellectuals or even any subaltern populations (Chakrabarty [2000] 2008). Because translocal centers on only one scale—the local—and on horizontal connections thought through trans, it risks erasing other scales and their interlinkages.

Transversal

Another possibility is transversal, a concept I briefly addressed in chapter 1. Transversal is mobilized in Italian feminism and in some left movements in France, but it is much less known in the English-speaking world. Transversal is a specifically sociospatial concept that brings into relief lines and points of contact among similar or disparate entities across any human or geographical scale, thereby resolving one of translocal's problems. The Italian feminist usage of transversal is based on Félix Guattari's social and geopolitical thinking wherein the term aims to generate "new universes of reference" and "breaks in habits and conditioned uses of space and place" to create "new possibilities of life" (Kanngieser 2019, 283, 269; Deleuze and Guattari 1980; Guattari 1977, 1972). For Deleuze and Guattari, transversal describes how any number of like or unlike entities can become connected and in doing so produce radical subjects and new conditions of alliances (Deleuze and Guattari 1980; Guattari 1972, 1977; Yuval-Davis 1998). Their main concern is not successes or failures of political action but rather the novel knowledge and relations that links open up. When thought in relation to the qualities that Deleuze and Guattari assign it, transversal is in many ways commensurate with and helpful to *planetarities*. It prevents *planetarities'* simplistic reduction to everything-everywhere, a too-muchness, an unproductive all-over-the-placeness. Their idea of transversal helps describe how connections can happen across vast differences.

However, transversal also has limitations. Notably, at present transversal is used to recognize only human subjects, leaving all other sentient and nonsentient *beings-becomings* under erasure. It does, however, productively relate to a part of the many dimensions, registers, and *operabilities* that *situated planetarities* aims to open up.

Planetarities in Situated Planetarities

Unlike prior concepts, *planetarities* in *situated planetarities* understood in its geopolitical dimension invites us to perceive the planet as a living entity with its own genealogies, *co-presences* and futurities, manifold dimensions, registers, scales, *co-present temporal-spatialities*, and subjects and *beings-becomings* across the *dominant-to-subaltern continuum*. *Planetarities* emphasizes interconnectedness across geopolitical scales and sites. It encourages *freedom-exigent co-motion* across radical differences.

This way of thinking about *planetarities* is informed by multiple strands. Many Indigenous peoples have long conceptualized the planet as a living *being-becoming*, often specifically as a respected elder: grandmother or mother (Kim 2016). Gloria Anzaldúa helpfully imagines the planet as a human, ecological and spiritual-energetic space that includes many scales (2009b, 312). She hopes we will not think "in terms of 'my' country or 'your' nation' but rather 'our' planet" (Alarcón, forthcoming). She advises that we imagine all other humans as "*vecinos* (neighbors) whether they live across the street, across national borders, or across oceans" (Anzaldúa

2009b, 312). For *planetarities*, all *beings-becomings* are included as *subjects-in-socialities and another*.

Spivak's usage of planetary, too, is immanently fruitful for thinking *planetarities*. She suggests "planet-thought" to understand "the earth" as "paranational" thereby resolving the problem of the nation form posed in transnational and international (2003, 95). She considers this approach productively utopian for it does not reference a defined topos or ground. Planetary is associated with an "(im)possibility" that is simultaneously within and out of reach (72). Spivak, of course, is not referring to a view from nowhere—that is, a dominantly located view with universalist pretentions. Instead, she is invoking an exit from it altogether. Kwok Pui-Lan observes that Spivak's planetary when combined with love insists on connections between sentient and nonsentient beings (Moore and Rivera 2011; Gnanadason 2010). For my concept of *situated planetarities*, however, love is not necessarily a solution. If love is made the criterion for recognition or mattering it can constitute a stumbling block to the total *freedom-exigency* of all who/that exist(s). Many humans, animals, insects, plants, and substances are not so readily lovable by humans. What of poisonous snakes? Angry wasps that attack? Ground that forms sinkholes? The sea in its tsunami state-of-being? For *planetarities*, whether we like them or not they are included, not eliminated. With *planetarities* we need to shift how we understand them.

Planetarities expressly has no limits as to who or what constitutes a subject or *being-becoming* that should receive full consideration as a subject. Agencies and capacities belong not only to humans and other sentient and nonsentient *beings-becomings* that at present can be known as such. They equally belong to *beings-becomings* that are yet to be recognized and named as subjects—the air, the spirits of future cats or long disintegrated flowers—and subjects and *beings-becomings* who/that are not yet imagined at all. *Planetarities* is always in the plural to acknowledge an infinity of coinhabitants, of relatives, across a multitude of *co-present temporal-spatialities* across the planet.

Situated Planetarities

To think with *situated planetarities* is to reconsider the place of power in how we understand *co-present temporal-spatialities*, subjects, relationalities, and epistemic openings.

Co-Present Temporal-Spatialities, Power, Subjects

An important aspect of the conjoined third term *situated planetarities* that is not generally found in other imaginings of situated or of the worldwide scale is *co-present temporal-spatialities*. From the tiniest to the most expansive, *co-present temporal-spatialities* are scattered across all dimensions of existence at varying intensities at any moment anywhere. Here I will engage primarily with just two registers of *co-present temporal-spatialities*: power and subjects.

A key point of departure for thinking about power and subjects with *co-present temporal-spatialities* is Foucault's notion of heterotopia (*hétérotopie*), which he first presented in 1967 in Paris. Interestingly, he wrote the text while living in Tunisia, which was newly independent from France (since 1956) and a site where he spoke only the ex-colonial language and not the peoples' Arabic or Amazigh languages. While Foucault does not reference this geopolitical displacement, if we read his text with this understanding in mind, we might sense something of how he might have intuited and felt the violent, fragmenting effects that the French colonial imposition and erasures induced, especially in Tunisia but also eventually in France. For us, a most important aspect of heterotopia is its juxtaposition "in a single real place of several spaces, several sites that are in themselves incompatible" (2004, 12). In the text Foucault writes that the present moment is an "epoch of simultaneity," "of juxtaposition," "of the near and far, of the side-by-side, of the dispersed" (12). Heterotopia incites us to consider how distinct spaces inhabit a common *co-present* and how the experience of time can shift historically.

Yet, heterotopia, notwithstanding Foucault's extreme antiessentialism elsewhere, is unfortunately consistent with the idea of relative space (see chapter 2). To mobilize heterotopia with *situated planetarities* is to reimagine heterotopia through notions of space as a production. Moreover, while heterotopia focuses primarily on space, *situated planetarities* concerns *co-present temporalities* and *spatialities* inseparably.

Let us consider the *co-present temporal-spatialities* of coloniality that the notion of *situated planetarities* allows to unfold. Colonialism, a genealogical component of coloniality, can be understood via a *longue durée* spread across the globe for over five hundred years. It unfolds in many disparate *co-present temporal-spatialities*. It has many different manifestations: settler, administrative, military, commercial, internal, external, etc. It has an array of actors: national governments (Britain, France, Spain, Portugal, Italy, Germany, etc.), commercial entities, missionaries, academics, artists, travelers (Bacchetta 2023; 2025a). Colonialism entails a plethora of practices: genocide, massacre, theft of lands, enslavement, torture, maiming, epistemicide, psychic violence, spiritual annihilation, eradication of the colonized's history and language, the imposition of cultural, juridical, and administrative systems, etc. In each colonial context the colonizing entity thrusts its *hegemonic temporal-spatiality* on the colonized whose own temporal-spatialities remain *co-present* even if in newly subalternized forms. Ultimately, each *co-present temporal-spatiality* is its own world. Each has distinct zones of intensities, densities, speeds, and fields of intelligibility. The presence of each strand within a given assemblage of *co-present temporal-spatialities* is evident for some, hidden for others. Each temporal-spatiality has forms of light that produce specific luminosities and shadows (Deleuze 1986, 60). The perceptible and imperceptible in *co-present temporal-spatialities* act on conditions and subjects in myriad ways. Derrida proposes "ghost logic" to account for whatever is unseen and nevertheless hovers and haunts (1993).

In any context of power, generally one dominant temporal-spatiality is hegemonic while others are subjugated. In colonialism, the colonizer's temporal-spatiality is hegemonic while the temporal-spatialities of the colonized are subjugated. In general (not always), the hegemonic temporal-spatiality is hypervisible and the subjugated ones are shadowed to imperceptible. A hegemonic temporal-spatiality will seem to structure all of life, to be exclusive and eternal. Yet, it is always co-constituted and coexistent with many other *co-present temporal-spatialities* that it dominates. This means that subjects and *beings-becomings* across the *subaltern-to-dominant continuum* within a same context do not necessarily live in a fully same temporal-spatiality. They may live in different *co-present temporal-spatialities* within a same moment.

The disparately situated subjects across the *subaltern-to-dominant continuum* within a same site are co-constituted in and in relation to the same *co-present temporal-spatialities* but differently so and with disparate consequences. This point can be illustrated through the relation between (temporal) velocity and (spatial) location and mobility. In Delhi, India, as in most major urban centers on the planet, the lives of people of different classes unfold inside a same hegemonic temporal-spatiality yet therein at different paces in disparate smaller-scale spaces. In Delhi the wealthy live in one place, the poor in another even if in the case of *bastis* (suburban slums) they are often directly side by side. They have dissimilar inorganic and organic prostheses to enable speed and movement, thus disparate degrees of space-time compression. The upper middle classes might employ a live-in personal driver for their (imported) SUVs and other luxury cars. The middle classes might have a full- or part-time driver for their (Indian-made) cars. The lower middle classes use bicycles, rickshaws, and buses, and walk. The making-ends-meet poor take buses and walk; in an emergency, they might take a rickshaw. The very poor walk; in an emergency they might take a bus. These distinct assemblages of subjects and transport have unequal degrees of protection from sun, rain, wind, extreme heat, bitter cold, overexertion, road accidents, police harassment, and other people with less than honorable intentions. This situation is a cumulative effect of ongoing assemblages of power and of subject co-constitution itself.

For *situated planetarities*, an aspect of *co-present temporal-spatialities* is that they tend to produce relative coherency, or states of *being-in-sync* and *being-in-place*, with the hegemonic temporal-spatiality in dominant subjects and states of estrangement in subalterns. Subaltern alienation in time and space has quite a thick history of theorization. W. E. B. Du Bois accounts for it with the concept of "Black double consciousness" (1994). Frantz Fanon highlights the colonized's internal splitting and reiterations of the colonizer's value system (1952). Gloria Anzaldúa posits a fractured subject in the borderlands/*la frontera* who becomes conscious of *la facultad* (faculty, ability, capacity) of "perceiving doubly" ([1987] 2007). Ralph Ellison says this about a US Black male who comes to know and name the effects of what, for me, is a racialized temporal-spatial disjuncture: "Invisibility, let me explain, gives one a slightly different sense of time, you're never quite on the beat. Sometimes you're ahead and sometimes behind. Instead of the swift and imperceptible flowing of time, you're aware of its nodes, those points where time stands still or from where it leaps ahead" ([1947] 1980, 8). Here, Ellison identifies a certain vertigo, a leaning within a different temporal-spatiality, in Black subjective disconnection from the dominant setting. Albert Memmi highlights the doubled psychic conflict of subgroups among colonizers who disidentify with colonization (1973). J. Jack Halberstam underscores a divide between queer times and places, and normative reproductive and hetero-familial time-space (2005). José Esteban Muñoz names a queer futurity in a present that cannot include nonnormativity (2009). Lisa Lowe and David Floyd highlight alternative temporalities in relation to dominant Global Northern narratives of progress (1997). For me, in all these cases the subaltern's near-awareness of *out-of-sync-ness* and *out-of-place-ness* reveals a world of *co-present temporal-spatialities*.

Another important feature of subject co-constitution inside *co-present temporal-spatialities* is how the dominant agentically situates the subaltern in time and space. For Irigaray, in Eurocentric discourse "man" associates himself with time and becoming and equates "woman" with space, nature, and stasis. She remarks that "a change of epoch . . . requires a change in the perception and conception of space-time" (1984, 15). Johannes Fabian demonstrates how dominant subjects envision themselves in the present and imagine their Others in the past (1983, 143–44). They erase their own self-referentiality to represent their Others in colonial-racialized terms as perpetually backward, stagnant, traditional, and underdeveloped. Fabian's insights help explain what goes on in colonial progress and savior narratives. He proposes that the dominant learn to meet the Other "on the same ground, in the same Time" (165). The idea of multiple differential and unequal temporal-spatialities abounds in much subalternist and *subaltern-complicit* work even when the concept-term *co-present temporal-spatialities* itself does not appear. Nearly all of postcolonial and decolonial theorizing usefully highlights the coexistence of past and present. Some feminist and queer of color theorizations point to the present's coexistence in possible futurity (Sithole 2020; Muñoz 2009).

Perhaps one can measure the force of relations of power, and thus the intensity of subaltern construction and suppression, according to degrees of subaltern erasure in a hegemonic temporal-spatiality. In the United States, the dominant *national-normative temporal-spatiality* relies on *colonialism-class-race-caste-misogynarchic amnesia*. It represents, legitimizes, and glorifies settler colonial subjects by forgetting genocide and the historical and ongoing theft of Native land. The US nation's rituals and festivities celebrate erasure and substitution. Thanksgiving Day operates to rewrite violent colonialism and occupation as consensus. Veterans Day functions to glorify the US military apparatus and induce both docile and active patriotism. It effaces the internal class and race politics of "recruitment" and the lethal anti-other use to which mainly subaltern enlisted bodies are put in war. An annual White House Christmas tree lighting ceremony reinforces white Anglo-Saxon Protestant Christianity as the unavowed *national-normative* religion while masking its hegemony to keep the myth of US secularism and multiculturalism intact. Mother's Day and Father's Day bolster the institution of the heteronormative nuclear family and heterosexual cisgender reproduction, while capitalist consumption as affect is attached to purchases of gifts and cards. In this scene of heteronormative familiality, queers are exiled or "murderously included" (Haritaworn et al. 2014). Each moment of *national-normative* chronological time is narrowed to hide the subaltern *co-present temporal-spatialities* that form its underside.

The *co-present temporal-spatialities* with potential to displace, disperse, reverse, marginalize, or otherwise dethrone the dominant's central status are the most vehemently repressed, negated, or erased. To disclose them becomes an act of resistance. The poster in figure 4.1, circulated on Global Northern anglophone social media, becomes a potential insurgency-inciting object precisely because it juxtaposes an ongoing present that the dominant keeps under erasure. The poster invokes past and present in *co-presence*. It exposes a temporal-spatiality (1492) that the hegemonic temporal-spatiality has *whited-out* and written over. It makes clear that this history is *co-present*. The poster's uncloseting of *suppressed co-present temporal-spatialities* makes a mockery of the US state's notion of "homeland," "security," "terrorism," and "borders." It induces a pause in the ongoing (genocidal) erasure of Native lives. It reminds the viewer of whose homeland "the homeland" is, whose "security" has long been at stake, who has performed "terrorism" on this land (since 1492), who constructed and who polices the borders that now divide Indigenous communities and kin from each other. It exposes the hypocrisy of the US state's construction of dominant (non-Native, presumably white, entitled) US citizen-subjects as *more-vulnerable-than-thou*. It can do this work because it visibilizes several temporal-spatialities in *co-presence*.

Yet, if we consider this poster through *situated planetarities*, it can incite some different questions about power and subjects. Concerning power, it can link to various sites, scales, and *operabilities*, such as other settler colonialisms and occupations (Palestine, Kurdistan, Kashmir, the Pacific Islands, Australia, New Zealand, and more), genocides (across all of Turtle Island and Abya Yala and beyond), theft of land (as in all forms of settler colonialism and occupation), extractivism (across settler, administrative, commercial, military and other forms of colonialism), impositions of borders, etc. It can conjoin Native peoples in Turtle Island with Native peoples elsewhere across the planet. Moreover, to make *situated planetarities* central means bringing the trees, land, birds, energies, sea, wind, rain, and all other *beings-becomings* into the analysis. Such a rereading would require a different poster and slogan.

4.1 The *co-present* articulation of the erased past with the present has a capacity to incite (Dull-Pianist-6777 2023).

Power, Subjects, Relationalities

Indeed, *situated planetarities* hopes to radically open up who and what gets considered as a valuable subject, *being-becoming*, form of life, or *presence-absence*, and how. *Situated planetarities* is concerned with all humans and equally so with the insects that humans smash without a second thought, the fish they massively confine and inject with hormones and consume, and the animals they keep as pets or torture in scientific experiments and/or for profit, enslave to work, imprison, force feed, mass slaughter, and eat. It hopes to incite different, more livable relationalities for all. *Situated planetarities* also emphasizes mindfulness of *beings-becomings* who/that do not appear in human perception at all. It aims to respect embodied and unembodied entities: water, minerals, earth, air, ether, the partially manifested, the fully unmanifested. *Situated planetarities* includes *beings-becomings* across many dimensions, such as the ghosts and spirits of ancestors and progenitor of all forms of life. It acknowledges *beings-becomings* who/that may seem like *beings-without-becoming*, perhaps because the temporalities in which they unfold in space are to humans too slow to be perceived: a rock, a mountain, an acre of flat land. *Situated planetarities* includes *beings-becomings* who/that do not show up in recognizable ways at all in human *sensing, perception*, or fields of *intelligibility*. It encompasses totally absent *beings-becomings*—the *x* of chapter 2 and thereafter—who/that humans have yet to dream exist.

All these entities have different kinds of capacities, agencies, forms of stasis, movement, and other existences. Their modes of *togethering* exceed dominant human logics of interrelations. They are beyond oppositionality (humans vs. other forms of existence), sameness (the claim that other *beings-becomings* are like humans), continuity (others as same with variable difference), and semblance (alike but not identical). *Situated planetarities* invites us to scramble and dissolve current dominant categories and logics of subjecthood, *being-becoming*, and relationality. It hopes to induce different, *subalternative* forms of recognition and respect. The notion of *subjects-in-sociality and another*, explained in chapter 2, can help us consider all these entities, regardless of whether they are likable or *perceptible* or imaginable. In turn, the *subaltern-to-dominant continuum* can help us reflect on how entities are co-constituted, maintained, or eliminated in relations of power in any given *co-present temporal-spatiality*.

Situated planetarities is in conversation with multiple other approaches to subjects and relationalities. The *subalternative* epistemologies of some Native peoples loom large (Kimmerer 2015). They are not simply perspectives from subalterneity, nor solely oppositional to relations of power such as coloniality or capitalism. Instead, they preexist these conditions. Their continual dynamism is often so dramatically *out-of-sync* with imposed colonial relations of power that, while selected aspects may be appropriated and reframed, they are not always so easily fully co-opted. Some can totally open the idea of who/what counts as a subject or as kin (TallBear 2017, 2011; Deloria 2001; Cajete 1994; Hau'ofa 1993). Some can entail an expansive way to think about subjects, *beings-becomings*, and relationalities together. With some of them, *situated planetarities* includes the *co-presence* of *beings-becoming* who/that leave no traces and in fact may be as yet unthought.

Currently some other imaginings of human to nonhuman relations are close to but not necessarily *in-sync* with *situated planetarities*. For instance, some abolitionist animal rights groups usefully reconceptualize humans and animals in a same category that philosopher Tom Regan calls "subjects-with-a-life" (2004). This classification posits sentience as justification for extending human recognition and legal entitlements to animals (Regan 2004; Francione and Garner 2010; Francione 2008). *Colonialism-class-race-caste-misogynarchic amnesia* feminist abolitionist animal rights theorizations from the work of Carol Adams onward critically highlight how animals have the same function in (presumably Global Northern heteronormative) sexist societies as (presumably white) women. They are used, exploited, commodified, made to serve others, considered irrational, objectified, turned into targets of desire including sadistically, and equated with nature while (presumably white) men are equated with culture (Adams 1996). Scholars of European scientific racism point to how zoology served directly as a model for human racial construction and classification and how the dehumanization of subalternly racialized groups was effected by animalizing them (Jackson 2020; Bancel et al. 2004; Guillaumin 1972). Asis Nandy demonstrates that the colonial representation of subalterns in Indian society (Dalits, Bahujans, Adivasis) entailed their animalization (1983). From Dr. B. R. Ambedkar to the Dalit Sahitya Akademi group in Bangalore, Dalit intellectuals have long highlighted how the caste system constructs equations between Dalits, Adivasis, wild animals, and wilderness. Dominant vocabularies of racial differentiation—"primitive," "backward," "out of control," "wild," etc.—suggest an evolutionary Darwinist vision in which certain categories of humans are imagined as beasts or nature (Jackson 2020; Sithole 2020; Guillaumin 1972). Thus, the end of animal exploitation would have many additional reverberations.

Unfortunately, the sentience criteria for animal respect can reinforce human-centrism. It often depends on logics of sameness-with-humans and continuity-with-humans that produce yet other exclusions: of all nonsentient *beings-becomings* and *beings-becomings* whose existence is as yet unacknowledged. The idea of subjects-with-a-life, even if extended beyond *sentient-centrism*, does not necessarily (although it could) recognize, oppose or transform the relations of power in which humans, animals and other *beings-becomings* are co-constituted and caught. Some strains of "new" materialism extend the logics of the same and of continuity to plant life without dissolving human-centricity at all. Kim TallBear (2017) points to how Indigenous feminisms have long undone the colonial Eurocentric life vs. nonlife binary. Indeed, new materialism, species inclusions, and related imaginings and ideas are "new" in dominant European and US thought but, again, have a long history in some Native epistemologies. Today, research reveals that fungi construct underground solidarity networks to sustain multiple trees in a same forest, an ensemble that some scientists call the "woodwide web." Recently botanists have "discovered" that plants have feelings and that trees act in solidarity with each other. These are important developments. But they do not automatically lead to valuing nonhuman *beings-becomings* beyond their use-value to humans or beyond their conformity with human values.

Perhaps emerging queer scholarship participations in the "nonhuman turn" offers a different contribution. Much of it flags that the category human has been overly present in critical thought and seeks to change that. In an issue of the *Journal of Lesbian and Gay Studies*, Mel Chen and Dana Luciano (2015) highlight a particular queer affinity with the nonhuman and propose that queer subjects have often been identified as nonhuman life. Queerphobic discourses often place queers outside the social realm and thus outside human life. Yet queer, in its incarnation as trans, can signal self-identification with a desirable posthuman life. Lest this give rise to premature celebrations, Chen and Luciano include in their discussion some words of caution from Jin Haritaworn for whom the nonhuman turn is not necessarily more liberatory than human-centrism for some of the planet's most subaltern human subjects. For Haritaworn, radical environmentalists—who helpfully attack capitalism—have yet to consider how in colonial moralizing discourse Indigenous people are represented both as too close to nature and as destructive of nature. These contradictions are conveyed in colonial-racialized controlling images such as of drunken adult Natives on reservations littering beer cans everywhere. This reinforces the long continuum in colonial, Eurocentric discourses of constructing Black and brown bodies of any gender or sexuality through animal imagery and tropes (Jackson 2020; Bancel et al. 2002; Guillaumin 1972). With centuries of the colonial, racist animalization of people of color in mind, we might contemplate Haritaworn's important questions: "For whom might the non-human be too risky a move?" And, "To what degree does the turn to animal studies reflect a desire to protect or save that which does not talk back?" (2015a).

This queer work can be put in conversation with other queer work that is presently emerging against the grain of the racialized human-animal analogy and the human vs. animal binary that Chen and Luciano rightly critique. P. J. Di Pietro (2020b) deconstructs and decolonizes it, and creates an elsewhere from it, when they describe the trans body as outside the colonial-racial categorizations of human, animal, and monster. Sharon Holland subverts it by claiming Black relationality to animals as she studies how African Americans associate with horses (2015). This question of radical difference-in-relationality is important to *situated* and to the idea of plurality in *situated planetarities*.

Another point of dialogue for *situated planetarities* is Deleuze and Guattari's work on becoming-animal. They advocate an exit from the dominant field of intelligibility by reimagining subjecthood through molecularity as assemblages (see chapter 3). They hope to push the human-animal relation beyond oedipality and hierarchy, and to create new forms of transspecies solidarity. But what happens to the animal when humans imagine themselves as animal? What kind of assimilative power *in-relationality* risks getting reproduced? Donna Haraway feels that Deleuze and Guattari unjustifiably reduce relations between animal pets and their humans to oedipality. For Haraway, they idealize wild animals as an abstraction but have no idea what it is to create an emotional relation with an animal (2008). Instead of becoming-animal, Haraway advises becoming with animals in ways that do not privilege humans over animals.

Some Deleuze-Guattari-inspired scholars argue that the human-animal hierarchy is now dissolving on its own. Some sustain that in our times animals are no longer the referent for human otherness that was constructed under colonialism and in (white) Eurocentric scientific discourse (Braidotti 2009). For *situated planetarities*, a key question is this: What localized and planetary conditions of power make such claims possible while public officials' discursive assaults abound, such as French President Sarkozy's 2005 call to "clean up" youth of color "with bleach"; Hillary Clinton's 2016 use of "predator" to denote African American men as sexual criminals; or Brazilian President Jair Bolsonaro's 2020 characterization of Indigenous people as wild animals?

Another site of engagement for *situated planetarities* is critical discussions of the Anthropocene. Notwithstanding important differences and disparate designations—Capitalocene (Moore 2014), Plantationocene (Haraway 2015; Tsing 2025), white supremacy scene (Mirzoeff 2018), Terracene (Mameni 2023)—this scholarship draws mutual attention to the lifeworld's exposure to human destruction. The human degradation factor is also now part of common sense. We saw it reverberate transnationally when journalists across the globe remarked during COVID-19 (human) confinement how animals returned to city streets and the air cleared, suggesting what pre- and posthumanity might be like.

Since Paul Crutzan first proposed the concept-term *Anthropocene* in 2000 and 2002 to describe in geological terms a temporality of planetary human destruction of other species and the environment, scientists have disagreed about how to define it and when to date it (Mameni 2023; Erickson 2020). Neoliberal scientists point to technology, not relations of power, as its motor and defining criteria. For Marxist scientists, capitalism with its appropriation, destruction, extractivism, and exploitation of land, natural resources, waters, and air for profit is the Anthropocene's cause. For Jason Moore it is more accurately named Capitalocene (2014). For Simon L. Lewis and Mark A. Maslin (2015), the period of decline began with colonial genocide in the Americas that caused a rapid loss of CO_2. Kathryn Yusoff (2016) sustains that in an early phase of discussion, the category human appeared undifferentiated and was inserted into a human vs. nature binary. She highlights racism and dominant Eurocentric thought structures in hegemonic definitions of the Anthropocene and points to how they frame white people as both the cause and the saviors of environmental problems, thus erasing everyone else. Mameni (2023) rethinks the place of war, militarism, and massive destruction wrought by colonialism, capitalism, and racism to suggest instead the concept of Terracene, which links the earth, humans, nonhumans, the colonial-racialized construction of the terrorist as outside humanity, the terror induced by colonial and capitalist forces of planetary destruction and annihilation, and territorialization. The disparate defining criteria and the differential identification of agents in the debates around Anthropocene and its critics lead to quite a variability in dating the Anthropocene: from 1610 with colonial genocide, 1784 with the rise of the Industrial Revolution, 1945 with the testing of the first atom bomb, and others (Erickson 2020).

Current critiques of the Anthropocene generally propose that humans begin to respect animals. They rarely recall the Indigenous and other subaltern southern epistemologies that have long held such values. The dominant non-Indigenous literatures often represent animal-human relations as either resemblance or continuity or superiority. In resemblance, humans project a (human-like) culture onto nonhumans to emphasize their ostensible similarities with humans. Scholars note the intelligence, intracommunication, and creativity of nonhumans, and even how they steal from each other. This move enfolds animals into (human) neoliberal racial-diversity discourses that propose greater inclusion of "marginalized" or "underrepresented" (human) "minorities," all concept-terms that distinctly avoid remembering genocide, slavery, racism, sexism, queerphobias, speciesism, ableism, and other practices of power. "Minorities" calls to mind a numerical issue. "Marginalized" invokes a spatial problem. "Underrepresented" summons discursive representation abstracted from material power relations.

In turn, continuity discourse entails the projection of animalness and thingness onto subaltern humans who are presumed to need to be "cultivated." Continuity is akin to anthropological "gone native" discourses that produce and valorize the supposedly "primitive" characteristics of colonized humans as possible helpful supplements to colonizer subjects. Continuity discourse simply directly reverses progress narratives, thereby reinforcing the latter's referentiality. It posits that the (dominant) human can be humanized by adopting some characteristics of the nonhuman or the less-than-human.

Resemblance and continuity share human-centricity and erasures of power. New Anthropocene activisms that seek to undo some relations of power by revalorizing nonhuman life sometimes constructively promote practices such as veganism to undermine the *species-murder-industrial-complex*. However, they also risk reproducing colonial-racial relations of power as they figure the human as undifferentiated, in relations of equality with nonhuman life. Insofar as there are vast inequities among humans and prior presumptions of the nonhumanity or less-than-humanity of some categories of humans, these activisms risk inadvertently placing some non-human life above subaltern human life.

Situated planetarities invites us to co-generate dramatically different *sensings, perception, intelligibility*, relationality, and ultimately social organization for our times. *Situated planetarities* includes yet exceeds all human and animal subjects of the most recent version of "We Are Family" that we saw in chapter 1. *Situated planetarities* carries the hope of inciting the uncompromising *alter-kinship* of all *beings-becomings* as integral *subjects-in-socialities and another* as conceptualized in chapter 2. *Situated planetarities* recognizes kinship with ducks, a mountain, a spirit, the air, the unthought, the unimagined. In an early poem, Chrystos (1981), a working-class lesbian Native Mamaceqtaw poet from the *territory-in-coloniality, territory-in-capitalism*, now called Wisconsin in the United States, expresses such a relationship beyond human-other resemblance or continuity: "No bird ever called me crazy. No rock scorns me as whore."[1] Her bird, her rock, are elsewhere. Chrystos thereby offers a vibrant point of departure for thinking the simultaneity of worlds and relationalities of subjects and *beings-becomings* in *situated planetarities*.

For *situated planetarities*, relationalities unfold in *co-presence*, near or far. Since there is quite a bit of related literature, I will distinguish how I think of *co-presence* from it. For instance, Irving Goffman offers the term "copresence" to signal human relations in immediate "micro and macro levels" (1996). Some scholars prior to and after Goffman emphasize that subjects do not have to be in a same location or register. People can have a copresent relation with the dead or with fictional characters. Celeste

Campos-Castillo and Steven Hitlin rethink Goffman's "copresence" to make subjective perception central and to include nonimmediate relations such as cyber communities. They posit four criteria for a redefinition of copresence: subjectivity, variability for each subject in an ensemble, responsiveness to contextual factors, and influences on interactional outcome (2013). They define copresence primarily in relation to mutual attention, emotion, and conduct.

These ideas about copresence inform the *co-presence* that *situated planetarities* makes possible. Yet *co-presence* in *situated planetarities* differs sharply. First, the subjects of relationality in *co-presence* are not exclusively humans who may be alive, deceased, in cyberspace, etc. The subjects are also other sentient and nonsentient *beings-becomings* in this and other dimensions. *Co-presence* is attached not to classic scales such as micro and macro, but rather to historical contextuality, genealogy, and to the relationality that Deleuze and Guattari call molecular and molar (see chapter 3). *Co-presence* includes subjects, *beings-becomings, co-present temporal-spatialities*, and relations of power that in current dominant human fields of intelligibility may seem unrelated to each other, or further, may not seem to exist at all.

Epistemic Openings

The work of analyzing relations of power that *situated planetarities* hopes to enable centrally entails an epistemic dimension. The current hegemonic fields of intelligibility—with their categories, logics, presuppositions, and conclusions—that are present in and carried by dominant Global Northern languages across the North(s) and many parts of the South(s)—are saturated in colonialism, coloniality, capitalism, imperialism, racism, *misogynarchies*, speciesism, and ableism. *Situated* in *situated planetarities* invites us to recognize the most minute subalternized fields of intelligibility across the Global North(s) and South(s). It incites us to consider many ways of *sensing, perceiving, rendering intelligible*, and relating in the world. It invites us to understand that much of what exists is far beyond human perception and imagination.

Situated planetarities assumes that every episteme, every field of intelligibility is limited, partial, is only one in a plurality across the planet. Each is incomplete without *and another* (see chapter 2). *Situated planetarities* opens the possibility of equitable dispositions toward the perspectives of all *beings-becomings* across *co-present temporal-spatialities* by considering them not as the same, equivalent, or in continuity, but rather as differentially equally vital.

We can already get a glimpse of possibilities for opening *subalterna-tive sensing, perception,* and *intelligibility* to ever more subaltern fields of intelligibility. Some current theorizations are already *in-sync* with this as-pect of *situated planetarities* and vice versa. They bring into relief a world of ecologies, spirits, liminalities, differential realities, and dreamscapes. For instance, Gloria Anzaldúa helpfully addresses states of becoming and how they are conjoined with othered ways of knowing, such as the ecstatic, the spiritual, and trance (Anzaldúa 2009a, 2009b, [1987] 2007, 2002). Laura Pérez and P. J. Di Pietro engage hallucination as a site of knowl-edge production that is inscribed in Chicana/x art and in trans life (Di Pietro 2020a; Pérez 2019, 2007). M. Jacqui Alexander explores differential, heightened perception, as theorized and experienced in African-descended spiritual practices. In a discussion of "making the invisible tangible" she suggests reconceptualizing "the spiritual as epistemological" in reference to "terms, symbols, and organizational codes that the Bantu-Kongo people used to make sense of the world" (2005, 287, 293). She explains that "the in-visible constitutes its presence by a provocation of sorts, by provoking our attention. We see its effects, which enable us to know it is there. By perceiv-ing what it does we recognize its being and by what it does, we learn what it is" (307). In the process, "the praxis of the senses involves the rewiring of the senses" (328). This reorganization of sensibilities also implies a shift in embodiment. Alexander notes that many unseen others—ancestors, spir-its, and deceased contemporaries—walk with us (328). Yet much remains unknown about power and subjects.

Concluding Remarks

Situated planetarities can hopefully open up yet other analyses, imaginings, practices, and activisms. The next chapter will mobilize *situated planetari-ties* alongside other concepts to consider power, subjects, and *co-motion* in one small place within our vast world.

Ne me libérez pas. Je m'en charge. (Don't liberate me. I'm taking care of it myself.)

    Chant by racialized feminists in France

One of authority's most insidious effects may well be to confine definitions of resistance to only those that appear to oppose it directly, in the open, where it can be made and seen to fail.

    Steve Pile, "Opposition, Political Identities
    and Spaces of Resistance"

How might the concepts suggested across this book's chapters animate and *operate* in analytics and praxes *in-context*?

    This chapter concentrates attention on a very small context: *freedom-exigent co-motion* in Paris, France, and its banlieues by a specific activist sector: radically critical, subalternly racialized queer+, trans+, and dyke+ subjects and allies. I use this term for the subjects instead of the English language designations QTPOC (queer trans people of color) and BIPOC (Black, Indigenous, and other people of color) because the former makes best sense *in-context*.[1] I bring in QTPOC only where it is a self-designation by the subjects whose *co-motion* I discuss. I use *subalternly racialized* and more often (as is habitual in the French-speaking world) just the shorter term *racialized* to translate two self-designations: *racisé.e.s* (literally, "racialized," with the *.e.* to flag women, femininity, and all other genders, alongside an otherwise presumably masculine term, *racisés*); and *nonblanc(he)* (nonwhite, with the *he* signifying a similar inclusive gender designation). The + in queer+, trans+, and dyke+ has three meanings. It is to recognize suppressed self-designations in languages in France's former and present colonies (see, for example, Garaoun 2022). It brings into the analysis the *etcétera* as placeholder, as not merely additive but instead as the gender, sexuality, or subject who is unknown-knowable in the dominant field of intelligibility. And it reminds us of the constant presence of the *x* that represents the unknown-unknown gender, sexuality, or subject. (On *etcétera* and *x*, see chapter 2, and Bacchetta and Crawford forthcoming). The notion of racialized queer+, trans+, dyke+ puts into relief that there is always an outside to the genders, sexualities, and subjects that are named, and that context is vital. Importantly, this term and all its components are all approximations, for we have as yet no adequate ways of speaking about, naming, or translating them.

The *freedom-exigent co-motion* here is a fraction alongside many kinds of formations—*subaltern, subalternist, subalternative, liberation-oriented,* or others with which it is sometimes entwined. I make no claims as to this fragment's superiority over others elsewhere. Instead, I aim to put into relief instances of coming together from which there is much to learn. The *freedom-exigent co-motion* here is complex, plural, messy. Some of it is magnificent. All of it is imperfect. None of it is as yet completely free of toxicities. It is always in process.

It warrants outing up front (again) that I expressly do not desire to "apply" the concept-terms in this book to this or any other empirical situations. "Apply" is out of place in such an *in-context* analytic. The "apply" approach, or imposing concepts with their specific genealogies and uses in one site onto another, risks obscuring or concealing important relations of power and rendering some *subjects-in-socialities and another* imperceptible. As I first mentioned in this book's introduction, the concept-terms here are not magical universal formulas. Rather, they are minute potential points of departure, infinitely small lines of escape, for possible *critical conceptual wanderings* to elsewhere places for thinking and imagining. In this chapter I do not try to make use of every concept. Only some are helpful to my discussion. Yet, this chapter orbits back into the empirics that—along with the other sites in this book—first lay bare the limitations of some of the dominant, now self-universalized critical vocabularies whose constraints provoked me to try to create more useful concepts *in-context*.

Many studies of different forms of *co-motion*, including this one, are at least partially motivated by a desire to expand solidarities. Given the numerical smallness and dismissability of radically critical, racialized queer+, trans+, and dyke+ subjects and allies in France, one may wonder: Why focus on their *co-motion* at all? I suggest, first, that this fragment is in and of itself important, not to be discarded. Second, reflection from and with it enables a reach far beyond the small scale of the *co-motion*'s emergence within it. Again, with Kabir, who is quoted at the beginning of this book's introduction, any place can be a point of departure.

To consider the expansive capacities of any small site with *situated planetarities* in mind, Arjun Appadurai's (2006) approach to the social scientific disdain for small numbers and Gyanendra Pandey's (1992) thinking on the fragment are helpful (see also Bacchetta 2018). For Appadurai, dominant negative affect toward small numbers and the will to expel them from analysis are effects of classical liberal notions of the nation as a homogenous, cohesive entity that, in the context of globalization's deterritorialization, "minorities" ostensibly threaten. The dominant seeks to strip "minorities" of difference or otherwise eliminate them from the scene of sense making. In turn, Pandey argues that a tiny, seemingly insignificant social fragment can be a vital part of an extensive context that is incomprehensible without it. With *situated planetarities* in mind, the life conditions and political work of these specific subalternized subjects can reveal a world.

Archival Matters

The sources for understanding this small and extremely subaltern social sliver, its relationalities and connectivities, are material and immaterial traces of events, representations, analyses, collective action, spaces, energies of bodies, affect, relationalities, creations, and practices by and among subalternly racialized queer+, trans+, and dyke+ subjects and allies in France today. The archive here includes insights from semidirective interviews that I conducted by Zoom in COVID-19 confinement in summer 2020 and in person conversations in January, February, April, and May 2022 in Paris.[2] It encompasses observations about coming together in action and becoming together in practices such as *entr'aide* (mutual help) or social solidarity. Other sources are written calls for political action, statements, posters, websites, art, social media, but also forms of embodiment, ways of speaking, and silence. I willfully omit some elements to respect the nondisclosure desires of authorial subjects such as in the aftermath of extreme colonial-racialized lesbophobic, queerphobic, or transphobic physical violence, or for the preservation of subjects' dignity as in the wake of their agentic life-endings. The chapter is informed by my own activism and extended conversations with coparticipants since the 1980s. Additionally I take the gossip of racialized queer+, trans+, and dyke+ seriously as a subaltern mode of producing data and analysis, but also relationality.[3]

I construct this heterogeneous archive against the grain of an over-whelming absence in the public space of identifiable traces of racialized queer+, trans+, and dyke+ life in France. The analytics, activisms, and artivisms here are shut out of dominant historiographies. Most signs of racialized queer+, trans+, and dyke+ life that exist are scattered, uncollected, forgotten. There are currently some projects bringing them together (Cheikh 2021; Danjé 2021; Bacchetta and Crawford, forthcoming; Bacchetta 2020, 2009a).[4] But at this time, they do not register in the hegemonic *national-normative* field of intelligibility. The speaking subjects and kinds of political projects they entail are often elsewhere from that field's capacities for recognition. They pass below its radar. When an item does surface it is often erroneously resignified in ways that make it unrecognizable to the subjects who created it.

Though there is as yet no physical or electronic archive by, about, or that speaks centrally to racialized queer+, trans+, and dyke+ in France, such subjects are far from archiveless. There are elders and next generations. Each is (already) a living archive, a work of memory, representation and *re-presentation*, order, *x*, art, *etcétera*, chaos (Bacchetta 2018). Some of the subjects are walking emergencies. Some you may find beautiful, others horrific. All are vital. Whatever they invent together attests to life, stubbornness, obstinacy, a refusal to disappear, but also to their immense creativity and desires for a *freedom-exigent elsewhere-present* and a *freedom-sustaining elsewhere-futurity*.

I think of the archival traces of racialized queer+, trans+, and dyke+ *co-motion* here as *critical luminosities* in a seemingly unending night. They defy claims that the subjects have no history. They illuminate power. They make perceptible multiple dimensions of the *co-motion* of which they are a part.

To suggest *critical luminosities*, I draw from the thought of Dalila Kadri Cheriet, the Algerian-French lesbian filmmaker, poet, essayist, and activist.[5] One of Kadri's films, *Lucioles* (Fireflies), specifically about racialized lesbians+, is the first documentary about racialized queers+ in France. For Kadri racialized lesbians emerge as momentary illuminations in a long night. Her notion can be thought together with Gilles Deleuze's reflections on the hidden and the perceptible in Foucault, and on sensing in Nietzsche. Deleuze highlights how for Foucault power conceals some of its most ferocious operations; yet meaningful encounters, events, and objects can bring them briefly into light (Deleuze 1986). In *Nietzsche and Philosophy* (1962)

Deleuze writes that "the point of critique is not justification but a different way of feeling: another sensibility." In sum, with Kadri and Deleuze we can consider how *co-motion* and its archival traces appear and disappear as *critical luminosities* that cannot be fully captured, that open up other senses, affect, and ways of knowing and living.

In-Context

With *situated planetarities* as a point of departure (not arrival) we can put into relief how relations of power at disparate scales saturate and co-constitute racialized queer+, trans+, and dyke+ subjects across the subaltern pole of the *subaltern-to-dominant continuum in-context* in France. This social fragment includes French citizens and documented and undocumented immigrants with various statuses. They are working class, middle class, employed, unemployed. They have disparate relations to France's former and present colonial empire.

The *co-productions* colonialism, capitalism, imperialism, and *misogynarchies* loom large in the lives of all subalternly racialized people in France whether citizens or not, new immigrants or not. The specific situated site of Paris and its banlieues are incomprehensible without an understanding of the *co-present temporal-spatialities* that constitute it and continue to saturate it. France is often imagined from outside as a site of human rights and liberation. Yet, it is also a global colonial power since the sixteenth century: across the Americas, in North and sub-Saharan Africa, the Middle East, the Pacific, South Asia, and East Asia. France has enacted multiple colonialisms: settler, commercial, administrative, military, missionary, external, and combinations thereof (Bacchetta 2023). These disparate forms are not analogous or parallel but rather interconnected, enmeshed, even entrapped. One stylistic arrangement and practice informs, enables, and reinforces another. They are often merged.

Along with other Western European colonial powers, France imposed current borders across the Global South(s). It carried out colonial genocide in North America and the Caribbean. In many places it forcibly inserted the French education system and language, thereby producing devastating cultural and linguistic alienation. It imposed *political amnesias* and induced assimilation policies that left psychic, cultural, spiritual, and social damage. France was a major enslaver, trader of enslaved peoples, and direct financial beneficiary of enslaved people's labor in its colonies. It did not broadly recognize its role in slavery until 2001 and has done almost nothing reparative about it. Via its colonial interventions, France forced vast parts of the planet into global capitalism. It pillaged natural resources in the colonies. It continues to play a massive role in postcolonial economies including a determinative one via the Central African franc (CFA) for six countries in Africa.

Like other Western European colonial powers, France imagines itself as eternally *more-gender-and sexuality-egalitarian-than-thou*. Yet, it has since colonial times left a trail of gender and sexuality damage. Its particular formations of *misogynarchies* are two: *fraternarchy* among the (white) French and *colonial patriarchy* in relation to colonized subjects. France intervened in gender and sexuality constructions in its colonies through judicial and military means (Dorlin 2006).

Multiple kinds of national movements for independence and decolonial politics emerged inside French colonial borders. They are *subalternist, subalternative, liberation-oriented*, and *freedom-exigent* or simultaneous combinations of these (see chapter 2). For example, enslaved people in Saint Domingue revolted, freed themselves, and in 1804 successfully created the world's first Black republic, Haiti. In Algeria, the independence movement militarily humiliated France and forced former colonial settlers back to France. The overwhelming majority of racialized subjects in France today have these and other genealogies in direct resistance to colonialism.

Across academic, popular, mediatic, and artistic genres, French colonialism has been radically critiqued within and beyond France for its economic and cultural devastation, epistemic violence and annihilation, orientalism, racism, exoticization, commodification, distortion, spiritual annihilation, queerphobia, and transphobia. For example, Michaëla Danjé (2014) remarks: "Your world is just a small destructive bit of perceptible universes. Ours include the invisible, faith, the irrational and all of it makes sense. You have disarticulated peoples and histories. Stop moving. Pay attention if you are capable of doing so." Joao Gabriell (2021) highlights how all Black gender and sexualities are constructed as anormative in French colonial-racial discourse such that for Black trans people the transition to Black manhood sheds light on the racial-gendered violence that targets Black men. For Gabriell, "To transition is, in fact, just another way to be Black." In another example, Yuki Kihara illustrates how the celebrated (white) French artist Paul Gaugin erased trans subjects and imposed his version of cisgender women in their place (Palumbo 2022a, 2022b). In a reparative move, Kihara recomposed Gaugin's iconic *Two Tahitian Women* from 1899 by eliminating Gaugin's subjects (figure 5.1) and reinserting trans subjects in their place (figure 5.2).

Today, France remains a major, direct global colonial power. It has five *départements d'autre-mer* (overseas departments) with the same juridical status as its ninety-six metropolitan departments, yet they each have a very high rate of poverty: 77 percent in Mayotte, 53 percent in Guyane, 42 percent in Réunion, and 30 percent in Martinique and Guadeloupe. France possesses several *collectivités d'autre-mer* (overseas collectivities) with various classifications: French Polynesia with Tahiti and other islands (overseas country), Saint Barthélemy (overseas collectivity), Saint Martin (overseas collectivity), Saint Pierre and Miquelon (territorial collectivity), Wallis and Futuna (territory), and New Caledonia (autonomous overseas collectivity). It holds an uninhabited island, Clipperton Island, off the coast of Mexico.

The majority of racialized peoples in Paris today come from places France directly colonized. They are concentrated in racialized working class urban outskirts where they face *segregationality* or multidimensional partitioning that manifests (beyond segregation's spatial separation and hierarchization) in territorial, economic, epistemic, linguistic, cultural, symbolic, psychic, spiritual, and energetic disconnection and degradation (see chapter 4; also Bacchetta 2020, 2016). The *racialization of space* and *spatialization of race* there implicate all dimensions of life. The outskirts have the highest rates of unemployment, lowest average salary per capita, least access to education, and highest rates of employment rejection even when all the right diplomas are there (Beaman 2017). The French government self-identifies as egalitarian and color-blind (Soumaharo 2022, 2020; Boubeker 2005). It gathers no distinct statistics on racialized peoples and thus can ignore inequities in hiring, firing, and education.

Colonial-racism, sexism, and queerphobia across all registers are inscribed in France's juridical and political apparatuses. Some of its laws perform biopolitics on bodies such as by forcibly unveiling Muslim women (see below). Its "counterterrorism" laws are mobilized to target Muslims. It imposes heterosexist *sanguinal*-based familiality for postcolonial subjects such as obligatory DNA tests for "family regrouping" for immigrants. As mentioned earlier, it enforced *calculated amnesia* by making it mandatory to teach French colonialism in a "positive" light in schools and universities.[6] Its refusal of Global Southern languages is inscribed in the 1994 Toubon Law.[7] Its colonial rhetoric persists in France today, generally

5.1 Paul Gauguin's *Two Tahitian Women* (1899), the object of painter Yuki Kihara's critical and reparative artivism.

unmodified and denied as colonial rhetoric at all (Frith et. al. 2023; Stora 1999, 1994). France also has a life of its own in the societies and literatures of some former colonies where it is variably internalized, rejected, resisted, or circumvented (Azzouzi 2023; Mbembe 2021). In France, during the 2022 presidential election—when in the final round 42 percent of the French vote went to the fascist Marine Le Pen and the rest to the colonial-capitalist Emanuel Macron—the colonial-racist term "assimilation" (see chapter 1)

5.2 Critical and reparative painting by Yuki Kihara, picturing the subjects of Paul Gauguin's painting in their original form as trans ("Yuki Kihara, *Paradise Camp*" 2022).

was a major point of agreement across the political spectrum. Following massive demonstrations against racist and Islamophobic police murders and brutalities—in connection with the now transnational Black Lives Matter movement—in 2021 the French government outlawed "separatism" to prohibit autonomous groups of racialized people. The first banned was Collectif contre l'Islamophobie en France (CCIF, Collective Against Islamophobia in

France), France's only group documenting Islamophobic incidents in the country. Since the law does not distinguish between autonomy and separatism, any of the autonomous groups of racialized queer+, trans+, and dyke+ that I discuss here could be next.

What today manifests as the *freedom-exigent co-motion* of racialized queer+, trans+, and dyke+ subjects in France has a long history that remains *co-present* in spirit (Bacchetta 2020, 2009a; Bacchetta and Crawford, forthcoming). While Europe is dominantly imagined as homogenously white, subalternly racialized people have been in France (and other European countries) from its beginnings as a nation-state (El-Tayeb 2011). Since France made several colonies administratively French, the creations, inventions, *co-motion*, and silences of racialized queer+, trans+, and dyke+ in all those sites over centuries are part of this genealogy.

The bulk of immediate racialized queer+, trans+, and dyke+ ancestors, predecessors, and family members in Paris are entangled with massive colonial and postcolonial immigration primarily following Europe's World War II. The first such sizable colonial-racialized population was comprised of men. Between the two world wars, France solicited workers from its (ex)colonies to fill lower-rung positions in factories. Some became activists around their labor conditions. Women and children did not enter in larger numbers until the 1970s "family grouping" laws that allowed nuclear family members to join a male counterpart. In some cases, lone subjects could enter as refugees but those were limited in number. A fraction of single women and non-women-identified single trans subjects, often from Brazil or other sites in Abya Yala that were not directly colonized by France, entered, too, for disparate reasons including to escape political persecution, for university studies, and for sex work (Gomes Silva 2022; Georgette 2016; Moujoud and Pourette 2005; Goldberg-Salinas 2000).

The "family regrouping" laws were explicitly colonial, paternalistic, sexist, and queerphobic. They are stunning examples of how *misogynarchies* opens our analytics as opposed to reducing everything to patriarchy. As mentioned in chapter 4, the modern French state is organized as a *fraternarchy* historically and at present symbolically. However, the same state manifests as patriarchal in relation to postcolonial subjects. It wifeifies colonized men by making them dependent helpers of the *fraternarchal* French state, corporations, and population while excluding them from positions of power. The gender and sexuality of postcolonial subjects are pathologized as excess or lack (Bacchetta 2009a, 2017). Colonized men are represented as incapable of leadership or self-control, thus infantilized, pathologized, and criminalized.

Historically, the French state presumed that all subjects migrating from colonized space were heterosexual. While white heterosexual and queer mobility tend to be celebrated, often the mobility of colonized and postcolonial subjects is demonized (Bacchetta et al. 2015; El-Tayeb 2012). The French government defined and reified the family according to the dominant white French nuclear model that does not correspond to extended family structures in many parts of the Global South(s). State laws made colonial-racialized immigrant women's status dependent on and subordinated to the (differently subordinated) status of male counterparts. Colonized women were confined to the position of wives and daughters of (wife-ified) colonized men.

This situation of immigrant women's forced dependency would soon lead them to organize for "autonomous rights for immigrant women" (Bacchetta 2009a). Because their legal status was determined by their country of origin's bilateral treaties with France, they first came together in nation-based groupings. They created the Association des femmes khmères (Association of Khmer Women, Paris, 1977); Groupe femmes algériennes (Algerian Women's Group, Paris, 1978); and Groupe femmes marocaines (Moroccan Women's Group, Paris, 1980). Some coalitional exceptions are Groupe latino-américain des femmes (Latin American Women's Group, Paris, 1972); the Coordination des femmes noires (Network of Black Women, Paris, 1976); and Association des femmes arabes immigrées (Arab Immigrant Women's Association, Gennevilliers, 1982). Lesbians+ were in these groups but did not generally publicly declare themselves as such. By 1984, among the fifteen feminist groups housed at the *Maison des Femmes de Paris* (Paris Women's Center) the majority were racialized women's groups.

In 1999, racialized lesbians formed their first fully autonomous group, the Groupe du 6 novembre: Lesbiennes issues du colonialisme, l'esclavage et l'immigration (6 November Group: Lesbians begotten of/out of colonialism, slavery, and immigration) (Bacchetta and Crawford, forthcoming; Bacchetta 2019b, 2009a). In 2009 they created a second autonomous group, Lesbiennes of Color (LOCs, or Lesbians of Color).[8]

More broadly, racialized queers+, trans+, and dykes+ began to construct national and regional social and solidarity networks in France in the 1980s. Today, as more racialized queer+, trans+, and dyke+ are citizens, counter to divide-and-rule politics most groups are heterogeneous in national origin, class, racialization, documentation status, and sexuality and gender identifications. For example, LTQ révolutionnaires (Lesbian Trans Queer Revolutionaries) includes subjects from all geopolitical genealogies, statuses, queer genders, and sexualities. The Black feminist and lesbian+ group Collectif afroféministe MWASI (Afrofeminist Collective MWASI) draws members from across Africa and French-speaking Black diasporic geographies.[9] Increasingly, as the autonomous groups have confronted *colonialism-and-racism-amnesia* and opened dialogues, a critical mass of white queer and trans people and allies are now committed to *accomplicity-comradeship* and their numbers are growing.

Backwards-Sideways

To discuss instances of *freedom-exigent co-motion* here, I mobilize what we can call a *backwards-sideways* approach. It is directly informed by *situated planetarities* and by the idea of *co-present temporal-spatialities*. It is about thinking the small-scale genealogy (*backwards*) and *co-present* horizontal interconnectivity (*sideways*) in the *situated* site of Paris and its racialized working-class outskirts with small-scale to planetary relations of power at once.

The orientations implicated in the *backwards-sideways* approach directly circumvent dominant modes of social movement historiography that by contrast proceed with what we might call a *forward-thinly-linear* approach. Dominant historiographies generally commence in the past and move *forward* in linear chronology to arrive in the present. They are *thinly linear* insofar as they focus on one (dominant) set of subjects, movement, and group of events, and delete the rest. They are *mono-focal* in that they revolve around one relation of power (gender, sex) as though it were (colonially, class, racially) neutral, as opposed to multiplicities of relations of power inseparably that *co-formations* and *co-productions* implicate. Dominant historiographies are often disconnected from (*sideways*) other subjects and movements *in-context* and beyond. The dominant *forward thinly linear* approach tends to exclusivize, universalize, and naturalize the dominant subjects, movement, and events it features while erasing all the rest.

In contrast, a *backwards-sideways* approach begins with the *co-present* and proceeds *backwards* to offer a *thick historiography* of the *co-present* (Bacchetta 1996). It makes apparent interconnections between multiple *co-present temporal-spatialities* of past and present struggles. It refuses dominant historiographies' selective erasures of the *co-motion* of ancestors and elders. It opens *sensing, perception,* and *intelligibility* to the relations of power that precede, get reiterated, transform, and accumulate or not, in the present. This approach rethinks the present as a *co-present* comprised of many temporalities: pasts, points zero, cyclicalities, futurities, etc. The *sideways* in the *backwards-sideways* approach elucidates how any *freedom-exigent co-motion* is connected to simultaneous contemporary movements, struggles, and *co-motion in-context.*

The *backwards* in the *backwards-sideways* gesture here is inspired by Foucault's (1977, 1976, 1971, 1966) genealogical method, or a reading of the present with and through the past. For Foucault, genealogy is distinct from the search for origins and from linear development. It is far from a quest for a "truth" and far from a colonial or other progressive narrative. Instead, genealogy is about multiple moments that help illuminate the present. We find here a different conception of historical time; it unfolds in plurality. This notion is somewhat distinct from Christina Hanhardt's interesting approach to "Looking 'Backward'" yet is resonant with the importance that Hanhardt assigns to the "backstory" (2013, 26).

In turn, the *sideways* in *backwards-sideways* is about *co-presence* and interrelationality. It draws inspiration from P. J. Di Pietro's (2016b) suggestion that *travestis* in Argentina invent "sideways relationality," a kind of decolonial horizontality that I find fruitful for considering *co-motion.* Further back, it is also informed by Siobhan Somerville's (2005) useful "sideways" approach that she discusses in her critique of gay marriage. For Somerville, "sideways" is a strategy to consider laws around sexuality in their "inter-relatedness," "simultaneity" and "embeddedness" (338) as opposed to "analogous thinking" (247). The *backwards-sideways* approach that I propose is not to establish a reverse linear chronology based in a presumably seamless, knowable, even taken-for-granted past. Those presuppositions most often serve the dominant. Instead, a *backwards-sideways* approach mobilizes thicker genealogical elements to open perception to both flagrant and indiscernible relations of power, subjects, and *co-motion.*

There is something very queer happening here. *Backwards-sideways* is especially useful to subjects whose histories have been distorted, thinned out, debased, and/or erased in the name of forced assimilation or unity. A *backwards-sideways* orientation understands events not in isolation or as serial but rather as entangled and *co-present.* In it, *critical luminosities*—that contribute to knowing precisely because of what they make perceptible—can surface. With it, sometimes multiple contexts appear in a sole incident, or a sole incident appears in multiple temporalities.

Backwards-sideways helps us put into relief enactments that constitute "events" for the racialized queers+, trans+, and dykes+ and allies here. In a different vein, in a dialogue about 9/11, Jacques Derrida (2004, 88, 93) remarks that (in dominant perception) the "event" is demarcated by, among other factors, a powerful political and military apparatus and hegemonic "international law, diplomatic institutions, the media, and the greatest technoscientific, capitalist, and military power" (88). The "event" is also about affect that reverberates widely, a doing that, as he points out, is never neutral but always already socially conditioned. These and Derrida's many other critical observations are helpful to understand how dominants construct events. However, this angle of perception about what constitutes events is limited for our purposes. In it, the category events is slanted to the dominant's perspective and all the rest is ignored, erased. In the case Derrida analyzes, the notion of events relies on the dominant's hegemonic *selective empathy* for specific violated dominant subjects, while occurrences that destabilize or destroy subaltern subjects—colonial-racial genocide, mass murders, a racialized or gendered murder, or other devastations of subaltern others—get dismissed.

A *backwards-sideways* approach shifts the focus of what is important, of what reverberates, and for whom. It discloses that what constitutes an event for racialized queer+, trans+, and dyke+ subjects—and certainly for other multiply subalternized subjects—is tied up with subaltern survival and thriving in contexts where many constituencies would like to see us dead.

Freedom-Exigent Co-Motion in the Co-Present

I will begin with a form of *co-motion* that while seemingly very useful does not at first glance seem to offer anything *freedom-exigent* or even politically pertinent: the coming together of heterogeneous ensembles of racialized queers+, trans+, and dykes+ during the COVID-19 pandemic to organize food, clothing, shelter, legal aid, funds, employment, transport, and especially relational solidarity for the community. Yet in the present state of the world, with its increasing loss of humanity, decency, and grace, we might reconsider—among other things—how we imagine the political significance of such against-the-grain, loving relationality.

Because multiple groups are involved, there are many points of entry to describe this work. One path inside is November 6, 2020, when the genderly and racially plural group called QTPOC autonomes (Autonomous QTPOC) surfaced a call.[10] It proposed three actions: (1) urgently raising funds; (2) Zoom meetings for isolated folks and the creation of a structured team of listeners; and (3) organizing alternative holidays to prevent isolation during official ones—Christmas, New Year—because "not only has COVID-19 killed since March but so has solitude."[11] The funds paid for shelter, food, clothing, and sociality. Some collective houses opened their space to those who could not live with their families, whether for reasons of adequate space, queerphobia, or transphobia. Some individuals who could do so moved in with family members to make space for those who need it. Yet others took in animals of the displaced. QTPOC autonomes is one example; many other groups—e.g., Queers racisé.e.s autonomes (Autonomous Racialized Queers) and LOCs—did similar work. At points they came together.[12]

From a dominant *forwards-thinly-linear* point of view, these enactments during COVID-19 could be framed as simply intracommunity charity. Yet, from this dominant angle of vision, the political process of subalternized subjects producing this reflective, proactive collectivity and its radical political significance gets lost entirely. Instead, a *backwards-sideways* approach clarifies how the *co-productions* colonialism, capitalism, imperialism, and *misogynarchies*, and the *co-formations* racism, class, and Islamophobia, make such organizing necessary. It exposes how this fragment draws on prior and current racialized queer+, trans+, and dyke+ critiques of relations of power. It brings to mind how this work is informed and bolstered as a continuation of genealogies (the *backwards* in *backwards-sideways*) of *entr'aide* (mutual solidarity) in anticolonial struggles, marronage, immigration, shared organization of daily life in the racialized working-class urban outskirts that I mentioned in this book's introduction, and in histories of racialized and allied queer+, trans+, and dyke+ work around HIV/AIDS and refugee statuses. It is also inscribed in longstanding racialized queer+, trans+, and dyke+ understandings of visibilities, invisibilities, and spirit worlds that I discuss below.

This solidarity activism is about staying alive together and thrival (Jolivette 2015). It proceeds with knowledge that it is useless to ask the state or dominant society for solidarity. It moves against the grain of neoliberal individualist solutions. The subjects do not demand equality in the mess that the *operations* of power together make. Instead, their survival and thrival labor corresponds to *freedom-exigent* desires, hallucinations, and revelations. They prioritize relationality, intimacy, friendship, revolutionary love, a totally different life. The subjects of this *co-motion* move far beyond the kind of *affective, sanguinal, alter-kinship*, and *common conditions* alliances that I discussed in chapter 1. Their work constitutes an event because of how it moves the subjects involved, what it opens up, and what it transforms.

Accomplicity-Comradeship in Process

If we turn *sideways*, still under COVID-19 conditions, some related simulta-neous political actions, fruit of this same social fragment, glide into light and help clarify this COVID-19 solidarity work. An example is the autonomous contingent that racialized queers+, trans+, and dykes+ created at the left Pride March that the mainly white left group Pride politique auto-gérée (Au-tonomous Political Pride) organized on July 4, 2020, in Paris. The contin-gent was a convergent point for both *liberation-oriented* and *freedom-exigent* desires and a space of encounter. It was politically supported by white left queer and trans *accomplices-comrades*.

The left Pride March has its own genealogy. It was created in 2015 in opposition to the Pride March planned by the neoliberal dominant group l'Inter-associative lesbienne, gaie, bi et trans (Inter-Associative Lesbian, Gay, Bi, and Trans; hereafter Inter-LGBT). Founded in 1999, Inter-LGBT is a co-alition of about thirty mainly white queer groups. It organizes the official Marche de la fiérté LGBT (LGBT Pride March) every year. Radical queer and trans people periodically protest its homonationalism, state repres-sive apparatus inclusions (such as of queer police and military unions), and *white-centricity*. In 2015, Act-Up and other radical groups split off to establish a separate—albeit smaller—demonstration called *Pride de nuit* (Night Pride), which every year draws many racialized queer and trans groups and individuals.

Like many other official Pride marches across Europe today, the ones that Inter-LGBT arranged in Paris had become ever more right-leaning with time (Haritaworn 2015; Bacchetta and Haritaworn 2011; Haritaworn et. al. 2013). In 2020, two Inter-LGBT actions deeply irritated radical queer and trans people. First, Inter-LGBT (again) framed the Pride March as a celebratory integrationist, homonationalist commercial festival. Second, at a time when much of the left was protesting the French government's ban on political protests, after calling the March for June 27, 2020, Inter-LGBT canceled it (ostensibly due to COVID-19) and reset the date for Novem-ber 7, 2020. Unfortunately, Inter-LGBT called for the postponed march with a poster featuring a lone heroic white cisgender male, bearer of the official LGBT flag, leading everyone else (see figure 5.3). The poster spoke to the dominant, *mono-focal, colonialism-racism-class-misogynarchy*, indeed *homo-colonial*, cisgender spirit of the official March and to what kind of subjects would be legitimate and intelligible in it.

5.3 Inter-LGBT poster calling for the LGBT Pride March in 2019, featuring a lone white gay man leading everyone (Inter-LGBT 2019).

In response, the group Pride politique auto-gérée announced their own march to be held on July 4 with a different poster and the slogan "Pride 2020: Our Pride is Political" (see figure 5.4).[13] Pride politique auto-gérée then organized a series of open meetings to prepare the march. They invited radical racialized queers+, trans+, and dykes+. Those who attended proposed to form an autonomous leading racialized queer contingent. Pride politique auto-gérée agreed.

The group Queers racisé.e.s autonomes, a heterogeneous collective born in October 2019, soon emerged as the main organizer of the autonomous contingent. In a friendly riff on the Pride politique auto-gérée poster, the collective announced the contingent with its own poster: "Pride 2020, Saturday July 4 Place Pigalle, Paris, Leading Contingent, Racialized Folks Autonomously" (see figure 5.5). The contingent's poster circumvents Inter-LGBT's political mono-focality, *colonialism-racism-class-misogynarchy*, cisgender ideal, and homonationalism as it portrays silhouettes of racialized queers across many national origins, gendered embodiments and political stances via hair varieties and head coverings or not. The poster suggests the *co-presence* of racialized queer+, trans+, and dyke+ subjects from all parts of the world. They undo the notion of a neutral universalized (white) queer subject who is explicitly figured by Inter-LGBT yet who does not need to

5.4 "Pride 2020: Our Pride is Political." Poster for a separate, more radical Pride March, issued by Pride politique auto-gérée in response to Inter-LGBT's poster (Gaelle 2020).

5.5 "Leading Contingent, Autonomous, Racialized" poster for 2020 Pride by Queers racisé.e.s autonomes (Autonomous Racialized Queers) (Gaelle 2020).

be portrayed because always already evident. The poster spontaneously enacts a *situated planetarities* analytic as it represents racialized French queer+, trans+, and dyke+ connectivities across the planet. It differs from the general *Pride politique* poster that does not suggest a broader world or multiplicities of relations of power. The poster uses parts of several flags in its background in recognition of the contingent's heterogeneous composition. It announces the meeting point not at the march's official commencement site but rather at Pigalle subway station, thus inside a working-class racialized neighborhood of Paris.

As planned, on the day of the march the group of racialized queers+, trans+, and dykes+ arrived and positioned itself in the lead with an in-your-face banner that read "*Queer et Trans Racisé.e.s*" (Racialized Queers and Trans) (see figure 5.6). This autonomous coalitionality marks a point of acceleration at the cusp of decades of racialized queer+, trans+, and dyke+ organizing. What is striking in 2020 is not the contingent's composition or insistence on primary placement in the march. This was the second time that an autonomous racialized coalitional sector coalesced in a broader queer pride march in Paris and led it (see below). Instead, most significant is the contingent's analysis in its call for participants. Drafted by members of Queers racisé.e.s autonomes, it was opened up for elaboration and transformed into a google doc to which others could contribute. The text was then jointly edited by members of thirteen racialized queer+ and trans+ groups. Ultimately, it was signed by fifty additional racialized queer+, trans+, dyke+, and feminist and/or "intersectional antiracism" groups.[14]

The text's title, "Our Queer Pride is Anti-Racist," announces a precise, situated perspective in relation to what white left queers had articulated as "Our Pride is Political." It foregrounds the *co-formations* racism and class, with reference to the violence of the *spatialization of race* and *racialization of space* in the racialized working-class urban outskirts (see full text in appendix A). It begins with a hailing: "We, racialized dykes, bis, trans, faggots, and intersex people call for bringing our queer and antiracism demands into an autonomous contingent of the queer pride demonstration this Saturday, July 4." It then denounces conditions of subalterneity, stigmatization, and criminalization. It decries the French state's deportation of undocumented people; the letting die of Black, sex-worker, and trans subjects; indifference about COVID-19 killing "the most precious among us"; police bullying, violence and murders; and more. It reiterates "We are in mourning and we are angry" three times, thereby emphasizing collective affect and determination but also echoing call-and-response

5.6 Photo of 2020 LGBT Pride with banner by *Queer et trans racisé.e.s* (Racialized Queers and Trans) announcing the autonomous contingent of racialized queer and trans people (Raha and Baars 2021).

and repetition in many forms of subaltern music, sacred chants, and oral communication. The text proclaims, "We are the Adama generation"—the generation of uncompromising racialized activists and allies sparked by the 2016 racist murder of Adama Traoré (July 19, 1992–July 19, 2016), a young Malian French Black male, in the Parisian banlieue Beaumont-sur-Ois. In a *sideways* gesture, the text references queer inseparability and *accomplicity-comradeship* with movements that racialized people are leading: pro-immigration, labor, for trans lives, for sex workers' lives, abolitionist, against all forms of police brutality, etc.

The text circumvents dominant mono-focal logics. It refuses everything that separates struggles such as for racialized queer+, trans+, and dyke+ life, for workers' equity, or ending police murders and brutality. The text undoes the idea of racialized queers as a monolith. Its speaking subjects are plural we-subjects. The text names dykes (first), thereby preventing their otherwise habitual erasure in the exclusive foregrounding of queer and trans. It explodes the rubric "racialized queer" by articulating multiple kinds of conditions, *situated* relations to French *national-normativities* and desires. The text's authors sometimes self-designate as fully autonomous ("We, racialized dykes, bis, trans, faggots, and intersex people"). At other times they present as fused with all racialized people—for example, in reference to police terror. In yet other instances they merge with racialized people and white allies together, as in the invocation of the "hundreds of thousands" (*gilets jaunes*, or yellow vests) who are subjected to violent police repression. The text ultimately forms a broad community in *liberation-oriented co-motion*.

Unfortunately, however, lest we become prematurely celebratory, we need to note that the text also resulted in internal alienations. Some racialized dyke+ groups and individuals did not attend because they felt the "dyke" appellation was simply decorative because the text's analysis ignored their conditions of colonial-racialized sexism and lesbophobia. By leaving some registers of contextual relations of power unthought, they were inadvertently bolstered. Here a *backwards-sideways* perspective that keeps entire communities (and historical exclusions, see below) in view *critically illuminates* how the march call's partial articulation (just the term dyke without a dyke analysis) obstructed from within the potential for unified *co-motion*.

Already Elsewhere

At this point if we turn *sideways*, we can open up yet another moment of *critical luminosity*. It revolves around the racialized dyke+ concerted critique of a Pride March that Inter-LGBT and SOS Homophobie (SOS Homophobia) tried to organize in 2019 in Saint-Denis, a banlieue of Paris, with the financial support of Saint-Denis's city council. SOS Homophobie, like Inter-LGBT, is predominantly white. It was founded in 1994 by the centrist Socialist Party and modeled on the Party's preceding group, SOS Racisme that it had used to substitute for and destroy the radical grassroots *beur* movement of the 1980s (Bacchetta 2017, 2016). Neither Inter-LGBT nor SOS Homophobie had a history of concern for racialized queer+ and trans+ people. They had never held activities in banlieues. Unsurprisingly, many racialized queer+, trans+, and dyke+ people inside Saint-Denis and beyond experienced the projected march as a colonial, racist intrusion.

Indeed, a brief *historical-contextualization* of the space of Saint-Denis will help to clarify this position. In the dominant French imaginary and in official political discourse and policies that draw on it, Saint-Denis—specifically—serves as an iconic controlling image saturated with dominant imaginings and projections about banlieue life. Informed simultaneously by earlier colonial-racial-sexual fantasies and present *colonialism-racism-class-misogynarchies-amnesias*, Saint-Denis is dominantly hallucinated as a foreign site, dense with out-of-control Black and brown bodies, confusion, periodic riots, sexual violence, and other disorders ostensibly requiring constant heavy police presence. This racialized fantasy projection actually directly defies the reality of organized, meaningful life in the banlieues. As mentioned in this book's introduction and above, habitually—and under COVID-19 conditions—banlieue residents step up to fill the lacunae of the colonial-racial state by organizing their own childcare, informal taxis, homemade food, tutoring, internet services, basement mosques, and more. They create life sustainment inside imposed conditions of *segregationality*.

In the dominant queer and nonqueer imagination, the banlieue and its racialized subjects, especially men, are assigned excessive queerphobia. Ironically, the largest queerphobic demonstration ever in France, *La Manif pour tous*—"The demonstration for everyone," an insulting riff on the homonationalist gay marriage slogan "Marriage for everyone"—held on January 13, 2013, was overwhelmingly white and took place not in a banlieue but instead in central Paris.

On June 6, 2019, the group LOCs, mentioned above, dropped a public political response to Inter-LGBT and SOS Homophobie's march announcement. Founded by the Djibutian French Sabreen Al Rassace and the Indian French Moruni Turlot in 2009, LOCs, which comprises both immigrants and citizens, mobilizes and defends racialized lesbian+, mainly refugees, from everywhere.[15] The group is open to all lesbians+: women-identified, nonbinary, trans, etc. Many members are refugees from across the Global South(s). LOCs also works in coalitions with racialized trans+ groups. It takes an uncompromising position against lesbophobia and sexism everywhere.

The LOCs statement on the march, entitled "Pride for Whom? Pride for What? The Opportunism of Alliances and Visibility," takes no prisoners (see appendix B). It clarifies itself as a "Statement in Response to the Call for a First 'Pride March in the Banlieue.'" It presents a forceful analytic of the *co-productions* colonialism and capitalism, and the *co-formations* racism, class, and sexism. It critiques Inter-LGBT and SOS Homophobie for ignorance about racialized lesbians lives, genealogies, heritage, life issues, and ways of living. It frames the Inter-LGBT and SOS Homophobie march as an unwanted invasion for dominant queer and trans performative wokeness.

The statement decries the projected march's "pinkwashing" that "leaves intact the effects of racist, sexist, and capitalist policies that crush the lives of our families, our communities, friends, and comrades, here and elsewhere." It affirms "we are actors of our spaces and struggles." It invokes an earlier issue wherein LOCs vehemently publicly opposed a racist Inter-LGBT march poster (see below). It remarks that the march "smacks of racist, sexist, nationalist, and even Pétainist overtones." It highlights Inter-LGBT and SOS Homophobie's silence about sexism and the "unbridled capitalism that oppresses us and prevents us from flourishing and even from simply living." It observes that Inter-LGBT and SOS Homophobie do not "publicly speak out against unbridled racism, nor even actively fight it within their own organizations." LOCs refuses the march's complicity with the city's gentrifying plans that aim to provide space to white "homoparental" couples, as elsewhere in Western Europe and in the United States (Haritaworn 2015b; Bacchetta et. al. 2015; Hanhardt 2013). For LOCs, it is all part of displacing racialized lesbians who "do not feel less safe" in the banlieue than in central Paris where they are "forced by police to show their ID documents, are attacked, harassed, but also exoticized, depoliticized, ignored, or invisibilized." The statement critiques the city of Saint-Denis for funding the march while not investing in improving conditions for banlieue residents who continue to die in fires or get relocated when buildings burn.

The LOCs statement makes an important decolonial epistemic intervention as it refuses dominant norms of visibility. It highlights the work of LOCs and its invisibilization in dominant perception. It presents a specifically *situated planetarities* kind of analytic as it connects the banlieue to the world:

> Our life experiences are those of lesbians from postcolonial migrations, exiles, refugees, caught up in community and family networks of complex solidarities that cannot be reduced to the sole rhetoric of coming out and public visibility. We fight to support lesbian refugees and against the fascisms that restrict our lives. We know how and when to be visible. We did not wait for any authorization to organize ourselves, to build safe spaces, and to build international solidarity. . . . Our lesbian bodies may be invisible and inaudible to many, but we will continue to fight in line with our experiences and the neighborhoods in which we live.

The statement goes on to denounce a party the march organizers have announced for the evening after the march in a gentrified enclave of Saint-Denis where the only racialized people are staff who will serve the white partiers. It ends powerfully with "Anything that is done without us cannot be done for us!"

With this, LOCs incited a debate with the march organizers. Other groups of racialized queers+ got involved, too. Soon the event was reconceptualized. Ultimately the critical *articulations* of LOCs provoked a radical reframing of the march such that in the end LOCs agreed to participate.

A *backwards-sideways* perspective makes clear how LOCs's exposure of Inter-LGBT and SOS Homophobie's violent reproduction of relations of power incited extreme divisions, and how the refusal of LOCs to compromise opened up the possibility of coming together.

No Return

Yet, the above would be incomprehensible without another *backwards* moment. The prior year's Pride March in Paris, on June 30, 2018, had constituted a stunning point zero of departure for what followed. It was the first time racialized queer+, trans+, dyke+ groups and individuals came together in a same autonomous leading contingent in the official Pride March in Paris organized by Inter-LGBT. Given the history of conflict with Inter-LGBT, they did not seek cooperation or permission. They just arrived—about one hundred strong—with their banner and placed themselves at the front of the march to enact their desire to subvert it. The banner read "*Queer et Trans Racisé.e.s contre le Homonationalisme*" (Racialized Queers and Trans Against Homonationalism) (figure 5.7). This action publicly articulated a strong refusal of assimilation but also of *segregationality* as a condition inside Paris and its banlieues. It also pushed against the dominant conception of a visibility-invisibility binary.

The main organizer of the 2018 contingent of queer+, trans+, and dyke+ subjects was a newly formed coalition: Qitoko. To bring folks together, Qitoko issued a call, the title of which was later inscribed on the banner mentioned above (see appendix C). In the call, Qitoko critiqued Inter-LGBT for its homonationalism, white supremacy, collusion with the officials of the City of Paris, and for speaking in place of and about racialized queer+, trans+, and dyke+ subjects while silencing and invisibilizing them. Qitoko exposed Inter-LGBT's support for the mayor's plan for Gay Games as "a springboard for the 2024 Olympics" and its "gentrifying effect" for sites where working-class racialized people live. The group cited the iconic spatiality of colonial-racialized fantasies—the working-class city of Saint-Denis, where Inter-LGBT and SOS Homophobie would later try to organize the march that LOCs critiqued and fundamentally modified.

The 2018 Qitoko statement pointed to Inter-LGBT's collusion with the City of Paris's plan for "attracting gay, white, wealthy tourists" while excluding precarious racialized queer+ and trans+ people. It highlighted the "murderous police who infiltrate our spaces" thereby putting racialized queer+ and trans+ people into ever more danger. It emphasized that "while

5.7 LGBT Pride March from 2018 with banner reading
"Racialized Queers and Trans Against Homonationalism"
(*Manifesto 21* 2018).

this same police is violently hunting down migrants and murdering our
brothers, our sisters, our siblings, our mothers, and our fathers in working-
class neighborhoods, while this police is repressing social movements
and establishing colonial order in France, the organizers of the march are
rolling out the red carpet for them." Qitoko's call flagged that (white) queer
police were planned to be on a float shooting water pistols into the air
"for fun," a terrifying insult to all racialized people, including queer and
trans people, who are faced with real police violence. The statement un-
derlined that Inter-LGBT fully ignored that year's Asylum-Immigration
Law that puts the lives of all racialized people including queer and trans
people at risk. The law "deprive[s] undocumented people who are HIV-
positive or are undergoing hormonal treatment or medical treatment"
of health care. The statement affirmed that since racialized queers and
trans are not wanted in the march they would take it over, positioning
themselves at its head.

An important footnote in the call clarifies: "We refuse the command
that we be out implied by this kind of autonomous contingent, but we want
to assert ourselves at the head of the march because our issues and our lives
must be defended." This rejection of what we could call the dominant queer
outness imperative, which is also an *outness imposition*, affirms a totally

different paradigm by and for racialized queer+ and trans+ people. The *outness imperative* refers to the colonial-racist notion of "out" of the closet as a sign of queer pride and radicality, and "in" as shame, cowardice, and complicity. The *outness imperative* proceeds with zero consciousness that racialized queers+, trans+, and dykes+ come from sites and situations devasted by colonial gender and sexuality impositions and that have vastly different heterosexual and queer kinds of socialities and relationalities (Danjé 2021; Fernandes 2021; Di Pietro 2020b, , 2016; Driskill et al. 2011; Lugones 2008; Driskill 2004; Oyěwùmí 1997). For example, the kind of display of heterosexuality that is normative in French public space is considered extremely vulgar across the Maghreb. Thus, queer visibility cannot have the same meaning across those sites. A combination of colonial-racializing factors—including colonial French sexualized representations of colonized-racialized bodies—*operate* in ways that can make racialized queer+ visibility in France variably harmful. Further, the *outness-imperative* can unfold in France as epistemic violence that suppresses racialized queer+, trans+, and dyke+ distinct categories, logics, presuppositions, conclusions, and self-designations (Garaoun 2022; Cheikh and Garaoun 2022). The Qitoko statement thereby confirms racialized queer+, trans+, and dyke+ subjects' right to what below and elsewhere I call *radical critical silence, in-context* (Bacchetta 2009a).

The solidarity in the march in Paris by antiracist, antihomonationalism white queers who sandwiched between the autonomous racialized contingent and Inter-LGBT was wholeheartedly welcome. Yet, it was not completely without problems. While passing a statue of Jeanne D'Arc some white queers suddenly broke ranks, climbed up it, and unfolded a banner. The police rushed in and predictably instead of arresting them came for nearby racialized queers+, trans+, and dykes+. The latter managed to escape into the crowd before arrest. Afterwards some radical white queer groups critiqued the action and vowed it would not happen again. Some imagined the arrest risk as an instance of rogue police racism. For others it was much more. It entailed dominant queer *political amnesia, nonsensing,* and *imperception* about how racism operates to create murderous conditions for racialized subjects.

R-assemblage

To understand the complexities of danger here, let us move *backwards* to a slightly earlier *critical-luminosity* moment of *freedom-exigent co-motion*: the March 10, 2017, coalitional autonomous racialized queer+, trans+, and dyke+ day of panels, film, art exhibits, dialogue, and meal sharing during Queer Week in Paris. It was one of several entry points for broadening racialized queer+, trans+, and dyke+ intellectual, activist, and artivist solidarities.

Co-organized by activists in the Decolonizing Sexualities Network and some France-based racialized queer+, trans+, and dyke+ groups, the day was called Journée R-assemblage lesbien, trans, queer décolonial et anticapitaliste (Day of Lesbian, Trans, Queer Decolonial and Anti-Capitalist Assemblage). The title invokes the specifically French meaning of *assemblage* that I explain in this book's Introduction and chapter 3. The event was a first collective attempt in Paris to gather disparate autonomous racialized queer+, trans+, and dyke+ people from different perspectives into a same sustained conversation. It was also fully open to allies. Free and open to the public, it took place at ~~La Colonie~~, a space founded by the Algerian French artist Kader Attia at 128 Rue Lafayette in Paris's center, for decolonial art exhibits, meetings, conferences, workshops, films, and other events. It was at once a space of *common conditions* and *affective alliances* with *alter-kinship co-motion* potentialities, in the sense of chapter 1. To choose ~~La Colonie~~ meant affirming that racialized queers+, trans+, and dykes+ are inseparable from broader racialized communities and from other decolonial movements. Some allies would have to enter a potential discomfort zone to hear them.

That day was the first queer event ever at ~~La Colonie~~ but would not be the last. It drew an audience that packed ~~La Colonie~~'s large conference room and overflowed into the street. The public came from many different movements. The walls held an art exhibition of photos by the Black Caribbean French lesbian Estelle Prudent and paintings by the queer New Caledonian artist Alexandre Erre.

The event began with the film *diaspora/situations* by the Moroccan French artist, filmmaker, and poet Tarek Lakhrissi. Next was a panel on *Trans anti-capitaliste et décolonial* (Anti-Capitalist and Decolonial Trans) and then a panel on *Décoloniser les sexualités* (Decolonizing Sexualities). Finally, I gave a short closing talk, "*Construire ensemble les alliances queer et trans racisé.e.s*" (Constructing Racialized Queer and Trans Alliances Together) which developed some of the thematics of this book. It was followed by a long discussion. Importantly, during the conversation the Afro-Caribbean photographer and activist Richard Mar raised (to everyone) the question of racialized queer+, trans+, and dyke+ people's decolonial solidarity with nonhuman *beings-becomings*.

The brilliance of Mar's question can best be understood *in-context*. In France the main critical literature on human to nonhuman relationality is located in sociological deconstructions of the colonial-racist animalization of colonized subjects specifically in nineteenth- and twentieth-century scientific discourse. It is continued in many ways, including the publication of the highly sensationalized account of French colonial universal exhibitions, *Zoos humaines* (Human zoos) (Bancel et. al. 2004). Whereas in many other European countries human-nonhuman relationality is discussed in environmental movements, France has no such substantial movement (Bahaffou and Gorecki 2022). In France veganism and vegetarianism are not widespread. Right and left are overwhelmingly uninterested in human to nonhuman relationality. Speciesism in France remains largely *unsensed, imperceptible*, and *unintelligible* as a relation of power. Animals, fish, fowl, and plant life as *and anothers* who/that would be integral to thinking about *subjects-in-sociality and another* are beyond such radar in France. Among racialized queers+, trans+, and dykes+, views are split between valorizing "traditional" nonvegetarian or nonvegan Global Southern foods and a desire to disrupt the essentialization of "traditional" and to rethink it as crystallized practices that can be redynamized otherwise. It is thereby significant that many racialized queers+, trans+, and dykes+ in the room followed Mar to express that queer relationality to nonhuman *beings-becomings* is a vital question for queer lives.

A few weeks after the above event, the French branch of Decolonizing Sexualities Network began organizing vegan and vegetarian events.[16] First a dinner at Café Falafel, then a collective lunch in the Buttes Chaumont Park provided time-spaces for connections, socializing, fun, and political conversations. The lunch became an annual occurrence. With discussion—such as of caste-based forced vegetarianism in India—the food options were opened to nonvegetarianism. The gatherings were interrupted due to COVID-19 confinement. Yet, they contributed to creating solidarities that continue at present.

Homo-Colonial Violence

To understand something of the *freedom-exigent* analytics around which the COVID-19 solidarity referenced above converges, we can shift a bit further *backwards*. From there we can see that the clashes between racialized queers+, trans+, and dykes+ and Inter-LGBT in 2020, 2019, and 2018 are but surface points to a deeper *co-present* history of discord.

To cite one meaningful conflict moment, let us turn to the 2011 poster proposed by Inter-LGBT for that year's LGBT Pride March that the 2019 LOCs statement (above) critiqued (figure 5.8). The 2011 Inter-LGBT poster displayed a white rooster or cock draped with a red boa against a blue back-drop with the words *"Pour l'Égalié: en 2011 je marche, en 2012 je vote"* (For Equality: In 2011 I march, in 2012 I vote). In contrast to prior years in which rainbows abounded, the 2011 poster was suddenly saturated with toxic masculine, nationalist symbols: the cock representing France, the blue-red-white of the French flag, and words that offer an I speaking subject position previously reserved exclusively for the properly documented cisgender heterosexual male citizen-subject, now extended to (white) queer citizen-subjects. In the terms of chapter 1, this new *homo-inclusion* calls to mind a (white*) sanguinal alliance*. It also collapses all white queer subjects under the rubric of the gay male citizen-subject, thereby erasing all other white queers. It directly excludes undocumented queers who cannot vote and all racialized queers+, trans+, and dykes+ whose "equality" requires more than laws that protect anormative gender embodiment and queer sexuality.

The poster presents the condensed figure of the white gay male with French citizenship as *more-nationalist-than-thou*. Historically, in France the brown cock was an antiroyalist symbol of the French revolution. The chromatic shift from brown cock to white cock could hint at a further *white supremacistization* requiring the erasure of racialized subjects and their presumed out-of-control sexuality to achieve patriotic respectability (Guénif-Souilamas 2006a; Bilé 2005; Guénif-Souilamas and Macé 2004). The boa as effeminacy symbol draped on the white cock provides a homo twist to *national-normative* white citizen-subjectivity while genderly serving as contrast to enhance the cock's virility. This scene recalls Irigaray's (1977, 1985) insistence that the only I speaking subject in French (and Italian and English) is male. The sexual politics remain intact: in everyday parlance in French the cock is a (white) Don Juan figure. A sexist cisgender hetero-sexual male trying to seduce a woman is described thus: *"Il fait le coq"* (He's acting like a rooster or cock).

If we move *sideways* a bit we can observe that this poster's reductive figuration of white queers as national subjects under the sign of the white gay male *homo-citizen* did not stand alone. Transnationally, it resonated with public, racialized Gay Pride disasters across Europe, from Berlin to East London to Brussels (Bacchetta 2020; Haritaworn 2015b; El-Tayeb 2011; Bacchetta and Haritaworn 2011). It corresponded to right-wing nationalist resurgences in France and across Western Europe. In France, the fascist

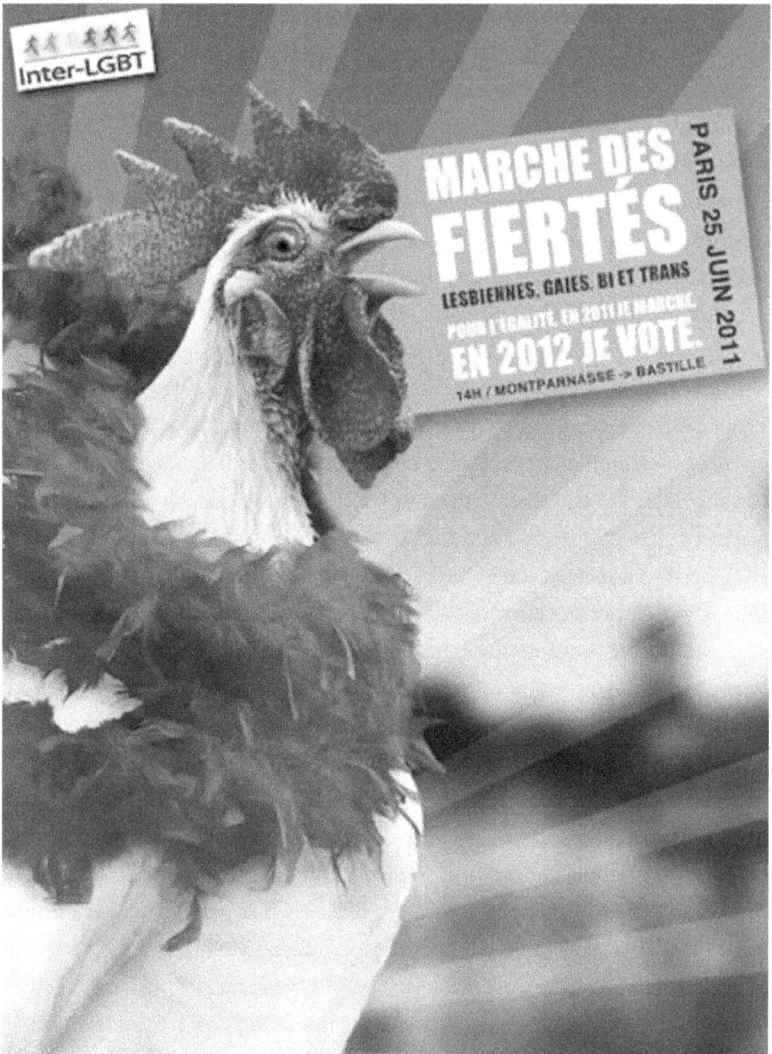

5.8 Inter-LGBT poster calling for LGBT Pride March in 2011: white rooster or cock, red boa, and the words "Pride March, Lesbians, Gays, Bi, and Trans" and "For equality, in 2011 I march, in 2012 I vote" (*Libération* 2011).

National Front worked to seduce (white) queer votes by presenting Muslim, Arab, and Black (presumably straight) men as *more-queerphobic-than-thou*. The figuring of out-of-control, presumed-to-be-straight racialized men as threats unfolded parallel to new laws demonizing racialized communities such as the "security" legislation banning employment of airport workers who travel to specified Muslim countries, and the April 2011 outlawing of the burka in public space.

Unsurprisingly then, within twenty-four hours of its release, the 2011 poster incited a public clash between homonationalists in Inter-LGBT and racialized queers+, trans+, and dykes+ and allies on Facebook and in the then Twittersphere. This is not the place to detail all responses. My focus is on racialized queer+, trans+, and dyke+ analytics. For that, I will highlight the main coalitional Facebook group, L'affiche officielle de la Marche des Fiértés parisienne 2011 DOIT DÉGAGER (The Official Poster of the 2011 Paris Pride March has to GET OUT; in caps in the original).

If we remain with a *backwards-sideways* analytic, the apparition of DÉGAGER (GET OUT) in the antiposter coalition's name already preannounces the coalition's critique. During the 2011 North African, sub-Saharan African, and Middle Eastern revolutions against dictatorships, degrading economic conditions and assaults on poor peoples' dignity induced in neocolonial relations especially to France, *dégager* (get out) became a clarion call in Tunisia and its diaspora against the dictator Ben Ali: *Ben Ali Dégage!* (Ben Ali Get Out!). The racialized queer Facebook group thereby directly linked its resistance to the Inter-LGBT poster to the *co-present* Jasmine Revolution in Tunisia.[17]

A first post on the group's Facebook page declared: "The French universalist republican nation was constructed on the backs of racialized and/or sexual and gender minorities. . . . The gay nationalists ask us to march in the name of the French Republic that persists in refusing equal rights to LGBT people and/or immigrants and to *des français louches pas de souche*." The latter is a political play on words: *francais de souche* means the proper white middle-class French, and *francais louche*, which rhymes, means the suspect French. *Francais de souche* had particular resonance for racialized people as it had recently been an object of controversy. Houria Bouteldja, spokesperson for the then active decolonial Parti des indigènes de la République (Party of the Indigenous of the Republic) had called the collectivity of dominant French people *les souchiens* in a TV interview. While ostensibly invoking dominant (white) citizen-subjects, her reformulation phonetically rings as *sous chiens* (those below the dogs). Bouteldja's sarcastic reversal of dominant racialized animalization (see above) incited white supremist outrage. Importantly, throughout, francophone orality (rhyme, phonetics, poetics) looms large in all the decolonial critiques offered here.

Facebook page authors denounced the slogan "I march, I vote" as resounding with military orders: "You will have to march, you will have to vote." They proclaimed: "You will march without LGBT people who are racialized, trans, undocumented, foreign, whores, sex workers, HIV-precarious folks and foreigners deprived of access to medical care, the faggots, and all those who for quite a long time no longer identify as homosexual, transsexual, gay, or lesbian. Without your voting card, without your Socialist Party card, without your membership to Inter-LGBT you are nothing." They wrote: "We're against integration. We're against assimilation. . . . We demand that the poster be taken away immediately." The insertion of this *subalternist* oppositionality amplified the "DÉGAGER" (GET OUT) demand.

Some other individuals and racialized queer+, trans+, and dyke+ groups posted statements, too. They exposed how the poster was haunted by other *co-present temporal-spatialities*. For instance, LOCs called the poster "racist, macho and Pétainist" in a reference to Henri Philippe Benoni Omer Pétain, the head of Vichy France, collaborator with Nazis. In everyday French, the referent *Pétainisme* is used to describe extreme right-wing and fascist politics. But for LOCs it is not lost that Pétain was also a sexist womanizer.

Some dominant queer groups, too, expressed discontent on the page, for different reasons. For instance, *Le Refuge* (The Refuge) attacked the poster for what it termed its femme-phobic fixation on the boa, an assault to (their desired) *homo-respectability*. Jacqueline Julien, president of *Bagdam espace lesbien* (Bagdam Lesbian Space) in Toulouse, called the cock a "hideous" and "viriloid symbol." Unfortunately, the majority-white queer groups consistently left out colonial-racism, thereby precluding broader alliances.

Inter-LGBT responded by claiming that the poster was meant to "*detour*" (divert, parry, reappropriate) the cock, to develop "pride," to speak to a broader public. They imagined the boa as "transgression" and the poster's words as a warning about their demands for the 2012 presidential elections: gay marriage, *homo-parenté* (gay and lesbian adoption and parental rights), trans reforms, and other kinds of integration and assimilation. In the end, Inter-LGBT had alienated multiple constituencies and was forced to withdraw the poster.

Deadly Encounter

If we remain with the *backwards-sideways* gesture, we will recall a related *critical luminous* clash point during Pride week just one year earlier. It began when some white French lesbians in Paris and white Spanish lesbians from the Girlie Circuit Festival in Barcelona joined forces. They issued a very colorful, bilingual (French and English), strikingly colonial-racialized poster announcing an "Official Lesbian Party" in Paris on June 26, 2010.[18] The poster displays the words "Official Lesbian Party," the initials "RG" (which stand for Rive Gauche, or the left bank of the Seine, thus the Latin Quarter), along with "Girls Club Paris," "*Samedi 26 juin*" (Saturday, June 26), "*Dès 22h30*" (From 10:30 p.m.), "Gay Pride *événement*" (Gay Pride event), and "Happy Hour Pride" (in English). It shows two cisgender white women who correspond neatly to the hegemonic model for proper cis femininity, dressed in bikinis and black high-heeled sandal-like shoes, both wearing fake, cartoonish, rainbow-colored Indigenous headdresses. One woman is on all fours and the other is sitting on her back mock riding her. The rider is holding a rainbow-colored whip in a position to use it on the woman on all fours.

This French and Spanish lesbian *co-motion* that the poster hoped to induce must be read *in-context* with what it disappears, *re-presents*, and invokes (Bacchetta 2018). It spectacularizes white French and Spanish lesbian subjects, and Indigenous objects (not subjects). Both France and Spain have spent over five hundred years as planetary colonial powers across multiple forms: settler, mercantile, administrative, majoritarian, minoritarian, external, break-away (Bacchetta 2022). Both countries lost settler colonies through military defeat: France, Algeria; and Spain, most of Abya Yala. They both carried out genocide, land theft, enslavement, and human traffic in "the Americas." Today both are sites of *segregationality*. Yet, on the poster French and Spanish colonialism are absent, displaced, replaced with reference to an elsewhere, the United States. The poster thus reflects a variant of the logic of elimination (Lee-Oliver 2019; Barker 2017; Wolfe 2006). Its procedure of *in-context* repression and recurrence elsewhere (a kind of return of the repressed) inscribes it in Native *repression-displacement-elimination*. Simultaneously, because the poster includes (here imported) Native objects from the United States, a powerful elsewhere, in the site of French and Spanish Native elimination, it also enacts Native *obliteration-with-trace*.

On the poster, the (white) French-Spanish lesbian alliance is a *deadly encounter* for it is constructed on the *murderous backdropification* of (displaced) Native life (Bacchetta 1999, 2019c). It foregrounds white lesbian bodies performing colonialism. The bodies are accompanied by sacred Native items that are habitually transformed into props in US colonial-racialized anti-Native discourse—headdress, feathers—along with a slave-master prosthesis, the whip, specifically from Turtle Island (Berkhofer 1978). The headdresses and feathers are extracted from Native space, painted rainbow-colored, and resignified for white French and Spanish lesbian erotic pleasure. In this *xenophobic lesbophilic* scenario the instrumentalization of feathers is an unspeakable violation. In Native cultures, feathers are sacred symbols of deep respect that must be earned. Leaders wear headdresses. The representation of headdresses on the poster without Native bodies reiterates the eliminative logic of "vanishing" and replacement (Wolfe 2006). The poster transforms Natives simultaneously into *etcéteras* and a forcibly disappeared *and another* who cannot according to the logic of elimination be recognized as alive in the present. White French and Spanish lesbian unity is achieved through colonial-racial complicity and mono-focality (see chapter 3). Across national divides the lesbians become indistinguishable in their Europeanness. They produce a *sanguinal alliance* of the most reactionary type (see chapter 1).

On the poster, the image of one white lesbian riding another like a horse is meant to induce an erotic effect. Yet, this visual references Hollywood "cowboys and Indians" scenarios that habitually construct and spectacularize white male bravado and Native incapacity, an assemblage that depends on *colonialism-racism-class-misogynarchies amnesia*. The white lesbians' bikinis are color-coded in a queer gender and speciesist set of binarisms: the rider's, which is blue, dominantly codes top, while the horse's, which is pink, suggests bottom. This scene is reinforced by the dichotomous positioning of a resignified Native item (colorful headdress) on both heads and a settler item (black high-heeled shoes) on the feet. The poster represents Natives via things and white people as subjects. Its announcement of the party's venue in Paris's Latin Quarter reinforces the ostensible harmonious relation of the category lesbian to a site of colonial-racial anxiety for many racialized people in France including racialized dykes+ (see introduction).

A brief *backwards-sideways* shift here clarifies that the *backdropification* of subalternly racialized subjects-objects to assert dominant (white) lesbian subjectivity has a long genealogy in France. N. Doumia of the 1990s autonomous racialized lesbian *Groupe du 6 novembre* highlights how during public debates about PACS (*pacte civil de solidarité*, "civilian pact of solidarity," or domestic partnership) an all-white queer group sold T-shirts reading: "All homophobes will be reborn as undocumented Black lesbians" (Doumia

2001, 23). The slogan's "humor" depended on white (queer and straight) people's understanding that they will never become undocumented Black lesbians. The white queer activists were having a dominant-to-dominant discussion wherein Black lesbians were made absent, reduced to objects. Doumia critiqued the slogan's instrumentalization of undocumented Black lesbians and suggested replacing it with "All homophobes will be reincarnated as orange pricks without pubic hairs" (24).

On the French-Spanish lesbian party poster, Native obliteration unfolds both via substitutive redface and via the horse image that signals Natives' racist animalization, a process that is never far from massacre (Jackson 2020; Sithole 2020). Jacques Semelin (2011, 59) remarks: "We begin to kill" when we "disqualify" the Other "from humanity"; indeed "massacre" etymologically signals killing animals.

The poster's phrase "Official Lesbian Party" hints at how *political amnesias* operate in representations of the universalized lesbian subject as white (i.e., "official") while marginalizing or erasing all Others. In France, "official" has deep resonances. Almost two decades prior to this poster, Dalila Kadri Cheriet, mentioned above, coined "Official French Lesbian Movement" (MLFO) as a humorous critical riff on the classic phrase Women's Liberation Movement (MLF). MLFO describes white lesbians who feel entitled to speak for all lesbians without the latter's consent (Cheriet 2001, 20). This speaking-for, a form of *re-presentation*, is yet another mode of annihilation (Bacchetta 2018).

Notwithstanding the above, such *deadly encounters* and *backdropifications* are not reducible to enactments by *politically amnesic* white queers. Unfortunately, any feminist or queer coalitionality inside a settler colony (e.g., "the Americas," Australia, New Zealand, etc.) that forgets Native subjects where it is located can inadvertently reproduce elimination.

Non-Encounter Co-Motion

To provide insight into "official," into the *outness imperative*, and into life below the dominant radar let us move *backwards* again to another point of *critical luminosity* that remains unseen and yet is deeply telling: the *co-motion* of some veiled Muslim lesbians against the March 15, 2004, French law banning Muslim veils in schools.[19] Much scholarship, journalism, and social media has exposed the law. Thus, nearly everyone in France and many people globally now feel they know everything about it. I will not repeat that important work here. Instead, I am interested in events outside the spotlight. One of these is a quiet protest enactment by veiled Muslim lesbians who did not out themselves as lesbians in the action. I will explain below, but for now some introductory comments about the *articulation-inarticulation continuum, co-formations*, and *co-productions* will help to contextualize.

Earlier I mentioned that, with Foucault in mind, it can be productive to reveal and *articulate* all relations of power, especially those that power itself hides. Here I will suggest that whether disclosing power is useful or not depends on the *situated* relation between exposure, power, forms of subalterneity, and scale. Sometimes uncovering power can participate in ocular-centrism's murderous effects. Heidegger and Benjamin highlight how (European) modernity is characterized by the hegemony of visuality. For Foucault, visualization (panopticon, mapping, revealing) is a technique of disciplinary power and biopolitics (Foucault 2003, 1977). We saw above how some racialized queers+ contest the *outness imperative*. Disability activists highlight that reliance on visuality discounts subjects who "see" otherwise. Rey Chow, with reference to US drone warfare, posits an intimate connection between seeing and destroying (2006, 25–43). For Gilles Deleuze (1986; 1962) and Jacques Rancière (2001), visualization and all perception depend less on senses than a shared field of intelligibility. Finally, calling for always-already systematically revealing ever more relations of power can imply that all power is eventually knowable even if at present still unseen. The *obstructed-perception* requiring *perception-liberation* presupposition risks functioning as Reich's "repressive hypothesis" with all the latter's problems (Foucault 1972). So here, let us consider how at times exposing some relations of power can reinforce them and how sometimes the most effective *freedom-exigent* strategy is *radical critical silence*.

To do so, let us first distinguish between different forms of silence. One kind is *dominant silencing*. In the outpouring of discourse on the law, the voices of covered Muslim women were made inaudible. This was problematized by racialized feminist, dyke+, and lesbian+ activists. It was also critiqued in art. An example is the installation *Ghost* by Kader Attia, mentioned above (Vitrani 2011; figure 5.9). Attia's piece consists of 560 veiled silhouettes made of aluminum paper, arranged in rows, praying. Conceptualized during the expansion of zealous Islamophobia between September 11, 2001, and 2005, it was inspired by the artist's mother.[20] *Ghost* speaks to how individual Muslim women *in-context* are hailed to reimagine themselves as part of a homogenized, serialized group. The aluminum foil invokes their fragility; they can easily be crushed. The piece visualizes how Muslim women in

5.9 Kader Attia, *Ghost*. Photo by Hugo Vitrani (Attia 2011).

dominant colonial-racist imaginaries are constructed as voiceless, without brains or heads, reduced to the veil. *Ghost* brings into play multiple dimensions and registers of *co-formations* and *co-productions*. It also situates the women both within and beyond murderous relations of power *in-context*. *Ghost* belongs to many *co-present temporal-spatialities* and dimensions of life at once. It invokes invisibilization but also a haunting that insists on *co-presence*. In a possible move toward *situated planetarity* here the silhouettes are praying together, thus opening a line of flight through relationality to the divine and to a community of Muslim women beyond France's borders.

During the 2004 law debates across registers (political discourse, scholarship, media, etc.) Muslim women's voices were resoundingly unheard. In their place the law's nonveiled non-Muslim supporters (right, left, and center, including feminists and lesbians) occupied most of the space. Across the political spectrum they projected the usual colonial-racialized figurations of Muslim women as eternal victims of brutal hypersexed Muslim men (Karimi 2023; Moujoud 2025, 2015; Guénif-Souilamas 2006a, 2006b; Kaddour 2001; Yegenoglu 1998; Kabbani 1986; Mernissi 1983). They spectacularly reinforced the *co-productions* colonialism, coloniality, and colonial-racialized *misogynarchies*. These representations were deployed to legitimize the state's violent biopolitical hold over Muslim women's bodies. They directly resonated with the colonial French army's humiliating forced unveiling of women in Algeria as an assimilationist strategy. A highly articulate sector of white French feminists and leftists mobilized what Nacira Guénif-Souilamas (2006a) calls "virtuous racism," here racism connected to colonial savior narratives.

In demonstrations against the law, veiled Muslim women gathered massively. A national demonstration on February 14, 2004, organized by Une école pour tous (One School for All) drew thousands. Though unknown then and mostly ignored today, a small group of veiled lesbian-identified Muslims marched together without specific banners, signs, or chants (Bacchetta 2009a). They stayed in group formation, without identifying themselves as lesbians to other marchers or spectators.

Read through a colonial-racist field of intelligibility in which all Muslims are deemed *more-queerphobic-than-thou*, the *non-outness* of veiled Muslim lesbians in the march will automatically seem motivated by fear of rejection or violence from other Muslims, including family members. In daily life, as the meticulous ethnographic work of Salima Amari has shown, many Muslim lesbians—not unlike non-Muslim lesbians nearly anywhere—do negotiate silence around familial (in)acceptability (2018).

However, here I point to other registers. I suggest the veiled Muslim lesbians' obscuring their lesbianism in the march might be elsewhere from familial and community pressure or even from resistance to both the white queer *outness imperative* and its long-standing "dream" of lesbian of color silence and erasure (Bêtes noires 2001).

I open the possibility that it is a *freedom-exigent* stance primarily designed to divert their violent reframing in the dominant field of intelligibility. The Muslim lesbians in question are members of activist groups with a long practice of analyzing Islamophobia, gender, and sexuality. They know their bodies are (mis)read within the dominant French field of intelligibility with its specific signifying conventions, regulations of the visible and invisible, authorized subject positions, and voids. They understand their place in the distribution of (non)intelligibility. The early autonomous racialized lesbian group, the *Groupe du 6 novembre*, had written this: "Our words" are "considered as an immense brouhaha, cry of savages, incoherent and inconsistent screams" that "as soon as constructed are already deconstructed" and promptly "buried" (Groupe 2001, 25–26).

The veiled lesbians in the march were acutely aware that Muslim lesbianism is figured in colonial-orientalist-racialized discourse not as love between women but rather as a sign of frustration ostensibly due to Muslim male barbarism, polygamy, and the harem. In such discourses Muslim lesbianism is lesbophobically disconnected from lesbian desire, capacity, and agency. It is colonially-racially framed as part of all Muslim women's sexual excess and/or lack in relation to colonial gender and sexuality normativity. Therein, Muslim women are variously represented in reductive ways: (1) as perfect victims-to-be-saved by white French men, women, or civilization or (2) as imperfect victims who are non-victim-victims.[21] The first rubric references French colonial-racialized savior narratives and the second their demonization narratives.

Historically and in the march, veiled Muslim women are made to serve as what I have called *reductive evidence* of the supposed evils of Muslim society. In *reductive evidence* one sign or practice in a society—which manifests in only a fractional portion of the society—is selectively extracted, resignified, and repositioned to represent the essence of an entire society (Bacchetta 2025d). *Reductive evidence* is mobilized to pathologize, demonize, criminalize, or even to annihilate the society in question. Some examples—beside the veil—are the harem in the Middle East, sati in India, "honor killing" in Pakistan, and genital cutting in Africa.

A particularly toxic aspect of *colonial savior solidarity* is the dominant's self-satisfaction around rescuing ostensible victims. Sara Ahmed suggests that the savior-saved relation provides dominant pleasures connected to charitableness (2004). Saviors find gratification in neocolonial generosity. Certainly, other sentiments, too, are involved: brief diversion, x, momentary concern, temporary outrage, excitement, *etcétera*, fascination, attraction, or entertainment.

In France there is a long history of those *targeted-for-saving* talking back. For example, Houria Bouteldja recalls that in the 2011 International Women's Day demonstration in Paris when white French women started chanting "Solidarity with women in the Maghreb!" and "Solidarity with women in Africa!" a contingent of racialized women responded, "Solidarity with women in France!" and "Solidarity with women in Switzerland!" (Bouteldja 2011). They refused to be considered victims who require white feminist saviors. They escaped from *colonial savior solidarity* obliteration.

Accordingly, as the quote at the beginning of this chapter hints, a popular antisavior demonstration slogan among racialized women in France today is "Don't liberate me. I'm taking care of it myself."

To shift back *sideways*, the veiled Muslim lesbians' silence about their lesbianism in the march can be read as *freedom-exigent critical silence*. In a dominant field of intelligibility overdetermined by colonial-orientalist representations, their *outness* would only be weaponized against them. *Beur* fiction writers have long expressed a similar understanding of the limits of articulation and *intelligibility*, and a sense of play and war with it (Talahite 2001).

In-context the women's *self-unmarkedness* as lesbians might be understood elsewhere from a facile self-renunciation of lesbian identity or speech. It can signal both an oppositional and nonoppositional political enactment in the sense of Steve Pile's (1997) reading of Fanon. The *self-unmarkedness* is oppositional, for it directly defies colonial-racial Islamophobic representations and *political amnesias* in which the signifiers "veiled Muslim woman" and "Muslim lesbian" are trapped (Bacchetta 2009a). It is nonoppositional in that the lesbians remain below the radar of power, creating safe space and an *otherwise-collectivity* together.

Both oppositionality and nonoppositionality come into play as the veiled lesbians confront dominant misrecognition with their silence as a shield. They know the dominant will assign them to the place of the colonial-racialized fantasy figure of the victimized straight Muslim woman (Karimi 2023; Alloua 2001; Bacchetta 1994). Meanwhile they are totally elsewhere. Escaped. Together. Their agentic *critical silence* undermines the Global Northern notion of transparent observation. They circumvent a *deadly encounter* with the obliterating onlooking colonial gaze. Their *non-encounter co-motion* can be understood as revolutionary self-preservation, a vital component of *freedom-exigency*, while bolstering *in-context* solidarity against the law.

Concluding Remarks

I will conclude with three brief observations.

First, in this chapter a *backwards-sideways* approach opens insights into *freedom-exigent co-motion* primarily in two ways. The *backwards* movement exposes serial reproductions and accumulations of *co-productions* and *co-formations* of power and how their reiteration precludes or enables *freedom-exigent co-motion in-context*. The *sideways* gesture reveals a world of racialized queer+, trans+, and dyke+ intertextualities with other move-ments, events, and subjects. The *backwards-sideways* orientation discloses densities and intensities that open many dimensions to our comprehension.

Second, in this chapter three key concepts from the *theory-assemblages* this book suggests—*co-formations, co-productions, situated planetarities*—are especially salient for understanding saturations of power and its *operability in-context*. *Co-formations* and *co-productions* comprise condi-tions, co-constitute subjects, and intervene in *freedom-exigent* analytics, practices, and *co-motion*. We saw that any relation of power that was left intact, or worse left unthought, risked becoming a new point of depar-ture for power's reorganization, reproduction, and expansion. Ignoring relations of power produced divisions and closures, while understanding and engaging them (openly or with silence) strengthened possibilities for *freedom-exigent co-motion*. We also saw here the relation between a *situated planetarity* analytic and the possibility of a *freedom-exigent present* and *futu-rity*. The subjects of the above *co-motion* attempted to uncompromisingly identify and transform power *in-context*, and in ways to preempt harmful side effects elsewhere.

Third, beyond this chapter and this book, *co-productions, co-formations*, and the *political amnesias* they induce operate from one generation to the next to make *freedom-exigent co-motion* seem new, a wonder that drops from the sky. Without a long and wide *backwards-sideways* understanding, each generation is left to reinvent the wheel. Yet, we are not alone. We are the *co-present* of multiple genealogies of struggle and creation. They left us seeds, fruits, all along. We need to reconnect with them, meticulously ana-lyze power for our times, invent yet other ways of coming together in broad *accomplicity-comradeship*, and grow as subjects in the process to create a pre-sent and futurity wherein everyone/everything can thrive *in-relationality*.

Together, we already are, we already have, the potentiality to reorganize life. The *theory-assemblages* that this book suggests hope to make a contri-bution even if miniscule to that process. Together, infinitely more efforts in all directions are absolutely vital. With many voices, hands, contributions, with many kinds of *sensings, perception and intelligibilities*, with ever more precise, uncompromising analytics and practices, it can be done. Now.

Appendix A

"Our Queer Pride Is Anti-Racist"

We, racialized dykes, bis, trans, faggots, and intersex people call for bringing our queer and antiracist demands into an autonomous contingent of the queer pride demonstration this Saturday, July 4.

This year, again, we are outraged to see that we are still precarious, stigmatized, discriminated against, violated, abused, and killed without any public authority deigning to take the urgency of our situations seriously.

We are in mourning and we are angry. The undocumented among us are being forced out of France. The Black people and our sex-worker trans sisters among us are dying. Colonial and Islamophobic institutions that claim to protect us display their indifference to hide their complicity.

We are in mourning and we are angry. While the most precarious among us have succumbed to the disease to which they were exposed because of the incompetence of our leaders, the one measure taken to minimize contamination with COVID-19 was just a pretext for the police to freely terrorize and violate racialized people in racialized working-class neighborhoods.[1]

We are in mourning and we are in revolt. The health crisis has exposed the scam that our health system represents. Unable to deal with a pandemic, though it was announced in advance, this same system refuses us parenthood, mutilates intersex people, pathologizes our identities, and lets us die.

We are in mourning and we are in revolt. While hundreds of thousands demonstrate for our lives despite the threat posed to us by the security forces that bully us, gas us, exert violence, and rape us, the Interior Ministry gets emotional about the filmed performances of a few cops fearing for their impunity.[2]

We have had enough. Our lives are not secondary. Our lives matter. We are the queer community of the Adama generation and the situation in France calls for us, too, to revolt.[3]

Open call for signatures (of racialized queer, racialized feminist and/
or intersectional anti-racism organizations).

Queers racisé.e.s autonomes, 2020
(Eventually joined by fifty racialized queer+, trans+, dyke+, feminist,
and intersectional anti-racism groups)

Appendix B

Pride for Whom? Pride for What?
The Opportunism of Alliances and Visibility

Statement in response to the call for a first "Pride March in
the Suburbs" on June 9, 2019, in Saint-Denis.

Many of us, LOCs—Lesbians of Color—have grown up in the racialized working-class suburbs, currently live there, work there, fight there, or we take refuge there, in particular in Saint-Denis where the first "Pride March in the Suburbs" will take place. This march, proposed by an organization whose goal is, among other things, to give "a better image of the city of Saint-Denis" provokes us to ask many questions.

Why and how are we supposed to build alliances with institutionalized organizations such as Inter-LGBT or SOS Homophobie that have no knowledge of our lives, our issues, our ways of living? We cannot accept that Saint-Denis is the showcase of a French-style pinkwashing that, lurking behind pseudovisibility, leaves intact the effects of the racist, sexist, and capitalist policies that crush the lives of our families, our communities, friends, and comrades, here and elsewhere. In this way of investing in Saint-Denis and THE suburb we cannot see anything other than a desire to purchase an unburdened conscience and, at the same time, to sell out the history of our struggles. We are actors of our spaces and our strategies. We attach great importance to the heritage and the transmission of our struggles and analyses, which is why we do not forget the French rooster proudly represented on the first poster of the Parisian March 2011, proposed by Inter-LGBT. Since this proposal, which smacks of racist, sexist, nationalist, and even Pétainist overtones, we have not seen Inter-LGBT publicly speak out against unbridled racism, nor even actively fight it within its own organizations. So why come and give us lessons about intersectionality in Saint-Denis?

We Lesbians of Color refuse to see this march become one more sign sent by the city council to gentrifiers of all stripes, transforming our neighborhoods into opportunities for white and wealthy homoparental families to the detriment of subalternized lesbians who do not feel less safe here than in Paris, where they are forced by police to show their ID documents, are attacked, harassed, but also exoticized, depoliticized, ignored, or invisibilized. The city council is funding this event, but where is the money when it comes to housing us in decent apartments or simply not letting us die and relocating us when our buildings collapse or burn down? Our lesbian lives should be proud of having comfortable beds to welcome our companions, families, and refugee friends with dignity.

Be visible on Saturday, June 9, but with what objectives and what consequences for our struggles, our communities, and our sisters who are not protected the rest of the year? Our life experiences are those of lesbians from postcolonial migrations, exiles, refugees, caught up in community and family networks of complex solidarities that cannot be reduced to the sole rhetoric of coming out and public visibility. We fight to support lesbian refugees and against the fascisms that restrict our lives. We know how and when to be visible. We did not wait for any authorization to organize ourselves, to build safe spaces, and to build international solidarity. For years we have resisted and proven our worth, our strengths in the battles we lead, in a network combining many Dionysian collectives and beyond, far from the total disinterest that these organizations have in our lives, outside of their codes and their spaces. To whom does a march ultimately bring value? Always the same people. Those who know how to value it in fundraising cases where the money does not serve our interests.

They are organizing a party at 6B in the wake of this march, a gentrified place known to have no connection with the rest of the city. Most of the racialized people there work as security guards or in the kitchens. Dionysian racialized LGBTQI+ are not welcome there. Events there are mostly designed for party people and consumers of culture who only know Saint-Denis for its train station, its basilica, and its infamous neighborhoods. All of this seems quite revealing to us. The city council that is funding this march and the organizations that support it do not care about the total lack of space for LGBTQI+ communities in the segregated suburbs. Racialized LGBTQI+, especially those living in these suburbs, are not immune to the racism, Islamophobia, police violence, and the hunt for migrants that racialized non-LGBTQI+ people face. We cannot fight without taking this context into account.

No word either in the call broadcast by the organizers of this march on the sexism that is present in all the places where we are. The organizations that fight against homophobia should, however, forcefully take this into account. They also say nothing about the unbridled capitalism that oppresses us and prevents us from flourishing and even from simply living. We sincerely regret these hazardous alliances, the meager fruits of which we know will be stolen.

We see it as just a turnkey pinkwashing kit logic—how else to see it? Our lesbian bodies may be invisible and inaudible to many, but we will continue to fight in line with our experiences and the neighborhoods in which we live because, as bell hooks says, "the margins are a place imposed by oppressive structures but also a space of radical possibility and resistance."

Let's be radical. Let's not be fooled. Anything that is done without us cannot be done for us!

June 6, 2019
LOCs Group—Lesbians of Color

Appendix C

Racialized Queers and Trans Against Homonationalism

The Qitoko collective is calling for a contingent led by racialized queer and trans people for the Pride March on June 30, 2018.[1]

This contingent will be situated at the head of the larger Pride Leading Contingent—Stop Pinkwashing!—and will take the lead. We, racialized queer and trans folk, many of whom are Muslims and/or from the racialized, working-class suburbs, who are directly affected by the repressive, racist, homonationalist, and gentrification policies of which the march is the relay, affirm our place at the head of the march. Against the Inter-LGBT that claims to erase our existence and spits in our face, against Paris's City Hall and Mayor Anne Hidalgo, against the racist government, against the murderous police who infiltrate our spaces, against the neoliberal political parties that hide behind an inclusive veneer, we revolt.

The organization of this march by Inter-LGBT is a triple attack on our lives and our rights.

The choice of a slogan around sport shows Inter-LGBT's indifference to current government policies. The organization's focus is on a derisory aspect of the violence we suffer in a racist and cis-hetero-patriarchal system. Moreover, it was chosen for the sole purpose of communicating around the Gay Games, a sporting event that is fully part of Anne Hidalgo's pinkwashing strategy. Hidalgo and the government claim inclusion while excluding racialized queer and trans people. Indeed, the "Gay Games" are explicitly a springboard for the 2024 Olympics, whose gentrifying effect for working-class neighborhoods and in particular the city of Saint-Denis are well known. Attracting gay, white, wealthy tourists on the one hand, excluding precarious racialized queer and trans people on the other: this is the policy supported by this Pride March.

Just as gentrification is always accompanied by a reinforcement of police presence, always making life for racialized queer and trans people more dangerous, this march welcomes the police and gives them a comfortable space. While this same police is violently hunting down migrants and murdering our brothers, our sisters, our siblings, our mothers, and our fathers in working-class neighborhoods, while this police is repressing social movements and establishing colonial order in France, the organizers of the march are rolling out the red carpet for them. So, in defiance of the hundreds of victims of police murders, in defiance of our lives, in defiance of the history of Pride celebrating a riot against police brutality in nonwhite trans and queer spaces, the FLAG float will be able to parade in uniform and shoot the crowd with water pistols "for fun."

Finally, it is through its guilty silence that Inter-LGBT participates in the violence that we suffer. This year was marked by the Asylum-Immigration Law: a nationalist and racist law that puts all migrants in danger of death, including LGBTQI migrants. Many are refused asylum on the pretext that they failed to "prove" their sexual orientation and/or gender identity. This law limits access to asylum rights on the one hand but also penalizes illegal residence again by justifying longer imprisonment terms of undocumented migrants, including children, under the guise that longer "administrative detention" is necessary for "identity verification." By refusing to make this law and its consequences on LGBTQI people visible during this march, by refusing to firmly oppose and resist all these repressive policies and those who propose them and put them into practice, Inter-LGBT endorses these same policies that in particular deprive undocumented people who are HIV-positive or are undergoing hormonal treatment or medical treatment of care. Worse, it collaborates with the agents of these repressive and racist policies that are the government or the City of Paris by offering them the best spaces in the march.

This year again, it is clear that our presence is undesirable at this Pride March, reserved for white bourgeois privileged gays, lesbians, and bisexuals who continue to benefit from the white privilege conferred on them by white supremacy. We therefore organize our resistance to them by taking the lead in the Pride March, which belongs to us, and we call on all racialized queers who share our analyses to join us at the head of the procession.

Qitoko, 2018

Notes

Introduction

In this introduction and throughout the book, I use italics for concepts that I propose or reimagine and for words in languages other than English that I translate in the text. In cases where an author expressly does not translate a non-English word—such as in Gloria Anzaldúa's writing—I respect the author's desire and leave the word untranslated.

1   Importantly, Angela Davis draws attention to this situation in her blurb on the back of a recent collection of Lélia Gonzalez's work published in Brazil by writing that Brazilians can learn much more from Gonzalez about Black women in Brazil than from her work about the United States.

2   Abya Yala is a Native name for the life space encompassed by what colonizers call Latin America or Central and South America. It comes from the Guna language, where it means, literally, "land in its full maturity," and where it invokes a specific kind of affective and ancestral relation to the land. Prior to colonialism, the Guna lived on what is now the northern coast of Colombia. Today they live on the northern coast of Panama. The term came into broader use after it emerged in the context of the Second International Summit of Indigenous Peoples and Nationalities in Abya Yala, held in Quito in 2004. Many scholars argue that the term Latin America erases Native, Black, and other subjects of color while Eurocentrically foregrounding the Spanish, Portuguese, and other (white) Europeans. The idea of North, Central, and South America presumes colonial history as origin (i.e., via Amerigo Vespucci) while disappearing Native prior, contemporary, and future existence.

3   Turtle Island is a Native name for the life space that colonizers call the United States, Canada, and Mexico. It is linked to the turtle creation stories of many peoples. Aotearoa is the Native Maori name for what colonizers call New Zealand.

4   I use the concept-term *misogynarchies*—a combination of *misogyny* and *archy*—as a large rubric to acknowledge many disparate kinds of systematizations of gender and sexuality relations of power, including but also beyond patriarchy. *Misogynarchies* is a specifically decolonial,

co-formational, and *co-productional* concept. For more elaboration, see especially chapter 4 and Bacchetta (2025d).

5   When discussing people in the French context, who in the United States and elsewhere identify as people of color, I use the term *racialized,* as it makes more sense in the French context. See also note 8 herein, as well as chapter 5.

6   See, for example, PIR (n.d.).

7   Conversation about intersubjectivities in *feminismo communitario* (community feminism) with Julieta Paredas, Salvador, Bahia, Brazil, December 5, 2018.

8   In chapter 5 I explain why, in the French context, the term *racialized queer+, trans+,* and *dyke+* makes more sense than LGBTIQ+ or *queer and trans of color.*

Chapter 1. Co-Motion at Present

Epigraph 1: In the 1990s the slogan was readapted as "An army of lovers cannot lose" by Queer Nation and other groups.

1   Historically, there are multiple, conflicting, racialized constructions of Henry Louis Gates as a Black male intellectual. See Hazel Carby's analysis of the pimp-like "Moghul" image assigned to him in a 1990 *New York Times* article (1992, 187).

2   See the initial critique of the universalization of the notion of patriarchy and my discussion of *misogynarchies* in note 4 of this book's introduction and the more extensive treatment in chapter 4. See also Bacchetta 2025c.

3   I am grateful to Sandhya Luthar and Sonia Jabbar, leaders of the CALERI uprising, for our conversations about CALERI over many decades, including during and since the events.

4   Many subaltern groups articulate nation rhetoric without qualifying as nation projects. An example is the 1990s US group Queer Nation, which had neither territorial space nor classic or alternative nation aspirations.

5   Entitled *Non credere d'avere dei diritti* (Don't think you have any rights), a quote from Simone Weil.

6   Podcasts of the panel are available on the DSN website: https://decolonizingsexualities.org/decolonialcafes.

7   *Cracker* is a sarcastic term to designate a white person, especially of the popular class and in the US South. Its origins are many: *cracker* as in *cracking corn* because too poor to afford the mills; *whip cracker* as the foreman for the slave owner; or to invoke white biscuits in a way similar to the related expression "white bread."

8   I am grateful to Donatella D'Angelo and Paolo Guera for multiple conversations on the drag queen readings in March and April 2020.

Chapter 2. Imaginings Otherwise

1 These practices are distinct from some other kinds of surgeries, such as trans surgeries. They are vastly differentially located in relations of power. In the case of those mentioned in-text, the subjects seek to become another by achieving greater sameness with dominant corporealities. In the case of trans surgeries, the subjects seek embodied coherency of the self.

2 Here I call this the Borgesian-TCEBK's because, as Maciel notes, there is no trace of the TCEBK's existence outside Borges's essay.

3 This analysis is based on the classic English translation (see Akhmatova 2000). I thank Harsha Ram for our conversations on Akhmatova. Any errors in my analysis are my own.

4 The reader will note a discrepancy in the translations of this question between Agambem's and Akhmatova's texts. While the difference is extremely interesting, addressing it is beyond the objectives of this chapter, and it is not relevant to my immediate argument here.

Chapter 3. Co-Formations, Co-Productions

1 Translations often reduce Gramsci's work on this topic to questions of consent. Instead, Nicole-Claude Mathieu (1985) elegantly elaborates its many dimensions in theorizing how "to concede is not to consent."

2 In the monolingual English language world there is confusion around French-to-English translations of some everyday terms-made-concepts. A similar chaos surrounds *dispositif*. In Deleuze and Guattari, *dispositif*'s English translation is (like *agencement*) "assemblages." Yet *agencement* and *dispositif* have vastly different signifieds in French. In English translations of Foucault, *dispositif* is sometimes left in French. Such disparities make it difficult to understand these authors and their intertextualities without French.

3 Merah's multiple constructions are more complex but far from my objectives here to fully address.

Chapter 4. Situated Planetarities

1 *Mamaceqtaw* in the language of the nation literally means "humans."

Chapter 5. Other Sensings in Praxes

1 While *queer* is widely used in France, I invoke it here in English, conscious that it is an imperfect translation from the French notion of queer. The term has a distinct genealogy and some distinct meanings on each side of the Atlantic. *Queer* arrived in France from the United States but developed *in-context*. In France, *queer* does not necessarily signal radical or

coalitional politics. Some cisgender heterosexual white French people self-identify as queer. Some radically critical racialized dykes+ and trans+ disidentify with queer because they feel it has been co-opted into neoliberalism and erases sexism, lesbians, and trans. And so to respect the latter, I adopt their self-designations outside *queer*. BIPOC, another US term, productively highlights specific genealogies of power and subjects in Turtle Island. It usefully invokes the United States as a site of settler colonialism, the system of slavery, and multiple kinds of racializations. Yet in other contexts, people subjected to settler colonialism do not necessarily self-define as Indigenous. Instead, they might prefer Native, First Nations, Seneca, Wayuu, Maori, etc. In France, Indigenous relates to many other forms of colonialism besides settler colonialism and it continues to carry overwhelming colonial-racial insulting connotations even if, like the terms *dyke* and *queer*, radically critical postcolonial subjects have resignified it and adopted it as their own.

2   I am deeply grateful to the twenty-three intellectuals, artivists, and activists, organizers of and participants in the collective work mentioned here, whom I was able to interview in 2020, and to all the *accomplices-comrades* for our ongoing conversations before and after the 2022 polylogues discussed here. As requested for political reasons and safety, you remain anonymous here unless you have specifically given permission for or requested nonanonymity.

3   Gossip, of course, is not neutral fact but rather *situated* in context. It is dependent on contextual relations of power and the speaking subjects, their personalities, moods, and many other factors. To ignore gossip in queer and trans communities is to miss something important. To take it seriously—which is not the same as to uncritically treat it as "truth"—is to open important dimensions to the analysis.

4   The Archives de recherche et de cultures lesbiennes (ARCL, Archives of Lesbian Research and Cultures, a.k.a. Archives lesbiennes or Lesbian Archives) at La Maison des Femmes de Paris (Paris Women's Center) has some files on racialized lesbians and the curators are interested in expanding the collection. A new queer archives project spearheaded by queer theorist Sam Bourcier and others in Paris is also compiling racialized queer+, trans+, and dyke+ archival traces.

5   Dalila Kadri Cheriet signed her writings and films, variously, as Dalila Cheriet, Dalila K. Cheriet, and Dalila Kadri. Throughout she was known in the movement as Dalila Kadri, and in her later life she signed her writings and films with that name. To respect her later self-designation, regardless of how she signed earlier works, I refer to her as Dalila Kadri here. For citation purposes I attribute each text or film to the name with which she signed it because it is the name under which the reader can locate her work.

6   *La lois n° 2005–158 du 23 février 2005 portant reconnaissance de la Nation et contribution nationale en faveur des Français rapatriés* (Law no. 2005–158 of February 23, 2005, regarding recognition of the nation and national contribution in favor of French repatriates) made it mandatory to teach the "positive values" of French colonialism in high school (art. 4, para. 2). After left historians protested it for censorship (not for racism) in 2006 it was repealed.

7   *La loi no 94–665 du 4 août 1994 relative à l'emploi de la langue française* (Law No. 94–665 of August 4, 1994 relative to the use of the French Language) prohibits other languages in government, state institutions and commerce including advertising, etc. While for some the law protects French against the onslaught of English, for postcolonial subjects in France it signals the prohibition of languages such as Arabic, Amazigh, Wolof, etc., thus parts of their heritage and present.

8   This is the first use of "of color" by a racialized queer group in France. In brief, from this point on the use of an English term in a group name is often a sign of a desire for transnational legibility beyond the French-speaking world and is in fact resistant to dominant French-centricity. For farther discussion of naming and language see Bacchetta and Crawford (forthcoming).

9   MWASI means woman in Lingala. Interestingly in the group's analysis of the form of *misogynarchies* that is most relevant to their conditions is "whitearchy," or white supremacy and patriarchy together. For more information in MWASI's own words, see Ghorbani 2015.

10   This is the first use of these particular English terms together in such a group.

11   Published on Facebook on the group's page on that day.

12   On a whole range of similar creative solidarity work in Germany, Canada, and elsewhere, see the new work of Jin Haritaworn, including their podcast at decolonizingsexualities.org.

13   In French, the phrase "Our Pride is Political" is in the plural, as is customary to account for all recognized positionalities in LBTIQ+. This differs from the inclusion operation in the Queers racisé.e.s autonomes poster, for the latter includes multiple racialized positionalities, as discussed below.

14   The signatories are: 343 racisé.e.s; Les colleuses Afroféministes; Extimité; Mille et une queer—Nouveau collectif de féministes queer issuEs de l'immigration; LOCS (Lesbiennes of color); MWASI—Collectif Afroféministe; Nta Rajel officiel Collectif féministe décolonial de la diaspora nord-africaine; Qolors; Queers racisé.e.s autonomes; Membres racisé-e-s de la Queer Week; the Paris Xclusive House Of LaDurée; Collectifsesamef 芝麻社; Trace ta voix.

15   For LOCS, the term *lesbian* is a political choice: it is intentionally in the title of the group. Out of respect, I refer to the members on their own terms.

16 Information on this and other activities of the Decolonizing Sexualities Network can be found on their website: https://decolonizing sexualities.org/

17 What the Global North(s) called the Arab Spring, Tunisians called the Jasmine Revolution.

18 Unfortunately, the poster was not in shape to be able to be printed here, but a copy is available in two places: the personal collection of Paola Bacchetta and the Archives Recherches Cultures Lesbiennes, located at La Maison des Femmes, 163 rue de Charenton, 75012 Paris, France.

19 Here again, I use the subjects' self-designation.

20 I am grateful to Kader Attia for our conversations about this piece. Any errors in interpretation are my own.

21 For insightful discussions on dominant representations of victims, see Fukushima 2012 and Shrikantia 2007.

Appendix A

1 Translator's note: Reference to the French state's imposition of the obligation to wear a mask and to carry a form stating one's identification information and the purpose of one's foray outside the home (grocery shopping, post office, etc.) and the times of departure and return.

2 Translator's note: Reference to Yellow Jackets movement.

3 Translator's note: Reference to the generation now working to end racist police violence, sparked by the racist murder of Adama Traoré (July 19, 1992–July 19, 2016), a young Malian French Black male, in the Parisian banlieue Beaumont-sur-Ois in 2016. In France, groups against racist police brutality have existed for decades, but only recently is there a mass movement.

Appendix C

1 We refuse the command that we be out implied by this kind of autonomous contingent, but we want to assert ourselves at the head of the march because our issues and our lives must be defended.

References

Abdulhadi, Rabab, Suzanne Adely, Angela Davis, and Selma James. 2021. "Confronting Apartheid Has Everything to Do with Feminism." *Mondoweiss*, March 17. https://mondoweiss.net/2017/03/confronting-apartheid -everything/.

Adams, Carol J. 1996. *The Sexual Politics of Meat: A Feminist-Vegetarian Critical Theory*. New York: Continuum.

Agamben, Giorgio. 1999. *Potentialities: Collected Essays in Philosophy*. Edited and translated by Daniel Heller-Roazen. Stanford, CA: Stanford University Press.

Agamben, Giorgio. 2001. *La comunità che viene*. Torino: Bollati Boringhieri.

Agamben, Giorgio. 2007. *L'amitié*. Paris: Payot et Rivages.

Ahmed, Sara. 2004. *The Cultural Politics of Emotion*. New York: Routledge.

Ahmed, Sara. 2006. *Queer Phenomenology: Orientations, Objects, Others*. Durham, NC: Duke University Press.

Ait Ben Lmadani, Fatima. 2025. "Fatema Mernissi's Situated Perspective: 'The Mirror Effect.'" Translated by Paola Bacchetta. In *Fatema Mernissi for Our Times*, edited by Minoo Moallem and Paola Bacchetta. Syracuse, NY: Syracuse University Press.

Ait Ben Lmadani, Fatima, and Nasima Moujoud. 2012. "Peut-on faire de l'intersectionnalité sans les ex-colonisé-e-s?" *Mouvements* 4 (72): 11–21.

Akhmatova, Anna. 2000. *The Complete Poems of Anna Akhmatova*. Edited by Roberta Reeder. Translated by Judith Hemschemeyer. Edinburgh: Canongate.

Alarcón, Norma. 1990. "The Theoretical Subject(s) of *This Bridge Called My Back* and Anglo-American Feminism." In *Making Face, Making Soul / Haciendo Caras*, edited by Gloria Anzaldua. San Francisco: Aunt Lute.

Alarcón, Norma. 2013. "Anzaldúan Textualities: A Hermeneutic of the Self and the Coyolxauhqui Imperative." In *El Mundo Zurdo 3: Selected Works from the 2012 Meeting of the Society for the Study of Gloria Anzaldúa*, edited by Larissa M. Mercado-López, Sonia Saldívar-Hull, and Antonia Castañeda. San Francisco: Aunt Lute.

Alasah, Eman. 2023. "An Interview with Raja Shehadeh: Documenting the Ordinary in an Unordinary Place." *Journal of Palestine Studies* 52 (1): 92–99.

Alcoff, Linda Martin. 2024. "The Roots (and Routes) of the Epistemology of Ignorance." *Critical Review of International Social and Political Philosophy* 27 (1): 9–28.

Alexander, M. Jacqui. 2002. Remembering *This* Bridge, Remembering Ourselves: Yearning, Memory, and Desire. In *This Bridge We Call Home: Radical Visions for Transformation*, edited by Gloria Anzaldúa and AnaLouise Keating. New York: Routledge.

Alexander, M. Jacqui. 2005. *Pedagogies of Crossing: Meditations on Feminism, Sexual Politics, Memory, and the Sacred*. Durham, NC: Duke University Press.

Alexander, M. Jacqui, and Chandra Talpade Mohanty. 1997. Introduction to *Feminist Genealogies, Colonial Legacies, Democratic Futures*, edited by M. Jacqui Alexander and Chandra Talpade Mohanty. New York: Routledge.

Alloua, Malek. 2001. *Le harem colonial*. Paris: Séguier.

Alqaisiya, Walaa. 2022. *The Politics and Aesthetics of Decolonial Queering in Palestine*. London: Routledge.

Althusser, Louis. 1965. *Pour Marx*. Paris: Maspéro.

Althusser, Louis, and Étienne Balibar. 1977. *Reading Capital*. London: Unwin Brothers.

Amar, Paul. 2013. *The Security Archipelago: Human-Security States, Sexuality Politics, and the End of Neoliberalism*. Durham, NC: Duke University Press.

Amari, Salima. 2018. *Lesbiennes de l'immigration: Construction de soi et relations familiales*. Paris: Editions Le Croquant.

Ambai, C. S. Lakshmi. 2000. "One Person and Another." In *Same-Sex Love in India*, edited by Ruth Vanita and Saleem Kidwai, translated by Kanchana Natarajan. New York: Palgrave.

Andersen, Chris. 2009. "Critical Indigenous Studies: From Difference to Density." *Cultural Studies Review* 15 (2): 80–100.

Anderson, Benedict. 1994. *Imagined Communities. Reflections on the Origins and Spread of Nationalism*. New York: Verso.

Anzaldúa, Gloria. (1987) 2007. *Borderlands/La Frontera*: *The New Mestiza*. San Francisco: Aunt Lute.

Anzaldúa, Gloria. 2002. "Now Let us Shift . . . The Path of Conosciemento . . . Inner Work, Public Acts." In *This Bridge We Call Home: Radical Visions for Transformation*, edited by Gloria Anzaldúa and AnaLouise Keating. New York: Routledge.

Anzaldúa, Gloria. 2009a. "Border Arte: Neplanta, el lugar de la frontera." In *The Gloria Anzaldúa Reader*, edited by AnaLouise Keating. Durham, NC: Duke University Press.

Anzaldúa, Gloria. 2009b. "Let Us Be the Healing of the Wound: The Coyolxauhqui Imperative—La sombra y el sueno." In *The Gloria Anzaldúa Reader*, edited by AnaLouise Keating. Durham, NC: Duke University Press.

Appadurai, Arjun. 1984. "Disjuncture and Difference in the Global Cultural Economy." In *Colonial Discourse and Post-Colonial Theory*, edited by Patrick Williams and Laura Chrisman. New York: Columbia University Press.

Appadurai, Arjun. 2006. *Fear of Small Numbers: An Essay on the Geography of Anger*. Durham, NC: Duke University Press.

Ariés, Philippe. 1960. *L'Enfant et la vie familiale sous l'Ancien Régime*. Paris: Plon.

Arnold, Emily, and Marlon Bailey. 2009. "Constructing Home and Family: How the Ballroom Community Supports African American GLBTQ Youth in the Face of HIV/AIDS." *Journal of Gay and Lesbian Social Services* 21 (2–3): 171–88.

Atkinson, Ti-Grace. 1984. "Le nationalism féminine." *Nouvelles Questions Féministes*, no. 6/7 (Spring): 35–54.

Attia, Kader. 2011. "Ghost @ Galerie Christian Nagel." Flickr, February 7. https://www.flickr.com/photos/michleemans/5424580024.

Azzouzi, Najah. 2023. "The Aesthetics of French Taste: How French Colonial Epistemologies Shapeshift into Class-Oriented Practices in Modern Egypt in the 1826–1950 Period." PhD diss., University of California, Riverside.

Bacchetta, Paola. 1994. "All Our Goddesses Are Armed: Religion, Resistance and Revenge in the Life of a Militant Hindu Nationalist Woman." In *Against All Odds: Essays on Women, Religion and Development from India and Pakistan*, edited by Kamla Bhasin, Nighat Khan, and Ritu Menon. New Delhi: Kali for Women.

Bacchetta, Paola. 1996. *La construction des identités dans les discours nationalistes hindous: Le Rashtriya Swayamsevak Sangh et la Rashtra Sevika Samiti (1939–1992)* [The construction of identities in Hindu nationalist discourse: The Rashtriya Swayamsevak Sangh and Rashtra Sevika Samiti (1939–1992)]. PhD diss., A.N.R.T, Université de Lille III.

Bacchetta, Paola. 1999. "When the (Hindu) Nation Exiles its Queers." *Social Text*, no. 61 (Winter): 141–66.

Bacchetta, Paola. 2002. "Extra-Ordinary Alliances: Women Unite Against Religious-Political Conflict in India." In *Feminism and Anti-Racism: International Struggles*, edited by Kathleen Blee and France Winddance Twine. New York: New York University Press.

Bacchetta, Paola. 2004. *Gender in the Hindu Nation: RSS Women as Ideologues*. New Delhi: Women Unlimited.

Bacchetta, Paola. 2009a. "Co-Formations: Sur les spatialités de résistance de lesbiennes 'of color' en France." *Sexualité, genre et société* 1 (1). https://doi.org/10.4000/gss.810.

Bacchetta, Paola. 2009b. "Dyketactics! Notes Towards an Un-Silencing." In *Smash the Church, Smash the State: The Early Years of Gay Liberation*, edited by Tommi Avicoli Mecca. San Francisco: City Lights.

Bacchetta, Paola. 2013. "Queer Formations in (Hindu) Nationalism." In *Sexuality Studies*, edited by Sanjay Srivasta. Oxford: Oxford University Press.

Bacchetta, Paola. 2015. "Décoloniser le féminisme: Intersectionnalités, assem-blages, co-formations, co-productions" [Decolonizing feminism: Inter-sectionalities, assemblages, co-formations, co-productions]. *Cahiers du CEDREF*, no. 20. https://doi.org/10.4000/cedref.833.

Bacchetta, Paola. 2016. "Segregationality and QTPOC Subalternative Spatalities in France." Keynote at Sexuality and Space Pre-Conference, American As-sociation of Geographers, San Francisco, March 28.

Bacchetta, Paola. 2017. "Murderous Conditions and LTQ+ POC Decolonial, Anti-Capitalist and Anti-Misogyny *Life* Imaginings in France." In "Postcolonial Queer Europe." Special issue, *Lambda Nordica* 22 (2–3): 153–73.

Bacchetta, Paola. 2018. "'Re-Présences': Les forces transformatives d'archives de queers racisé.e.s." *Friction*. https://friction-magazine.fr/re-presence-les-forces-transformatives-darchives-de-queers-racise-e-s/.

Bacchetta, Paola. 2019a. "Dyketactics!" In *Global Encyclopedia of Lesbian, Gay, Bisexual, Transgender, and Queer History*, edited by Howard Chiang. New York: Macmillan Reference.

Bacchetta, Paola. 2019b. "Groupe du 6 Novembre: Lesbiennes Issues du Co-lonialisme, de l'Esclavage et de l'Immigration." In *Global Encyclopedia of Lesbian, Gay, Bisexual, Transgender, and Queer History*, edited by Howard Chiang. New York: Macmillan Reference.

Bacchetta, Paola. 2019c. "Queer Presence in/and Hindu Nationalism." In *The Majoritarian State: How Hindu Nationalism is Changing India*, edited by An-gana Chatterji, Thomas Hanson, and Christophe Jaffrelot. London: Hurst.

Bacchetta, Paola. 2020. "Decolonial Sexualities." In "Decolonial Trajectories," edited by Sandeep Bakshi, Suhraiya Jivraj and Silvia Posocco. Special issue, *Interventions: International Journal of Postcolonial Studies* 22 (4): 574–85.

Bacchetta, Paola. 2022. "Francophoning Anzaldúa's *Borderlands/La Frontera: The New Mestiza.*" Preface to Gloria Anzaldúa's *Terres Frontalières/La Frontera: La nouvelle mestiza*, by Gloria Anzaldúa, translated into the French by Nino DuFour and Alejandra Soto. Paris: Courambakis.

Bacchetta, Paola. 2023. "What Does It Mean to Decolonize?" In *Decolonizing Europe*, edited by M. Faye-Rexhepi, M. de Groot, E. Inghelbrecht, et al. Amsterdam: Common Grounds. https://decolonial.eu/booklet.

Bacchetta, Paola. 2025a. "Decolonizing Sexualities." *Kohl* 11 (1): 6.

Bacchetta, Paola. 2025b. "Toward Decolonial Translating: Reflections on 'Francophoning-Anglophoning' 'Les Lionnes.'" In *Fatema Mernissi for Our Times*, edited by Minoo Moallem and Paola Bacchetta. Syracuse, NY: Syracuse University Press.

Bacchetta, Paola. 2025c. "Misogynarchies." *Kohl* 11 (1): 17.

Bacchetta, Paola. 2025d. "Reductive Evidence." *Kohl* 11 (1): 20.

Bacchetta, Paola, and Nawo Crawford, eds. Forthcoming. *Lucioles: Théories et pratiques de lesbiennes racisées en France, du 1970 au présent*.

Bacchetta, Paola, Jules Falquet, and Norma Alarcón. 2012. Introduction to "Théories féministes et queers décoloniales: Interventions Chicanas et Latinas états-uniennes," *Cahiers du CEDREF*, no. 18, 7–40.

Bacchetta, Paola, and Jin Haritaworn. 2011. "There Are Many Transatlantics: Homonationalism, Homotransnationalism and Feminist-Queer-Trans of Color Theories and Practices." In *Transatlantic Conversations*, edited by Kathy Davis and Mary Evans. Farnham, UK: Ashgate.

Bacchetta, Paola, Jin Haritaworn, and Fatima El Tayeb. 2015. "Queer of Color Formations and Translocal Spaces in Europe." *Environment and Planning D: Society and Space.* 33 (5): 769–78.

Bacchetta, Paola, and Margaret Power, eds. 2002. *Right-Wing Women: From Conservatives to Extremists Around the World.* New York: Routledge.

Back, Les, and John Solomos, eds. 2000. *Theories of Race and Racism: A Reader.* London: Routledge.

Bahaffou, Miriam, and Julie Gorecki. 2022. Introduction to *Feminism or Death: How the Women's Movement Can Save the Planet*, by Françoise d'Eaubonne. London: Verso.

Bailey, Marlon. M. 2013. *Butch/Queens up in Pumps: Gender, Performance, and Ballroom Culture in Detroit.* Detroit: University of Michigan Press.

Bailey, Marlon M. 2021. "Structures of Kinship in Ballroom Culture." *Architecture Review*, no. 1479 (March): 16–19.

Bailey, Marlon M., Priya Kandaswamy, and Mattie Udora Richardson. 2004. "Is Gay Marriage Racist?" In *That's Revolting! Queer Strategies for Resisting Assimilation*, edited by Mattilda Bernstein Sycamore. Brooklyn, NY: Soft Skull.

Bakan, Joel. 2005. *The Corporation: The Pathological Pursuit of Profit and Power.* New York: Free Press.

Bakhtin, Mikhail. 1980. "The Law of Genre." *Glyph*, no. 7, 203–4.

Bakhtin, Mikhail. 1981. *The Dialogic Imagination.* Edited and translated by Caryl Emerson and Michael Holquist. Austin: University of Texas Press.

Bakhtin, Mikhail. 1984. *Problems of Dostoevsky's Poetics.* Edited and translated by Caryl Emerson. Minneapolis: University of Minnesota Press.

Bakshi, Sandeep. 2022. "Celebrating Queerness.: Notes on Queer of Color Critique and Queerness in India." *GRAAT On-Line*, no. 25 (February): 9–31. http://www.graat.fr/LGBTQ02.pdf.

Bakshi, Sandeep, Suhraiya Jivraj, and Silvia Posocco, eds. 2016. *Decolonizing Sexuality.* London: Counterpress.

Bakshi, Sandeep, Suhraiya Jivraj, and Silvia Posocco. 2020. "Decolonial Trajectories: Praxes and Challenges." In "Decolonial Trajectories," edited by Sandeep Bakshi, Suhraiya Jivraj, and Silvia Posocco. Special issue, *Interventions: International Journal of Postcolonial Studies* 22 (4): 451–63.

Balasurya, Tissa. 1984. *Planetary Theology.* New York: Orbis.

Balibar, Étienne. 1991. "Is There a 'Neo-Racism'?" In *Race, Nation, Class: Ambiguous Identities*, edited by Étienne Balibar and Immanual Wallerstein. London: Verso.

Ballhatchet, Kenneth. 1980. *Race, Sex and Class Under the Raj: Imperial Attitudes and Policies and Their Critics, 1793–1905*. London: Weidenfeld and Nicolson.

Bancel, Nicolas, and Pascal Blanchard. 2002. *De l'indigène à l'immigré*. Paris: Découvertes Gallimard Histoire.

Bancel, Nicolas, Pascal Blanchard, Gilles Boetsch, Éric Deroo, and Sandrine Lemaire. 2004. *Zoos humains: Au temps des exhibitions humaines*. Paris: La Découverte Poche.

Banerjea, Niharika, Debanuj Dasgupta, Rohit K. Dasgupta, and Jaime M. Grant. 2022. *Friendship as Social Justice Activism: Critical Solidarities in a Global Perspective*. Chicago: University of Chicago Press.

Barker, Joanne. 2015. "Indigenous Feminisms." In *Oxford Handbook of Indigenous People's Politics*, edited by José Antonio Lucero, Dale Turner, and Donna Lee VanCott. January. http://www.oxfordhandbooks.com/view/10.1093/oxfordhb/9780195386653.001.0001/oxfordhb-9780195386653-e-007.

Barker, Joanne, ed. 2017. *Critically Sovereign: Indigenous Gender, Sexuality, and Feminist Studies*. Durham, NC: Duke University Press.

Beaman, Jean. 2017. *Citizen Outsider: Children of North African Immigrants in France*. Berkeley: University of California Press.

Bénani, Hamid, Jalil Bennani, and Fatema Mernissi. 2025. "The Lionesses: A Film Project (1981)." Translated by Paola Bacchetta. In *Fatema Mernissi for Our Times*, edited by Minoo Moallem and Paola Bacchetta. Syracuse, NY: Syracuse University Press.

Benasayag, Miguel, and Diego Sztulwark. 2009. *Du contre-pouvoir*. Paris: La Découverte.

Ben-Ghiat, Ruth, and Mia Fuller. 2005. *Italian Colonialism*. New York: Palgrave.

Bennani, Jalil. 2022. *Des Djinns à la psychanalyse: Nouvelle approche des pratiques traditionnelles et contemporaines*. Dijon, France: Les presses du réel.

Benslama, Fethi. 2011. "Soudain, la revolution!" *Jamiat Al Hurriyat*, February. Accessed March 3, 2012. http://jamiatalhurriyat.org/blog?p=12.

Bergozza, Marina, Francesca Coco, and Scott Burnett. 2024. "#Gays for Trump: 'Coming Out' as Republican on Twitter." *Journal of Language and Sexuality* 13 (1): 51–75.

Berlant, Lauren. 2008. *The Female Complaint: The Unfinished Business of Sentimentality in American Culture*. Durham, NC: Duke University Press.

Berlant, Lauren. 2012. *Desire/Love*. New York: Punctum.

Berkhofer, Robert F. 1978. *The White Man's Indian: Images of the American Indian from Columbus to the Present*. New York: Random House.

Bertrand, Pierre. 2007. *L'intime et le prochain: Essai sur le rapport á l'autre*. Montréal: Liber.

Bêtes Noires. 2001. "Des lesbiennes blanches revent notre silence." In *Warriors/Guerrieres*, edited by Groupe du 6 Novembre. Paris: Nomades'Langues Editions.

Bharati, Agehananda. 1985. "The Self in Hindu Thought and Action." In *Culture and Self: Asian and Western Perspectives*, edited by Anthony J. Marsala, George DeVos, and Francis L. K. Hsu. New York: Tavistock.

Bhatia. Sunil. 2020. "Decolonizing Psychology: Power, Citizenship and Identity." *Psychoanalysis, Self and Context* 15 (3): 257–66.

Bhatia, Sunil, and Kumar Ravi Priya. 2021. "Coloniality and Psychology: From Silencing to Re-Centering Marginalized Voices in Postcolonial Times." *Review of General Psychology* 25 (4): 422–36.

Bhavnani, Kum-Kum, John Foran, and Priya A. Kurian, eds. 2003. *Feminist Futures: Re-Imagining Women, Culture and Development*. London: Zed.

Bilé, Serge. 2005. *La légende du sexe surdimensionné des Noires*. Monaco: Le serpent à plumes.

Bilge, Sirma. 2013. "Intersectionality Undone: Saving Intersectionality from Feminist Intersectionality Studies." *Du Bois Review: Social Science Research on Race* 10 (2): 405–24.

Blackwomon, Julie. 1976. "Revolutionary Blues." *Hera Feminist Newspaper*. Dyketactics! Archive.

Blackwomon, Julie. 1984. *Revolutionary Blues and Other Fevers*. Publisher unknown. Dyketactics! Archive.

Borges, Jorge Luis. 1965. "El idioma analítico de John Wilkins." Accessed May 5, 2025. https://sites.evergreen.edu/wp-content/uploads/sites/226/2016/09/jorge-luis-borges-the-analytical-language-of-john-wilkins-1.pdf.

Boubeker, Ahmed. 2005. "Le 'creuset francais' ou la légende noire de l'intégration." In *La fracture coloniale*, edited by Pascal Blanchard, Nicolas Bancel, Sandrine Lemaire. Paris: La Découverte.

Bouteldja, Houria. 2011. "Femmes blanches et le privilège de la solidarité." Presentation at IVème congrès international du féminisme islamique. https://indigenes-republique.fr/les-femmes-blanches-et-le-privilege-de-la-solidarite/.

Brah, Avtar, and Ann Phoenix. 2004. "Ain't I a Woman? Revisiting Intersectionality." *Journal of International Women's Studies* 5 (3): 1–12.

Braidotti, Rosi. 2009. "Animals, Anomalies, and Inorganic Others." PMLA 124 (2): 526–32.

Brass, Paul. 1992. *Ethnicity and Nationalism: Theory and Comparison*. Delhi: Sage.

Browne, Irene, and Joya Misra. 2003. "The Intersection of Gender and Race in the Labor Market." *Annual Review of Sociology* 29:487–513.

Bruno, Tianna. 2023. "More Than Just Dying: Black Life and Futurity in the Face of State-Sanctioned Environmental Racism." *Environment and Planning D: Society and Space* 42 (1). https://doi.org/10.1177/02637758231218101.

Bugnon, Fanny, ed. 2022. *Actes du colloque, Femmes de droite*. Paris: Presses Sciences Politiques.

Byrd, Jodi A. 2011. *The Transit of Empire: Indigenous Critiques of Colonialism*. Minneapolis: University of Minnesota Press.

Byrd, Jodi A., and Michael Rothberg. 2011. "Between Subalternity and Indigeneity: Critical Categories for Postcolonial Studies." In "Between Subalternity and Indigeneity." Special issue, *Interventions: International Journal of Postcolonial Studies* 13 (1): 1–12.

Cabnal, Lorena. 2010. *Feminismos diversos: El feminismo comunitario*. Spain: ACSUR-Las Segovias. https://porunavidavivible.wordpress.com/wp-content/uploads/2012/09/feminismos-comunitario-lorena-cabnal.pdf.

Cajete, G. A. 1994. *Look to the Mountain*. Durango, CO: Kivaki.

CALERI (Campaign for Lesbian Rights). 1999. *Lesbian Emergence: A Citizen's Report*. New Delhi: Usha.

Calhoun, Craig. 1997. *Nationalism*. Minneapolis: University of Minnesota Press.

Campari, Maria Grazia, Rosaria Canzano, Lia Cigarini, Sciana Loaldi, Laura Roseo, and Claudia Shanmah. 1985. L'affidamento raggiunge il palazzo. *Il Manifesto*, March 29.

Campos-Castillo, Celeste, and Steven Hitlin. 2013. "Copresence: Revisiting a Building Block for Social Interaction Theories." *Sociological Theory* 31 (2): 168–92.

Canguilhem, Georges. 1988. *Ideology and Rationality in the History of the Life Sciences*. Cambridge, MA: MIT Press.

Carbado, Devon. 2013. "Colorblind Intersectionality." *Signs* 38 (4): 811–45.

Carby, Hazel. 1992. "The Multicultural Wars." In *Black Popular Culture*, edited by Gina Dent. Seattle: Bay Press.

Carrillo Rowe, Aimee. 2008. *Powerlines: On the Subject of Feminist Alliances*. Durham, NC: Duke University Press.

Césaire, Aimé. 1955. *Discours sur le colonialism*. Paris: Présence Africaine.

Chakrabarty, Dipesh. (2000) 2008. *Provincializing Europe: Postcolonial Thought and Historical Difference*. Princeton, NJ: Princeton University Press.

Cheikh, Malek, ed. 2021. "Transmettre." Special issue, *AssiégéEs: Citadelle des Résistances* 5 (Summer).

Cheikh, Malek, and Massinissa Garaoun. 2022. "Interventions." Conference on Decolonial and Queer of Color Archiving, University of Chicago in Paris, April 20. https://decolonizingsexualities.org/events.

Chekkat, Rafik, and Nadia Mokaddem. 2013. "*Caché* [Michael Haneke, 2005]: Le retour du refoulé du 17 octobre 1961." *État d'Exception*, October 17. Accessed December 26, 2013. http://www.etatdexception.net/?p=5981.

Chen, Adrian. 2011. "Is NYPD Sending Drunk Homeless People to Occupy Wall Street?" *Gawker*. Accessed January 4, 2012. https://gawker.com/5854870/is-nypd-sending-drunk-homeless-people-to-occupy-wall-street.

Chen, Mel, and Dana Luciano, eds. 2015. "Queer Inhumanisms." Special issue, *Journal of Gay and Lesbian Studies* 21 (2–3).

Cheriet, Dalila Kadri. 2001. "Lettre ouverte aux lesbiennes de France." In *Warriors/Guerriéres*, edited by Groupe du 6 Novembre. Paris: Nomades'Langues Edition.

Cheyfitz, Eric. 2002. "The (Post)colonial Predicament of Native American Studies." In "J. M. Coetzee's *Disgrace*." Special issue, *Interventions: International Journal of Postcolonial Studies* 4 (3): 405–27.

Cho, Sumi, Kimberlè Williams Crenshaw, and Leslie McCall. 2013. "Toward a Field of Intersectionality Studies: Theory, Applications, and Praxis." *Signs* 38 (4): 785–810.

Chow, Rey. 2002. *The Protestant Ethnic and the Spirit of Capitalism*. New York: Columbia University Press.

Chow, Rey. 2006. *The Age of the World Target: Self-Referentiality in War, Theory, and Comparative Work*. Durham, NC: Duke University Press.

Chrystos. 1981. "No Rock Scorns Me as Whore." In *This Bridge Called My Back*, edited by Gloria Anzaldúa and Cherríe Moraga. Watertown, MA: Persephone.

Churchill, Ward. 2004. *Kill the Indian, Save the Man: The Genocidal Impact of American Indian Schools*. San Francisco: City Lights.

Cixous, Hélène. 1979. *Vivre l'orange*. Paris: Des femmes.

Clough, Patricia Ticinet. 2007. Introduction to *The Affective Turn: Theorizing the Social*, edited by Patricia Ticinet Clough. Durham, NC: Duke University Press.

Cohen, Cathy J. 2005. "Punks, Bulldaggers and Welfare Queens: The Radical Potential of Queer Politics?" In *Black Queer Studies: A Critical Anthology*, edited by E. Patrick Johnson and Mae G. Henderson. Durham, NC: Duke University Press.

Colla, Elliott. 2011. "The Poetry of Revolt." *Jadaliyya*, January 31. Accessed February 1, 2011. http://www.jadaliyya.com/pages/index/506/the-poetry-of-revolt.

Collins, Patricia Hill. 1991. *Black Feminist Thought: Knowledge, Consciousness, and the Politics of Empowerment*. New York: Routledge.

Collins, Patricia Hill. 1997. "Comment on Hekman's 'Truth and Method: Feminist Standpoint Theory Revisited': Where's the Power?" *Signs* 22 (2): 375–81.

Collins, Patricia Hill. 1998a. *Fighting Words: Black Women and the Search for Justice*. Minneapolis: University of Minnesota Press.

Collins, Patricia Hill. 1998b. "It's All in the Family: Intersections of Gender, Race, and Nation." *Hypatia* 13 (3): 62–82.

Collins, Patricia Hill. 2005. *Black Sexual Politics: African Americans, Gender, and the New Racism*. New York: Routledge.

Collins, Patricia Hill, and Sirma Bilge. 2016. *Intersectionality*. Cambridge: Polity.

Combahee River Collective. 1997. "A Black Feminist Statement." In *The Second Wave: A Reader in Feminist Theory*, edited by Linda Nicolson. New York: Routledge.

Cosmic Debris. 2011. "Fighting Privatization of Sacred Lands: Occupy Tucson Joins Native Grass Roots 'Protect Chuk-Shon.'" *Daily Kos*, November 12. http://www.dailykos.com/story/2011/11/12/1035930/-Fighting -Privatization-of-Sacred-Lands:-Occupy-Tucson-Joins-Native-Grass-Roots -Protect-Chuk-Shon?via=spotlight.

Coulthard, Glen. 2010. "Place Against Empire: Understanding Indigenous Anti-Colonialism." *Affinities: A Journal of Radical Theory, Culture, and Action* 4 (2): 79–83.

Crenshaw, Kimberlé. 1989. "Demarginalizing the Intersection of Race and Sex." *University of Chicago Legal Forum* 1989 (1): 139–67.

Crenshaw, Kimberlé. 1991. "Mapping the Margins: Intersectionality, Identity Politics, and Violence Against Women of Color." *Stanford Law Review* 43 (6): 1241–79.

Crenshaw, Kimberlé. 2020. "Liberty. Equality. Intersectionality. An Antidote Against Fascism." Interview by Francesca Coin. *LeftEast*, June 26. https://lefteast.org/interview-w-kimberle-crenshaw-liberty-equality -intersectionality-an-antidote-against-fascism/.

Cusicanqui, Silvia Rivera. 2020. *Ch'ixinakax utxiwa: On Decolonising Practices and Discourses*. London: Polity.

Danjé, Michaëla. 2014. *J'ai séparé nos routes*. Paris: Cases Rebelles.

Danjé, Michaëla, ed. 2021. *Afrotrans*. Paris: Cases Rebelles.

Dar, Huma. 2015. "stargazing on the backs of our children." *Pulse*. Accessed December 29, 2018. https://pulsemedia.org/2016/07/23/stargazing-on-the -backs-of-our-children/.

Das, Veena. 1989. "Subaltern as Perspective." In *Subaltern Studies VI*, edited by Ranajit Guha. Delhi: Oxford University Press.

Da Silva, Denise Ferreira. 2007. *Toward a Global Idea of Race*. Minneapolis: University of Minnesota Press.

Da Silva, Denise Ferreira. 2017. "1 (life) ÷ 0 (blackness) = $\infty - \infty$ or ∞/∞: On Matter Beyond the Equation of Value." *Re-visiones* 7.

Davis, Angela. 1981. *Women, Race, and Class*. New York: Random House.

Davis, Angela. 1989. *Women, Culture, and Politics*. New York: Random House.

Davis, Angela. 1997. "Reflections on Race, Class and Gender in the USA: An Interview with Lisa Lowe." In *The Politics of Culture in the Shadow of Capital*, edited by Lisa Lowe and David Floyd. Durham, NC: Duke University Press.

Davis, Angela. 2003. *Are Prisons Obsolete?* New York: Seven Stories.

Davis, Angela. 2005. *Abolition Democracy: Beyond Empire, Prisons, and Torture*. New York: Seven Stories.

Davis, Angela. 2013. "Freedom is a Constant Struggle: Closures and Continuities." Birbeck Annual Law Lecture, London, October 25. *Critical Legal Thinking*. http://criticallegalthinking.com/2013/11/25/transcription-angela-davis -freedom-constant-struggle-closures-continuities/.

Davis, Angela, and Frank Barat. 2016. *Freedom Is a Constant Struggle: Ferguson, Palestine, and the Foundations of a Movement*. Chicago: Haymarket.

Davis, Angela, Gina Dent, Erica. C. Meiners, and Beth Ritchie. 2022. *Abolition. Feminism. Now*. Chicago: Haymarket.

Davis, Kathy, and Helma Lutz. 2024. *Routledge Handbook of Intersectionality Studies*. New York: Routledge.

Debord, Guy. 1977. *The Society of the Spectacle*. Detroit: Black and Red.

DeLanda, Manuel. 2006. "Deleuzian Social Ontology and Assemblage Theory." In *Deleuze and the Social*, edited by Martin Fuglsang and Bent Meier Sorensen. Edinburgh: Edinburgh University Press.

Deleuze, Gilles. 1962. *Nietzsche et la philosophie*. Paris: Presses Universitaires de France.

Deleuze, Gilles. 1986. *Foucault*. Paris: Les Editions de Minuit.

Deleuze, Gilles, and Félix Guattari. 1972. *L'Anti-Oedipe*. Paris: Les Editions de Minuit.

Deleuze, Gilles, and Félix Guattari. 1975. *Kafka: Pour une littérature mineure*. Paris: Les Editions de Minuit.

Deleuze, Gilles, and Félix Guattari. 1980. *Milles plateaux*. Paris: Les Editions de Minuit.

Deleuze, Gilles, and Félix Guattari. 2005. *Qu'est-ce que la philosophie?* Paris: Les Editions de Minuit.

Deloria, Vine, Jr. 2001. "American Indian Metaphysics." In *Power and Place: Indian Education in America*, edited by Vine Deloria Jr. and Daniel R. Wildcat. Golden, CO: Fulcrum.

Delphy, Christine. 1975. "Pour un féminisme matérialiste." *L'Arc* 61.

Delphy, Christine, and Diane Leonard. 1992. *Familiar Exploitation: A New Analysis of Marriage*. Cambridge: Polity.

Derrida, Jacques. 1980. "The Law of Genre." *Glyph*, no. 7, 203–4.

Derrida, Jacques. 1993. *Spectres de Marx*. Paris: Galilée.

Derrida, Jacques. 1994. *Politiques de l'amitié*. Paris: Galilée.

Derrida, Jacques. 2002. "Globalization, Peace and Cosmopolitanism." In *Negotiations: Interventions and Interviews, 1971–2001*, edited by Elizabeth Rottenberg. Stanford, CA: Stanford University Press.

Derrida, Jacques. 2004. "Autoimmunity: Real and Symbolic Suicides; A Dialogue with Jacques Derrida." In *Philosophy in a Time of Terror: Dialogues with Jurgen Habermas and Jacques Derrida*, edited by Giovanna Borradori, translated by Pascale-Anne Brault and Michael Naas. Chicago: University of Chicago Press.

Dhanaraj, Christina Thomas. 2018. "#SmashBrahminicalPatriarchy: Twitter's Apology Shows How Race Liberals Become Caste Conservatives." *Huffington Post*, November 22. https://www.huffingtonpost.in/2018/11 /22/smashbrahminicalpatriarchy-twitters-apology-shows-how-race -liberals-become-caste-conservatives_a_23596728/?ncid=tweetlnkinhp mg00000001.

Diallo, Rokhaya. 2014. "Femmes invisibles, prenons la une!" *Politis*, March 6. http://www.politis.fr/articles/2014/03/femmes-invisibles-prenons-la-une -par-rokhaya-diallo-25962/.

Dicken, Peter. 2000. "Globalization." In *Dictionary of Human Geography*, edited by R. J. Johnston, Derek Gregory, Geraldine Pratt, and Michael Watts. Malden, MA: Blackwell.

Di Pietro, P. J. 2016a. "Decolonizing *Travesti* Space in Buenos Aires: Race, Sexuality, and Sideways Relationality." *Gender, Place and Culture* (23) 5: 677–93.

Di Pietro, P. J. 2016b. "Of Huachafería, Así, and M' E Mati: Decolonizing Transing Methodologies." *TSQ* 3 (1–2): 65–73.

Di Pietro, P. J. 2020a. "Hallucinating Knowing: (Extra)Ordinary Consciousness, More-Than-Human Perception, and Other Decolonizing *Remedios* within Latina and Xicana Feminist and Queer Theories." In *Theories of the Flesh: Latinx and Latin American Feminisms, Transformation, and Resistance*, edited by Andrea J. Pitts, Mariana Ortega, and José Medina. New York: Oxford University Press.

Di Pietro, P. J. 2020b. "Ni humanos, ni animales, ni monstruos: La decolonización del cuerpo transgénero." *Eidos: Revista de Filosofía*, no. 34, 254–91.

Djebar, Assia. 1999. *Ces voix qui m'assiègent . . . en marge de ma francophonie.* Paris: Albin Michel.

Donadey, Anne. 1999. "Between Amnesia and Anamnesis: Re-Membering the Fractures of Colonial History." *Studies in 20th Century Literature* 23 (1): article 8.

Dorlin, Elsa. 2006. *La matrice de la race: Généalogie sexuelle et coloniale de la nation française*. Paris: La Découverte.

Doumia, N. 2001. "Le Groupe du 6 Novembre, notre Standing Up!" In *Warriors/ Guerrieres*, edited by Groupe du 6 Novembre. Paris: Nomades'Langues Editions.

Driskill, Qwo-Li. 2004. "Stolen from Our Bodies: First Nations Two-Spirits/ Queers and the Journey to a Sovereign Erotic." *Studies in American Indian Literatures* 16 (2): 50–64.

Driskill, Qwo-Li, Chris Finley, Brian Joseph Gilley, and Scott Lauria Morgenson, eds. 2011. *Queer Indigenous Studies: Critical Interventions in Theory, Politics, and Literature*. Tucson: University of Arizona Press.

Du Bois, W. E. B. 1994. *The Souls of Black Folk*. New York: Gramercy.

Duggan, Lisa. 2003. *The Twilight of Equality? Neoliberalism, Cultural Politics, and the Attack on Democracy*. Boston: Beacon.

Dull-Pianist-6777. 2023. "The utmost cruelty of New Mexico's first governor." Reddit, r/NewMexico. https://www.reddit.com/r/NewMexico/comments/17w8yk5/the_utmost_cruelty_of_new_mexicos_first_governor/.

Durham, Martin, and Margaret Power. 2010. *New Perspectives on the Transnational Right*. New York: Palgrave Macmillan.

Dutta, Anirudda. 2023. "Elsewheres in Queer Hindutva: A Hijra Case Study." *Feminist Review* 133 (1): 11–25.

Dyketactics! Archive. Author's collection. Beinecke Rare Book and Manuscript Library, Yale University. [Following Beinecke's release, digitized parts of the Dyketactics! Archive will be available at the John J. Wilcox Jr. Archives, William Way LGBT Community Center, Philadelphia.]

Egan, Frances. 2023. "Making Space for Queer Muslim Women: (Dis)orientation in Fatima Daas's *La Petite Dernière*." *Australian Journal of French Studies*. Vol. 60 (2): 161–74.

Ekers, Michael, Stefan Kipfer, and Alex Loftus. 2020. "On Articulation, Translation, and Populism: Gillian Hart's Postcolonial Marxism." *Annals of the American Association of Geographers* 110 (5): 1577–93. https://doi.org/10.1080/24694452.2020.1715198.

Ekine, Sokari, and Hakima Abbas. 2013. *Queer African Reader*. Nairobi and Oxford: Pambazuka.

El Forkani, H. 2011. "Ils sont libres et nous l'ignorons." *Webdo*. Accessed January 24, 2011. http://www.webdo.tn/2011/01/24/ils-sont-libres-et-nous-lignorons/.

El Général. 2011. "Rais Lebled." YouTube video. Accessed January 2011. http://www.youtube.com/watch?v=Q3tesjVIQGw.

Ellison, Ralph. (1947) 1980. *Invisible Man*. New York: Vintage.

El-Tayeb, Fatima. 2011. *European Others: Queering Ethnicity in Postnational Europe*. Minneapolis: University of Minnesota Press.

El-Tayeb, Fatima. 2012. "'Gays Who Cannot Properly Be Gay': Queer Muslims in the Neoliberal European City." *European Journal of Women's Studies* 19 (1): 79–95.

Eng, David, Judith Halberstam, and José Esteban Muñoz. 2005. "Introduction: What's Queer About Queer Studies Now?" *Social Text* 23 (3–4): 1–17.

Engels, Frederic. 2010. *Origin of the Family, Private Property and the State*. London: Penguin Classics.

Erickson, Bruce. 2020. "Anthropocene Futures: Linking Colonialism and Environmentalism in an Age of Crisis." *Environment and Planning D: Society and Space* 38 (1): 111–28.

Eriksen, Thomas Hylland. 2018. "Globalization." In *Handbook of Political Anthropology*, edited by Harald Wydra and Bjørn Thomassen. Elgar Handbooks in Political Science. Cheltenham, UK: Edward Elgar.

Fabian, Johannes. 1983. *Time and the Other: How Anthropology Makes Its Object*. New York: Columbia University Press.

Fabian, Johannes. 2000. *Out of Our Minds: Reason and Madness in the Exploration of Central Africa*. Berkeley: University of California Press.

Fanon, Franz. 1952. *Peau noire, masques blancs*. Paris: Seuil.

Fanon, Frantz. 1964. "Racisme et culture." In *Pour la révolution africaine*. Paris: Maspero.

Fantone, Laura. 2007. "Precarious Changes: Gender and Generational Politics in Contemporary Italy." *Feminist Review* 87:5–20.

Favret-Saada, Jeanne. 1985. *Les mots, la mort, les sorts*. Paris: Gallimard.

Federici, Silvia. 2004. *Caliban and the Witch: Women, the Body and Primitive Accumulation*. Brooklyn, NY: Autonomedia.

Ferguson, Roderick. 2012. *The Reorder of Things: The University and Its Pedagogies of Minority Difference*. Minneapolis: University of Minnesota Press.

Fernandes, Estevão Rafael. 2021. "Sexualidades divergentes em contextos indígenas: Estratégias para uma abordagem anticolonial." *Educação Em Foco* (Juiz De Fora) 26:1–9.

Foucault, Michel. 1966. *Les mots et les choses*. Paris: Gallimard.

Foucault, Michel. 1969. *L'archéologie du savoir*. Paris: Gallimard.

Foucault, Michel. 1971. "Nietzsche, la généalogie, l'histoire." In *Hommage à Jean Hyppolite*. Paris: PUF, coll. Épiméthée.

Foucault, Michel. 1972. *Histoire de la folie l'age classique*. Paris: Gallimard.

Foucault, Michel. 1976. *Histoire de la sexualité, vol. I: La volonté de savoir*. Paris: Gallimard.

Foucault, Michel. 1977. *Surveiller et punir: Naissance de la prison*. Paris: Gallimard.

Foucault, Michel. 1981. "De l'amitié comme mode de vie." *Gai Pied*, no. 25 (April): 38–39.

Foucault, Michel. 2000a. Preface to *Anti-Oedipus: Capitalism and Schizophrenia*, by Gilles Deleuze and Félix Guattari. Minneapolis: University of Minnesota Press.

Foucault, Michel. 2000b. "The Subject and Power." In *Power*, vol. 3 of *Essential Works of Foucault, 1954–1984*, edited by James D. Faubion. New York: New Press.

Foucault, Michel. 2000c. "Truth and Power." In *Power*, vol. 3 of *Essential Works of Foucault, 1954–1984*, edited by James D. Faubion.

Foucault, Michel. 2001a. "Le jeu de Michel Foucault (entretien sur *L'histoire de la sexualité*)." In *Dits et écrits*, vol. 2, *1976–1988*, edited by Daniel Defert, François Ewald, and Jacques Lagrange. Paris: Gallimard.

Foucault, Michel. 2001b. "Le pouvoir, une bête magnifique." In *Dits et écrits*, vol. 2, *1976–1988*, edited by Daniel Defert, François Ewald, and Jacques Lagrange. Paris: Gallimard.

Foucault, Michel. 2001c. "Le sujet et le pouvoir." In *Dits et écrits*, vol. 1, *1954–1975*, edited by Daniel Defert, François Ewald, and Jacques Lagrange. Paris: Gallimard.

Foucault, Michel. 2001d. "L'éthique du souci de soi comme pratique de la liberté: Entretien avec H. Becker, R. Fornet-Betancourt, A Gomez-Mulleer, 20 January 1984." In *Dits et écrits*, vol. 2, *1976–1988*, edited by Daniel Defert, François Ewald, and Jacques Lagrange. Paris: Gallimard.

Foucault, Michel. 2001e. "Michel Foucault: Une interview: Sexe, pouvoir et la politique de l'identité." In *Dits et écrits*, vol. 2, *1976–1988*, edited by Daniel Defert, François Ewald, and Jacques Lagrange. Paris: Gallimard.

Foucault, Michel. 2001f. "Préface in Deleuze (G.) et Guattari (F.), *Anti-Oedipus: Capitalism and Schizophrenia*." In *Dits et écrits*, vol. 2, *1976–1988*, edited by Daniel Defert, François Ewald, and Jacques Lagrange. Paris: Gallimard.

Foucault, Michel. 2003. *"Society Must Be Defended": Lectures at the College de France 1975–1976*. New York: Picador.

Foucault, Michel. 2004. "Des espaces autres. Hétérotopies. (Conférence au Cercle d'études architecturales, 14 mars 1967)." *CAIRN* 2, no. 54: 12–19.

Foucault, Michel. 2009. *Security, Territory, Population: Lectures at the College de France, 1977–1978*. Translated by Graham Burchell. New York: Palgrave Macmillan.

Francione, Gary. 2008. *Animals as Persons*. New York: Columbia University Press.

Francione, Gary, and Robert Garner. 2010. *The Animal Rights Debate: Abolition or Regulation?* New York: Columbia University Press.

Frith, Nicki, Sarah Arens, Jonathan Lewis, and Rebekah Vince. 2023. *Colonial Continuities and Decoloniality in the French-Speaking World: From Nostalgia to Resistance*. Liverpool: Liverpool University Press.

Fromm, Eric. 1941. *Escape from Freedom*. New York: Rinehart.

Fuglsang, Martin, and Bent Meier Sorensen. 2006. *Deleuze and the Social*. Edinburgh: Edinburgh University Press.

Gabriell, Joao. 2021. "Devenir l'homme noir." In *AfroTrans*, edited by Michaëla Danjé. Paris: Cases Rebelles.

Gaelle. 2020. "PRIDE 2020 will be more political than ever." *Friction Magazine*. https://friction-magazine.fr/pride-2020-sera-politique/.

Gago, Verónica. 2019. *La potencia feminista: O el deseo de cambiarlo todo*. Madrid: Traficantes de Sueños.

Galerand, Elsa, and Danièle Kergoat. 2014. "Consubstantialité vs intersectionnalité? À propos de l'imbrication des rapports sociaux." *Nouvelles pratiques sociales* 26 (2): 44–61.

Gandhi, Leela. 2006. *Affective Communities: Anticolonial Thought and the Politics of Friendship*. New Delhi: Permanent Black.

Garaoun, Massinissa. 2022. "A wīl-i žṛāhīm! An Introduction to a Moroccan Queer Language: Hədṛāt əl-Lwāba." *Decolonizing Sexualities Network Research Journal*. https://decolonizingsexualities.org/researchjournal/a-wl-i-hman-introduction-to-a-moroccan-queer-language-ht-l-lwba.

Gauguin, Paul. 1899. *Two Tahitian Women*. Oil on canvas, 37 × 28½ in. Metropolitan Museum of Art, New York. https://www.metmuseum.org/art/collection/search/436446.

Gellner, Ernest. 1983. *Nations and Nationalism*. Oxford: Blackwell.

Georgette, Crêpe. 2016. "Prostitution: L'invisibilité des femmes migrantes." STRASS: *Syndicat de Travailleuses de Sexe*. Accessed January 23, 2024. https://strass-syndicat.org/migrations-traite/.

Ghaziani, Amin. 2024. *Long Live Queer Nightlife: How the Closing of Gay Bars Sparked a Revolution*. Princeton, NJ: Princeton University Press.

Ghorbani, Mégane. 2015. "Afro-Feminism in France: The Struggle for Self-Emancipation." AWID, July 15. https://www.awid.org/news-and-analysis/afro-feminism-france-struggle-self-emancipation.

Gibson-Graham, J. K. 2002. "Beyond Global vs. Local: Economic Politics Outside the Binary Frame." In *Geographies of Power: Placing Scale*, edited by Andrew Herod and Melissa W. Wright. London: Blackwell.

Giglioli, Ilaria, Camilla Hawthorne, and Alessandro Tiberio. 2017. Introduction to *Etnografia e ricerca qualitative* 3 (September–December): 335–38.

Gilman, Sander. 1991. *The Jew's Body*. New York: Routledge.

Gilmore, Ruth Wilson. 2007. *Golden Gulag: Prisons, Surplus, Crisis, and Opposition in Globalizing California*. Berkeley: University of California Press.

Glenn, Evelyn Nakano. 1999. "The Social Construction and Institutionalization of Gender and Race: An Integrative Framework." In *Revisioning Gender*, edited by Myra Marx Ferree, Judith Lorber, and Beth B. Hess. Thousand Oaks, CA: Sage.

Glenn, Evelyn Nakano. 2002. *Unequal Freedom: How Race and Gender Shaped American Citizenship and Labor*. Cambridge, MA: Harvard University Press.

Gnanadason, Aruna. 2010. Review of *Planetary Loves: Spivak, Postcoloniality, and Theology*, edited by Stephen D. Moore and Mayra Rivera. Postcolonial Networks. Accessed June 1, 2013. http://postcolonialnetworks.com/2010/10/12/planetary-loves-spivak-postcoloniality-and-theology-eds-stephen-d-moore-and-mayra-riverafordham-university-press-new-york-2011-pages-414/.

Goffman, Irving. 1996. *Behavior in Public Places*. New York: Free Press.

Goldberg-Salinas, Anette. 2000. "Brésiliennes en exil." *Cahiers du CEDREF*, no. 8–9, 43–66.

Gomes Silva, Tauana Olivia. 2022. "Femmes noires brésiliennes en exil (1960–1980)." *Cahiers du CEDREF*, no. 25, 155–76.

Gómez-Barris, Macarena. 2017. *The Extractive Zone: Social Ecologies and Decolonial Perspectives*. Durham, NC: Duke University Press.

Gonzalez, Lélia de Almeida. 1988. "A categoria politico-cultural de Amefricanidade." *Tempo Brasiliero*, no. 92–93 (January–June): 66–81.

Gonzalez, Lélia. 2020. *Lélia Gonzalez: Por um feminismo Afro Latino Americano: Ensaios, intervenções e diálogos*. Edited by Flavia Rios and Marcia Lima. Rio de Janeiro: Zahar.

Gonzalez, Lélia, and Carlos Hasenbalg. 1982. *Lugar de negro*. Rio de Janeiro: Marco Zero.

Gould, Corinna, and Marcelo Garcia Montalvo. 2020. "A Conversation with the Segorae te Land Trust." Berkeley Center for New Media. YouTube video. https://www.youtube.com/watch?v=C4mj_gSZWGE.

Gramsci, Antonio. 1934. *Ai margini della storia: Storia dei gruppi sociali subalterni*. Quaderni del carcere 25.

Gramsci, Antonio. 1991. *Letteratura e vita nazionale*. Rome: Editori Riuniti.

Gramsci, Antonio. 1992. "Notes on Italian History." In *Selections From the Prison Notebooks*, edited and translated by Quintin Hoare and Geoffrey Nowell Smith. New York: International Publishers.

Gramsci, Antonio. 1995. *The Southern Question*. Translated and with an introduction by Pasquale Verdicchio. West Lafayette, IN: Bordighera.

Grande, Sandy. 2004. *Red Pedagogy*. Lanham, MD: Rowman and Littlefield.

Grech, Shaun, and Karen Soldatic, eds. 2015. "Disability and Colonialism: (Dis) encounters and Anxious Intersectionalities." Special issue, *Social Identities* 21 (1).

Green, Erica, Kate Benner, and Robert Pear. 2018. "Transgender Could Be Defined out of Existence Under Trump Administration." *New York Times*, October 21.

Greenberg, Zoe. 2023. "Dyketactics! Made History. Philly's Lesbian Memory Hotline Seeks Stories Like Theirs." *Philadelphia Inquirer*, April 9. https://www.inquirer.com/news/dyketactics-lesbian-memory-hotline-philadelphia-20230409.html.

Gressgård, Randi. 2008. "Mind the Gap: Intersectionality, Complexity and 'the Event.'" *Theory and Science* 10 (1). https://theoryandscience.icaap.org/content/vol10.1/Gressgard.html.

Grewal, Inderpal. 2005. *Transnational America*. Durham, NC: Duke University Press.

Grewal, Inderpal, and Caren Kaplan. 1994. Introduction to *Scattered Hegemonies: Postmodernity and Transnational Feminist Practices*, edited by Inderpal Grewal and Caren Kaplan. Minneapolis: University of Minnesota Press.

Grewal, Inderpal, and Caren Kaplan. 2001. "Global Identities: Theorizing Transnational Studies of Sexualities." GLQ 7 (4): 663–79.

Grewal, Inderpal, and Caren Kaplan. 2002. "Introducing Women's Studies in a Transnational World." In *An Introduction to Women's Studies*, edited by Inderpal Grewal and Caren Kaplan. New York: McGraw-Hill.

Grosfoguel, Ramón. 2013. "The Structure of Knowledge in Westernized Universities: Epistemic Racism/Sexism and the Four Genocides/Epistemicides of the Long

16th Century." *Human Architecture: Journal of the Sociology of Self-Knowledge* 11 (1): article 8. http://scholarworks.umb.edu/humanarchitecture/vol11 /iss1/8/.

Groupe du 6 novembre. 2001. *Warriors/Guerrieres*. Paris: Nomades'Langues.

Guardian. 2018. "Trump Administration Trying to Define Transgender out of Existence—Report." October 21. https://www.theguardian.com/world /2018/oct/21/trump-administration-define-transgender-out-of-existence -new-york-times.

Guattari, Félix. 1972. *Psychanalyse et transversalité*. Paris: François Maspero.

Guattari, Félix. 1977. *La révolution moléculaire*. Paris: Encres.

Guénif-Souilamas, Nacira. 2006a. "La Française voilée, la beurette, le garçon arabe et le musulman laïc. Les figures assignées du racisme vertueux." In *La république mise à nu par son immigration*, edited by Nacira Guénif. Paris: La Fabrique.

Guénif-Souilamas, Nacira, ed. 2006b. *La république mise à nu par son immigration*. Paris: La Fabrique.

Guénif-Souilamas, Nacira, and Eric Macé. 2004. *Les féministes et le garçon arabe*. Paris: l'Aube.

Guillaumin, Colette. 1972. *L'idéologie raciste*. Paris: Gallimard.

Guillaumin, Colette. 1978a. "Pratique de pouvoir et idée de Nature (1) L'appropriation des femmes." *Questions Féministes*, no. 2 (February): 5–30.

Guillaumin, Colette. 1978b. Pratique de pouvoir et idée de Nature (2) Le discours de la Nature. *Questions Féministes*, no. 3 (March): 5–30.

Guinhut, Hélène. 2020. "Maboula Soumahoro: Le racisme n'existe pas seulement aux États Unis." *Elle*, June 3. https://www.elle.fr/Societe/News/Maboula -Soumahoro-La-question-du-racisme-n-existe-pas-seulement-aux-Etats -Unis-3866688.

Guy-Sheftall, Beverly, ed. 1995. *Words of Fire: An Anthology of African-American Feminist Thought*. New York: New Press.

Halberstam, J. Jack. 2005. *In a Queer Time and Place: Transgender Bodies, Subcultural Lives*. New York: New York University Press.

Hall, Stuart. 1988. *The Hard Road to Renewal*. London: Verso.

Hall, Stuart. 2002. "Race, Articulation and Societies Structured in Dominance." In *Race Critical Theories*, edited by Philomena Essad and David Goldberg. Oxford: Blackwell.

Hanhardt, Cristina. 2013. *Safe Space: Gay Neighborhood History and the Politics of Violence*. Durham, NC: Duke University Press.

Haraway, Donna. 1988. "Situated Knowledge: The Science Question in Feminism and the Privilege of Partial Perspective." *Feminist Studies* 14 (3): 575–99.

Haraway, Donna. 2008. *When Species Meet*. Minneapolis: University of Minnesota Press.

Haraway, Donna. 2015. "Anthropocene, Capitalocene, Plantationocene, Chthulucene: Making Kin." *Environmental Humanities* 6 (1),159–65.

Hardman, Charlotte. 2020. *Other Worlds: Notions of Self and Emotion Among the Lohorung Rai*. New York: Routledge.

Haritaworn, Jin. 2015a. "Decolonizing the NonHuman." In "Theorizing Queer Inhumanisms," dossier in "Queer Inhumanisms," edited by Mel Chen and Dana Luciano. Special issue, GLQ 21 (2–3): 210–13.

Haritaworn, Jin. 2015b. *Queer Lovers and Hateful Others: Regenerating Violent Times and Places*. London: Pluto.

Haritaworn, Jin, Adi Kuntsman, and Silvia Posocco. 2013. "Introduction: Murderous Inclusions." *International Feminist Journal of Politics* 15 (4): 445–52.

Haritaworn, Jin, Adi Kuntsman, and Silvia Posocco, eds. 2014. *Queer Necropolitics*. New York: Routledge.

Hart, Gillian. 2007. "Changing Concepts of Articulation: Political Stakes in South Africa Today." *Review of African Political Economy* 34 (111): 85–101.

Hartman, Saidiya, 2007. *Lose Your Mother: A Journey Along the Atlantic Slave Trade*. New York: Farrar, Straus and Giroux.

Harvey, David. 1989. *The Condition of Postmodernity: An Inquiry into the Origins of Cultural Change*. Oxford: Blackwell.

Hau'ofa, Epeli. 1993. "Our Sea of Islands." In *A New Oceania: Rediscovering Our Sea of Islands*, edited by Epeli Hau'ofa, Vijay Naidu, and Eric Waddell. Suva, Fiji: University of the South Pacific.

Hawthorne, Camilla. 2022. *Contesting Race and Citizenship: Youth Politics in the Black Mediterranean*. Ithaca, NY: Cornell University Press.

Hessel, Stéfane. 2010. *Indignez-vous!* Montpellier, France: Indigène Éditions.

Hewitt, Andrew. 1996. *Political Inversions: Homosexuality, Fascism, and the Modern Imaginary*. Stanford, CA: Stanford University Press.

Hirsch, Marianne. 2012. *The Generation of Postmemory: Writing and Visual Culture After the Holocaust*. New York: Columbia University Press.

Hoad, Neville. 2000. "Arrested Development or the Queerness of Savages: Resisting Evolutionary Narratives of Difference." *Postcolonial Studies* 3 (2): 133–58.

Hobsbawm, Eric. 1990. *Nations and Nationalisms Since 1780: Programme, Myth, Reality*. Cambridge: Cambridge University Press.

Hobsbawm, Eric, and Terence Ranger. 1983. *The Invention of Tradition*. Cambridge: Cambridge University Press.

Holland, Sharon. 2015. "Vocabularies of the Vulnerable: HUM/ANIMAL/BLACKNESS." Keynote, Center for Race and Gender, University of California, Berkeley. November 2.

Hong, Grace Kyungwon. 2006. *Ruptures of American Capital: Women of Color, Feminism, and the Culture of Immigrant Labor*. Minneapolis: University of Minnesota Press.

hooks, bell. 1990. *Yearning: Race, Gender, and Cultural Politics*. Boston: South End Press.

hooks, bell. 1992. *Black Looks: Race and Representation*. Boston: South End Press.

hooks, bell. 2000. *All About Love: New Visions*. New York: HarperCollins.

Hunke, Sigrid. 1997. *Le soleil d'Allah brille sur l'Occident*. Paris: Albin Michel.

Iazzolino, Gianluca. 2020. "Power Geometries of Encampment: The Reproduction of Domination and Marginality Among Somali Refugees in Kakuma." *Geoforum* 110 (March): 25–34.

Ihmoud, Sarah. 2023. "On Love, the Palestinian Way: Kinship, Care and Abolition in Palestinian Feminist Praxis." *State Crime* 12 (2): 206–24.

Indigenous Action. 2014. "Accomplices Not Allies: Abolishing the Ally Industrial Complex." *Indigenous Action Media*, May 4. http://www.indigenousaction.org/accomplices-not-allies-abolishing-the-ally-industrial-complex/.

Inter-LGBT. 2019. "LGBT Pride March on June 29, 2019." May 5. https://www.inter-lgbt.org/marche-des-fiertes-lgbt-29-juin-2019/.

Invisible Committee. 2009. *The Coming Insurrection*. Los Angeles: Semiotext(e).

Irigaray, Luce. 1974. *Speculum de l'autre femme*. Paris: Minuit.

Irigaray, Luce. 1977. *Ce sexe qui n'est pas un*. Paris: Les Editions de Minuit.

Irigaray, Luce. 1979. *Et l'une de bouge pas sans l'autre*. Paris: Minuit.

Irigaray, Luce. 1981. *Le corps-à-corps avec la mère*. Montreal: Editions de la pleine lune.

Irigaray, Luce. 1984. *Ethique de la différence sexuelle*. Paris: Les Editions de Minuit.

Irigaray, Luce. 1985. *Parler n'est jamais neutre*. Paris: Editions de Minuit.

Irigaray, Luce. 1986. "Créer un Entre-Femmes." *Paris-Féministe* 31 (2): 37–41.

Jackson, Zakiyyah Iman. 2020. *Becoming Human: Matter and Meaning in an Antiblack World*. New York: New York University Press.

Jakobsen, Janet. 1998. *Working Alliances and the Politics of Difference*. Bloomington: Indiana University Press.

JanMohamed, Abdul. R. 2005. *The Death-Bound-Subject: Richard Wright's Archeology of Death*. Durham, NC: Duke University Press.

Jay, Martin. 1993. "From the Empire of the Gaze to the Society of the Spectacle: Foucault and Debord." In *Downcast Eyes*. Berkeley: University of California Press.

Jayawardena, Kumari. 1986. *Feminism and Nationalism in the Third World*. London: Zed.

Johnson, E. Patrick. 2004. *Appropriating Blackness: Performance and the Politics of Authenticity*. Durham, NC: Duke University Press.

Johnson, E. Patrick, and Mae G. Henderson, eds. 2005. *Black Queer Studies: A Critical Anthology*. Durham, NC: Duke University Press.

Jolivette, Andrew. 2015. *Research Justice: Methodologies for Social Change*. New York: Policy Press.

Jordan, June. 1982. "Moving Towards Home." *New York Times*, September 20.

Jordan, June. 2002. *Some of Us Did Not Die*. New York: Basic.

Kabbani, Rana. 1986. *Imperial Fictions: Europe's Myths of the Orient*. London: HarperCollins.

Kaddour, Hanan. 2001. "La continuité de la vision coloniale dans la pensée et analyse de lesbiennes francaises." In *Warrior/Guerrieres*, edited by Groupe du 6 Novembre, Paris: Nomades'Langues.

Kanngieser, Anja. 2019. ". . . And . . . and . . . and . . . The Transversal Politics of Performative Encounters." In "Félix Guattari in the Age of Semiocapitalism," edited by Gary Genosko. Special issue, *Deleuze Studies* 6 (2): 265–90.

Karimi, Hanane. 2023. *Les femmes musulmanes ne sont-elles pas des femmes?* Marseille: Hors Attente.

Kauanui, J. Kēhaulani. 2016. "'A Structure, Not an Event': Settler Colonialism and Enduring Indigeneity." *Lateral* 5 (1). https://doi.org/10.25158/L5.1.7.

Keating, AnaLouise, ed. 2009. *The Gloria Anzaldua Reader*. Durham, NC: Duke University Press.

Kelley, Robin D. G. 2017. "What Did Cedric Robinson Mean by Racial Capitalism?" *Boston Review*, January 12. http://bostonreview.net/race/robin-d-g-kelley-what-did-cedric-robinson-mean-racial-capitalism.

Kergoat, Danièle. 1978. "Ouvrières=ouvriers? Propositions pour une articulation théorique de deux variables: Sexe et classe sociale." *Critiques de l'Economie Politique*, n.s., no. 5, 65–97.

Kergoat, Danièle. 2004. "Division sexuelle du travail et rapports sociaux de sexe." *Dictionnaire Critique du Feminisme*, edited by Helena Hirata, Françoise Laborie, Hélène Le Doare, Danielle Senotier. Paris: PUF.

Kershaw, Sarah. 2009. "My Sister's Keeper." *New York Times*, January 30. http://www.nytimes.com/2009/02/01/fashion/01womyn.html?pagewanted=1&%2339&sq=sister&st=cse&scp=1&%2359%3Bs.

Khan, Riz. 2011. "The Political Power of Literature: What Role Do Artists and Intellectuals Play on the Frontline of Popular Uprisings?" *Aljazeera*, February 23. YouTube video. https://www.aljazeera.com/program/riz-khan/2011/2/23/the-political-power-of-literature/.

Khiari, Sadri. 2006. *Pour une politique de la racaille: Immigré-e-s, indigènes et jeunes de banlieues*. Paris: Textuel.

Khiari, Sadri, and Béatrice Hibou. 2011. "La révolution tunisienne ne vient pas de nulle part." *Politique africaine*, no. 121 (March): 23–34.

Kim, Seonghoon. 2016. "Newspapers, Environmental Justice, and Simon J. Ortiz's Poetry." *MELUS* 41 (2): 147–75.

Kimmerer, Robin Wall. 2015. *Braiding Sweetgrass: Indigenous Wisdom, Scientific Knowledge, and the Teachings of Plants*. Minneapolis, MN: Milkweed Editions.

Kingsley, Patrick. 2013. "80 Sexual Assaults in One Day—The Other Story of Tahrir Square." *Guardian*. July 5. https://www.theguardian.com/world/2013/jul/05/egypt-women-rape-sexual-assault-tahrir-square.

Knapp, G. A. 2005. "Race, Class, Gender: Reclaiming Baggage in Fast Travelling Theories." *European Journal of Women's Studies* 12 (3): 249–65.

Knudsen, Susanne V. 2007. "Intersectionality: A Theoretical Inspiration in the Analysis of Minority Cultures and Identities in Textbooks." In *Caught in the Web or Lost in the Textbook?*, edited by Éric Bruillard, Bente Aamotsbakken, Susanne V. Knudsen, and Mike Horsley. Eighth International Conference on Learning and Educational Media. https://iartemblog.wordpress.com /wp-content/uploads/2012/03/8th_iartem_2005-conference.pdf.

Kwok Pui-Lan. 2010. "What Has Love to Do with It? Planetarity, Feminism, and Theology." In *Planetary Loves: Spivak, Postcoloniality and Theology*, edited by Stephen D. Moore and Mayra Rivera. Oxford: Oxford University Press.

Laclau, Ernesto. 1977. *Politics and Ideology in Marxist Theory: Capitalism, Fascism, Populism*. London: NLB.

Laclau, Ernesto, and Chantal Mouffe. (1985) 1999. *Hegemony and Socialist Strategy: Towards a Radical Democratic Politics*. London: Verso.

Lambert, Gregg. 2008. "Deleuze and the Political Ontology of 'The Friend' (philos)." In *Deleuze and Politics*, edited by Ian Buchanan and Nocholas Thoburn. Edinburgh: Edinburgh University Press.

Lambert, Léopold. 2021. "Chronocartographie du massacre du 17 Octobre 1961 à Paris." *The Funambulist*, October 14. https://thefunambulist.net/editorials /chronocartographie-du-massacre-du-17-octobre-1961-a-paris.

Lavie, Smadar. 2011. "Staying Put: Crossing the Israel-Palestine Border with Gloria Anzaldúa." *Anthropology and Humanism Quarterly* 36 (1): 101–21.

Lee-Oliver, Leece. 2019. "Imagining New Worlds: Anti-Indianism and the Roots of United States Exceptionalism." In *Global Raciality: Empire, PostColoniality, DeColoniality*, edited by Paola Bacchetta, Sunaina Maira, and Howard Winant. New York: Routledge.

Lefebvre, Henri. 1974. *La production de l'espace*. Paris: Editions Anthropos.

Leong, Nancy. 2013. "Racial Capitalism." *Harvard Law Review* 126 (8): 2151. Also published as University of Denver Legal Studies Research Paper No. 13–30.

Lescure, Ryan M. 2023. "(Extra)ordinary Relationalities: Methodological Suggestions for Studying Queer Relationalities Through the Prism of Memory, Sensation, and Affect." *Journal of Homosexuality* 70 (1): 35–52.

Lewis, Simon L., and Mark A. Maslin. 2015. "Defining the Anthropocene." *Nature* 519 (7542): 171–80.

Libération. 2011. "Abandon de l'affiche de la Gay Pride avec un coq portant un boa en plumes." April 20. https://www.liberation.fr/societe/2011/04/20 /abandon-de-l-affiche-de-la-gay-pride-avec-un-coq-portant-un-boa-en -plumes_730361/.

Libreria delle Donne di Milano. 1987. *Non credere d'avere dei diritti*. Turin: Rosenberg and Sellier.

References

Lionnet, Francoise. 1989. *Autobiographical Voices: Race, Gender, Self-Portraiture.* Ithaca, NY: Cornell University Press.

Lionnet, Francoise, and Shu-mei Shih, eds. 2005. *Minor Transnationalism.* Durham, NC: Duke University Press.

Lombardi-Diop, Cristina, and Caterina Romeo. 2012. Introduction to *Postcolonial Italy: Challenging National Homogeneity.* New York: Palgrave.

Lorde, Audre. (1978) 1993. "The Uses of the Erotic: The Erotic as Power." In *The Lesbian and Gay Studies Reader*, edited by Henry Abelove, Michelle Aina Barale, and David M. Halperin. New York: Routledge.

Lowe, Lisa, and David Floyd, eds. 1997. Introduction to *The Politics of Culture in the Shadow of Capital.* Durham, NC: Duke University Press.

Lugones, María. 2003. *Pilgrimages Peregrinajes: Theorizing Coalition Against Multiple Oppressions.* New York: Rowman and Littlefield.

Lugones, María. 2008. "The Coloniality of Gender." In *On the De-Colonial (II): Gender and Decoloniality.* Vol. 2, dossier 2 of *The Worlds and Knowledges Otherwise Project*, edited by Manuela Boatcă. Center for Glabal Studies and the Humanities, Duke University. https://globalstudies.trinity.duke.edu/sites/globalstudies.trinity.duke.edu/files/file-attachments/v2d2_Lugones.pdf.

Lugones, María. 2020. "Gender and Universality in Colonial Methodology." *Critical Philosophy of Race* 8 (1–2): 25–47.

Lugones, María, and Elizabeth Spelman. 1983. "Have We Got a Theory for You! Feminist Theory, Cultural Imperialism, and the Demand for 'The Woman's Voice.'" *Women's Studies International Forum* 6 (6): 573–81.

Lykke, Nina. 2005. "Nya perspektiv på intersektionalitet. Problem og möjligheter" [New perspectives of intersectionality. Problems and possibilities]. *Kvinnovetenskaplig tidsskrift*, no. 2–3, 7–17.

Maciel, Maria E. 2006. "The Unclassifiable." *Theory, Culture and Society* 23 (2–3): 47–50.

Madhu. 2024. "Locating 'Selfhood' in Dalit Autobiographies." In *(Im)possible Worlds to Conquer: A Critical Reading of Dr. B. R. Ambedkar's Waiting for Visa*, edited by Mrunal Chavda. Singapore: Springer Nature.

Maitland, Padma. 2019. "Black Buddhist: The Visual and Material Cultures of the Dalit Movement and Black Panther Party." In *Global Racialities: Empire, Postcoloniality, and Decoloniality*, edited by Paola Bacchetta, Sunaina Maira, and Howard Winant. New York: Routledge.

Maldonado-Torres, Nelson. 2008. *Against War: Views from the Underside of Modernity.* Durham, NC: Duke University Press.

Mameni, Salar. 2023. *Terracene: A Crude Aesthetics.* Durham, NC: Duke University Press.

Manifesto 21. 2018. "Stop au pinkwashing: Les invisibles de la Pride voient rouge." 2018. July 3. https://manifesto-21.com/stop-au-pinkwashing-les-invisibles-de-la-pride-voient-rouge/.

Marx, Karl. (1859) 1970. *A Contribution to the Critique of Political Economy*. New York: International Publishers.

Marx, Karl. (1867) 1967. *Capital*. New York: International Publishers.

Massey, Doreen. 1991. "A Global Sense of Place." *Marxism Today*, June 24–29.

Massey, Doreen. 1993. "Power-Geometry and a Progressive Sense of Place." In *Mapping the Futures: Local Cultures, Global Change*, edited by Jon Bird, Barry Curtis, Tim Putnam, George Robertson, and Lisa Tickner. London: Routledge.

Massey, Doreen. 1994. *Space, Place, and Gender*. Minneapolis: University of Minnesota Press.

Massey, Doreen. 1999. "Spaces of Politics." In *Human Geography Today*. Cambridge: Polity.

Mathieu, Nicole-Claude. 1985. "Quand céder n'est pas consenter: Des déterminants matériels et pyschiques de la conscience dominée des femmes, et quelques une de leurs interprétations en ethnologie." *Cahiers de l'homme*. Nouvelle série XXIV: 169–245. Paris: Éditions de l'ecole des hautes études en sciences sociales.

May, Vivian M. 2015. *Pursuing Intersectionality, Unsettling Dominant Imaginaries*. New York: Routledge.

May, Vivian M. 2024. "Muted Tongues, Disappearing Acts, and Disremembered Subjects: Intersectionality and Black Feminist Intellectual History." In *Routledge Handbook of Intersectionality Studies*, edited Kathy Davis and Helma Lutz. New York: Routledge.

Mazouz, Sarah. 2017. *La République et ses autres*. Paris: ENS.

Mbembe, Achille. 2001. *On the Postcolony*. Berkeley: University of California Press.

Mbembe, Achille. 2019. *Necropolitics*. Durham, NC: Duke University Press.

Mbembe, Achille. 2021. *Out of the Dark Night: Essays on Decolonization*. New York: Columbia University Press.

McClintock, Anne. 1995. *Imperial Leather: Race, Gender, and Sexuality in the Colonial Contest*. New York: Routledge.

Mecca, Tommi Avicoli. 2008. "It's All About Class." In *That's Revolting!: Queer Strategies for Resisting Assimilation*, edited by Mattilda Bernstein Sycamore. Brooklyn, NY: Soft Skull.

Melucci, Alberto. 1991. *L'invenzione del presente: Movimenti sociali nelle societa complesse*. Bologna: Il Mulino.

Memmi, Albert. 1973. *Portrait d'un colonisée*. Paris: Payot.

Menon, Nivedita. 2015. "Is Feminism about 'Women'? A Critical View of Intersectionality From India." *Economic and Political Weekly* 50 (17): 37–44.

Mernissi, Fatema. 1983. *Sexe, idéologie, Islam*. Paris: Tierce.

Mernissi, Fatema. 2003. *Le harem européen*. Casablanca: Éditions Le Fennec.

Metzl, Jonathan M. 2019. *Dying of Whiteness: How the Politics of Racial Resentment Is Killing America's Heartland*. New York: Basic.

Mihesuah, Devon A., and Elizabeth Hoover, eds. 2019. *Indigenous Food Sovereignty in the United States: Restoring Cultural Knowledge, Protecting Environments, and Regaining Health*. Norman: University of Oklahoma Press.

Miladi, Nourreddine. 2011. "Tunisia: A Media Led Revolution?" *Al Jazeera*, January 17. https://www.aljazeera.com/opinions/2011/1/17/tunisia-a-media-led-revolution/.

Milan Women's Bookstore Collective. 1990. *Sexual Difference: A Theory of Social-Symbolic Practice*. Translated by Patricia Cicogna and Teresa de Lauretis. Bloomington: Indiana University Press.

Mitchell, Dan. 2020. "Anti-Libertarian Humor." International Liberty, December 13. https://danieljmitchell.wordpress.com/2020/12/13/anti-libertarian-humor-2/.

Mirzoeff, Nicholas. 2018. "It's Not the Anthropocene, It's the White Supremacy Scene; or, The Geological Color Line." In *After Extinction*, edited by Richard Grusin. Minneapolis: University of Minnesota Press.

Mitter, Partha. 1997. *Much Maligned Monsters: A History of European Reactions to Indian Art*. Chicago: University of Chicago Press.

Moallem, Minoo. 2005. *Between Warrior Brother and Veiled Sister: Islamic Fundamentalism and the Politics of Patriarchy in Iran*. Durham, NC: Duke University Press.

Mohammed, Wunpini Fatimata. 2022. "Why We Need Intersectionality in Ghanaian Feminist Politics and Discourses." *Feminist Media Studies* 23 (6): 3031–47.

Mohanty, Chandra Talpade. 1991. "Cartographies of Struggle." In *Third World Women and the Politics of Feminism*, edited by Chandra Talpade Mohanty, Anne Russo, and Lourdes Torres. Bloomington: Indiana University Press.

Moore, Donald S. 1997. "Remapping Resistance." In *Geographies of Resistance*, edited by Steve Pile and Michael Keith. London: Routledge.

Moore, Jason W. 2014. "The Capitalocene: Beyond Environment as the Zone of Consequence." https://jasonwmoore.wordpress.com/2014/03/26/the-capitalocene-beyond-environment-as-the-zone-of-consequence/.

Moore, Stephen D., and Mayra Rivera, eds. 2011. *Planetary Loves: Spivak, Postcoloniality, and Theology*. New York: Fordham University Press.

Moraga, Cherríe, and Gloria E. Anzaldúa, eds. 1984. *This Bridge Called My Back*. New York: Kitchen Table.

Morgan, Andy. 2011. "From Fear to Fury: How the Arab World Found Its Voice." *Guardian*, February 27. http://www.guardian.co.uk/music/2011/feb/egypt-tunisia-music-protests/.

Morgan, Jennifer. 2021. *Reckoning with Slavery: Gender, Kinship, and Capitalism in the Early Black Atlantic*. Durham, NC: Duke University Press.

Morrison, Toni. 1993. *Playing in the Dark: Whiteness in the Literary Imagination.* New York: Vintage.

Mosse, George L. 1985. *Nationalism and Sexuality: Middle Class Morality and Sexuality Norms in Modern Europe.* Madison: University of Wisconsin Press.

Moujoud, Nasima. 2015. "Talk: The Harem: A Western Colonial Invention." Conference on Colonial and Decolonial Struggles in France: Yesterday and Today. Université du Havre, France, November 30.

Moujoud, Nasima. 2025. "Fatema Mernissi, Intersectionality, and the Decolonization of Knowledge: Rural Women's Work Versus the Harem Myth." Translated by Paola Bacchetta. In *Fatema Mernissi for Our Times,* edited by Minoo Moallem and Paola Bacchetta. Syracuse, NY: Syracuse University Press.

Moujoud, Nasima, and Delorès Pourette. 2005. "'Traite' de femmes migrantes, domesticité et prostitution: À propos de migrations interne et externe. *Cahiers d'études africaines* 3–4 (179–180): 1093–1112.

Muñoz, José Esteban. 2009. *Cruising Utopia: The Then and There of Queer Futurity.* New York: New York University Press.

Nabulsi, Jamal. 2023. "Reclaiming Palestinian Indigenous Sovereignty." *Journal of Palestine Studies* 52 (2): 24–42.

Nancy, Jean-Luc. 1996. *Être singulier pluriel.* Paris: Galilée.

Nandy, Ashis. 1983. *The Intimate Enemy.* Delhi: Oxford University Press.

Nash, Jennifer. 2018. *Black Feminism Reimagined After Intersectionality.* Durham, NC: Duke University Press.

Nast, Heidi. 2004. "Mapping the 'Unconscious': Racism and the Oedipal Family." *Annals of the Association of American Geographers* 90 (2): 215–55.

Naterstad, Tora Berge. 2023. "The Reproduction of Nationalism and the Nationalism of Reproduction: Putin's Biopolitics of Defending Tradition, 2012–2021." *Nationalities Papers* 53 (1): 142–61. https://doi.org/10.1017/nps.2023.85.

Niang, Mame-Fatou, and Kaytie Nielsen, dirs. 2016. *Mariannes noires.* Film.

Nietzsche, Friedrich. 2006. *Thus Spoke Zarathustra.* Translated by Adrian Del Caro. Cambridge: Cambridge University Press.

Niumeitolu, Fuifuilupe. 2015. "Pacific Islanders March for Self-Determination." *Muliwai* (blog), March 2. https://morethantwominutes.wordpress.com /2015/03/02/pacific-islanders-march-for-self-determination/.

Niumeitolu, Fuifuilupe. 2019. "The Mana of the Tongan Everyday: Grief and Mourning, Patriarchal Violence, and Remembering Va." PhD diss., University of California, Berkeley.

Nixon, Rob. 2013. *Slow Violence and the Environmentalism of the Poor.* Cambridge, MA: Harvard University Press.

Nowak, Jörge. 2024. "Racial Capitalism and Global Labour Studies—a Missed Encounter?" *Global Labour Journal* 15 (1). https://doi.org/10.15173/glj.v15i1.5483.

Nyong'o, Tavia. 2005. "Punk'd Theory." *Social Text* 23 (3–4): 19–34.

O'Connor, Roisin. 2016. "Standing Rock: North Dakota Access Pipeline Demonstrators Say White People Are 'Treating Protest Like Burning Man.'" *Independent*, November 28. https://www.independent.co.uk/arts-entertainment/music/news/standing-rock-north-dakota-access-pipeline-burning-man-festival-a7443266.html.

Omi, Michael, and Howard Winant. (1994) 2015. *Racial Formation in the United States: From the 1960s to the 1990s*. New York: Routledge.

Omvedt, Gail. 1993. *Reinventing Revolution: India's New Social Movements*. New York: M. E. Sharpe.

Omvedt, Gail. 2016. *Understanding Caste: From Buddha To Ambedkar and Beyond*. Hyderabad: Orient BlackSwan.

Oyěwùmí, Oyèrónké. 1997. *The Invention of Women: Making an African Sense of Western Gender Discourses*. Minneapolis: University of Minnesota Press.

Palumbo, Jacqui. 2022a. "Powerful Photo by Pacific Indigenous Artist Reveals Truth About 1899 Painting." CNN, April 20. https://www.cnn.com/style/article/yuki-kihara-paradise-camp-snap/index.html.

Pandey, Gyanendra. 1992. "In Defense of the Fragment: Writing About Hindu-Muslim Riots in India Today." *Representations* 37 (Winter): 27–55.

Paolos, Mehdin, and Alan Maglio, dir. 2015. *Asmarina*. Film.

Patel, Geeta. 2002. "On Fire: Sexuality and Its Incitements." In *Queering India: Same-Sex Love and Eroticism in Indian Culture and Society*, edited by Ruth Vanita. New York: Routledge.

Patil, Vrushali. 2011. "Transnational Feminism in Sociology: Articulations, Agendas, Debates." *Sociology Compass* 5 (7): 540–50.

Patni, Gurgi, and Sheehan S. Khan. 2024. "Caste and Gender Politics: An Understanding of Dalit Consciousness in the Poems of Contemporary Dalit Writers." *Contemporary Voice of Dalit*, January 8. https://doi.org/10.1177/2455328X231209628.

Patterson, Orlando. 1982. *Slavery and Social Death*. Cambridge, MA: Harvard University Press.

Pêcheux, Michel. 1975. *Les vérités de la Palice*. Paris: Francois Maspero.

Pêcheux, Michel, and Catherine Fuchs. 1975. "Mises au point et perspectives à propos de l'analyse automatique du discours." *Langages* 37 (March): 7–80.

Pérez, Laura. 2007. *Chicana Art: The Politics of Spiritual and Aesthetic Altarities*. Durham, NC: Duke University Press.

Pérez, Laura. 2019. *Eros Ideologies: Writings on Art, Spirituality, and the Decolonial*. Durham, NC: Duke University Press.

Peterson, V. Spike. 2000. "Sexing Political Identities: Nationalism as Heterosexism." In *Women, States and Nationalism: At Home in the Nation?*, edited by Sita Ranchod-Nilsson and Mary Tétraut. New York: Routledge.

Phelan, Shane. 2001. *Sexual Strangers: Gays, Lesbians, and Dilemmas of Citizenship*. Philadelphia: Temple University Press.

Pile, Steve. 1997. "Introduction: Opposition, Political Identities and Spaces of Resistance." In *Geographies of Resistance*, edited by Steve Pile and Michael Keith. London: Routledge.

PIR (Parti des indigènes de la république). n.d. "Qui sommes-nous?" Accessed March 6, 2025. http://indigenes-republique.fr/le-p-i-r/que-voulons -nous/.

Puar, Jasbir. 2007. *Terrorist Assemblages: Homonationalism in Queer Times*. Durham, NC: Duke University Press.

Puar, Jasbir. 2012. "'I Would Rather Be a Cyborg Than a Goddess': Becoming-Intersectional in Assemblage Theory." *philoSophia*, 2 (1): 49–66.

Puar, Jasbir. 2013. "Rethinking Homonationalism." *International Journal of Middle East Studies* 45 (2): 336–39.

Purdie-Vaughns, Valerie, and Richard Eibach. 2008. "Intersectional Invisibility: The Distinctive Advantages and Disadvantages of Multiple Subordinate-Group Identities." *Sex Roles* 59:377–91.

Raha, Nat, and Grietje Baars. 2021. "'The Place of the Transfagbidyke Is in the Revolution': Queer and Trans Historical Imaginaries in Contemporary Struggles." *Third Text* 35 (1): 176–99. https://doi.org/10.1080/09528822 .2020.1864950.

Rajchman, John. 1998. "Foucault's Art of Seeing." *October* 44 (Spring): 88–117.

Ramirez, Jacobo, Claudia Patricia Vélez-Zapata, and Rajiv Maher. 2023. "Green Colonialism and Decolonial Feminism: A Study of Wayúu Women's Resistance in La Guajira." *Human Relations* 77 (7). https://doi.org/10.1177 /00187267231189610.

Rancière, Jacques. 2001. *L'inconscient esthétique*. Paris: Galilée.

Rankin, L. Pauline. 2000. "Sexualities and National Identities: Re-imagining Queer Nationalism." *Journal of Canadian Studies* 35 (2): 176–96.

Ransford, H. Edward. 1980. "The Prediction of Social Behavior and Attitudes." In *Social Stratification: A Multiple Hierarchy Approach*, edited by Vincent Jeffries and H. Edward Ransford. Boston: Allyn and Bacon.

Rao, Rahul. 2015. "Global Homocapitalism." *Radical Philosophy* 194 (November–December): 38–49.

Ray, Raka, and Seemin Qayum. 2009. *Cultures of Servitude: Modernity, Domesticity, and Class in India*. Stanford, CA: Stanford University Press.

Reagon, Bernice Johnson. 1983. "Coalition Politics: Turning the Century." In *Home Girls: A Black Feminist Anthology*, edited by Barbara Smith. New York: Kitchen Table.

Regan, Tom. 2004. *The Case for Animal Rights*. Berkeley: University of California Press.

Rege, Sharmila. 1998. "A Dalit Feminist Standpoint." *Seminar*, no. 710, 47–52. https://www.india-seminar.com/2018/710/710_sharmila_rege.htm.

Reich, Wilhelm. 2015. *The Mass Psychology of Fascism*. New Delhi: Aakar.

Revilla-Minaya, Caissa. 2023. "Persons, Agents, Objects and Everyone in Between: Diverse Perspectives of Non-Humans Among an Amazonian Indigenous Community." Unpublished paper presented at Max Planck Institute for Evolutionary Anthropology, Leipzig, Germany, June 23.

Rey, A., and J. Rey-Debove. 1984. *Petit Robert: Dictionnaire de la langue française*. Paris: Le Robert.

Rivas, Anthony. 2018. How Redefining Gender Under Trump Could Affect Transgender People's Health. *ABC News*, October 28. https://abcnews.go.com/Health/redefining-gender-trump-affect-transgender-peoples-health/story?id=58742630.

Robinson, Cedric. (1983) 1999. *Black Marxism: The Making of the Black Radical Tradition*. Chapel Hill: University of North Carolina Press.

Ruth, Barbara. 1976. "Poem to My Straight Sisters." In *From the Belly of the Beast*. Hardwick, MA: Four Zoas.

Ruth, Barbara. 1986. "The Eskimos." In *Past, Present, and Future Passions*. Oakland: Watr.

S., Kanika. 2017. "Brahmin Feminism sans Brahmin Patriarch." *Savari*, March 4. http://www.dalitweb.org/?p=3425.

Said, Atef Shahat. 2024. *Revolution Squared: Tahir, Political Possibilities, and Counterrevolution in Egypt*. Durham, NC: Duke University Press.

Said, Edward. 1978. *Orientalism*. London: Routledge.

Said, Edward. 1983. "Traveling Theory." In *The World, the Text, and the Critic*. Cambridge, MA: Harvard University Press.

Said, Edward. 2001. "Traveling Theory Reconsidered." In *Reflections on Exile and Other Literary and Cultural Essays*. London: Granta.

Salas-SantaCruz, Omi. 2023. "Nonbinary Epistemologies: Refusing Colonial Amnesia and Erasure of Jotería and Trans* Latinidades." *WSQ: Women's Studies Quarterly* 51 (3/4): 78–93.

Salas-SantaCruz, Omi. 2025. "Colonial Dysphoria." In "A Lexicon for Bridging Decolonial Queer Feminisms and Materialist Feminisms," edited by Paola Bacchetta, Soraya El Kahlaoui, and Sigried Vertommen. Special issue, *Kohl* 11 (1). https://kohljournal.press/colonial-dysphoria.

Sandoval, Chela. 2000. *Methodology of the Oppressed*. Minneapolis: University of Minnesota Press.

Sarkar, Tanika, and Urvashi Butalia, eds. 1996. *Women and Right-Wing Movements: Indian Experiences*. London: Zed.

Schneider, Jane, ed. 1998. *Italy's "Southern Question": Orientalism in One Country*. Oxford: Berg.

Segato, Rita Laura. 2015. *La critica de la colonialidad en ocho ensayos*. Buenos Aires: Prometeo.

Segato, Rita Laura, and Pedro Monque. 2021. "Gender and Coloniality: From Low-Intensity Communal Patriarchy to High-Intensity Colonial-Modern Patriarchy." *Hypatia* 36 (4): 781–99.

Semelin, Jacques. 2011. *Purifier et détruire: Usages politiques des massacres et génocides*. Paris: Seuil.

Shanin, Teodor. 1997. "The Idea of Progress." In *The Post Development Reader*, edited by Majid Rahnema and Victoria Bawtree. London: Zed.

Sharpe, Christina. 2016. "Lose Your Kin." *New Inquiry*, November 16. https://thenewinquiry.com/lose-your-kin/.

Shorter, Edward. 1977. *The Making of the Modern Family*. New York: Basic.

Silverman, Victor, and Susan Stryker, dirs. 2005. *Screaming Queens: The Riot at Compton's Cafeteria*. Film.

Singer, Linda. 1991. "Recalling a Community at Loose Ends." In *Community at Loose Ends*, edited by Miami Theory Collective. Minneapolis: University of Minnesota Press.

Sithole, Tendaye. 2020. *The Black Register*. Boston: Polity.

Smith, Andrea. 2008. *Native Americans and the Christian Right: The Gendered Politics of Unlikely Alliances*. Durham, NC: Duke University Press.

Smith, Anna Marie. 1994. *New Right Discourse on Race and Sexuality: Britain 1968–1990*. New York: Cambridge University Press.

Smith, Barbara, ed. 1983. *Home Girls: A Black Feminist Anthology*. New York: Kitchen Table.

Smith, Neil. 1984. *Uneven Development: Nature, Capital and the Production of Space*. Oxford: Blackwell.

Somerville, Siobhan. 2005. "Queer Loving." *GLQ* 11 (3): 335–70.

Soumaharo, Maboula. 2020. *Le Triangle et l'Hexagone*. Paris: La Découverte.

Soumaharo, Maboula. 2022. *Black Is the Journey, Africana the Name*. Cambridge: Polity.

Spade, Dean. 2011. *Normal Life: Administrative Violence, Critical Trans Politics, and the Limits of the Law*. Boston: South End Press.

Spiller, Hortense. 1987. "Mama's Baby, Papa's Maybe: An American Grammar Book." *Diacritics* 17 (2): 65–81.

Spiller, Hortense, Saidiya Hartman, Farah Jasmine Griffin, Shelly Eversley, and Jennifer L. Morgan. 2007. "'Whatcha Gonna Do?': Revisiting 'Mama's Baby, Papa's Maybe: An American Grammar Book': A Conversation with Hortense Spillers, Saidiya Hartman, Farah Jasmine Griffin, Shelly Eversley, Jennifer L. Morgan." *WSQ: Women's Studies Quarterly* 35 (1/2): 299–309.

Spivak, Gayatri. 1988. "Can the Subaltern Speak?" In *Marxism and the Interpretation of Culture*, edited by Cary Nelson and Lawrence Grossberg. Urbana: University of Illinois Press.

Spivak, Gayatri. 1995. Translator's preface and afterword to *Imaginary Maps*, by Mahasweta Devi, translated by Gayatri Spivak. New York: Routledge.

Spivak, Gayatri. 1996. "Subaltern Talk: Interview with the Editors." In *The Spivak Reader*, edited by Donna Landry and Gerald Mclean. New York: Routledge.

Spivak, Gayatri. 2003. "Planetarity." In *Death of a Discipline*. New York: Columbia University Press.

Spivak, Gayatri. 2004. "The Trajectory of the Subaltern in My Work." UCTV, September 13. YouTube video. https://www.uctv.tv/shows/Gayatri-Spivak -The-Trajectory-of-the-Subaltern-in-My-Work-8840.

Srikantiah, Jayashri. 2007. "Perfect Victims and Real Survivors: The Iconic Victim in Domestic Human Trafficking Law." *Immigration and Nationality Law Review* 87:205.

Stember, Charles Herbert. 1976. *Sexual Racism*. New York: Elsevier.

Stockton, Kathryn Bond. 2006. *Beautiful Bottom, Beautiful Shame: Where "Black" Meets "Queer."* Durham, NC: Duke University Press.

Stoler, Ann Laura. 2002. *Carnal Knowledge and Imperial Power: Race and the Intimate in Colonial Rule*. Berkeley: University of California Press.

Stoler, Ann Laura. 2011. "Colonial Aphasia: Race and Disabled Histories in France." *Public Culture* 23 (1): 121–56.

Stora, Benjamin. 1994. "Oublier nos crimes: L'amnésie nationale, une spécificité française?" *Autrement*, no. 144 (April): 227–43.

Stora, Benjamin. 1999. *Le Transfert d'une mémoire: De 'Algérie française' au racisme anti-arabe*. Paris: La Découverte.

Suárez-Krabbe, Julia. 2011. "Introduction: Coloniality of Knowledge and Epistemologies of Transformation." In "Epistemologies of Transformation: The Latin American Decolonial Option and Its Ramifications." Special issue, *Kult* 6 (Fall): 1–9.

Sukthankar, Ashwini, ed. 1999. *Facing the Mirror: Lesbian Writing from India*. Delhi: Penguin.

Talahite, Anissa. 2001. "Identity as 'Secret de Guerre': Rewriting Ethnicity and Culture in 'Beur' Literature." In *Cultures transnationales de France*, edited by Hafid Gafaiti. Paris: L'harmattan.

TallBear, Kim. 2011. Opening comments to symposium "Why the Animal? Queer Animalities, Indigenous Naturecultures, and Critical Race Approaches to Animal Studies," University of California, Berkeley, April 12. https:// indigenoussts.com/symposium-why-the-animal-queer-animalities -indigenous-naturecultures-and-critical-race-approaches-to-animal-studies -april-12th-uc-berkeley/.

TallBear, Kim. 2017. "Beyond the Life/Non-Life Binary: A Feminist-Indigenous Reading of Cryopreservation, Interspecies Thinking, and the New

Materialisms." In *Cryopolitics: Frozen Life in a Melting World*, edited by Jo-
anna Radin and Emma Kowal. Cambridge, MA: MIT Press.

TallBear, Kim. 2018. "Making Love and Relations Beyond Settler Sex and Family."
In *Making Kin Not Population: Reconceiving Generations*, edited by Adele
Clarke and Donna J. Haraway. Chicago: Prickly Paradigm.

Tasvuhein. 2012. "Derapage raciste de Sarkozy chez France Info: Musulman
d'apparence." March 26. YouTube video. https://www.youtube.com/watch
?v=yQKEtbE5Re4.

Teaiwa, Teresia. 1999. "Reading Paul Gauguin's Nau Nau with Epili Hua'ofa's
Kisses in the Nederends: Militourism, Feminism, and the 'Polynesian'
Body." In *Inside Out: Literature, Cultural Politics, and Identity in the New
Pacific*, edited by Vilsoni Hereniko and Rob Wilson. Lanham, MD: Row-
man and Littlefield.

Teltumbde, Anand. 2011. "Dalit Capitalism and Pseudo Dalitism." *Countercur-
rents*, March 7. http://www.countercurrents.org/teltumbde070311.htm.

Theweleit, Klaus. 1987. *Male Fantasies*. Vol. 1, translated by Stephen Conway.
Minneapolis: University of Minnesota Press.

Theweleit, Klaus. 1989. *Male Fantasies*. Vol. 2, translated by Erica Carter. Minneapolis: University of Minnesota Press.

Thrasher, Steven W. 2020. "An Uprising Comes from the Viral Underclass." *Slate*,
June 12. https://slate.com/news-and-politics/2020/06/black-lives-matter
-viral-underclass.html?fbclid=IwAR1xAn2nTHqCqiWJKYSFrHDiQOJ-
ClG7HeUZqRf2uD3vIGE1eDiudc3bGRec.

Tlatli, Moufida. 2011. *La Grande Table en direct de Tunis*. Part 1, "La révolution vue
par les artistes"; part 2, "La culture en Tunisie aujourd'hui." *Radio France Culture*, January 21. http://www.franceculture.com/emission-la-grande-table
-la-grande-table-en-direct-de-tunis-2011-01-21.html.

Tomassini, Lucia, and Elena Cavagnaro. 2020. "The Novel Spaces and Power-
Geometries in Tourism and Hospitality After 2020 Will Belong to the
'Local.'" *Tourism Geographies* 22 (3): 713–19.

Trinh T. Min-ha. 1989. *Woman, Native, Other*. Bloomington: Indiana University Press.

Trinh T. Min-ha. 2016. *Lovecidal: Walking with the Disappeared*. New York: Fordham University Press.

Tsing, Anna Lowenhaupt. 2015. *The Mushroom at the End of the World: On the
Possibility of Life in Capitalist Ruins*. Princeton NJ: Princeton University
Press.

Tuck, Eve, and K. Wayne Yang. 2012. "Decolonization Is Not a Metaphor." *Decolonization: Indigeneity, Education, and Society* 1 (1): 1–40.

Uberoi, Patricia. 1994. *Family, Kinship and Marriage in India*. Delhi: Oxford
University Press.

Vanita, Ruth, and Saleem Kidwai, eds. 2000. *Same-Sex Love in India*. New York: Palgrave.

Vaughan, Megan. 1991. *Curing Their Ills: Colonial Power and African Illness*. Stanford, CA: Stanford University Press.

Vergès, Francoise. 1999. *Monsters and Revolutionaries: Colonial Family Romance and Métissage*. Durham, NC: Duke University Press.

Vimalassery, Manu, Juliana Hu Pegues, and Alyosha Goldstein. 2016. "On Colonial Unknowing." *Theory and Event* 19 (4). https://muse.jhu.edu/article/633283.

Vitrani, Hugo. 2011. "Kader Attia, la sculpture en négatif et l'occupation du vide." *Mediapart*, January 19. https://www.mediapart.fr/journal/culture-idees/180111/kader-attia-la-sculpture-en-negatif-et-loccupation-du-vide.

Warren, Calvin. 2017. "Ontocide: Afropessimism, Gay Nigger #1, and Surplus Violence." *GLQ* 23 (3): 391–418.

"We Are Family: A Musical Message for All." n.d. Barney Wiki. Accessed November 8, 2024. https://barney.fandom.com/wiki/We_Are_Family:_A_Musical_Message_for_All.

Weheliye, Alexander. 2014. *Habeas Viscus: Racializing Assemblages, Biopolitics, and Black Feminist Theories of the Human*. Durham, NC: Duke University Press.

Weston, Kath. 1991. *Families We Choose: Lesbians, Gays, Kinship*. New York: Columbia University Press.

Willians, Tasha. 2018. "Research Shows Entire Black Communities Suffer Trauma After Police Shootings." *Yes Magazine*, August 3. https://www.yesmagazine.org/mental-health/research-shows-entire-black-communities-suffer-trauma-after-police-shootings-20180803?fbclid=IwAR02xvb1T-UagGwG1vlIjpnrBabnepkaFIzdyDIHhY5yFhotNQlwoWoIopc.

Willmott, Kyle. 2023. "Colonial Numbers: Quantification, Indigeneity, and the Politics of Fiscal Surveillance. *Surveillance and Society* 21 (1). https://doi.org/10.24908/ss.v21i1.14609.

Willsher, Kim. 2011. "Algerian-Born Man Living in France Is Refused French Nationality: Application Turned Down Because of Man's 'Degrading Attitude' Towards his Wife." *Guardian*, June 9. http://www.guardian.co.uk/world/2011/jun/09/man-refused-french-nationality.

Willoughby-Herard, Tiffany. 2016. Abolition and Kinship. *Abolition Journal*, May 24. https://abolitionjournal.org/abolition-and-kinship/.

Wittgenstein, Ludwig. 1984. *Remarques sur les couleurs*. Translated by Gérard Granel. Paris: Trans-Europ-Repress.

Wittig, Monique. 1992. *The Straight Mind and Other Essays*. Boston: Beacon.

Wolfe, Patrick. 2006. "Settler Colonialism and the Elimination of the Native." *Journal of Genocide Research* 8 (4): 387–409.

Wolpe, Harold. 1980. "Capitalism and Cheap Labor Power in South Africa: From Segregation to Apartheid." In *The Articulation of Modes of Production: Essays from Economy and Society*, edited by Harold Wolpe. London: Routledge and Kegan Paul.

Wong, Yen Nee. 2024. *Equality Dancesport: Gender and Sexual Identities Matter*. London: Routledge.

Wynter, Silvia. 2003. "Unsettling the Coloniality of Being/Power/Truth/Freedom: Towards the Human, After Man, It's Overrepresentation—An Argument." *CR: The New Centennial Review* 3 (3): 257–337.

Yegenoglu, Meyda. 1998. *Colonial Fantasies: Towards a Feminist Reading of Orientalism*. Cambridge: Cambridge University Press.

"Yuki Kihara, *Paradise Camp*." 2022. Contemporary Art Library. https://www.contemporaryartlibrary.org/project/yuki-kihara-at-pavilion-of-new-zealand-venice-23236.

Yusoff, Kathryn. 2016. "Anthropogenesis: Origins and Endings in the Anthropocene." *Theory, Culture and Society* 33 (2): 3–28.

Yuval-Davis, Nira. 1997. *Gender and Nation*. London: Sage.

Yuval-Davis, Nira. 1998. "Beyond Differences: Women, Empowerment and Coalition Politics." In *Gender, Ethnicity and Political Ideologies*, edited by Nickie Charles and Helen Hintjens. New York: Routledge.

Yuval-Davis, Nira. 1999. "What is Transversal Politics?" *Soundings*, no. 12 (Summer): 94–98.

Yuval-Davis, Nira. 2006. "Intersectionality and Feminist Politics." *European Journal of Women's Studies* 13 (3): 193–209.

Index

Page numbers in italics refer to figures.

Cittadini del Mondo (Citizens of the World), 67–68

Cixous, Hélène, 77

co-formations, 139, 211, 214–15; agencements/assemblages in, 121–26; articulation in, 109, 117–21; as co-motion clusters, 31, 33–34, 69, 109; intersectionality in, 109–15; misogynarchies and, 130, 137, 154–55, 189, 226n2; power matrix in, 115–17; racism as, 107–9, 119–20, 125–26, 130, 134, 138, 186, 189, 193, 196; together with co-productions, 129–38. See also alliances

Cohen, Cathy J., 62, 111

Collectif afroféministe MWASI (Afrofeminist Collective MWASI), 186, 229n9, 229n14

Collectif contre l'Islamophobie en France (CCIF, Collective Against Islamophobia in France), 183–84

Colletivo Diotima (Demeter Collective), 103

Collins, Patricia Hill, 59, 113–17, 124, 142

colonial dysphoria, 135–36

colonialism, 3, 8–9, 56–57, 71–75, 147–53, 169–71; British, 17, 26–30, 36–37, 45, 90, 127, 156, 161–62; Christianity and, 81; colonial dysphoria, 135–36; coloniality of power, 127–28; colonial-racial-sexual-amnesias, 1–2, 78, 84, 108–9, 114–15, 125, 154, 164, 167–68, 186, 191, 195, 208; colonial savior solidarity, 92, 212–14; Foucault on, 126–27; French banlieues and, 19–20, 61, 133–34, 179–86, 195–98; homo-colonial violence, 202–5; intersectionality and, 77, 109, 114, 121, 124, 127–28; operability of power and, 10, 31, 106, 108, 138, 165; orientalism and, 112, 127, 180, 213–14; police brutality and, 20–21, 135, 198–200, 217; privilege and, 21, 89, 93–94, 157; France and, 13, 20–21, 28–29, 112, 127, 130, 133, 161, 179–85, 199–200, 202, 205, 207, 212–13, 224, 227n1.4, 228n6; Italy and, 28; India and, 28, 36, 45, 63, 90, 127, 157, 168; United States and, 27–28, 37, 50, 63–64, 94, 130–31, 158, 164–65, 172, 227n1.4. See also activism: anticolonial; capitalism; France; postcolonial theory

Combahee River Collective, 16, 110–11, 142

co-motion, 74, 174, 176–79, 195, 207; definition, 4, 71–72; in methodology of book, 4, 6–9, 11–12, 14, 22, 24, 26, 33–34; non-encounter co-motion, 209–14; states' destructive power and, 11–13, 31, 33, 100, 104; in structure of book, 30–32. See also alliances; freedom-exigency: freedom-exigent co-motion

Coordination des femmes noires (Network of Black Women), 185

co-present temporal-spatialities, 22, 71, 119, 126, 131, 179, 186, 206, 211; situated planetarities and, 140, 148, 150, 159–67, 173

co-productions, 103–4, 127–28, 133, 150, 179, 211; misogynarchies and, 108, 126, 129–30, 137, 149, 189, 212, 225n4; political amnesias and, 137–38, 214–15. See also co-formations

COVID-19 pandemic, 58, 148, 170; deaths from, 6, 95, 189, 193, 217; in "Our Queer Pride Is Anti-Racist," 193, 217, 230n1.1; solidarity during, 177, 188–90, 196, 202

Crenshaw, Kimberlé, 77, 109, 114–15, 127, 137–38

critical conceptual wanderings, 27–30, 176

critical luminosities, 178–79, 187, 195, 200–201, 209

critical race theory, 44–45, 121

Critical Resistance, 66

critical silence, 200, 210, 214

Crowly, James, 40

Crutzan, Paul, 170

Cusicanqui, Silvia Rivera, 143

D'Angelo, Donatella, 68, 226n8

Danjé, Michaëla, 180

Dar, Huma, 63, 114

Darwinism, 168

Das, Veena, 89, 143

Davis, Angela, 9, 46, 60, 65–66, 100, 114–15, 225n1

deadly encounter, 207–9, 214

decolonial theory, 16, 126, 135, 143, 164

Decolonizing Sexualities Network (DSN), 63, 201–2, 229n16

de Lauretis, Teresa, 57

Deleuze, Gilles, 70, 106, 159, 173, 210; on assemblages, 77, 81, 121–25, 129, 227n2.2; on becoming-animal, 170; critical luminosities and, 178–79; etcétera and, 86; minor knowledges, 18, 62, 125; operability and, 3, 22, 120, 122, 124; on rhizome, 140

freedom-exigency, 3, 12, 22, 31, 33, 50, 60, 63, 94, 100, 105, 109, 157, 160, 178, 180, 190, 202, 210, 212; *freedom-exigent co-motion*, 7–11, 14, 32, 40, 62, 67, 69–73, 87, 89, 101–2, 104, 139, 159, 175–77, 184, 186–89, 200, 214–15; *freedom-exigent theory-assemblages*, 14–15; *freedom-exigent transformation*, 4, 9–10, 23. See also co-motion

freedom-life, 1, 4, 9–11, 31, 100–102, 140

Freud, Sigmund, 42, 83, 131–32

Fromm, Erich, 44–45

Fuchs, Catherine, 131–32

Gabriell, Joao, 180

Gandhi, Leela, 36–37, 39, 85, 127

Gandhi, Mahatma, 36–37, 39, 45, 85, 127

Gates, Henry Louis, 40, 226n1

Gauguin, Paul, 180, 183; *Two Tahitian Women,* 181–82

Gay and Lesbian Kingdom of the Coral Sea Islands, 49–51; "I Am What I Am," 52

Gays for Trump, 82

gender, 4, 26, 30, 54, 82, 135, 188; coloniality of, 127–28; as *co-production*, 107–9, 117, 121, 126–29, 137–38, 154; heteronormativity, 37, 40, 42–49, 51, 53, 65, 111, 157, 163–65, 168; intersectionality and, 77, 109–12, 114–16, 121, 124, 127–28, 138; Muslim racialization and, 46–48, 63, 128, 181, 209–14. *See also* feminism; *fraternarchy*; *filiarchy*; *misogynarchies*; misogynoir; patriarchy; queer+, trans+, and dyke+ subjects and allies; sexism

genocide, 11, 63–64, 72, 136, 147, 162, 188; in French colonial context, 179–80, 207; Palestinians and, 5–6, 152; United States and, 28, 44, 50, 92, 94–95, 150, 164–65, 171

Gibson-Graham, J. K., 148

Gilmore, Ruth Wilson, 6, 10

Girlie Circuit Festival (Barcelona), 207

Glenn, Evelyn Nakano, 112, 114–15, 124

Global North(s), 6–7, 16, 18, 23–25, 93, 112, 127, 135, 214; alliances and, 35–37, 43–44, 46, 53, 56, 58, 60, 63; lack of concern for coloniality, 1–3; limited theoretical tools of, 1–2; right-wing politics and, 11–12, 35, 56, 60; *situated planetarities* and, 141–48, 152–58, 163, 165, 168, 173;

subjects-in-sociality-and-another, 73–77, 83, 85–86. *See also individual countries*

Global South(s), 7, 12, 24–25, 28, 127, 179, 185, 196; alliances and, 44, 58, 60, 62–63; epistemologies of, 2, 6, 15–16, 18, 143, 147, 173, 181; *situated planetarities* and, 143, 145, 147, 153–54, 173. *See also individual countries*

global studies, 145

Goffman, Irving, 172–73

Goldstein, Alyosha, 135

Gonzalez, Lélia, 64, 143, 225n1

gossip, 25, 177, 228n3

Gould, Corinna, 30

Gramsci, Antonio, 66, 117, 120, 129, 227n1.2; on subaltern, 15–18, 31, 87–90, 93, 118–19

Gressgård, Randi, 86

Grewal, Inderpal, 129, 153, 156–57

Grosfoguel, Ramón, 143

Groupe du 6 novembre: Lesbiennes issues du colonialisme, l'esclavage et l'immigration (6 November Group: Lesbians begotten of/out of colonialism, slavery, and immigration), 185, 208, 212–13

Groupe femmes algériennes (Algerian Women's Group), 185

Groupe femmes marocaines (Moroccan Women's Group), 185

Groupe latino-américain des femmes (Latin American Women's Group), 185

Guattari, Félix, 70, 106, 140, 173; on assemblages, 77, 121–25, 129, 227n2.2; on becoming-animal, 170; on minor knowledges, 18, 62, 125; *operability* and, 3, 22, 120, 122, 124; on the transversal, 158–59

Guéant, Claude, 48

Guénif-Souilamas, Nacira, 16–17, 212

Guera, Paolo, 68, 226n8

Guha, Ranajit, 90

Guillaumin, Colette, 126, 134, 142

Gurr, Robert, 23

Halberstam, J. Jack, 163

Hall, Stuart, 81, 117, 119–20

Hands Across America, 84

Hanhardt, Christina, 187

Haraway, Donna, 123, 142–43, 170

Haritaworn, Jin, 169, 229n12

Kihara, Yuki, 180–82; *Paradise Camp*, 183
Kipfer, Stefan, 120
Knudson, Susanne V., 111
Kwok Pui-Lan, 160

Laclau, Ernesto, 66, 119–20
Lakhrissi, Tarek: *diaspora/situations*, 201
language, 51, 76, 82–84, 120, 124; in as-
    similation, 136, 161–62, 179, 181; author's
    notes on terminology, 4, 56, 58, 175,
    225n0, 225nn2–4, 226n8.1, 226n7.2,
    227n1.3, 227n1.4, 229n8; English transla-
    tion and, 3, 25–26, 29–30, 85, 227n1.2,
    227n1.3, 227n1.4, 227n3.1, 227nn1–2.1;
    etcétera in, 85–86, 131–32, 134, 176,
    178–79, 208, 213; Gramsci and, 88–89,
    227n1.2; hegemony of English, 151;
    intersectionality and, 111–12; *La loi
    no 94–665 du 4 août 1994 relative à
    l'emploi de la langue française* (Law
    No. 94–665 of August 4, 1994 relative
    to the use of the French Language),
    229n7; lesbian-centrism in, 50, 57,
    229n15; on minoritarian, 92–94; on
    minorities, 171, 177; on precarious,
    92–93. *See also individual concept-terms*
Le Bon, Gustave, 23
Lefebvre, Henri, 83, 149
Le Pen, Marine, 182
lesbian nation projects, 58: rural settle-
    ments, 49. *See also* Van Dykes
Lesbiennes of Color (LOCs, or Lesbians
    of Color), 185, 189, 203, 206, 229nn14–15;
    Pride for Whom? Pride for What?,
    196–98, 219–21
lesbophobia, 30, 50, 148, 151–52, 177,
    195–96, 212–13
Lescure, Ryan M., 35
Levinas, Emmanual, 76
Lewis, Simon L., 171
liberation-orientation, 10, 96–102, 105;
    definition, 31, 94; logic of elimination
    and, 94–95
lines of flight, 30, 65, 70, 102, 138, 211;
    freedom-exigent transformation and,
    9–10; methodological *operability* and,
    22–24; power and, 10–14; *subalterna-
    tive sensing, perception, intelligibility*
    and, 14–22, 103, 125, 141, 174, 187
Lionnet, Françoise, 62–64, 92, 138
Loftus, Alex, 120

Lorde, Audre, 37, 70, 123
Lowe, Lisa, 163
LTQ révolutionnaires (Lesbian Trans
    Queer Revolutionaries), 186
Luciano, Dana, 169
Lugones, María, 36, 77, 127–29
Luxemburg, Rosa, 71

Maciel, Maria E., 85–86, 227n2.1
Macron, Emmanuel, 182
Maghreb, 21, 133, 200; *colonial savior soli-
    darity* and, 212–14. *See also individual
    countries*
Maison des Femmes de Paris (Paris
    Women's Center), 185, 228n4
Mameni, Salar, 147, 171
Mar, Richard, 201–2
Marx, Karl, 105, 110–11, 142, 149; on articu-
    lation, 81, 117–21; on blood family, 43;
    on capitalism, 107–8, 126, 146, 171; on
    friendship, 35–36
Maslin, Mark, 171
Massey, Doreen, 148–49
Massumi, Brian, 70, 124
matrix, 109, 115–17
May, Vivian, 116–17
Mbembe, Achille, 10
McClintock, Anne, 45, 121
McLuhan, Marshall, 146
Melucci, Alberto, 23, 37
Memmi, Albert, 163
Menon, Nivedita, 114
Merah, Mohammed, 133–34, 227n3.2
Mernissi, Fatema, 153
mimésis, 51–52
misogynarchies, 7–8, 10, 15, 27, 75, 93, 106,
    156; abstract space and, 83, 149; alli-
    ances and, 43, 50, 61; as *co-production*,
    31, 108, 126, 129–30, 137, 149, 189, 212;
    definition, 154–55, 225n4; France and,
    61, 179–80, 184, 212; *freedom-exigency*
    and, 100–101; patriarchy and, 43,
    154–55, 180, 184, 225n4; *political amne-
    sias* and, 84, 137, 164; whitearchy and,
    229n9. *See also* fraternarchy; filiarchy;
    misogynoir
misogynoir, 152
Misra, Joya, 112
Moallem, Minoo, 127
Mohanty, Chandra Talpade, 151, 156–57
Moore, Donald S., 117

Index

Wolfe, Patrick, 94
Wolpe, Harold, 120
Wynter, Sylvia, 81

"*x*," 131–32, 134, 167, 176, 178, 213; "add x
and stir," 82

Yellow Jackets movement, 194–95, 217,
230n2
Yusoff, Kathryn, 171
Yuval-Davis, Nira, 45

Zuma, Jacob, 120–21

www.ingramcontent.com/pod-product-compliance
Lightning Source LLC
Chambersburg PA
CBHW032345280326
41935CB00008B/458